McGraw-Hill Higher Education
A Division of The **McGraw-Hill** *Companies*

LEADERSHIP IN RECREATION, SECOND EDITION

Published by McGraw-Hill, an imprint of The McGraw-Hill Companies, Inc., 1221 Avenue of the Americas, New York, NY 10020.

This book is printed on acid-free paper.

1 2 3 4 5 6 7 8 9 0 QPF/QPF 0 9 8 7 6 5 4 3 2 1 0

ISBN 0-07-012330-6

Vice president and editor-in-chief: *Kevin T. Kane*
Executive editor: *Vicki Malinee*
Developmental editor: *Tricia R. Musel*
Senior marketing manager: *Pamela S. Cooper*
Project manager: *Mary E. Powers*
Production supervisor: *Enboge Chong*
Coordinator of freelance design: *Rick D. Noel*
Cover designer: *A. M. Design*
Interior designer: *Kathleen Theis*
Senior photo research coordinator: *Carrie K. Burger*
Compositor: *Interactive Composition Corporation*
Typeface: *10/12 Times New Roman*
Printer: *Quebecor Printing Book Group/Fairfield, PA*

Library of Congress Cataloging-in-Publication Data

Russell, Ruth V., 1948–
Leadership in recreation / Ruth V. Russell.—2nd ed.
p. cm.
Includes bibliographical references and index.
ISBN 0-07-012330-6
1. Recreation leadership. I. Title.

GV181.4 .R87 2001 00-022121
CIP

www.mhhe.com

Leadership in Recreation

SECOND EDITION

Ruth V. Russell, Re.D.
Department of Recreation and Park Administration
Indiana University
Bloomington, Indiana

Boston Burr Ridge, IL Dubuque, IA Madison, WI New York San Francisco St. Louis
Bangkok Bogotá Caracas Lisbon London Madrid
Mexico City Milan New Delhi Seoul Singapore Sydney Taipei Toronto

For
Patricia Setser

Table of Contents

Preface

Over the past century men and women have been professionally guiding others in the wise use of free time. Since the pioneering efforts of people like Joseph Lee, Henry S. Curtis, Jane Addams, Dorothy Enderis, Lebert Weir, Steven Mather, and Juliette Low, a great deal of volunteer and salaried time, expertise, and energies have been devoted to the provision of recreation leadership.

Many of us look with a great deal of respect and fond memory to that special individual who first showed us the wonder of a night sleeping under the stars, or the thrill of a checkmate in chess, or the glorious exhaustion of mastering a dance movement, or the pride of a hand-molded clay pot.

PURPOSE OF THE TEXT

The ability to guide with wisdom, to implement with knowledge, to provide with appreciation, and to help with sensitivity is the task of those who lead in recreation. This task requires study, training, and practice if it is to be done well. *Leadership in Recreation*, in this second edition, as well as the first, is intended to assist with the study, training, and experiences of students of recreation leadership.

The roles, types, and tasks of leaders in recreation services have changed over the years. The recreation leader is no longer *just* the supervisor of children's play periods, the instructor of nature crafts, or the police in the gymnasium. In addition, the recreation leader is a counselor, a social worker, a technician, a teacher, a decision maker, a resource protector, a risk manager, a skilled helper, and a humanitarian. The recreation leader of today must be a master at holistically converting the needs and interests of people into meaningful and personally fulfilling leisure experiences.

WHO IS IT WRITTEN FOR?

Leadership in Recreation is designed and written primarily as a text for the undergraduate student. Its coverage includes the concepts and skills needed by persons who are beginning to work with recreation participants or beginning to supervise staff who work with recreation participants. It can be used for a course on recreation leadership, recreation supervision, recreation activity methods, and management of people in recreation settings. Because of its comprehensiveness, it also may be useful in introducing the professional fields of recreation services, parks, therapeutic recreation, sport and fitness management, and tourism management.

FEATURES OF THIS EDITION

This text provides a sound basis for both student learning and professional practice in the recreation fields. It maintains a strong research base and a practical usefulness. Specifically, there are six reasons why you are encouraged to use *Leadership in Recreation*:

1. *Balanced perspective on the subject matter*: Along with a strong conceptual foundation on the theory and research of leadership, this book equally teaches the practical need to develop skills in leading people.
2. *Distinctive coverage*: The topics of the history and goals of recreation leadership are included as important to establishing a student's foundational understanding. An entire chapter is devoted to the important communication skills needed by recreation leaders. Such abilities as successfully getting organized, managing time, working within a team, and being supervised are also covered. Conflict management and innovation in leadership are also newly featured.
3. *Comprehensive coverage*: This text also incorporates the most complete treatment of the subject matter currently available. Because of its balance between concept and practice, the chapter topics are not only comprehensive in their inclusion but also comprehensive in their discussion. Equal and thorough emphasis is placed on traditional perspectives and on popular new perspectives.
4. *Systemic approach*: The abundance of material is presented within a logical framework. Part 1 establishes a foundation for the study of recreation leadership. In this section the chapters include the context, the definition, the theory, the types, and the goals of leading in recreation. Part 2 concentrates on the general competencies needed to be a successful recreation leader. It includes such skills as decision making, problem solving, group management, communication, change and innovation management, participant motivation, facilitating and managing participant behavior, and teaching. Part 3 rounds out the text with up-to-date information on using resources, managing the workload and leader skills according to participant age groups and abilities. The appendixes provide thorough, easy to follow, step-by-step instruction on leading in fifteen specific recreation activity areas. This second edition contains approximately 40 percent new material.
5. *Case studies*: Numerous relevant case studies occur throughout the text to realistically demonstrate important concepts. The examples are selected from many of the employment areas including public recreation, therapeutic recreation, private recreation, commercial recreation, armed forces recreation, corporate recreation, and voluntary youth agencies.
6. *Readable writing style*: The language and sentence structure in the text is lively, fresh, and highly readable. The undergraduate student has been the focus not only in the inclusion of content but also in the appropriateness of writing style.

PEDAGOGICAL AIDS

To facilitate its use by instructors and students, *Leadership in Recreation* employs the following important learning aids:

- Succinct statements of focus opening each chapter to explain the relevancy of the topic to the student and to introduce the key concepts to be learned
- Summaries conceptually concluding each chapter to review the major points for the student
- Review and discussion questions to enhance student interest and to check comprehension
- Internet addresses for concepts, agencies, or programs mentioned in the chapter
- Key terms for each chapter with page numbers for term definitions
- Boxed material to highlight special support topics for the reader
- Exercises for individual and group active learning
- Figures and tables to illustrate key concepts
- Photographs that realistically depict a variety of actual recreation leaders
- References in each chapter providing the most up-to-date resources available

ACKNOWLEDGEMENTS

A textbook is never the sole effort of one person. This book is also the result of the committed hands and hearts of many people. Although I have spent many years synthesizing the ideas in this book, they would never have gotten between two covers without the help of friends and colleagues.

First, I am grateful to the reviewers of the manuscript. Their combined contributions have added much to the quality of the text. Grateful appreciation is extended to the following colleagues:

- Susan J. Hastings-Bishop, Ph.D.
  Ferris State University
- Cynthia Moyer, MS.
  California Polytechnic State University
- Rebecca McCann, Ph.D.
  Central Michigan University
- Nancy Pittman, Ph.D.
  St. Charles Community College, St. Pete, MO
- Jeff A. Stuyt, Ph.D.
  Texas Tech University

I also would like to sincerely acknowledge the assistance of Tricia Musel and Gary O'Brien, my editors from McGraw-Hill who worked enthusiastically with me on the text; Lee Furr, librarian and archivist at the National Recreation and Park Association, who helped with the acquisition of historical leader photographs; Jack Lefkowitz, art director for *Parks & Recreation* magazine, who provided the contemporary leader photographs; Danelle Stebleton, a master's degree student at Indiana University, who helped with a wide variety of tasks including locating Internet resources and case studies; Alex Russell for photo organizational assistance, and Patricia D. Setser, who drove rental cars and managed data files and much more.

This text is designed to teach. Ideal teachers are those who use themselves as bridges over which they invite their students to cross, then having facilitated their crossing, joyfully collapse, encouraging them to create bridges of their own. This is my hope.

Ruth V. Russell
October 1999

PART ONE

A Foundation

CHAPTER 1

The Context of Recreation Leadership

Leading edge influencing skills are needed today more than ever before in human history.
—Lambert, 1996, p. 4.

LEARNING OBJECTIVES

To establish a beginning foundation of commitment and perspective, you will learn the broader context of recreation leadership as it emerges from:

• history • society • definition • theory

KEY TERMS

pioneer leaders p. 11
social class differences p. 11
leadership p. 12
power p. 14
legitimate power p. 14
reward power p. 14
coercive power p. 14
expert power p. 14
information power p. 14
referent power p. 14
trait p. 15
autocratic leader behavior p. 16
democratic leader behavior p. 16
laissez-faire leader behavior p. 17
task-oriented behavior p. 17
relationship-oriented behavior p. 17
The Managerial Grid ® p. 18
Fiedler's contingency theory p. 18
leader-member relations p. 18
task structure p. 20
power position p. 20
path-goal theory p. 20
directive leader p. 20
supportive leader p. 20
participative leader p. 20
achievement-oriented leader p. 21
transactional leader p. 22
transformational leader p. 22
charisma p. 22

Our way of life is still changing rapidly. Over the past three decades, examples of social and cultural change are numerous: doubling of the world's population; greater celebration of ethnic, gender, and ability diversity; a new basis of wealth as information and technical ability; and expanded options for conserving the environment. It has been a period when we could relish the luxury of dreaming about what was "possible" and then use our intellect to set that possibility into motion.

Our way of life is still changing rapidly. The countervailing forces that erupted since the 1970s have ushered in such challenges as stiffer competition for tax dollars, increased demands for services to an aging population, a shrinking workforce, and a lack of citizen involvement.

There is little doubt, that during the opening years of the new century we will continue to experience rapid, pervasive, and dramatic change. As Goodale (1980) pleaded, "For a number of reasons, those working in the field of recreation . . . will be 'front and center' through these decades of change and will bear their share and more of the burden" (p. 211).

Change can bring both crisis and opportunity. In times of rapid change, progress is possible that could never be accomplished in times of stability. As demanded by Gray (1984), "Flexibility, recognition of opportunity, escape from pessimistic thinking, and leadership are required to respond to this period" (p. 47). Now is the time for those who lead in the recreation, park, sport, and tourism services fields to escape yesterday's success and bring new dreams into reality.

This calls for creative, courageous, and thoughtful leadership. Leaders in leisure services must be prepared to confront today's and tomorrow's problems. We must come to grips with rapidly changing attitudes, behavior patterns, and lifestyles as they affect leisure interests and practices. Recreation leaders must seek to build in others a total awareness of the significance of play in modern life and to promote its constructive participation. This calls for leadership that is committed to the enhancement of the human being.

This book will not teach you this commitment. You must discover that yourself. This text will introduce you to the leadership techniques, skills, and strategies that you will need to improve your creativity, to refine your courageousness, and to enlighten your thoughtfulness.

To begin your introduction to recreation leadership an overview of the historical, social, definitional, and theoretical circumstances that encase our professional efforts is important.

HISTORICAL CONTEXT

To many the recreation and park movement was one of the outstanding social service developments of the twentieth century (Butler, 1965), owing much of its growth and success to the efforts of many dedicated people. Early leaders in particular are responsible for the imagination, foresight, conviction, and action that caused recreation to be recognized as a basic human and societal need.

Those persons who were our professional predecessors were radicals for their time. They continually fought city hall; organized people at the grass roots; gave public speeches; and wrote articles deploring the life conditions of the poor, the disenfranchised, the enslaved, and the immigrant. Our founders faced up to many social and economic problems with strength and skill. They were not meekly intimidated by political systems or politicians (Duncan, 1980).

Because of the dedicated service of these first advocates of recreation, among many other opportunities we now have playground programs that are safe and fun, outdoor recreation resources that are aesthetic and challenging, sport facilities that are convenient and useful, and cultural art programs that are vital and meaningful. We enjoy a wide variety of recreational opportunities that are made available to us by the priceless legacy bequeathed by many of our early leaders.

Yet despite such a significant contribution, even the names of many of our pioneers have been forgotten. The purpose of this section is to share major activities, distinctive ideas, and personal characteristics of selected recreation leaders from history to provide a comparison with today's recreation leadership styles and goals. Within this historical context it is hoped that among other benefits you will be able to broaden your appreciation for your chosen profession. Figure 1.1 helps us keep track of this history.

FIGURE 1.1. Recreation leaders in American history: 1850–1950

1950s	Beatrice Hill is instrumental in development of recreation services for persons who are ill or disabled Josephine Randall is first woman to choose recreation as full-time career Jackie Robinson becomes first black athlete to play for major professional team TV ownership grows rapidly
1940s	World War II begins: recreation provided at home and abroad Courses in recreation management begin at colleges Franklin Roosevelt's work program provides recreation facilities and opportunities
1930s	Great Depression begins Henry Curtis promotes recreation for older adults 1,700 U.S. cities have organized park systems
1920s	The Weekend founded: more workers get Saturday off Juliette Low organizes first Girl Scout group World War I – recreation provided on military bases Joseph Lee conceives Boston recreation department program as wider than just playgrounds
1910s	Eleven States have state forests Mass produced cars revolutionize tourism Based on Luther Gulick's suggestion, Playground Association of America organized
1900	Sierra Club founded 100 U.S. cities have organized park systems Joseph Lee establishes model playground in desolate Boston neighborhood Boom in professional sports and commercial recreation
1890s	Hull House settlement house in Chicago Judge William Gladstone Steel views Crater Lake in Oregon for first time Sand Garden movement introduced from Germany American Association for Health, Physical Education, and Recreation founded Joseph Lee surveys play opportunities in Boston
1880s	Twenty U.S. cities have organized park systems Yellowstone set aside as national "pleasuring ground"
1870s	First railroad across U.S. – starts modern era of tourism Yosemite State Park in California established Boys Club founded; YMCAs offer recreation programs Luther Gulick's ideas influence YMCA, school athletics, Boy Scouts of America, and Camp Fire Girls programs
1860s	NYC authorizes development of Central Park; industrialization, immigration, urbanization grows at a rapid pace

According to most historical writings, *Joseph Lee* was the most beloved and influential of the public recreation leaders. He is considered to be the "Father of the American Playground Movement" (Butler, 1965, p. 1; Weiskopf, 1982, p. 93).

Lee's first activity in the interest of playgrounds was his help in an 1882 community survey conducted by a social work agency in Boston (Butler, 1965). He surveyed play opportunities, including graveyards, in several crowded neighborhoods. Some time later he was shocked to see neighborhood boys arrested for merely playing in the streets. To correct a situation that, as he commented, was equal to being arrested for living, he secured permission to use an empty lot for a neighborhood play area. He provided planks, boxes, barrels, and game equipment and told the children it was their playground (Butler, 1965).

Leader Profile: The Past
Joseph E. Lee
(on the bottom in a game of leap-frog). Father of the American Playground Movement.

Soon the children began to fight and break up their games unless Lee was there to supervise; it became apparent that the children did not know how to play well. Day after day Lee spent several hours observing the children's play activity and noting their reactions to play leadership.

In 1898 Lee helped to create a model playground in a desolate Boston neighborhood (Butler, 1965). It included a program of basketball, bowling, club activities, and gardening. Two leaders were employed, and Lee paid the total expenses of the playground's operation for the next six years.

This close involvement with Boston's playgrounds over several years convinced Lee that children needed opportunities to play under competent leadership. When a recreation department was organized in Boston in 1913, Lee conceived its program as involving not only playgrounds but also gardening, concerts, donkeys to ride, wading, ice skating and sledding, dancing, and storytelling for all ages throughout the year. He asserted that its leaders should not be chosen mainly for their proficiency in baseball but should instead have the qualities of a social worker (Butler, 1965).

As his influence expanded, Lee came into great demand as a speaker and writer. He recognized the great creative abilities of leaders and argued that the key element in a municipal recreation organization was the individual who headed it (Weiskopf, 1982).

Lee also argued that quality was more important than quantity in individual and societal efforts. It was better, he felt, to meet a few needs effectively than to obtain mediocre results in numerous areas. The key to quality was through well-planned goals, efficiency and organization, and educated expertise (Hartman, 1937). Today recreation professionals still maintain this leadership philosophy.

No recreation leader personally practiced the leisure ethic more fully than Lee. As a youth he played football, rowed, boxed, sailed, ice skated, and bicycled. Lee was also an avid reader, loved to paint, took great delight in conversation, enjoyed music and the theater, and—although "no great fisherman"—considered the opening day of fishing season an important one (Butler, 1965, p. 15). Lee cared deeply for a quality life for all persons because he lived richly and fully.

Dr. Luther H. Gulick's chief contributions to our fields' history were his primary role in establishing the Playground Association of America and his effective leadership of the association as its first president (Butler, 1965). Unlike most of the other early leaders, he devoted only a few years of service to the recreation field, but his brief efforts were significant. He is noted most for his successful organizing. His leadership style was to take an idea, develop it, get it organized, turn it over to others to carry on, and then tackle a new idea. Gulick was a capable, inventive, and energetic leader.

An unusual person, even a bit eccentric, he was impulsively willing to accept anything once. The story is told, for instance, that one day he even jumped out of his moving automobile in an attempt to force his wife to learn to drive (Knapp, 1972). In addition, Gulick's leadership style sometimes antagonized others, since he criticized persons who fell behind his active pace or who held what he considered to be weak concepts. Nevertheless, Gulick was remembered as a highly effective organizer who could draw out the best efforts and ideas of his colleagues.

The Playground Association of America originated in a suggestion made by Gulick to other playground leaders in 1905 (Butler, 1965). Under his leadership as its first president, the association made amazing progress. In addition to his early advocacy for playgrounds, Gulick maintained a conviction that the association's scope should be broadened to all public recreation. During his life Gulick also assumed leadership responsibility in the YMCA, school athletics, the Boy Scouts of America, Camp Fire Girls, Inc., and recreation services in the U.S. Armed Forces.

Recreation was also an important part of Gulick's own life. He played several musical instruments and was an enthusiastic swimmer, sailor, and camper. An avid entertainer, he also enjoyed giving unusual parties and leading discussion groups.

Leader Profile: The Past
Dorothy Enderis
Founder of the Lighted School House Movement.

Dorothy Enderis is the name usually associated with Milwaukee's fame as "The City of Lighted Schoolhouses" (Butler, 1965, p. 142). For more than three decades she was in charge of the United States' most widely known and highly respected recreation program under school auspices.

Born in 1880, her first introduction to recreation leadership came when as a fourth grade teacher she and two other teachers were asked to assist in the school board's newly formed recreation extension service (Butler, 1965). The new school-based recreation program grew, and Enderis became its director in 1920. By the time she retired in 1948, Milwaukee's Recreation and Adult Education Department was operating thirty-two indoor centers and sixty-two playgrounds in addition to other citywide services (Butler, 1965). Informality and organized activity were stressed in the program. For example, two of the popular features of the indoor centers were "roughhouse" rooms where young boys could burn up excess energy and "drop-in" rooms where young adults could dance and socialize.

In the following quotation from her leader's manual, Enderis sets a high aim for recreation leaders:

> A play leader who perfunctorily carries on activities and guards his playground against physical mishap has a job. He who adds skill and technique to these duties creates a profession, but he who crowns his profession with consecration and devotion performs a mission, and the children, youths, and adults who come to him for play and sport carry away deeper values and greater riches than the mere memory of a happy day (Butler, 1965, p. 146).

Another equally prominent person who influenced therapeutic recreation leadership in the United States was *Beatrice Hill.* During a period of volunteering in a tuberculosis sanitarium and a personal bout with tuberculosis, her interest in the development of recreation service for institutionalized persons was inspired.

As Director of Recreation at Goldwater Memorial Hospital on New York's Welfare Island, she initiated many of our current concepts of leadership in therapeutic recreation (Avedon, 1974). As a member of the staff of the National Recreation Association, she was instrumental in encouraging the development of recreation services for persons who were ill or disabled. In 1960 she formed a separate national service agency,

Comeback, Inc., which expanded her therapeutic recreation consultation services to Canada, Mexico, and various European countries (Avedon, 1974).

Hill was also one of the first to recognize the recreation needs of the noninstitutionalized disabled person and advocated focusing service attention on such settings as sheltered workshops, clinics, nursing homes, and the neighborhood. Her efforts during this period led to the acceptance of therapeutic recreation as a professionally valid service.

Outdoor recreation owes much of its growth to the vision of a small number of idealistic persons who were able to have the early foresight to see the long-range, natural resource-based recreation needs of the people. The national park concept in the United States, which originated around a camp fire in the Yellowstone area, succeeded mainly as a result of the single-minded devotion of such individuals as *George Catlin, John Muir, Theodore Roosevelt, Steven Mather, Gifford Pinchot, William Steel, John Lacey*, and many others (McCall & McCall, 1977).

For example, the story of how Crater Lake National Park was founded is a tale of one person's devotion to a single concept. Judge William Gladstone Steel viewed Crater Lake in Oregon for the first time in 1885 and, looking into its blue 2,000-foot depth, vowed to devote the rest of his life to establishing it as a national park. It was a vow he kept (McCall & McCall, 1977).

The tale is told of how Steel carried rainbow trout from Medford, Oregon, to Crater Lake, which because of no inlet or outlet was without fish. It is told that he walked for three days where no roads existed, carrying a pail of minnows. Although only half his trout survived, it was enough to start a sporting population that exists to this day.

Josephine Randall was one of the first women in the United States to choose recreation leadership as a field of full-time work. During the twenty-five years that she was the director of the San Francisco Recreation Department, outstanding drama groups were organized, the roving leader concept was developed, recreation services for public housing residents were created, and a renowned nature program for youth was initiated.

Just as Boy Scouting was brought to the United States by an individual who had become acquainted with the program in Great Britain, so was Girl Scouting. *Juliette Gordon Low* had led Girl Guide groups in Scotland and England, and in 1912 on one of her visits to her native city of Savannah, Georgia, she organized the first Girl Scout group in the United States. By the 1930s the Girl Scout national membership had outstripped that of any other membership organization for girls.

Leadership in recreation has been rather dramatically modified since the early influences of Lee and other founders. Many of the social and economic problems faced by the early leaders have been solved only to create new paradoxes for today's professional recreation leaders. Modern society's efforts to industrialize were so successful that now countries face an uncertain energy future. Modern sewage and medical systems have brought most communicable diseases under control, only to find that stress related diseases have taken their place. Government at all levels has recognized its responsibility in providing recreation and park services for all people, but the growing demands for austerity by taxpayers now threaten some of these same services.

Additionally, leadership styles and approaches have changed for those working in the leisure services fields. In our early professional history, the leaders completely dominated the form and content of all services. Many times those with visions of their own solely determined the objectives of the recreation service. In the 100 years since the first U.S. playground opened, the leader's role has been altered in primarily four ways.

First, society has become increasingly more democratic. Likewise recreation participants, clients, and guests have demanded more opportunities to contribute to their own leisure service decision making. This has caused recreation leadership over the years to become less autocratic and more participatory or democratic.

Second, as a result of an information and technology explosion, recreation leaders must be more diversified, more knowledgeable, better trained, and more global in perspective. There is greater diversity than ever in what programs we offer, who sponsors them, and how we pay for them. As a result, the contemporary leader is required to have the ability to integrate program services of a wide and complex array.

Third, present-day recreation leaders are affected by the sheer size of our leisure service industry. This growth has increased the diversity of the clientele served. In Lee's day the participants were mainly young, inner city boys; today the recreation leader's constituency ranges widely in chronological age, economic affluence, ability, interests, needs, and amount of free time.

Fourth, the styles and approaches of recreation leadership have been altered by increased recreation facility resources. Now, in addition to playgrounds there are athletic stadiums, natatoriums, velodromes, golf courses, ski slopes, community centers, tennis courts, marinas, horse and rider campgrounds, water parks, off-road vehicle parks, softball complexes, theme parks, and more. Within these new circumstances, the recreation leader is charged with not only directing people but directing people in a dozen different environments, each with its own unique management requirements for success.

Do these four transformations mean that old-fashioned styles of recreation leadership known to our pioneers are obsolete? To some degree the answer is yes. The autocratic style of leadership that predominated the approach of our early leaders is no longer as useful. What has primarily changed over the last 100 years is the role of the leader in delivering recreation services. The leader has evolved from "the one who makes all the decisions to the one who develops a system and a process by which decisions can be made" by those served (Davis, 1978, p. 122). The recreation leader of today is to a large extent a manager.

However, let us hope that the spark of individuality and the deeply rooted sense of purpose that characterized the leadership of Lee, Hill, Steel, and others will continue to have a decisive effect on today's recreation organizations. As it was for the profession's pioneers, enthusiasm, adaptability, creativity, sensitivity, readiness to meet new challenges, and energy will likely remain hallmarks of successful recreation leadership in the future.

Perhaps the greatest lesson to be learned from studying our pioneer leaders is the necessity for the leader to manage change. The refusal or inability to recognize and adapt to emerging social, economic, and psychological patterns is a dangerous pattern for recreation professionals. The leader of leisure services today must be prepared with the attitude and the skills to seek out and foster change.

SOCIETAL CONTEXT

In the United States, Canada, and many other nations recreation represents a major area of social service responsibility for a wide array of governmental agencies, nonprofit service organizations, and commercial enterprises. In the United States, for instance, numerous towns, cities, counties, and special districts provide extensive systems of parks, playgrounds, community centers, athletic fields, gardens, and other services to meet the needs of their residents. Voluntary, nonprofit organizations such as Boys' and Girls' Clubs, YMCAs, YWCAs, Boy Scouts, Girl Scouts and Big Brothers/Big Sisters provide recreation to millions of youth and adult members. Special organizations that serve the recreation needs of special populations with mental and physical illnesses or disabilities are flourishing under private and commercial sponsorship. Thousands of companies and industries sponsor recreation services for their employees. Colleges and universities provide extensive recreation programs for students, faculty, staff, and their broader community. Commercial recreation enterprises focus on provision of recreation as a business investment in greatly increasing numbers. Hospitality services for tourists are increasing and becoming more comprehensive. The family members of those in the armed forces receive recreation services that are unprecedented in military history.

Contemporary society the world over is calling on the leadership expertise of many men and women employed in leisure-related settings. These persons do not carry out their professional endeavors in an isolated vacuum, however. The recreation leader's styles, approaches, and worth are influenced by the broader society. Social factors influence what is done, how it is done, and how successfully it is done. Today's leadership in recreation is primarily shaped by the context created by the following social factors.

A *troublesome economy* with the cumulative effect of inflation, energy costs, unemployment, and national debt increases has greatly affected the efforts of those working in recreation. Although this has not meant that the total amount of money spent on recreational pursuits has changed (spending for recreation has risen more rapidly than consumer spending as a whole), it has meant that the sponsorship and the forms of recreation have changed. For instance, an increase in the role of private and commercial agencies and a decrease in the role of government agencies have resulted. It has also meant a greater interest in home-based entertainment and local community-based pursuits. Additionally, people expect fewer free services and have become adjusted to the concept of paying for what they get.

Contemporary recreation leaders also work within the context of *shifting attitudes on work and leisure*. In the United States requirements of settling the frontier and industrializing production set the stage for early Americans to highly value work. Early society was a work society. As such there was little room for leisure pursuits or leisure values. During the 1960s work went out of vogue. This was a time of relative affluence and rebellion against traditional societal standards. In the leisure services field it was popular to conclude that work values were becoming less important, while leisure values were becoming the fulcrum of life (Kraus, 1983). However, the economic conditions of the late 1970s and early 1980s, and resulting heavy unemployment, created a renewed respect for work. With work becoming hard to get, it became more precious. In addition, there was a strong resistance to compulsory retirement.

According to data from time diaries, Americans now have more leisure—at least more time for leisure. Since 1965 Americans have gained nearly one more free hour per day (Robinson & Godbey, 1997). This may seem at odds with what most American adults say they experience. Many complain of hectic and rushed work lives. Where has the free time gone? According to numerous time-budget studies it has gone to television. Sitting on the couch in front of the television takes up 40 percent of the free time of the average American adult (Robinson & Godbey, 1997).

The *aging of society* is also having a profound effect on leadership in recreation. The proportion of older persons in our society is increasing, and more Americans are retiring (or reducing work hours) at an earlier age (Robinson & Godbey, 1997). This has shifted the programs and facilities leaders offer, as well as the nature of that leadership. Now the attention paid to the needs and powers of an older constituent is much more than a token provision.

Yet the aging of society is not the only demographic change affecting the nature of recreation leadership. For example, a *changing family structure* means today's leaders are focused on providing services for wide ranges of family types. Fewer Americans are married than a generation ago, and fewer still are parents. For those who are, most are employed full-time outside the home. Yet, the evidence of recent studies indicate the amount of time spent by parents on child care has remained essentially constant over recent decades (Robinson & Godbey, 1997). Nonetheless, today's recreation leader is likely to be focused on the *problems of youth*. Problems created by youth dropping out of school, using drugs or alcohol, joining gangs, becoming teenage parents, and being involved in antisocial and delinquent acts are widely recognized (Witt & Crompton, 1996). Many leisure service organizations are responding to these issues through targeted prevention and intervention strategies—ironically, in similar ways as those used by our **pioneer leaders** of a century ago.

Another demographic context for recreation leadership is increasing **social class differences**. As conclusions from the research of Robinson and Godbey (1997)

Case in Point: Over 50 Baseball

"My name is Howard Rollin, and I am the founder and national director of OVER 50 BASEBALL based in Denver, Colorado. I have been involved in adult senior baseball for over 10 years. In 1988, the Men's Senior Baseball League (MSBL) came to Denver, and I was an original member of that year's 8-team league. I was 40 years old at that time playing in a 30 and over league. It was great fun. Although the Denver MSBL was just a 30 and over league, a Denver 40 and over team was created to compete in the MSBL's 40 and Over World Series each fall in Phoenix, Arizona. Many players from those 40 and over teams would have liked to stay and play together during the regular season, but a 40 and over league was denied by the Denver MSBL's board of directors, even though there were over 120 players over the age of 40 already in the league by 1991. The Denver MSBL was convinced that 40 and over baseball would not work.

"Since I have been just an average player, I was finding it more and more difficult by the time I reached my mid-forties to compete with those young 30 and over "whippersnappers" who were coming fresh into the league each year. So I decided to retire from baseball in the fall of 1991, or so I thought.

"In early 1993, the National Adult Baseball Association (NABA) came to Denver. The NABA national director promised me that if their organization would be successful with 30 and over baseball in Denver, I would be given the opportunity to start a 40 and over league in 1994. And so I did! When I started that league, I told everyone that 'within 5 years, there will be a 50 and over league.'

"This past year was the inaugural year for the DENVER OVER 50 BASEBALL LEAGUE. There were 4 teams competing in the Denver metro area. This year we will expand to at least 6 teams."

From "Over 50 Baseball: Who Created Over 50 Baseball and Why?" (November, 1998).

http://www.over50baseball.com/webdoc3.htm

indicated:

> The most worrisome social trend in America over the last several decades has been the widening gap in wealth and income between the social classes. There is also a less noticed counterpart trend: less well educated Americans appear to be 'enjoying' more free time, whereas their college-educated counterparts, for the most part, are not (p. xviii).

Today's society supports the *importance of the individual* in ways previously unknown. Accordingly in recent years, we have seen an increased awareness for the diversity of people. Such dimensions of diversity as gender, race, ethnicity, sexual orientation, and physical/cognitive abilities tell recreation leaders that people must be served according to their backgrounds and cultures. The quality of the individual's life experience and of how an individual prepares to realize her fullest potential is at the core of our societal system. It should also be at the philosophical core of those who lead in recreation. It is this concern for the human being and human development, rather than activities or services per se, that forms the operational context of recreation leaders.

There are, of course, social factors in addition to these that could be cited as important to the context of recreation leadership. Changing technology, social problems such as substance abuse and violent crime, and increased concerns for health and wellness are other factors that make up the context within which leaders professionally exist. The point is, however, that no matter the changes in society, recreation leadership should continue to strive for equitable opportunity; the possibility of success; the development of talent; and the positive social, psychological, and physical welfare of people.

DEFINITIONAL CONTEXT

Leadership appears to be a rather complex and culture-specific concept. Words meaning *chief* or *king* are the only words found in many languages to distinguish a ruler from other members of the society. The *Oxford English Dictionary* (1933), on the other hand, noted the appearance of the word *leader* in the English language as early as the year 1300. However, the word **leadership** did not come into use until around 1800 (Stogdill, 1974).

The Latin and Greek words for leadership shed the most light on our efforts to define the concept. The English word *leadership* is derived from a Greek verb meaning to act, to begin, to achieve, to finish. The corresponding word in Latin means to set in motion, to bear (Sessoms and Stevenson, 1981).

Despite these definitional foundations, there continues to persist as many different definitions of leadership as there are persons who consider themselves leaders. Nevertheless, there is enough similarity between definitions to permit at least a basic description of the concept. In this text leadership is defined as *interpersonal influence exercised by a person or persons, through the process of communication, toward the attainment of an organization's goals.*

This definition recognizes that leadership is typically an ongoing activity and involves influencing a person or group toward the accomplishment of certain goals. It suggests that leadership is oriented toward having an impact on the behaviors of others. This impact may be direct, such as a leader who relates as a director to others, or this impact may be more indirect, such as a leader who relates as an enabler with others.

Leadership influence is exercised by persons; leaders are persons others want to follow. They usually possess certain abilities, attitudes, or qualities that facilitate their role. Leaders have been generally described, for example, as being confident, trustworthy, motivated, visionary, and aware. Persons who follow leaders also usually possess certain qualities that facilitate their role because the relationship is only successful as long as the followers wish to follow the leader. Followers acknowledge and accept one (or more) person(s) as the leader(s).

The process that links the leader's and followers' influence on each other is communication. Both formal and informal means of communication are used by leaders and followers. This linking process is considered so important to successful leadership that an entire chapter is devoted to it later in this text.

Finally, all communication influence between leaders and followers is targeted toward the achievement of something specific. The existence of any group is evidence of the willingness of the members (both leader and followers) to work together, rather than alone, toward a goal. Working or playing together is a give-and-take proposition, and the leader is the catalyst of the process. The leader and the group are considered successful when the group's accomplishments are viewed as greater than those that could have been achieved by individuals.

Figure 1.2 depicts the definitional context of leadership in a recreation setting. It graphically shows the influence between leaders, participant or staff followers, and the achievement of their goals. Leadership is the process of helping people move toward desired recreational outcomes.

Recreation leaders work with groups of participants or with coworkers to mobilize successful recreation for others. In some cases recreation leaders may work with highly structured and stable activity groups where there is a considerable amount of close interaction in even one-to-one roles. In other cases, recreation leaders may be involved in large or loosely structured activity groups without significant interpersonal interaction. Additionally, recreation leaders may make use of their influence with coworkers,

FIGURE 1.2. Leadership: influence toward the attainment of recreation goals

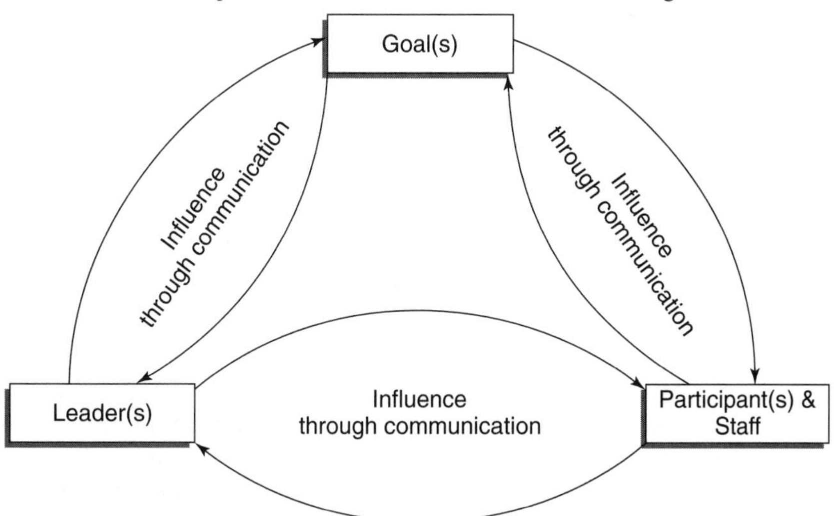

representatives of other organizations, members of professional associations, volunteers, community officials, and other groups not directly linked with recreation goals.

The recreation leader, nonetheless, is an individual who through specific values and abilities in recreation attempts to meet the needs of others by influencing them in the achievement of worthwhile recreational goals. Thus a fun water carnival, a highly reviewed art exhibit, or an adventuresome fifty-mile backpack trip is only worthwhile if it has afforded significant outcomes for the participants—if it has meaningfully satisfied the attainment of their recreational goals. It is the recreation leader who attempts to influence this attainment.

Leader Profile: The Present
Kathy Bayless
Director, Division of Recreational Sports, School of Health, Physical Education, and Recreation, Indiana University, Bloomington. Recreation leaders rely on several different types of power to be effective.

How do recreation leaders influence others? Why do participants accept the influence of a leader? Some would say that this happens because the leader has power. **Power** is the capacity to influence the behavior of others (Mintzberg, 1983). According to Bartol and Martin (1998) there are many sources of leader power.

1. **Legitimate power.** Power comes from a position's location in the organization's hierarchy. Legitimate power comes from the position, rather than from the person per se. Employees follow the directions given by the executive director of a YMCA, because she holds a position of authority.
2. **Reward power.** Power is based on ability to provide valued reward to others. Leisure service organizations offer a variety of rewards to employees and participants including pay raises, prizes, bonuses, interesting assignments, promotions, praise, office space, support for training, time off, and blue ribbons. The greater the leader's control over valued rewards, the greater that leader's reward power.
3. **Coercive power.** Power relies on ability to punish others. Forms of punishment in managed recreation situations include criticism, termination, reprimands, warnings, suspensions, negative performance appraisals, and getting kicked off or out. The greater the leader's freedom to punish, the greater that leader's coercive power.
4. **Expert power.** Power is based on valued expertise. Leaders in recreation, parks, tourism, and sport typically have considerable knowledge, technical skills, and experience important to participants' success in the leisure activity or experience. A rock climbing instructor, for example, possesses a great deal of power with participants in a beginning rock climbing course because of expert power.
5. **Information power.** Information power comes from access to and control over the distribution of information about organizational operations and future plans deemed important by others. Often accompanying legitimate power, directors and supervisors typically have more information about what is going on in the organization than subordinates. This can extend to the power between activity leaders and participants. For example, on a group tour travelers confer power on the trip leader because of his possession of information about the next hotel, restaurant stop, and sightseeing event.
6. **Referent power.** When we like people, want to be like them, and feel friendly toward them, we are more willing to follow their directions. The more the recreation leader is able to cultivate the liking, identification, and admiration of others, the greater her referent power.

Although the six types of power are useful means of influencing others, in recreation leadership situations which are best? Let's consider this question in terms of the likely reactions of subordinates and followers. Expert power and referent power are most likely to lead to participant commitment, while legitimate power, information power, and reward power tend to result in participant compliance (Yukl, 1989, p. 44). The use of coercive power tends to provoke resistance in subordinates, therefore recreation leaders tend to minimize its use.

THEORETICAL CONTEXT

The successful recreation organization has one major attribute that sets it apart from unsuccessful recreation organizations: dynamic and effective leadership. Leadership in recreation is a basic resource. Commercial, governmental, private, outdoor, therapeutic, tourist, and corporate recreation agencies continually search for persons who are able to lead effectively.

Yet, what does it mean to be "able to lead effectively"? For many years theorists have contemplated why and how there is leadership. What makes a leader recognizable as a leader? How is it that a group of persons can be led toward achievement of a common goal? Is leadership inferred by the behavior of leaders or the behavior of followers? Over eleven thousand books and articles have been written about the nature of leadership, seeking to identify what signals leadership effectiveness (Bass,1990). It is the intent of this section of the chapter to overview this theoretical foundation of leadership as it applies to recreation.

The typical question is "What are the specific parameters that are associated with the leadership process?" The research strategies used to answer this question have been varied. One approach has been to determine the general underlying personality and/or physical characteristics that contribute to the presence of leadership. Another research tactic has been to examine leadership behavior to determine common modes of response or characteristic forms of behavior exhibited by persons in leadership positions. A third theoretical premise analyzes the situational characteristics that set the stage for leadership to occur. Finally, leadership has been explained as a reciprocal process.

Trait Approach to Leadership

Probably the earliest research studies into the nature of leadership were those attempts to describe physical and personality characteristics of a leader. This approach suggests that there are certain inherent personal qualities, or traits, that are essential for effective leadership.

In our observation of recreation leaders, it has been suggested that there are certain traits, such as physical energy and friendliness, that are essential. According to the **trait** approach, such universal personal qualities as intelligence, pleasing appearance, and verbal communication ability are inherent and thus transferable from one situation to another.

Additionally, this approach holds that since all individuals do not have these traits, only those who naturally have them can be considered as potential leaders. Consequently, this approach seems to question the worth of training individuals to assume leadership positions; leadership training would thus be useful only to those with the inherent leadership traits.

This theoretical perspective has lost favor with some researchers and theorists. Essentially, studies have failed to find those traits that consistently distinguish leaders from nonleaders. Yet although more recent views on the study of leadership are different than this early trait approach, the ultimate impact of personal qualities on the recreation leader's effectiveness is still viewed in our field as important. Researchers have suggested that it may be possible to isolate leadership traits that are optimal for specific types of situations (House & Baetz, 1979). For example, research reported by McGuire (1983) indicated that the leader characteristic preferences of older recreation participants were activity-specific but tended to be focused toward a preference for older leaders rather than younger leaders.

Behavior Approach to Leadership

Since the trait approach does not seem to provide all the answers, the focus of some research has shifted to the behavior of the leader. That is, many believe that leadership is best explained by what leaders actually do rather than the traits they possess. Thus, leader actions have been the concern of numerous studies.

For example, early attempts at scientifically identifying the most effective leader behaviors were those by University of Iowa researcher Kurt Lewin and his colleagues (Lewin & Lippitt, 1938). Their focus was on three leader behaviors: autocratic, democratic, and laissez-faire. **Autocratic** behavior describes a leader-centered, authoritarian, close supervision type of action. Autocratic leaders usually make unilateral decisions

A Leadership Profile Exercise

What leadership traits do you have? If you are reading this book, it's assumed that you're interested in improving your leadership style and effectiveness or at least interested in learning more about what you already do well and what you might be able to develop further. Recognizing that everyone has ideas about the qualities of good leaders, let's examine what you respect and admire in a leader.

Step 1: A Leader I Know. Do some thinking. To help, grab a blank sheet of paper or use the margin of this book. Bring to your mind at least one recreation leader with whom you have had an experience. This person should be someone you think does an above-average job as a leader. It could be a coach, a scout leader, a camp counselor, or so on. Now identify in your mind an experience where this person was leading. Reflect, in as much detail as you can, on what this person did. How did she/he create a successful recreation experience? Why do you feel she/he did a good job? List on the paper, as specifically as possible, the qualities or skills that you feel made that person a good recreation leader.

Step 2: An Ideal Leader. Let's build on this list. In creating it, did you think of any qualities or traits that, in addition to those demonstrated by the leader you chose, would be desirable? Make a second list and include any other qualities that you think an excellent recreation leader should possess. Make this list as comprehensive as possible. Include any qualities you value from step 1.

Step 3: A Personal Profile. Consider yourself as a recreation leader. Think about experiences where you were leading. Think about what you do, what you say, what qualities allow you to be effective. Create a third list, this time focus on the specific qualities and traits that you feel help you to be a good leader. Don't be overly modest—don't miss anything. If you are new to recreation leadership, don't worry. Just create a list of qualities based on what you think you can do well.

Step 4: Self-Evaluation. Look at all the profile lists you have created. How do you compare? What are your personal traits and abilities in comparison to those of someone you respect or those of your ideal leader? What are the similarities? What are the differences? Make a note on those qualities that you admire but feel you need to develop to count them on your profile. These may be the specific ones in which you will want to focus as you study this book and take this course.

(Adapted from Rohnke & Butler, 1995, pp. 16–19)

and specify activities for others to follow. In contrast, **democratic** leaders involve the group in decision making. Typically the democratic leader is encouraging and helpful; requests the cooperation of others; and as distinguished with autocratic behavior, "shares" the leadership with the members of the group. In **laissez-faire** leadership the group has complete decision-making freedom without leader involvement. Literally meaning "let it be," the laissez-faire leader serves as a resource and participates only when requested by the group.

In one of the original studies (Lewin, Lippitt, & White, 1939) it was strikingly demonstrated that the same group of followers will behave in markedly dissimilar ways under these different leader behaviors. In the study, groups of ten- and eleven-year-olds in a club setting were led at separate times by three adults who behaved according to each of these three leader behaviors. When the groups were under an autocratic leader, they were more dependent on the leader and more egocentric in their peer relationships. The children responded with submissive and generally subdued behavior. Also the amount of hobby projects completed (e.g., model building, soap carving, and other hobbies) was high.

When rotated to a democratic leader behavior, the same children responded with more self-initiative, friendly, and responsible behavior. More group-mindedness and sharing behaviors were evident. Although the quantity of completed projects was not high, the quality of the completed projects under the democratic leadership was better than under the autocratic leader behavior. In response to laissez-faire leadership, hostility and aggressive behavior by the children was more prevalent. Also there was a fair amount of haphazard activity with the children feeling less of a sense of accomplishment because the hobby task progressed slowly and randomly.

Unfortunately, later research results produced more mixed results. Sometimes democratic leadership produced higher performance, and at other times performances were lower to that under autocratic leader behavior. Building on this early work, another classification of leader behavior was developed. First suggested by Fiedler in 1964, developed by University of Michigan researchers in the 1970s, and further studied by Hersey and Blanchard in the 1980s, leadership behavior was described by a leader's tendency toward either task or relationship concerns.

Generally, in **task-oriented behavior** the leader is concerned with productivity, and the satisfaction is derived from the completion of the task. A task-oriented leader would advocate completing the job at hand to the cost of other group needs. In the **relationship-oriented behavior**, by contrast, the leader is mostly concerned for establishing and maintaining good group interpersonal relationships. This leader is focused on the personal welfare of the participants. The emphasis is on human dynamics rather than the completion of the work. The studies by Hersey and Blanchard (1982) found that some leaders focus mainly on directing task accomplishment-related activities, whereas other leaders concentrate on providing emotional support through relationships with their followers. Rarely would a leader be completely task oriented or completely relationship oriented. Most persons in leadership positions have concerns for both, although to varying degrees.

For example, we might suspect that a task-oriented leader would be best for coaching a sport team. However, one study (Danielson, Zelhart, & Drake, 1975) concluded otherwise. These researchers asked 160 junior and senior high school ice hockey players to indicate whether the behavior the researchers described was characteristic of their coach. They found that the coaching was mainly of a communicative nature with a strong focus on the development of the players.

One popularized outgrowth of the research on leader behavior was the **Managerial Grid®** developed by Blake and Mouton (1985). Rather than using a leader behavior continuum, as was used in the University of Michigan studies, the grid used parallel leader behaviors—concern for people and concern for task. Depending on the degree of concern for people and task, a leader can fall anywhere on the grid. However, Blake and Mouton argue that the most desirable leadership behavior is the "9,9" grid location, which involves a high concern for both people and task. (See figure 1.3.)

Situational Approach to Leadership

Although earlier researchers and theorists were aware that the effectiveness of leader traits and leader behaviors may be contingent on factors external to the leader, only more recently has a systematic analysis of the situational characteristics of leadership been undertaken. The various situational explanations claim that effective leadership is ascribed by the leader's trait and behavioral appropriateness to such external factors as the followers, the entire group structure, and the characteristics of the organization. This approach assumes, therefore, that leadership occurs only within the context of a specific situation. Several theories can be grouped under this approach to explaining leadership.

Arguably the most well known of the situational approaches is **Fiedler's contingency theory** of leadership. Fiedler postulated that "leadership effectiveness depends upon the leader's style of interacting with his (or her) group members, and the favorableness of the group-task situation" (Fiedler & Chemers, 1974, p. 81). Thus the existence of leadership in a particular situation is contingent on (1) the appropriateness of the leader's style of relating to group members and (2) the nature of the group or task situation. Figure 1.4 outlines this theory.

According to Fiedler, the leader's style of interacting refers to her motivational orientation (i.e., task versus interpersonal). The favorableness of the group-task situation, on the other hand, is viewed as being a product of three subfactors: leader-member relations, task structure, and power of the leader.

The subfactor of **leader-member relations** refers to the quality of the personal relationship between the leader and followers. Thus, if the followers like the leader, it will be easier for the leader to exert influence. Fiedler views this subfactor as the most important in the determination of situational favorableness.

Case in Point: What Works for the Gander Does Not Work as Well for the Goose

A research study conducted by Hutchison, Valentino, and Kirkner in 1998 examined the effects of leader behaviors and leader gender on employees' perceptions. Ninety-one employees completed a survey measuring leader behaviors, perceived organizational support, and organizational commitment. Results confirmed the hypothesis that a high interpersonal orientation and high task orientation had the most positive effect on employee attitudes. However, the high interpersonal orientation and high task orientation were not equally effective for both female and male leaders. Only those employees who work for a male supervisor high in relationship and task orientations were more committed to the organization.

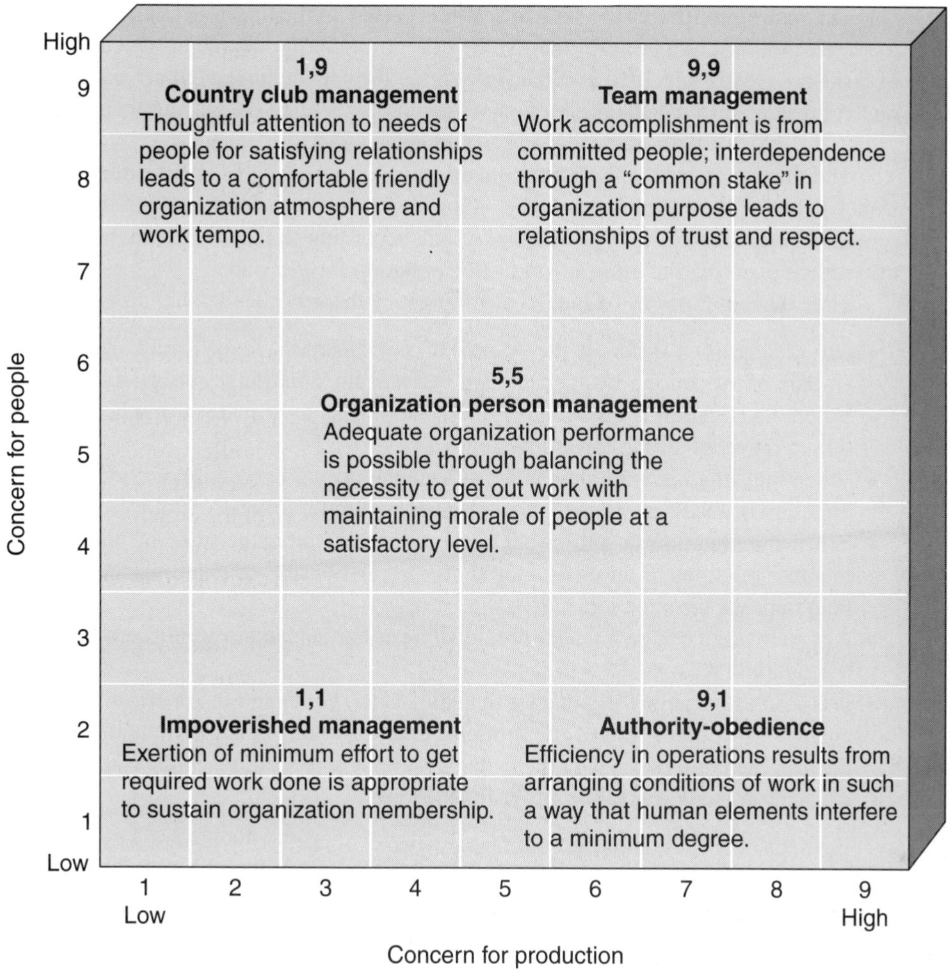

High
9
8
7
6
5
4
3
2
1
Low

Concern for people

1,9
Country club management
Thoughtful attention to needs of people for satisfying relationships leads to a comfortable friendly organization atmosphere and work tempo.

9,9
Team management
Work accomplishment is from committed people; interdependence through a "common stake" in organization purpose leads to relationships of trust and respect.

5,5
Organization person management
Adequate organization performance is possible through balancing the necessity to get out work with maintaining morale of people at a satisfactory level.

1,1
Impoverished management
Exertion of minimum effort to get required work done is appropriate to sustain organization membership.

9,1
Authority-obedience
Efficiency in operations results from arranging conditions of work in such a way that human elements interfere to a minimum degree.

1 Low 2 3 4 5 6 7 8 9 High

Concern for production

FIGURE 1.3. The Managerial Grid (Reprinted with permission from Robert A. Blake and Jane S. Mouton, The Managerial Grid ®, Houston: Gulf Publishing, 1985, p. 12)

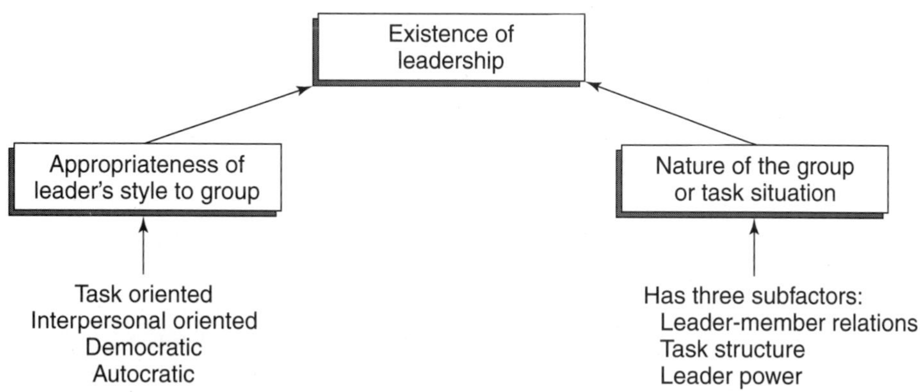

FIGURE 1.4. Outline of the basic assumptions of Fiedler's contingency theory

The **task structure** or the second subfactor refers to the differences among tasks in the degree of structure present; that is, the differences in the degree to which the goals of tasks are clearly specified and the procedures for goal achievement are not ambiguous. A postulate of Fiedler's theory is that the more structured the task performed by the group, the easier it is for a leader to exert influence.

The third subfactor is the **power position** of the leader. This is determined by the leader's control over group awards, his authority over group members, and the support provided the leader by the organization. Again, according to Fiedler, the more powerful the leader's position, the more favorable the situation for the leader.

Thus the major points of Fiedler's contingency theory of leadership are as follows:

- Group situations differ in the degree of favorableness for a leader. That is, the amount of influence a leader can exert varies from situation to situation.
- When the situation is unfavorable, the leader needs to provide strong task orientation to move the group toward its goal.
- When the situation is favorable, a task-oriented leader can easily provide whatever direction is necessary because the followers willingly follow.
- When the situation is only moderately favorable, either because of poor leader-member relations or an unstructured task, a relationship-oriented leader is best to help improve the situation.
- Any individual can be a leader provided his or her leadership style is matched with the situation.
- It is easier to change the situation than the leader. For example, an organization can change the composition of the group to alter the leader-member relations, change the task structure by varying the extent of rules and procedures in the task situation, or increase the power (authority) of the leader.

Leader Profile: The Present
R. Dean Tile
Executive Director, National Recreation and Park Association. His leadership demonstrates all four leader behaviors: directive, supportive, participative, and achievement-oriented.

Fiedler's introduction of the contingency theory of leadership generated a multitude of research studies. However, there has not been consistent support for his theory. On the other hand, a number of other theorists have attempted to account for the process of leadership by centering on the behaviors of the leader across different situations. One of these theories is the path-goal theory.

The **path-goal theory** of leadership places emphasis on the needs and goals of the followers. That is, as the follower moves along the "path" toward her goal, the appropriate function of the leader is to provide the coaching, guidance, support, and rewards necessary. Thus a major notion of the path-goal theory is that the leader's function is a supplemental one. The leader's efforts are directed toward assisting the subordinate or follower in reaching his goals by reducing road blocks and increasing the opportunities for personal satisfaction en route (House & Dessler, 1974).

To affect recreation participant "paths" and "goals" four leader behaviors are employed according to their appropriateness to the situation (Bartol & Martin, 1998).

1. **Directive leader** behavior involves letting participants know what is expected of them, providing guidance, and identifying standards. This behavior strongly demonstrates task orientation.
2. **Supportive leader** behavior shows concern for the well-being and needs of participants, and being friendly and approachable. This behavior is strongly relationship oriented.
3. **Participative leader** behavior consults with participants, encourages their suggestions, and considers their ideas when making decisions.

4. **Achievement-oriented leader** behavior involves setting goals, expecting a high level of achievement, and conveying a high degree of confidence in participants.

But this isn't all there is to it. To enhance the path-goal of participants, leaders also need to consider two types of situational factors: participant and environmental characteristics (Bartol & Martin, 1998).

1. Participant characteristics include personality traits, skill levels, abilities, and needs. Persons with low skills in a particular recreation pursuit are likely to thrive best under directive leadership, while highly skilled persons are apt to appreciate a participative leader.
2. Environmental characteristics fall into three categories: the task, the group, and the organization's authority system (such as levels in the hierarchy). For example, supportive leaders may be what is needed when the task is boring, while achievement-oriented leaders may increase motivation on an interesting task.

In using the path-goal theory to determine appropriate leader behavior, leaders need to assess the various situational factors. Several examples of how this might work are shown in figure 1.5.

Because the path-goal theory can account for multiple leader behaviors and possibly large numbers of situational factors operating simultaneously, only limited research testing of the theory has been conducted, yet a recent evaluation of studies does indicate general support (Indvik, 1986).

Reciprocal Approach to Leadership

Since the development of the path-goal theory, a newer "family" of leadership theories emerged that focus on the relational and reciprocal nature of the leader-participant interaction. These approaches emphasized the mutual goals and motivations of both leaders and followers and elevated the importance of the role of followers in the leadership process (Komives, Lucas, & McMahon, 1998). There was also a renewed recognition of the importance of leader traits and behaviors, something ignored by the situational theories (Weese, 1995). These reciprocal approaches are referred to as transactional and transformational leaders.

FIGURE 1.5. Path-goal theory examples

Leader behavior		Situational factor		Goal
Directive	→	Children in an after-school playground program	→	Control of the group
Supportive	→	Patients dealing with monotony in a residential rehabilitation center	→	Increase the sense of the intrinsic value of the therapy regime
Participative	→	An unstructured group task, such as making a ship out of scrap materials for adults on a cruise	→	Goal achievement
Achievement oriented	→	Outdoor challenge program for adolescent girls with low self-confidence	→	Increase effort and performance expectations

Transactional leaders motivate subordinates and participants to perform at expected levels by helping them recognize task responsibilities, identify goals, acquire confidence about meeting desired performance levels, and understand how the needs and the rewards they desire are linked to goal achievement (Bartol & Martin, 1998). As you have probably recognized, transactional leadership is similar to the path-goal theory. In contrast, **transformational leaders** motivate individuals to perform beyond normal expectations by inspiring them to focus on broader missions that "transcend" their immediate self-interests, to concentrate on intrinsic higher-level goals (such as self-actualization) rather than extrinsic lower-level goals (such as safety), and to have extraordinary confidence in themselves (Bartol & Martin, 1998). Transformational leadership is transactional leadership with what we might call add-ons: performance beyond expectations. Figure 1.6 helps us visualize this idea.

A transformational, or visionary, leader:

1. has a mental image of both the current and possible future status of the group or organization,
2. understands the critical components that need to be carried out to realize this desired end, and
3. has the ability to relate this focus to others in a charismatic fashion so that they take responsibility for the vision and are committed to making it a reality (Sashkin, 1986).

According to Bass (1985) three leader factors are particularly important to transformational leadership: charisma, individualized consideration, and intellectual stimulation. **Charisma** is the leader's ability to convey a sense of vision that inspires followers. Classic examples of leaders in history said to have had charisma are Martin Luther King, Jr., Mahatma Gandhi, and John F. Kennedy. Leaders with charisma inspire pride, respect, and faith in a group. The second factor in transformational leadership, individualized consideration, involves delegating projects to help develop group members' capabilities. Also, transformational leaders do not treat all people the same. Instead they consider each individual's situation as unique and make varied and different decisions accordingly (Weese, 1995). Finally, an intellectually stimulating leader influences participants and subordinates to think about problems and situations in new and

FIGURE 1.6. Transactional and transformational leadership (based on Bass, 1985, p. 23)

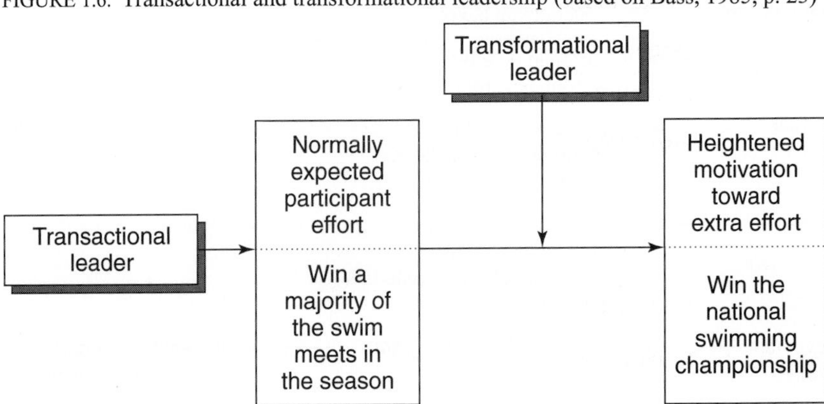

creative ways. These leaders offer new ideas to stimulate people to rethink old ways of doing things.

Leadership is a complex, frequently misunderstood term that has been studied from nearly every conceivable angle, in a multitude of settings. In this section of the chapter, we have looked at the path of leadership theory development from this research literature. Earliest studies focused on the traits and characteristics deemed important to leaders. While the trait approach to explaining leadership served as a useful starting place it was too narrowly focused. To follow was the behavioral explanation of leadership. This second thrust tried to identify leader behaviors that would be most effective in managing groups of people. However, similar to the trait approach, the behavioral theories of leadership also fell out of favor, because specific leader behaviors were not effective in all situations. So, these theories gave way to the situational theories of leadership. This third approach held that the specific situation played a major role in determining leadership effectiveness. Today, theorists believe that certain traits and behaviors are descriptive of the great leaders, and their transformational approach with groups of people is what makes for effective leadership. A summary of this leader theory development path is in figure 1.7.

Summary

Recreation leadership does not exist within a vacuum. Instead leadership is a professional resource operating within the context of its history, its society, its definitions, and its theories.

In the historical context early leaders such as Lee, Gulick, Enderis, Hill, and many others can be cited as responsible for the imagination, foresight, conviction, and action that helped recreation become recognized as a basic human and societal need. Yet the leadership that these pioneers expressed is different from what it is today. In our early professional history, the leaders completely dominated the form and the content of recreation services. Today's leader in recreation deals within a more democratic relationship with participants; is more knowledgeable, better trained, and more global in perspective; works with a more diversified clientele; and is responsible for a more diversified and sophisticated recreation setting.

FIGURE 1.7. Summary of leadership theories

Approach	Period	Examples	Major points
Trait	1907–1947	Physical energy, friendliness, intelligence	Leaders have natural physical and personality characteristics
Behavior	1950s–1980s	Lewin's autocratic democratic and laissez-faire; Hersey & Blanchard's task-oriented and relationship-oriented leaders; The Managerial Grid ®	Leaders behave in certain ways
Situational	1950s–1980s	Fiedler's contingency theory	The situation determines the optimal leader traits and behaviors
Reciprocal	1980s–present	Transactional and transformational leaders	Leadership is a relational process

Within the societal context, recreation represents a major area of service responsibility for various governmental levels, private service organizations, and commercial enterprises. Modern society the world over is increasingly calling on the leadership expertise of many women and men employed in leisure-related settings. This may be attributed to society's recognition that recreation is a highly significant and inseparable aspect of contemporary life.

Leadership also exists within a definitional context. In this book leadership is defined as a communicated interpersonal influence in behalf of other persons' goal attainment.

Finally, it is the theoretical context that attempts to answer "What does it mean to be able to lead effectively?" The research strategies used to answer this question have been leader traits, behaviors, situations, and leader-follower relations (reciprocal).

Questions and Activities for Review and Discussion

1. The professionalization of leisure in the United States began around the turn of the last century with the leadership efforts of urban playground organizers and supervisors. Why is the early leadership of people like Lee important to our current professional efforts?
2. Has the role of recreation leaders in service provision changed since the early work of Gulick, Hill, and the others? In what ways?
3. What do you see as the appropriate role of professional leadership for recreation in the midst of contemporary demographic changes?
4. The Greek verb for leadership means to act, to begin, to achieve, to finish. How would you apply these meanings to recreation leadership?
5. What is meant by the statement "leadership involves influence"? In terms of recreation leadership, influence for what?
6. Why is an overall theoretical understanding of leadership important? Can you name some ways in which knowing theory can be useful in an actual recreation leadership situation?
7. What personal traits or characteristics would you use to describe the recreation leader? Why is this approach inadequate for a complete theoretical explanation of the leadership phenomena?
8. According to the various behavioral theories of leadership, what determines effective leadership? Can you illustrate this with an example from your own experience in leadership?
9. Describe Fiedler's contingency theory of leadership. How would you interpret this theory so that it has application to the recreation leader?
10. How is transformational leadership an "add-on" to transactional leadership? Can you cite an example from your own experience?

References

Avedon, E. M. (1974). *Therapeutic recreation service: An applied behavioral science approach.* Englewood Cliffs, NJ: Prentice-Hall.

Bartol, K. M., & Martin, D. C. (1998). *Management* (3rd ed.). New York: McGraw-Hill.

Bass, B. M. (1985). *Leadership and performance beyond expectations*. New York: Free Press.

Bass, B. M. (1990). *Stogdill's handbook of leadership*. New York: Free Press.

Blake, R. A., & Mouton, J. S. (1985). *The Managerial Grid® III*. Houston: Gulf Publishing.

Butler, G. D. (1965). *Pioneers in public recreation*. Minneapolis, MN: Burgess Publishing.

Danielson, R. R., Zelhart, P. F., & Drake, C. J. (1975). Multidimensional scaling and factor analysis of coaching behavior as perceived by high school hockey players. *Research Quarterly*, *46*(3), 323–424.

Davis, M. J. (1978). Leadership in leisure service. In H. Ibrahim & F. Martin (Eds.), *Leisure: An introduction*. Los Alamitos, CA: Hwong Publishing.

Duncan, M. (1980). Back to our radical roots. In T. L. Goodale & P. A. Witt (Eds.), *Recreation and leisure: Issues in an era of change.* State College, PA: Venture Publishing.

Fiedler, F. E., & Chemers, M. M. (1974). *Leadership and effective management.* Glenview, IL: Scott, Foresman.

Goodale, T. L. (1980). Of godots and goodbars: On waiting and looking for change. In T. L. Goodale & P. A. Witt (Eds.), *Recreation and leisure: Issues in an era of change*. State College, PA: Venture Publishing.

Gray, D. E. (1984). Managing our way to a preferred future. *Parks and Recreation, 19*(5), 47–49.

Hartman, E. T. (1937). Joseph Lee, creative philanthropist. *Recreation, 31*, 546–547, 583.

Hersey, P., & Blanchard, K. H. (1982). *Management of organizational behavior: Utilizing human resources* (4th ed.). Englewood Cliffs, NJ: Prentice-Hall.

House, R. J., & Baetz, M. L. (1979). Leadership: Some empirical generalizations and new research directions. *Research in Organizational Behavior, 1*, 341–423.

House, R. J., & Dessler, G. (1974). The path-goal theory of leadership: Some post hoc and a priori tests. In J. G. Hunt & L. L. Larson (Eds.), *Contingency approaches to leadership*. Carbondale, IL: Southern Illinois University Press.

Hutchison, S., Valentino, K. E., & Kirkner, S. L. (1998). What works for the gander does not work as well for the goose: The effects of leader behavior. *Journal of Applied Social Psychology, 28*(2), 171–182.

Indvik, J. (1986). Path-goal theory of leadership: A meta-analysis. In J. A. Pearce & R. B. Robinson (Eds.), *Best Paper Proceedings*. Chicago: Academy of Management.

Knapp, R. F. (1972). Play for America: The national recreation association, 1906–1950. *Parks and Recreation, 7*(10), 20–27, 43–47.

Komives, S. R., Lucas, N., & McMahon, T. R. (1998). *Exploring leadership: For college students who want to make a difference*. San Francisco: Jossey-Bass.

Kraus, R. (1983). The changing role of government in recreation, parks, and leisure services. In The Academy of Leisure Sciences, *Values and leisure and trends in leisure services*. State College, PA: Venture Publishing.

Lambert, T. (1996). *The power of influence: Intensive influencing skills at work*. London: Nicholas Brealey Publishing.

Lewin, K., & Lippitt, R. (1938). An experimental approach to the study of autocracy and democracy: A preliminary note. *Sociometry, 1*, 292–300.

Lewin, K., Lippitt, R., & White, R. K. (1939). Patterns of aggressive behavior in experimentally created social climates. *Journal of Social Psychology, 10*, 271–301.

McCall, J. R., & McCall, V. N. (1977). *Outdoor recreation: Forest, park, and wilderness*. Beverly Hills, CA: Bruce.

McGuire, F. A. (1983, October). *Factors influencing leadership preferences of the elderly: Perceived personal competence versus perceived leader competence*. Paper presented to the Leisure Research Symposium, Kansas City, MO.

Mintzberg, H. (1983). *Power in and around organizations*. Englewood Cliffs, NJ: Prentice-Hall.

Oxford English Dictionary (1933). London: Oxford University Press.

Robinson, J. P., & Godbey, G. (1997). *Time for life: The surprising ways Americans use their time*. University Park, PA: The Pennsylvania State University Press.

Rohnke, K., & Butler, S. (1995). *Quicksilver: Adventure games, initiative problems, trust activities and a guide to effective leadership*. Dubuque, IA: Kendall/Hunt Publishing.

Sashkin, M. (1986). *Becoming a visionary leader.* King of Prussia, PA: Organizational Design and Development, Inc.

Sessoms, H. D., & Stevenson, J. L. (1981). *Leadership and group dynamics*. Boston: Allyn & Bacon.

Stogdill, R. M. (1974). *Handbook of leadership: A survey of theory and research*. New York: The Free Press.

Weese, W. J. (1995). A synthesis of leadership theory and a prelude to the five "C" model. *European Journal of Sport Management, 2*(1), 59–71.

Weiskopf, D. C. (1982). *Recreation and Leisure: Improving the Quality of Life*. Boston: Allyn & Bacon.
Witt, P. A., & Crompton, J. L. (1996). *Recreation programs that work for at-risk youth: The challenge of shaping the future*. State College, PA: Venture Publishing.
Yukl, G. A. (1989). *Leadership in organizations* (2nd ed.). Englewood Cliffs, NJ: Prentice-Hall.

Web Resources

American Therapeutic Recreation Association: www.atra-tr.org/

Boys Scouts of America: www.bsa.scouting.org/

Characteristics of charismatic leaders:
http://home.ubalt.edu/ntsbmilb/ob/ob10/sld008.htm

Characteristics of transactional and transformational leaders:
http://home.ubalt.edu/ntsbmilb/ob/obl0/sld009.htm

Girl Scouts of America: www.girlscouts.org/

Leader behaviors: www-unix.oit.umas.edu/~mee/leadership_theories_mm3.htm

Leadership development: www.smartbiz.com/sbs/columns/abu19.htm

Leadership theory: www.fhsu.edu/htmlpages/faculty/cocc/org-link.htm
http://cbpa.louisville.edu/bruce/rfct600/schwart2.htm

National Adult Baseball Association: www.dugout/org/about/About/htm

National Park Service: www.nps.gov/

National Parks and Conservation Association: www.npca.com/

National Parks Magazine: www.ncpa.com/newsstand.html

National Recreation and Park Association: www.nrpa.org

National Recreation Database: www.lin.ca/findrs.htm

National Therapeutic Recreation Society: www.nrpa.org/brances/ntrs.htm

Organization change by design: www.gridsmi.com/

YMCA: www.ymca.org/

YWCA: www.ywca.org/

CHAPTER 2

Who Is The Recreation Leader?

Leadership goes beyond management as it provides the vision of the future for the field.
—Mobley, 1996, p. 35.

Learning Objectives

To continue to establish an introductory foundation for understanding leadership, you will be able to appreciate recreation leaders' customary:

• settings • types • functions • roles

Key Terms

municipal and county government p. 28
state, provincial, and federal government p. 29
therapeutic recreation p. 30
commercial recreation p. 30
corporate recreation p. 31
private recreation p. 31
human service organizations p. 31
direct service leader p. 32
supervisory leader p. 32
administrative leader p. 33
technical functions p. 34
human relations functions p. 34
conceptual functions p. 34
communicator p. 39
enabler p. 39
innovator p. 39
intrapreneur p. 40
idea champion p. 40
sponsor p. 40
orchestrator p. 40
dreamer p. 41
teacher p. 41
coordinator p. 41
motivator p. 41
problem solver p. 41
decision maker p. 42

Beth Monroe is the special programs coordinator for a small city. It is her responsibility to plan and conduct (with the assistance of other staff and volunteers) recreation programs for community residents with mental or physical disabilities. She also plans and leads citywide special events such as kite flying tournaments, summer musical concerts in the parks, and big band era dances. Beth is thirty years old and has a bachelor's degree in recreation.

Randy Marks is director of employee recreation services for a large manufacturing company. Bobbie Levine directs the cultural, educational, and recreational activities at a community center for older adults. One of Melanie Christiansen's first professional positions was as special groups program coordinator for a commercial theme park. Van Alderson is the director of guest services for a convention hotel. Doug Percival is a recreation center director for a U.S. Air Force base in Europe. Lorraine Binkley directs the outdoor recreation and outings program at the student union for a university. Sally Williams plans and leads social, dramatic, music, craft, and trip programs for residential clients in a convalescent center.

Sandy Preston is a Girl Scout leader, and Denise Setser spent last winter coaching a 9–11 year old basketball league at the YMCA. Bret Keeling is spending his college summers assisting with interpretive programs for the National Park Service, while Susie Morris spends her summers as a lifeguard at a fitness center. Linda Montague is a recreation student intern for a community theater.

Who are recreation leaders? They are Beth, Randy, Bobbie, Melanie, Van, Doug, Lorraine, Sally, Sandy, Denise, Bret, Susie, and Linda. These fictional examples based on real people filling actual positions as recreation leaders show that some leaders are full-time, salaried employees of large organizations; others are part-time or seasonal workers; and others are leading in recreation as volunteers. These persons, and their settings, functions, and roles, illustrate recreation leadership.

Some argue that the importance of leadership is greatly overrated and that in many contexts, leaders make little or no difference (Yukl, 1989). As we learned in chapter 1, there has been extensive research, yet we are still trying to pinpoint what leadership is. Because of this some critics argue that leaders may not be as important as we sometimes think (Bartol & Martin, 1998). This chapter takes aim at this criticism by defending the importance of the settings, types, roles, and functions of recreation leaders.

SETTINGS FOR RECREATION LEADERS

Perhaps one of the most unique and exciting realizations about recreation leadership is the wide diversity of settings within which it may be found. Recreation leaders carry out a variety of functions in a variety of places.

Leader Profile: The Present
Tracey Crawford
Superintendent of Recreation, Northern Suburban Special Recreation Association. Her duties include: development, maintaining, and acquiring programs for citizens with disabilities in Northfield, Illinois.

Municipal and County Government

Local governments have traditionally been one of the major providers of recreation and park services in North America. Most Americans depend on **municipal and county government** to provide many important leisure services. Literally thousands of towns and cities and hundreds of counties, sponsor recreation services through full-time agencies. In some areas, public school districts provide recreation facilities and programs, and in others (such as Illinois), special districts have been established by local governments to provide these services. In addition to these, many other local government agencies such as housing authorities, police departments, public museums and libraries, and youth and aging commissions often share the sponsorship of recreation services.

Municipal and county governments acquire, develop, and maintain facilities needed for the leisure participation of local citizens. They also provide the program structure for the use of these facilities. This makes them the prime government source of sport, recreation, and park services. This is because local governments reach more people in providing services as they are closest to their daily lives. For example, most towns and cities provide softball, baseball, tennis, swimming, basketball, picnic, playground, fitness, and community center services. Medium to large cities also offer golf, other sports such as soccer and biking, nature and garden, cultural art, museum, and library services.

In local government agencies recreation leadership positions are available for administrators, supervisors, center directors, sport and fitness specialists, cultural arts program coordinators, youth specialists, planners and researchers, public relations officers, special program directors, and park superintendents.

State, Provincial, and Federal Government

Numerous organizations at the **state, provincial, and federal government** levels sponsor recreation services. As a recreation leader, you could find yourself working in morale, welfare, and recreation services for a branch of the U.S. Armed Forces or in campground planning for the Tennessee Valley Authority.

In the United States, for example, the federal government provides a broad assortment of leisure services. While difficult to count from election to election, there are more than ninety federal departments, bureaus, commissions, councils, divisions, and authorities that have at least some responsibility for park and recreation provisions (Russell, 1996). The notion that recreation services are also a state responsibility emerged in the 1960s and 1970s as the federal government gave states more authority to dispense federal funds to their own agencies. Accordingly, states are diverse in the manner in which they sponsor these services, yet typically provide parks, forests, historical and cultural preserves, and lakes and beaches for recreational use. States also promote tourism to the state through departments of commerce, planning, highways, natural resources, and tourism. At this moment you might also be a beneficiary of another state function in leisure—state colleges and universities that offer professional curriculums to prepare students for careers in leisure services.

Recreation leadership positions in state and federal agencies in the United States include rangers, naturalists, outdoor education specialists, park superintendents, planners, extension agents, conservation workers, museum directors, grant and technical assistance coordinators, tourism directors, and even college professors.

Voluntary Organizations

Major contributors to a community's recreation services are the nongovernmental, nonprofit agencies sponsored by private citizens. Almost all of us have been touched by

Case in Point: Big Brothers/Big Sisters

The idea behind the Big Brothers/Big Sisters program is simple: to involve adults in the life of a young person, to be a friend, a role model, and a hero. Men and women are matched with young boys and girls who need more adults in their lives. There are several ways this can happen. First, is the one-on-one match of an adult with a child—a "big brother" or a "big sister." Someone the child can count on for a few hours week after week—count on for going to a movie, playing in the park, doing homework, or hanging out. There is also "first friends," a program that provides activities for children who are waiting to be matched with a big brother or big sister. Volunteers can sign up for as many activities with small groups of children as they wish—such things as horseback riding, picnics, basketball games, and ice skating. Finally, "school friends" is available as a school-based mentoring program helping children improve their self-esteem and academic skills. An adult volunteer is paired with a student for a weekly session together at the school under the direction of the classroom teacher.

these services. These include 4-H Clubs; Girls' and Boys' Clubs; Girl Scouts of America; Boy Scouts of America; Camp Fire, Inc.; religiously oriented social agencies such as YMCA, YWCA, and CYO; Easter Seal Society; Special Olympics, Inc.; and the American Association of Retired Persons. These organizations are defined for the most part as groups that provide recreation experiences for their members. In addition to their more traditional programs of outdoor recreation, cultural arts and sports, these voluntary organizations have tried hard in recent years to help solve social problems. Through their recreation services, they have focused on problems of interracial and intercultural relationships, poverty, youth-at-risk, teenage parenting, and violence. Their programs have broadened to include such atypical recreation services as vocational guidance, school subject tutoring, and family counseling.

Positions are available for activity specialists, program supervisors, counselors, facility managers, and administrators.

Therapeutic Recreation Settings

There are many professional opportunities for those whose prime concern is promoting the well-being of persons who have disabilities that limit their full involvement in recreation. **Therapeutic recreation** is the provision of recreation services and opportunities to assist individuals in establishing and expressing an independent leisure lifestyle. Therapeutic recreation specialists use leisure as a treatment for disability or illness. Working with other medical specialists, they focus on the healing potential of leisure.

Job opportunities range from working with substance abusers to children with physical disabilities to patients in convalescence to adjudicated youth.

In addition to community-based therapeutic recreation leadership efforts, many therapeutic recreation specialists work within an institutional setting. Such facilities as psychiatric hospitals, rehabilitation centers, chronic disease centers, children's hospitals, convalescent and other extended care facilities, schools for persons with mental disabilities, correctional institutions, special camps, group homes, and others maintain professional positions for administrators, supervisors, and program specialists.

Commercial Organizations

There has been a dramatic growth in the number, variety, and scope of enterprises that provide recreation services as a financially profitable business, called **commercial recreation.** As a result, this category represents, perhaps, the largest provider of organized recreation in North America. This is because in industrialized societies, people are willing (and often eager) to pay for leisure. Recreation services operated for commercial purposes include a wide variety from shopping malls to ski resorts. There are commercial campgrounds, golf courses, tennis courts, bowling centers, riding stables, health spas, museums, game rooms, playgrounds, theaters, dance studios, sport stadiums, racetracks, music halls, and gymnasiums. Despite this variety, certain types of recreation are regarded the domain of mainly commercial sponsorship. Commercial enterprises are more likely to be associated with entertainment, popular culture, spectator sport, theme park, tourism, food and drink, and shopping facilities and programs.

Positions in commercial recreation include managers, directors, sales personnel, and planners. Of particular interest to today's newly trained recreation professional is a career in the tourism occupations. These professionals organize conferences and meetings, market the attractions of a particular site or facility, and manage vacation destinations.

Other Settings

Other settings for recreation leadership can also be identified. The recreation services that corporations and companies make available to employees and their families, for example, are typically part of more comprehensive personnel service efforts. This form of **corporate recreation** sponsorship has grown rapidly with more than 3,000 companies and industries providing a wide scope of recreation, fitness, educational, cultural, and social services (Nudel, 1984, p. 41). When professional leadership is used in this setting, such career options as recreation program director; facility manager; resort, camp, or center director; fitness specialist; wellness program coordinator; sport coach; and retirement counselor are possible.

Country clubs, yacht clubs, fraternities and sororities, service clubs, churches, and synagogues represent **private recreation** membership organizations that frequently provide recreation programs and facilities for their members. In some cases recreation staff are employed to carry out membership recreation services.

Colleges and universities also employ recreation leaders in functions ranging from intramural and sport club programming; to student union activities; to the development and implementation of special events, dances, lecture series, film fests, and tours.

The scope of leadership settings is truly unlimited. Do you want to become a cruise ship activity director, leisure education specialist, concert promoter, tour guide, youth sports coach, stadium manager, aquatics specialist, environmental interpreter, church recreation director, fitness specialist, or museum guide?

Despite this far-ranging assortment of settings and wide diversity of positions, those individuals working in recreation and park organizations are a part of a more broadly conceptualized mission. "Human services" is the label used to describe those organizations and their staff whose goal is the enhancement of the quality of life for those served.

This means that human service professionals are concerned with the promotion of human happiness and life satisfaction and seek to realize this objective by providing opportunities for mental, physical, social, cultural, educational, and spiritual well-being. Recreation leaders, along with other professionals from fields such as health, education, religion, and social welfare, are considered to be a part of this human services mission.

Such **human service organizations** as medical facilities, mental health centers, social service agencies, schools, churches and synagogues, colleges, police departments, career-consulting firms, and recreation organizations are numerous in our society and provide many of the services we have come to consider an essential part of our culture. As an integral part of this broader perspective, the recreation leader works in a variety of settings to join with the efforts of other societal leaders.

How is this achieved? Leaders in all settings assume specific levels of responsibility and roles, while performing certain tasks that make it possible to achieve their missions. Recreation leaders are no exception. These may be described in terms of types, roles, and functions. The focus of the remainder of this chapter is to overview recreation leadership in terms of levels of responsibility, professional capacities, and performance tasks.

TYPES OF RECREATION LEADERS

Who is the recreation leader in terms of different levels of responsibility? For leader types, recreation leader responsibilities can be summarized according to three categories: direct service, supervisory, and administrative. These categories can be viewed as a vertical differentiation among leaders because they match the three typical hierarchical levels of recreation, park, and sport organizations. This is illustrated in figure 2.1. Even though the actual job titles of recreation leaders are nonstandardized and numerous, it is still possible to broadly summarize everyone's level of responsibility according to these three types.

Direct Service

The **direct service leader** in recreation organizations is involved in face-to-face, front line contact with those persons the organization serves. The direct service leader could be a playground leader, a tennis coach, a dance instructor, a camp counselor, a tour guide, or one of many positions found within recreation agencies. These leaders work directly with constituents, guests, or clients. This type of leader has the most immediate and constant contact with program participants and facility users. The attitudes and skills taught in this text are most vital to this type of recreation leader.

Supervisory

A **supervisory leader** within a recreation organization is usually considered to be working at a middle management job level. Supervision is a process that involves the coordination, direction, and evaluation of other staff and volunteers in the organization. The primary objective of the recreation supervisor is to facilitate the agency's services by helping other staff members become more effective. This means that supervision is an

FIGURE 2.1. Hierarchical levels of recreation leaders and organizations

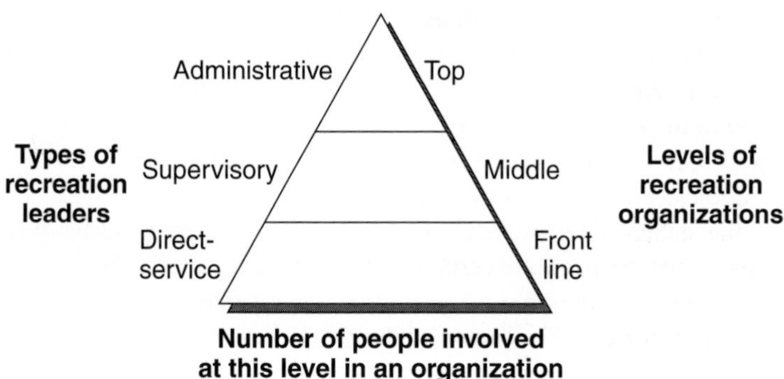

enabling endeavor; supervisors enable direct-service leaders to use their abilities to achieve the organization's goals.

As is true with all three types of recreation leaders, the exact tasks of supervisors vary according to their employment assignments. For example, area supervisors are usually responsible for overseeing the staff and services within a single geographical area such as a district of a city or a designated floor in a hospital. In contrast, facility supervisors oversee a single major building or property such as a community center, softball complex, or off-road vehicle park. Usually facility supervisors are responsible for supervising the work of the direct service program leaders as well as facility maintenance personnel. Finally, a program supervisor is usually a specialist in a particular type of program service such as older adults, performing arts, or fitness. They are responsible for carrying out programs and services within the program specialty area for the entire organization.

The attitudes and skills discussed in this book are also important to this type of recreation leader.

Leader Profile: The Past
Randall Balon
Former Chief Deputy, Los Angeles County Department of Parks and Recreation. He served at the administrative leader level.

Administrative

An **administrative leader's** (top level) major focus is on planning, developing, controlling, and evaluating services for the entire recreation organization. The executive director for a Girl Scout council, the general manager for a resort island, and the administrator of a municipal recreation and park department also require an underpinning of the leadership skills and attitudes discussed in this book to guide their organization toward the accomplishment of its goals. This book does not, however, offer information beyond these basic competencies because the administrator's responsibilities also usually include fiscal management and control, long-range strategic planning, resource development, and policy implementation.

Although the basic leadership processes apply to all three leader types, there are differences. We will learn in the next section the functional differences of recreation leaders.

RECREATION LEADER FUNCTIONS

Who is the recreation leader in terms of the functions performed?

Leadership functions are those professional and personal tasks that enable leaders to influence others. They are those performance methods that, in essence, make it all possible. By leadership's definition, a person is considered to possess leadership abilities when he is able to influence others toward certain predetermined ends.

Although you may have the title of leader such as waterfront director, leadership does not occur until you behave in certain ways. In other words, if a waterfront director not only has the authority that is inherent in the title, but also performs the functions of a waterfront director, then it is more likely that she will be able to help other staff and pool users achieve their objectives.

If we were to list them, we would discover many functions that describe the actions and methods of the recreation leader. Therefore it may be useful to categorize these numerous functions according to three types of tasks. According to Hersey and Blanchard (1982), these are labeled technical, human relations, and conceptual functions. These function categories are defined as:

- **Technical functions:** The use of knowledge, methods, techniques, and equipment necessary for the performance of specific tasks as acquired from experience, education, and training. A common example is computer-based skills.
- **Human relations functions:** Working with and through people, including the use of motivation and an application of effective leadership styles. Conflict management is an example.
- **Conceptual functions:** An understanding of the complexities of the overall organization, where one's responsibilities fit in, and how the organization relates to its world outside. Strategic planning is an example of this function.

Within the technical, human relations, and conceptual function categories, specific recreation leadership tasks can be discussed. The following material overviews those particular tasks that describe the day-to-day functioning of a typical recreation leader. Many of these functions are also discussed in later chapters.

Technical Functions

The Recreation Leader Plans Programs

The primary goal of any recreation organization is to provide recreation experience opportunities. Ultimately all the energies of the agency are devoted to this objective. The "package" of recreation experience opportunities the organization provides is usually termed its program. Program planning is a fundamental function for recreation leaders and can range from preparing an individualized treatment program for a hospital patient to establishing a year-round cultural arts program for a state park system.

The Recreation Leader Carries Out Organizational Management

Organizational management entails ability in those overall agency operations that support the program. For example, the recreation leader needs competency in various computing operations, budgeting, staffing, scheduling, training, facility development, public relations, and marketing. This function requires the ability to know what monies are available, what physical facilities can be used, and what equipment and staff resources can be put to best use. Organizational management requires that the leader effectively employs all available resources in planning, organizing, and implementing services.

The Recreation Leader Evaluates

The process of evaluation is basic to the operation of a recreation agency. Evaluative information is necessary to determine whether the agency is adequately serving its constituency. Most recreation organizations evaluate three aspects of their operation: programs, maintenance, and staff. The evaluation process involves the designation of objectives, then the measurement of the extent to which the objectives have been met. The recreation leader's task is to be able to judge when evaluation is necessary, to select and use appropriate measurement techniques, to interpret the results, and to implement the recommendations so that the program offerings or staff performances are improved. The competent leader is constantly able to evaluate the efficiency and effectiveness of her services to the participant and the quality of her own professional functioning within the agency.

The Recreation Leader Is Aware of and Works Within a Legal Framework

The operating practices of most recreation organizations are subject to the regulatory stipulations of provincial, state, local, and federal laws. For example, state codes often specify the conditions under which camps and other residential centers must operate, state and local codes also regulate the operation of swimming pools, and the services offered by municipal recreation and park agencies are based on the designation of legal authority. The recreation leader must be able to conduct his work so that it is consistent with legal regulations and authorization. Furthermore, every recreation leader (as well as the agency) assumes a legal responsibility to provide service in a reasonable, prudent, and safe manner with a constant concern for avoiding negligent and potentially harmful conduct. The function of risk management, therefore, pertains to recreation leadership.

The Recreation Leader Accomplishes General Office and Technical Tasks

Regardless of the leader's job description, she should most likely be able to make and receive phone calls; keep appointments; answer correspondence; maintain files; operate duplicating equipment; use movie, slide, and videotape projectors; operate a computer; keep records; and more.

Human Relations Functions

The Recreation Leader Acquires Relevant Information About Those Served

The leader must be thoroughly familiar with the needs and characteristics of the people served so that recreation services will be relevant and meaningful. This requires the ability to obtain and use demographic information and a basic knowledge of community organization, pressure groups, and bureaucratic functioning. In other words, the recreation leader should be able to obtain and interpret information about the people served to more effectively plan, implement, and evaluate recreation services. This further means that she must be able to operate within established power structures. The recreation leader must also be able to respect the unique needs of individuals and recognize the differences among them. This makes it necessary to balance the perspectives of individuals, groups, the organization, and the broader society.

The Recreation Leader Understands and Works with the Processes of Group Dynamics

An awareness of how individuals behave within and react to groups must be converted by the recreation leader into effective leadership approaches. Leaders must operate according to the uniqueness of a particular group to enable the group members to achieve the desired recreation experience. Many recreation leaders maintain the philosophy that participants should be exposed as fully as possible to democratic and shared group decision making and overall self-management.

The Recreation Leader Understands That Recreation Provides a Significant Outcome for Participants

The leader must constantly be concerned with what impact recreation activities, events, or other services can potentially have on the participant's psychological, physical, and social health. This accountability is an important human relations function for leaders. Thus a highly visible tournament championship, a large camp session enrollment, or a broadly acclaimed therapeutic technique has worth only if it contributes positively to the well-being of those involved. The recreation leader's main concern, in other words, should be with the results of leadership.

The Recreation Leader Develops Cooperative Relationships with Other Professionals and Organizations

In most situations, the organization in which the leader works is one of several in a community or area that provides park and recreation services. An awareness of these other organizations and the assumption of a team spirit with their staff enhance the options for more thorough and effective use of all resources. Given an appropriate rapport, resources can be shared, mutual problems can be solved, staff can be more efficiently trained and

A Leadership Profile Exercise

Try your hand with this case study, which illustrates some of the technical and human relations functions of recreation leaders.

SITUATION

M. Joachim, sixty years old, is currently a mechanic for the Four Corners Theme Park and Holiday World. He is responsible for the maintenance and repair of the fleet of cars and trucks and also the amusement rides at the park. He has served in this capacity for eight years, after retiring from his own garage, which he owned and managed for twenty-five years. Because of his experience and expertise Joachim feels strongly that the only way a job can be done right at Four Corners is to do it himself. This has been a problem because there is more work to be done than Joachim has time to do, and previous attempts to hire additional mechanics have resulted in resignations as the new hires found it difficult to work cooperatively with Joachim.

Several months ago the company reorganized the work of the maintenance shop into three categories: motor vehicle repairs, amusement ride maintenance, and amusement ride repairs. Joachim was given primary responsibility for motor vehicle repairs, and two new mechanics were hired and put in charge of the other two areas. The three mechanics were instructed by the park superintendent to coordinate their work with each other when appropriate.

Since these changes were made, however, Joachim has continued in his refusal to work collaboratively with the other mechanics. For example, when parts arrived in the shop for an amusement ride he made no attempt to advise the mechanic in charge of that repair area that the parts were in the storage shed. Also, when out in the park testing a truck repair Joachim discussed a maintenance problem with one of the rides with the ride operator but did not pass on the report to the mechanic in charge of ride maintenance. This has angered the other mechanics, and they have filed several grievance reports with the park superintendent.

The park superintendent has been hesitant to fire Joachim because of his years of service with the company, and even with such poor working conditions as bad lighting, insufficient tools, and small space, Joachim has worked hard and conscientiously to complete his repair work promptly. Joachim is also a friend of several other managers at the park.

SOLUTIONS

What are the technical functions that apply to this case? Describe those technical functions that if they had been carried out more fully may have prevented this problem, and also describe those technical functions that may be a part of its solution. What are the human relations functions that apply to this case? Describe those human relations functions that if they had been carried out more fully may have prevented this problem, and also describe those human relations functions that may be a part of its solution. What might be the reasons for Joachim's resistance to working with the other mechanics? How would you deal with Joachim? Should he be fired? How would you deal with the other mechanics?

(Adapted from Bannon & Busser, 1992, pp. 179–181)

placed, and overlap or underlap of services can be reduced. The end result of such a cooperative ability is better services for the constituents, the clients, and the guests.

Conceptual Functions

The Recreation Leader Works on the Basis of a Sound Philosophy of Recreation

You must understand and believe in the critical role of recreation in the life of the individual and society; its potential for contributing to human growth and development; and its potential for solving problems, improving motivation, and promoting social values.

The Recreation Leader Has a Sound Professional Philosophy

Leaders should have a set of professional beliefs relative to the practice of recreation services. The role of professional organizations should be understood and exercised, changing practices should be monitored, and trends in the provision of recreation services should be appropriately applied. This involves a commitment to the field. It involves being active as a professional in state, provincial, or national organizations. It means taking advantage of continuing education course and workshop opportunities, and it means performing ethically.

The Recreation Leader Contributes to, and Operates Within, Organization Philosophies and Goals

The recreation leader must not only be able to carry out services that complement the organization's overall mission but also be able to envision better missions. Such goals as broadening and intensifying volunteer involvement, playing the role of advocate by lobbying federal and state or provincial governments, providing a consultive service to other organizations requesting assistance, enhancing the field's national image, returning a higher proportion of clients to the community, or increasing net profits are examples of how some recreation organizations conceptualize their involvement in the provision of recreation services. The recreation leader must reflect such goals in all that he does.

The Recreation Leader Strives Toward the Achievement of a Better Society

Efforts such as incorporating persons with disabilities into the mainstream of society, reducing environmental pollution, enabling more satisfying retirement adjustment, and instituting leisure education programs reflect a leadership concern for meeting societywide priorities and needs. The recreation leader must be able to maintain a broad perspective. In so doing she remains constantly vigilant in promoting desirable and constructive social values.

The degree of functioning that the leader exhibits in technical, human relations, and conceptual areas varies according to the specific job description. For example, the exact mix of these tasks depends on whether you are a director of a large state tourism agency or the program coordinator for a 100-member Boys' and Girls' Club.

As indicated in figure 2.2, the degree of emphasis that a recreation leader places in technical, human relations, and conceptual functions also varies according to leadership type within the organization's responsibility hierarchy. Figure 2.2 suggests that as the recreation leader moves to higher levels of responsibility the use of conceptual functions increases, while the use of technical functions decreases. Therefore the waterfront director for a city's pools and beaches does not usually use as many of the technical skills necessary in teaching swimming and lifeguarding, but does make use of a

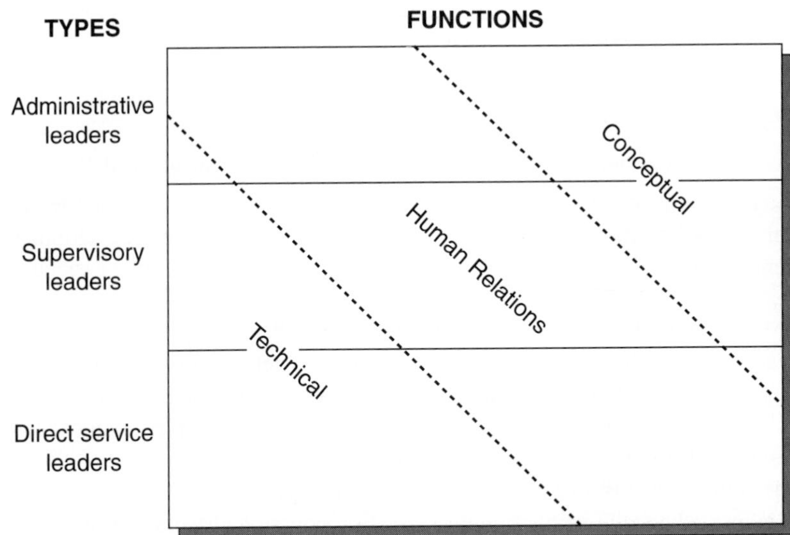

FIGURE 2.2. Recreation leadership functions according to leadership types (Redrawn from Hersey, P., & Blanchard, K. H. (1982). *Management of organizational behavior: Utilizing human resources* (p. 6). Englewood Cliffs, NJ: Prentice- Hall.)

thorough conceptual understanding of the philosophy of municipal recreation and the goals of the city for which she works. On the other hand, the beach lifeguards must daily use such technical functions as swimming, rescue techniques, small boat handling, CPR, and other tasks to provide direct service to the beach users. The lifeguard cannot completely do his job, however, without some appreciation as well for the objectives of the city as a whole.

Figure 2.2 also suggests that although the degree of technical and conceptual functions performed by the leader varies according to her leadership type, the degree of human relations skills used remains approximately constant for all types. The essence of leadership is, after all, the ability to work with, for, and through people. All types of recreation leaders must constantly perform human relations functions.

ROLES OF RECREATION LEADERS

Who is the recreation leader in terms of the roles assumed? Let's review an illustration.

> Elizabeth Tillett was making last minute changes to her notes about the weekly staff meeting for this afternoon at four o'clock. Each Thursday for the past three years Elizabeth (Director of Recreation Services for a large ski resort), Peter Hultsman (Director of Meetings and Conferences), Christine Williams (Director of Facilities), and Michael Ross (Director of Marketing) meet in Elizabeth's office to review the events of the past week and to coordinate the next week's happenings.
>
> Elizabeth looked over her notes again and ordered the numerous items for discussion: a complaint from the maintenance chief about vandalism at the ice rink after the dance last Friday, a request from the health club supervisor for a new floor in the sauna, a request from the resort general manager for justification of next year's proposed activity budget increase, the need to develop a creative strategy for training the seasonal

ski instructors next month, and the urgent need for the development of an up-to-date organization chart for the recreation services division.

"It was so much simpler when I started this job," thought Elizabeth. "How this organization has changed. Ten years ago a secretary, a few part-time ski instructors, and myself conducted primarily weekend programs. There was not much fuss. Our facilities were simpler; fewer customers that only had interests in skiing. Now I have so many 'hats' to wear in carrying out my job!" (Adapted from Edginton & Griffith, 1983.)

This fictional situation is useful in illustrating the multiple and complex "hats," or roles, undertaken by all types of leaders at all levels in recreation organizations. In today's society there are diverse postures of being and doing that swimming pool managers, camp counselors, fitness coordinators, resort managers, therapeutic recreation specialists, and others must take if they are to be identified as leading. The recreation leader often must assume many roles simultaneously. These include being a communicator, enabler, innovator, intrapreneur, dreamer, teacher, coordinator, motivator, problem solver, and decision maker.

The leader is a **communicator**. Communication processes are an integral part of a recreation leader's every effort and relationship with participants and colleagues. The success of leadership situations with participants, other staff, and the general public is based on communication. A leader who possesses the skills to communicate nonverbally, who has the ability to speak clearly and to write accurately, and who has developed an attitude for listening effectively is able to meet the recreation needs of individuals in a more productive manner. Communication is an important "hat" that should be studied and practiced; to this end an entire chapter is later devoted.

The leader is an **enabler**. The primary purpose of most recreation organizations is to provide opportunities for individuals, as well as groups, to engage in and enjoy recreation experiences. As an enabler the leader guides participants (and possible participants) in making choices, selecting directions, and matching opportunities in recreation. This role requires that the leader help people to grow in their ability to solve, cope with, or satisfy their own recreational needs and interests. In this sense recreation leaders wear a helping "hat." The leader outlines alternatives and provides resources so that the participant may independently take the most appropriate direction.

The leader is an **innovator**. The ability, as well as the attitude, of creativity is critically important to the recreation leader. Participants in recreation are more sophisticated. They have more complex requirements for fun. Their problems are more diverse than ever. The society within which today's recreation leader works demands that the content, marketing, and delivery of services be more innovative.

How can the camp director be more imaginative in conducting the postcamp evaluation this summer? How can the activities coordinator in the convalescent center creatively counteract the lack of participation by the ambulatory patients? How can the golf coach inventively teach the golf swing to ten- and eleven-year-old participants? Such now common activities as windsurfing, put/take fishing, land sailing, psychodrama, turf-skiing, water-walking, ski-bobbing, hot tubbing, flingbee, parasailing, par-course fitness, wallyball, flickerball, and swingball tennis are the result of recreation leadership that was able to conceptualize meeting the needs of the recreationist in a different way.

The recreation leader must be able to play with, to juggle, to rearrange, and to visualize old ideas so that they become new ideas. Tradition does play an important role in the success of many programs and facilities, but the leadership must also be flexible and know when tradition is useful and when it is not.

The role of innovator is closely allied with the *entrepreneurial process* in recreation organizations. More recently, individuals who engage in entrepreneurship are called **intrapreneurs**. This term is now used to differentiate innovators working inside existing organizations from individuals who innovate by creating new organizations (entrepreneurs) (Bartol & Martin, 1998). Being an intrapreneur takes special effort. Also, successful innovations are rarely the result of only one person's work. Instead, the process is much more likely to happen when persons at various levels of the organization work together. In fulfilling the intrapreneur role across an entire organization we can see that different people assume different innovator roles. As outlined by Bartol and Martin these are: idea champion, sponsor, and orchestrator.

An **idea champion** generates a new idea or believes in the value of a new idea and supports it in the face of numerous potential obstacles (Bartol and Martin, 1998, 26). Idea champions are usually at the direct-service level of the organization because they are at the front line level and more easily can recognize a problem that a new idea could solve. Because idea champions are relatively far down in the organization hierarchy, they often do not have the power and status to get their ideas accepted by the organization. This is why the sponsor is needed. A **sponsor** is often a supervisory level leader who due to her middle position in the organization can recognize the organizational significance of an idea and facilitate its implementation (27). Innovations in a recreation organization are not likely to happen without a sponsor, but they also depend on a third intrapreneur role—the orchestrator. The **orchestrator** is typically a top-level administrator who articulates the need for innovation, provides funding for new ideas, creates incentives for staff to produce ideas, and protects those with the new ideas (27). Sometimes new ideas are resisted by those in the organization who are comfortable with the

Case in Point: Innovation Self-Assessment

1. What is this a picture of?

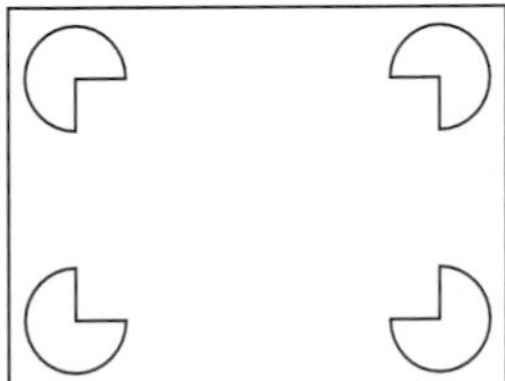

(Clues: A square. What else? Four hungry circles. What else? Mickey Mouse looking in a mirror. What else?)

2. Suppose you are the manager of a large sport and fitness center. By mistake an equipment order resulted in a shipment of $1,000 worth of ball bearings that you don't need. Furthermore, you can't return them to the vendor. Your task is to think of things to do with the ball bearings at the center, using them either one-at-a-time or in combination. What are your ideas?

   (Clue: Sew them into a canvas vest and use them as "weight clothing" for runners-in-training.)

3. What gives you courage to try a new idea?

   ___ Having a well-thought out plan
   ___ Past success
   ___ Big potential payoff
   ___ Encouragement from other people
   ___ Belief in yourself
   ___ Faith in the idea
   ___ Having a "Plan B"
   ___ Having no other alternative

   (Clue: Courage comes from the Old French word *cuer* and the Latin word *cor*, both meaning "heart." So, having courage to try a new idea means putting your heart into your effort.)

(Exercises adapted from von Oech, 1986)

status quo. An orchestrator provides the balance for trying out new ideas in the face of negative reactions by others.

The leader is a **dreamer**. The recreation leader constantly has sights set on the future. The future is looked forward to. The leader has enthusiastic visions of how recreation might better contribute to the quality of life for the individual and benefit society. This happens only from leadership that can respond to change.

The leader in recreation, in wearing the dreamer "hat," not only observes change but also responds to it and causes it. The recreation leader assumes an action-oriented role. This action occurs because dreams of better ways of facilitating "the good life" are the backdrop. Dreaming of better ways to achieve life quality requires a professional leadership capable of not only the rational techniques required in getting the job done but also the hope, the fantasy, and the playfulness to remain in touch with "why." This we address more thoroughly in the next chapter.

The leader is a **teacher**. Particularly for the direct service recreation leader the ability to teach those skills needed to meaningfully enjoy a recreation activity is important. The activity leader frequently needs to teach specific techniques and attitudes in activities such as backpacking and swimming for the activity to be experienced at all. As a teacher, the recreation leader must be able to understand and use the basic concepts of learning.

Although many persons seem to have a natural instinct for teaching, full awareness of the principles of skilled, effective teaching is necessary by all leaders. Breaking down activities into parts and communicating these parts to participants can be practiced and perfected.

The leader is a **coordinator**. The recreation leader brings people and resources together. The leader also brings together various program segments to yield a meaningful experience for participants. For example, if the leader is coordinating a three-day canoe trip, he must not only match or attract the most suitable people for this outing but also effectively coordinate methods of transportation, menus, location, safety procedures, equipment, evening camp fire programs, and much more so that those involved have a meaningful, pleasurable, safe, and appropriate trip.

The leader is a **motivator**. Sometimes a psychologist, sometimes an entertainer, sometimes an astute researcher—in wearing the motivator "hat," the leader seeks to stimulate participants to reach their fullest capacity for experiencing recreation. Although philosophical writings in the recreation, park, and sport field maintain that true leisure behavior is motivated by the rewards and values that are inherent to the experience, the leader must at least understand the nature of motivated behavior in recreation to lead appropriately. For this role the leader must understand what motivates people, how to influence what motivates people, how individuals react uniquely to different situations, and what motivational style is best for each setting. The leader's ultimate goal is to encourage participants to reach their highest level of involvement in recreation.

The leader is a **problem solver**. In a broad sense all that the recreation leader does could be called problem solving. The leader's aim is to "solve" (through the use of various resources) the needs of those persons the organization serves. Yet in a more narrow sense, problem solving is a process that leaders must draw on when those guidelines for handling routine situations are ineffective.

In recreation leadership, conditions arise from time to time requiring intelligent solutions. For example, a sudden rainstorm might flood the soccer field an hour before a city wide tournament, the local radio station fails to announce today's registration for next week's gourmet cooking class, only four percent of the resort's weekend occupancy takes advantage of the organized beach program, or the behavior of a child at camp is too difficult for the cabin counselor to control. These and other situations require that the leader not only be able to recognize and understand the cause of the problem but also be able to identify, select, and carry out courses of action that will solve the problem.

The leader is a **decision maker**. There can be no doubt that leading includes the often precarious role of making decisions. In every leadership situation and at every level of responsibility, it is necessary to make decisions. The ability to choose and the ability to help participants choose is vital in recreation leadership. How decisions are made depends on the type of decision that has to be made, the amount of available resources, and the situation within which the group exists. Beyond these factors, choices are much easier to make and bring into action if they grow from a sound and determined recreation philosophy. If we do not have a philosophy, we have little foundation to guide our professional decisions. This leader role is also covered more thoroughly in a later chapter.

Summary

Who is the recreation leader? Recreation leaders respond to the recreation needs of others through a wide diversity of settings. Yet, although they may be found working within governmental, voluntary, therapeutic, commercial, corporate, private, and other organizations, the recreation leader is also a professional in a more broadly conceptualized endeavor: human services. From a human services orientation, recreation leaders—along with other professionals from such fields as health, education, and entertainment—are concerned with the promotion of a holistic quality of life.

Recreation leaders who work in these varied settings within the overall human services focus can be further described from other vantage points. Because the labels commonly applied to those doing the work of recreation leadership are so diverse, it is more meaningful to investigate, as in this chapter, who the recreation leader is in ways other than job title. This chapter presents views of the recreation leader according to type, functions, and roles.

Leadership is pervasive. Throughout all organizations, leaders are usually identifiable according to three types:

- Direct service: that leadership involved in face-to-face contact with those persons the organization serves
- Supervisory: a middle management position concerned with helping direct service staff members become more effective
- Administrative: chief executive position with ultimate responsibility for guiding the organization toward the attainment of its overall goals

To effectively perform within these leader types the leader working in recreation needs to be accomplished in technical, human relations, and conceptual functions. For example, to perform the tasks of program planning, organizational management, evaluation, legal awareness, and assorted other technical procedures the leader must have an ability to use knowledge and techniques specific to recreation services. An ability to work with, for, and through people enables the leader to perform constituency needs research, group dynamics, and cooperative relationship tasks. Finally, the recreation leader requires conceptual skill to work from a sound philosophical and professional basis, as well as to contribute to organization goals and ultimately the betterment of society.

Regardless of the type of leadership, and the leader functions, recreation leaders assume similar complex roles. Ideally the leader's diverse postures of being and doing include communicating, enabling, innovating, dreaming, teaching, coordinating, motivating, problem-solving, and decision-making roles.

The levels of responsibility, the functions, and the roles that profile the recreation leader were overviewed in this chapter. The focus of later chapters is to teach the specific skills and abilities needed to assume these responsibility levels, fill these roles, and perform these functions.

Questions and Activities for Review and Discussion

1. Visit a recreation or park organization in your community and write a description of the human services approach according to this example. Is this organization providing services according to the human services mission? Give examples of how or how not.
2. What are the most common levels of responsibility for leaders working in recreation settings?
3. Interview a direct service leader working in a recreation organization in your community. Describe his or her day-to-day functioning according to the degree of technical, human relations, and conceptual tasks performed in his or her work.
4. Why are human relations functions equally employed by all types of recreation leaders?
5. Recall a recreation leadership role you have assumed in the past or are currently filling. Explain the many roles of leadership as presented in this chapter according to this experience.
6. Why is it so critically important that a recreation leader be able to be a dreamer? An innovator?
7. Which of the recreation leadership roles do you feel most comfortable in at the present time? In which roles do you need more training and experience? How will you go about becoming more comfortable in these roles?

References

Bannon, J. J., & Busser, J. A. (1992). *Problem solving in recreation and parks.* Champaign, IL: Sagamore Publishing.

Bartol, K. M., & Martin, D. C. (1998). *Management.* New York: McGraw-Hill.

Edginton, C. R., & Griffith, C. A. (1983). *The recreation and leisure service delivery system.* Philadelphia: Saunders College Publishing.

Hersey, P., & Blanchard, K. H. (1982). *Management of organizational behavior: Utilizing human resources* (4th ed.). Englewood Cliffs, NJ: Prentice-Hall.

Mobley, T. A. (1996). Leadership in recreation management. In F. J. Fu & P. P. C. Chan (Eds.), *Recreation, Sport, Culture, and Tourism for the 21st Century.* Hong Kong: Department of Physical Education, Hong Kong Baptist University.

Nudel, M. (1984). Employee recreation around the country. *Parks and Recreation, 19*(8), 40–43.

Russell, R. V. (1996). *Pastimes: The context of contemporary leisure.* Madison, WI: Brown & Benchmark.

Von Oech, R. (1986). *A kick in the seat of the pants: Using your explorer, artist, judge, and warrior to be more creative.* New York: Harper & Row.

Yukl, G. (1989). Managerial leadership: A review of theory and research. *Journal of Management, 15*, 251–289.

Web Resources

American Association of Retired Persons: http://www.aarp.org/

Boy Scouts of America: www.bsa.scouting.org/

Campfire—Boys and Girls: www.campfire.org/

Easter Seal Society: www.seals.com/

Girl Scouts of America: www.girlscouts.org/

Special Olympics: www.specialolympics.org/

Tennessee Valley Authority: www.tva.gov/

World Leisure and Recreation Society's International Centre of Excellence (WICE): www.worldleisure.org/wice.html

CHAPTER 3

Why Is There Recreation Leadership?

To be able to fill leisure intelligently is the last product of civilization.
—Bertrand Russell, 1946, p. 182.

Learning Objectives

This book is devoted to teaching the skills, abilities, and competencies important to the success of recreation leaders. What exactly is the "success" of a recreation leader? What do you ultimately want to accomplish with your leading? To complete the foundation for understanding recreation leadership, you will learn the goals recreation leaders have for:

- society
- the profession
- the sponsoring organization
- the participants

Key Terms

social responsibility p. 46
physical-social environment p. 48
leisure education p. 49
job description p. 51
performance appraisals p. 53
code of ethics p. 55
end-result ethics p. 56
rules ethics p. 56
organization's values p. 56
personal conviction p. 56
socializing behaviors p. 59
associative behaviors p. 59
acquisitive behaviors p. 59
competitive behaviors p. 59
testing behaviors p. 59
risk-taking behaviors p. 59
explorative behaviors p. 59
vicarious experience behaviors p. 59
sensory stimulation behaviors p. 59
physical expression behaviors p. 60
creative behaviors p. 60
appreciative behaviors p. 60
variety-seeking behaviors p. 60
anticipatory and recollective behaviors p. 60
socialization p. 63
social worlds p. 64

What are the goals of recreation leadership? What are we trying to accomplish? What is expected of recreation leaders by the participant, society, the sponsoring organization, and the profession? The aim of this chapter is to suggest that recreation leadership responsibility includes much more than providing entertainment and free-time fillers. Those who meet the challenges of the recreation mission measure their success by what they have achieved in making life better for others. Answering the question "How good a leader am I?" entails also asking the question "What have I accomplished?"

In the broadest sense, recreation leaders have a responsibility to society. The society within which you work places rather definite expectations on you, and these expectations must be met. Recreation leaders understand that recreation services are a key force in contemporary society. In addition to having a responsibility to society, recreation leaders also accomplish their goals within the context of a profession. As a competent leader, you have specific skills and knowledge that sets you apart and establishes you as a professional. As well, you have a responsibility to your employing organization. Regardless of the setting—commercial enterprises, corporations, governments, tourist sites, or therapeutic institutions—the recreation leader is the tool for translating organization purposes into productivity and effectiveness. Finally, leadership in recreation has a responsibility to its constituents, consumers, clients, and guests. Recreation is something that a person experiences and the leader's goal is to optimize the experience. To study each of these broad goals of recreation leadership further, we begin with society.

Leader Profile: The Past
Velma Ruth Baker
Former Service Club Director in the Fourth Army Special Services, 1969.

SOCIETAL GOALS

There are times when anything seems possible, even a world where social justice, human potential, wellness, and peace prevail. As we look through the course of human history, there do seem to have existed such times. Even as recently as the end of the Cold War in the late 1980s there appeared a glimpse of this possibility. But today this glimpse has faded. Societies around the world continue to struggle to find a more habitable world.

The recreation leader is integral to this effort. While you may consider it a matter of my professional pride, I believe that those working in our fields are central to creating a good society. To this point, the delegates from over fifty countries attending the International Recreational Management Conference held in December, 1995, in Hong Kong pledged to work for a society that:

- celebrates diversity
- empowers everyone socially and economically
- upholds social justice
- promotes equity
- values open space
- values heritage
- preserves and conserves unique natural resources
- measures quality of life by meaningful relations rather than material gain
- enables creative expression, freedom, and the expansion of the human potential
- considers wellness the norm (Edginton, 1996, pp. 138–139)

How might we help to accomplish such a vision of the perfect society? Recreation leaders contribute to "good" society through **social responsibility**. Social responsibility is our obligation to act in ways that protect and improve the welfare of society. What are specific social responsibilities of recreation leaders? In this section we explore the goals of social change, quality of life, and leisure education.

Social Change

There is little doubt that during the first decades of the century society will continue to experience dramatic social change. Those working in the recreation fields will be at the forefront through these decades of change and will need to assume their share of the responsibility for leading this change. The recreation profession must continue to be "change agents" in behalf of society. These efforts will be impacted by a variety of societal forces. These forces include ambiguity, globalization, and technology (Edginton, 1996).

First, ambiguity results from the rapid rate of change. Accelerated, quick-paced change is integral to our lives. Daily we are transformed—socially, politically, culturally, economically—by a rapid diffusion of ideas. This creates a tremendous uncertainty, requiring the ability to respond with great flexibility. As well, our daily lives are directly linked to the lives of others. Globalization is impacting our attitudes, values, and behavior. In some societies the result has been an increased desire to protect and promote geographical and cultural uniqueness. New technologies continue to drive our lives, too. Technology will enhance entertainment and education. It will enable us to "virtually leapfrog into new dimensions" (Edginton, 1996, p. 134). But it will also upset conventional ways of working, playing, and living. These and other forces ultimately mean challenges to religions, governments, environments, families, and other societal institutions such as education and the workplace. Even our values and behaviors in leisure are impacted.

Park, sport, tourism, and other recreation service fields have experienced, in recent years, a period of critical professional self-analysis. This undertaking has suggested the need for quite different means of service than those currently in operation. What do we want these new service modes to do? What specifically are our goals for real social change for society? A leisure service mode that creates social change might include:

- *Smaller role of government*: reduction in number of rules, regulations, and red tape governing recreational use; redistribution of government resources to community groups via grants; more incentives and more cooperation between government and private sectors; greater efficiency
- *Increased individual assumption of responsibility*: increase in volunteer services and self-help enterprises; increased flexibility in scheduling, such as fewer organized teams and classes; increased spontaneous activities
- *Greater community identity and autonomy*: reemphasis on smaller, decentralized, and community-controlled facilities; more emphasis on geographical community rather than on communities of interest; increased integration of age and interest groups; improved coordination among all community programs, facilities, and resources

Case in Point: The Facts

Leisure services provide more total benefits to quality of life than any other social service.

- recreation, along with crime, education, and housing costs, is significantly related to community migration patterns
- recreation is one of nine criteria used to judge the best places to live in the United States
- studies show that cultural resources such as number of museums, "good" restaurants, and "things to do" are significant in resident satisfaction with communities
- studies also show that well-maintained parks and playgrounds are significant in resident satisfaction with communities

Quality of Life

Those leading within the recreation fields maintain a societal goal for improving the quality of life. According to Mundy (1998), this goal can be understood from two perspectives. One perspective is that of the **physical-social environment**. This refers to the qualities of "community" life. Those qualities usually considered important include clean, safe, and interesting residential areas; aesthetically pleasing public areas and buildings; quality education and health services; convenient and enjoyable natural areas; convenient and attractive transportation; and socially and culturally stimulating events. For example, your home community could be compared with another community in terms of the qualities of its physical-social environment, and the results of your comparison could be interpreted to indicate which community was experiencing a higher quality of life. As recreation leaders we seek to enhance the physical-social environment of communities.

The second perspective from which we can consider the societal goal of quality of life involves the *meaning of life's experiences to the individual* (Mundy, 1998). This refers to the qualities of "individual" life. From this perspective we are concerned for the feelings and satisfactions attached to experiences. This means we want to promote such things as individual initiative, learning, growth, positive health, and self-actualization for those we serve. The aim for the recreation leader is to help people add to the quality of their lives by increasing the value of recreation experiences for them.

Indeed, a central tenet of modern Western cultures is the belief in progress, the belief that life should be (and is) getting better—healthier, wealthier, happier, more satisfying, and more interesting (Eckersley, 1999). Some commentators believe that if we continue on our present path of economic and technological development, humanity can overcome the obstacles and threats it faces and enter a golden age of peace, prosperity, and happiness. Others foresee an accelerating deterioration in the human condition leading to a major discontinuity, even perhaps extinction, of our species. Author Richard Eckersley, writing for *The Futurist* magazine in 1999 fears for the latter. "In developed nations, we have defined progress in mainly material terms. We equate 'standard of living' with 'quality of life.' . . . After 50 years of rapid growth, so many people today appear to believe life is getting worse . . . . Because wealth is a poor predictor of happiness, and more does not mean better if in our efforts to get more, we sacrifice what really matters to our happiness and well-being: the quality of our personal, social, and spiritual relationships that give us a sense of meaning, purpose, and belonging" (pp. 23–26). So, Eckersley suggests that a society can have a high standard of living, but a low quality of life.

Where does that leave us? Can the recreation leader enhance quality of life by improving the physical-social environment and by adding to the value and meaning of individual experiences? Yes, and research confirms this. For example, in a comprehensive review of numerous studies on quality of life, Allen (1991) found parks and playgrounds, clubs and social organizations, outdoor recreation, and entertainment facilities to be important predictors of community and personal life satisfaction.

Leisure Education

First grade children were once asked "Tell me what you think the word leisure means." In response to this request the replies included: "I don't know," "I think it means nothing," "It is a break in the skin," "Something you carry a dog around on," "Coloring," and

"It is a time when I can choose what I want to do." (Mundy, 1998, p. 54). Further, when the first graders were asked, "Who teaches you how to do some of the things you choose to do in leisure?" the responses were "mother," "daddy," and "my teacher." Not one child mentioned any type of recreation personnel, although 80 percent of the children were involved in some form of organized recreation program (Mundy, 1998, p. 54).

One possible avenue to the social change and quality of life goals is a third societal goal: **leisure education**. This is a major challenge to the leadership in recreation. It asks that we contribute to society's understanding and valuing of recreation. This means that the recreation leader needs to take responsibility for helping people of all ages understand the important role of leisure in their lives, as well as help them determine varied, enriching forms of recreational involvement.

The concept of leisure education carries diverse connotations even among those working in the recreation field. The most common image of leisure education is that of teaching what is worthy and wise use of free time. But, as recreation leaders, we are responsible for more than this. According to Navar and Tschumper (1999), leisure education seeks to help people:

- discover new interests
- explore community resources
- discover the benefits of leisure
- expand leisure choices
- learn how to establish and maintain friendships
- overcome barriers to enjoyment

It is important to make a distinction between education for leisure and leisure education. You have probably experienced education for leisure, but not leisure education. In sports, for example, we must learn physical skills and game rules to play well enough to enjoy it. The prerequisites of many artistic activities also require extensive education because some forms need a relatively high level of competence. The greater our leisure abilities, the greater are our leisure opportunities and satisfactions (Kelly, 1996). This is education for leisure.

Case in Point: Elderhostel

The Elderhostel organization, founded in 1975, has been called the greatest social movement of the twentieth century by *Time* magazine (Hyman, 1991, p. 1). Headquartered in Boston, Massachusetts, the program is based on the premise that people of all ages should have access to education. Founder Marty Knowlton, a social activist and educator, patterned the program on the worldwide youth hostel movement. One-to-three-week residential educational programs are offered each year for persons who are at least sixty years of age in over fifteen hundred institutions in fifty states, all ten Canadian provinces, and forty other countries. Major universities, community colleges, music schools, conference centers, and national parks are among the host institutions. Elderhostel courses are not for credit, and, except for a few intensive study programs, there are no exams, grades, or required assignments. It is learning for learning sake. For example, a course in Alaskan art is available at Alaska-Pacific University in Anchorage. Other examples include such courses as the "U.S. Presidents" at the Simpsonwood Conference and Retreat Center in Atlanta, "Mark Twain Studies" at Hannibal-La Grange College in Missouri, and "Jews and Arabs in Israel" at the Beit Berl University in Tel Aviv (Hyman, 1991). Elderhostel has over three hundred thousand alumni who have taken these and hundreds of other courses (Mills, 1993).

Leisure education, on the other hand, is learning to value and prioritize leisure. Teaching people that leisure has important benefits for personal and community lives requires teaching them how to make appropriate decisions for wholesome recreational pursuits; how to use leisure for optimal physical, social, and emotional health; and the importance of promoting leisure as socially, economically, and environmentally necessary for their community. Although learning how to perform well in a sport or musical performance is a necessary component for leisure education, leisure education is a broader goal.

Why are there recreation leaders? While all organizations and institutions in a society have a mandate for social responsibility, those who lead recreation, park, sport, and tourism organizations have a unique goal. We are charged with using recreation services to help create social change, enhance the quality of community and individual lives, and educate for wholesome leisure lifestyles. No other professions are singularly focused on these societal goals.

PROFESSIONAL GOALS

As a field of professional endeavor, recreation is neither a true science, a pure art, nor a classic profession—although it does have many components from each. The recreation leader's position most likely has no parallel in other occupations. It is often laden with political requirements and is fairly visible and exposed to demands by differing interest groups. There is usually competition for scarce resources and a typical requirement is to balance conflicting yet equally desirable goals. This means that recreation leadership can be an exciting, stimulating, and challenging occupation. How successfully you meet these challenges and opportunities depends not only on meeting expected service goals with competent skills and an enthusiastic attitude, but it also means performing according to honorable and appropriate standards and ethics. Often this involves attention to professionalism, performance standards, and ethics.

Leader Profile: The Past
Helen M. Dauncey
Former specialist in Leadership Training, National Recreation Association. The National Recreation Association was one of the professional organizations that merged in 1945 to form the National Recreation and Park Association.

Professionalism

Well-performed recreation leadership includes professionalism. As Niepoth (1983) pointed out, professionalism can be considered from three perspectives. First, a professional recreation leader may be thought of as anyone who is employed and receives pay for his efforts. Second, a professional recreation leader is one with a sense of commitment who is self-motivated to perform at a high level. Third, a professional recreation leader is a trained expert who carries out certain responsibilities according to standards of behavior. The second and third views have implications for the sense of professionalism as it is considered in this chapter. In this section professionalism is discussed as a special sense of commitment and in the following section professionalism is presented according to performance standards.

Professionalism as a commitment means that it is the responsibility of recreation leaders to behave with dedication, sincerity, and intelligence. Someone who is a professional in any occupation takes pride in her work and is singularly concerned for providing the best possible service. How does this happen? What exactly is professional commitment?

Professionals conduct, encourage, and use research related to recreation. They take time to read research; they cooperate with formally organized research projects; and they constantly carry out evaluative research on their own programs and services. Using relevant research findings as bases for direct leadership, and programming and administering efforts should provide you with greater confidence in the effectiveness of what you are doing.

Professionals also take advantage of continuing educational opportunities. They enroll for course work in colleges and universities even after the completion of their formal education. They attend conferences and workshops, and they read professional books and journals. They also encourage and participate in in-service training efforts sponsored by their own organizations.

Persons who demonstrate professional behavior take pride in their chosen career and encourage others in the career to develop a spirit of dedication and respect for the work that they do. Therefore they join and actively support local and national professional organizations, and they contribute to the continual development and improvement of the field.

Professionalism also means being interested in carrying out a task well for the sake of personal and organization pride in providing quality services. It means knowing what you are doing and being good at it. It means being willing to admit to mistakes and correct them and to improve performance and effort. It means being as technically knowledgeable as possible. As well, professional judgment distinguishes a professional. A true professional is marked by the possession of intellectual resources and the systematic ability to relate this to specific cases. A professional has the ability and the attitude for handling unfamiliar challenges and problems.

Performance Standards

Responsibility to the profession also means being systematically judged as competent. This is usually accomplished through performance standards. Performance standards spell out specific criteria for evaluating performance and capabilities. These can range from narrowly targeted standards for performance in a specific setting and for a specific task to broadly stated and universally applied standards for performance for an entire type of worker. An example of the first is a performance standard for the front reception staff of an older adults community center that stipulates that a staff member must greet everyone who enters the center within one minute of arrival. An example of broadly stated and universal standards of performance is the competencies for professional certification. Let's elaborate on each.

First, most organizations that you could potentially work within as a recreation leader will have specific expectations for your performance. These standards for performance are the expectations that your supervisor has for the conduct of your responsibilities. High standards mean that your best effort is expected, and your supervisor will compare you with your highest level of potential. To be successful in this, you must understand what is expected of you and have available the support and resources to meet this expectation. You should consider, therefore, your performance recordkeeping, performance evaluations, performance interviews, and even performance corrections as a positive opportunity for growth—not to mention justification for salary increases and promotions.

This all means that a clearly defined **job description** for your position is essential. A job description is important because it defines your required duties and scope of

Professional Organizations Serving the Recreation Fields

General.

Academy of Leisure Sciences
American Academy of Park and Recreation Administrators
American Alliance of Health, Physical Education, Recreation and Dance
American Association for Leisure and Recreation
American Recreation Coalition
Canadian Association for Leisure Studies
Canadian Parks and Recreation Association
International Council for Health, Physical Education, Recreational Sports, and Dance
National Recreation and Park Association (NRPA)
World Leisure and Recreation Association

Community, Corporate, and Commercial Recreation.

American Park and Recreation Society (NRPA)
Armed Forces Recreation Society (NRPA)
Association of Professional Directors of YMCAs
Boy Scouts of America
Campfire Boys and Girls
Commercial Recreation and Tourism Section (NRPA)
Girl Scouts of America
International Association of Amusement Parks and Attractions
National Employee Services and Recreation Association
Resort and Commercial Recreation Association

Higher Education.

American College Personnel Association
Society of Park and Recreation Educators (NRPA)

Outdoor Recreation.

American Alpine Club
American Camping Association
American Hiking Society
American Trails
American Whitewater Affiliation
American Wilderness Alliance
Association for Experiential Education
Association for Interpretive Naturalists
Canadian Parks and Wilderness Society
National Association of Recreation Resource Planners
National Forest Recreation Association
National Library for the Environment
National Park Foundation
National Parks and Conservation Association
National Society for Park Resources (NRPA)
National Wildlife Federation
Park Law Enforcement Association

Sport Management.

American College of Sports Medicine
American Running and Fitness Association
American Swimming Coaches Association
Canadian Professional Coaches Association
Club Managers Association of America
International Fitness Professionals Association
National Aquatics Section (NRPA)
National Association for Sport and Physical Education
National Association of Collegiate Directors of Athletics
National Association of Governor's Councils on Physical Fitness and Sports
National Athletic Trainers Association
National Intramural-Recreational Sports Association
North American Society for Sport Management

Therapeutic Recreation.

American Art Therapy Association
American Association of Music Therapy
American Dance Therapy Association
American Nursing Home Association
American Therapeutic Recreation Association
Leisure and Aging Section (NRPA)
National Council for Therapy and Rehabilitation through Horticulture
National Council on Aging
National Therapeutic Recreation Association (NRPA)
National Wheelchair Athletic Association

Tourism.

Ecotourism Society
National Tourism Association
Travel Industry Association of America

responsibilities; thus the job description can ultimately serve as a useful standard for evaluating your performance. If a job description is not automatically available to you, request that one be prepared—preferably with your input.

Systematic and regular **performance appraisals** are also essential to your working relationship with an organization. You should take every opportunity to interact with your employer, even on a day-to-day basis if possible, so that accurate and comprehensive information can be gathered about your performance. For example, a fitness leader teaching an exercise class should be able to expect an evaluation on his methods of presentation, the content of the class session, the depth of knowledge about fitness, rapport with the participants, and the degree of proficiency of the participants after the class has ended. These factors are evaluative information that can help the leader do an even better job. In other words, you should expect that your supervisor evaluate not only the amount of work that you accomplish but also the quality of your work.

In terms of the more broad and universally applied performance standards, we first consider that recreation leaders have special training. One of the mainstays of our profession is the professional preparation undertaken by those who enter the park and recreation fields. There are over 300 baccalaureate degree programs, 28 associate degree programs, and 100 graduate degree programs in leisure studies, park management, recreation administration, therapeutic recreation, sport management, tourism and others (NRPA, 1999). Students in these curricula take course work in the humanities, social and physical sciences, management, and recreation and leisure studies, as well as gain practical experience through internships in park and recreation organizations.

Professional certification is also an example of professionwide performance standards. Recreation leaders can seek certification in two areas—their area of leisure services expertise and health and safety abilities (Jordan, 1996). Many positions in recreation leadership require, for example, certification in first aid, CPR, and food handling. Some outdoor leaders must be certified in skiing, scuba diving, and small craft, and fitness leaders are increasingly required to be certified. Some certifications are absolutely required to qualify for a particular leader position, while others are voluntary. For example, the National Recreation and Park Association (NRPA), in conjunction with the American Association of Leisure and Recreation (AALR), conducts a voluntary program that certifies leisure services professionals. Other examples include the National Council for Therapeutic Recreation Certification (NCTRC), which provides a certification process for those working in therapeutic recreation, and the Certified Recreational Sports Specialist program offered by NRPA/AALR and the National Intramural-Recreational Sports Association (NIRSA).

Certification is the process of reviewing credentials. This review is based upon specifically identified competencies, or standards, that applicants must meet. In some cases, passing a written examination is required. For example, one of the ways to be a Certified Leisure Professional (CLP) is to hold a baccalaureate degree in a recreation field from an NRPA/AALR accredited college or university and pass the CLP examination. Certifications customarily require periodic renewal.

The purpose of all certification programs is to ensure that staff employed in recreation organizations meet high standards of performance. Becoming certified assures employers and constituents that certified job applicants meet prescribed education, experience, and continuing education requirements (Jordan, 1996).

Performing Ethically

From the news we see that contemporary organizations and their leaders are in the midst of ethics crises. A particular issue is the rising rate of white-collar crime. This form of crime includes fraud or embezzlement committed by someone who works for a company or organization. If you've ever taken a tablet of paper from the office for your own personal use, you are guilty of white-collar crime. According to one estimate, common street crime costs the nation approximately $4 billion a year, while white-collar crime annually costs over $40 billion to organizations and, eventually, to consumers and taxpayers (Bartol & Martin, 1998, p. 117).

Thus, ethics permeates our performance as recreation leaders. There are ethical implications to our decisions; we often face ethical dilemmas, and we many times encounter moral ambiguities. Our daily behavior is guided by our values-based ethical system. Such personal ethical systems come from the general norms and values of society; from individual experiences within family, religious, and educational settings; and from interpersonal interactions (Bartol & Martin, 1998, p. 117). Therefore, ethical standards may differ among recreation leaders. Yet, performing ethically is more than a belief. Successful leaders consider ethics an action. They take positive steps to address ethical issues and apply the practical tools of ethics in their leadership.

One way of helping leaders in an organization take the positive steps needed is through a code of ethics. It is estimated that 90 percent of organizations and companies in the United States have written codes of ethics (Otten, 1986). A code of ethics is a document prepared for the purpose of guiding members of the organization when they encounter an ethical dilemma. All sorts of organizations have codes of ethics, including most colleges and universities. For example, table 3.1 contains the code for students of the University of South Carolina.

Leadership Profile

Use the questions at the bottom to help you choose what to do in each of the following situations:

SITUATION 1

In a federally funded demonstration project for youth at risk, the supplies and equipment budget is running low and you need to purchase office supplies. Your supervisor instructs you to charge the supplies to the salary budget even though the terms of the grant forbid this. What do you do?

(1) explain to your supervisor that mischarging on a government contract is fraud
(2) refuse to mischarge
(3) do as your supervisor directed you
(4) buy the supplies with your own money

SITUATION 2

Your department wants to send you to a professional conference in Las Vegas. You have no interest in this conference because you believe it to be only minimally related to your job. However you are willing to go because you have never been there and enjoy gambling. What do you do?

(1) you think the conference might be of at least some value so you agree to attend
(2) reluctantly decline to go
(3) suggest that someone else attend who has more interest
(4) ask your supervisor what the organization hopes you will learn from the conference

GUIDING QUESTIONS

(1) What is your intention in making this choice?
(2) What will be the probable results from the choice?
(3) Will your choice be valid over a long period?

Codes of ethics in organizations, while they may differ in language and scope, essentially affirm the same thing: nobody should be hurt by the decisions and actions taken by others. At their core this means that the recreation leader must:

- Obey the law (both in letter and spirit).
- Tell the truth.
- Show respect for all people.
- Treat all people fairly.
- Do not harm people.
- Take action when you are needed and able.

(Adopted from Bartol & Martin, 1998, pp. 119–121)

TABLE 3.1. The Carolinian Creed

The Carolinian Creed was authored by a group of students, faculty, and staff and approved by the Faculty Senate, Student Senate, and the USC Board of Trustees.

The community of scholars at the University of South Carolina is dedicated to personal and academic excellence. Choosing to join the community obligates each member to a code of civilized behavior.

As a Carolinian . . . this introduction submits that membership in the Carolina Community is not without its obligations. It is assumed or understood that joining is evidence of a subscription to certain ideals and an agreement to strive for the level of achievement and virtue suggested by the following:

I will practice personal and academic integrity.
A commitment to this ideal is inconsistent with cheating in classes, in games, or in sports, it should eliminate the practice of plagiarism or borrowing another student's homework, lying, deceit, excuse making, and infidelity or disloyalty in personal relationships.

I will respect the dignity of all persons.
A commitment to this ideal is inconsistent with behaviors which compromise or demean the dignity of individuals or groups, including hazing, most forms of intimidating, taunting, teasing, baiting, ridiculing, insulting, harassing, and discriminating.

I will respect the rights and property of others.
A commitment to this ideal is inconsistent with all forms of theft, vandalism, arson, misappropriation, malicious damage to, and desecration or destruction of property. Respect for other's personal rights is inconsistent with any behavior which violates their right to move about freely, express themselves appropriately, and to enjoy privacy.

I will discourage bigotry, while striving to learn from differences in people, ideas, and opinions.
A commitment to this ideal pledges affirmative support for equal rights and opportunities for all students regardless of their age, sex, race, religion, disability, international/ethnic heritage, socioeconomic status, political, social or other affiliation or disaffiliation, affectional preference.

I will demonstrate concern for others, their feelings and their need for conditions which support their work and development.
A commitment to this ideal is a pledge to be compassionate and considerate, to avoid behaviors which are insensitive, inhospitable, or incitant or which unjustly or arbitrarily inhibit other's ability to feel safe or welcomed in their pursuit of appropriate academic goals.

Allegiance to these ideals requires each Carolinian to refrain from and discourage behaviors which threaten the freedom and respect every individual deserves.

This last clause reminds community members that they are not only obliged to avoid these behaviors, but that they also have an affirmative obligation to confront and challenge, to respond to, or report the behaviors whenever or wherever they are encountered.

For more information about the *Carolinian Creed*, contact the Office of the Vice President for Student and Alumni Services, 777-4172.

1998–99 Carolina Community: USC-Columbia Student Handbook and Policy Guide

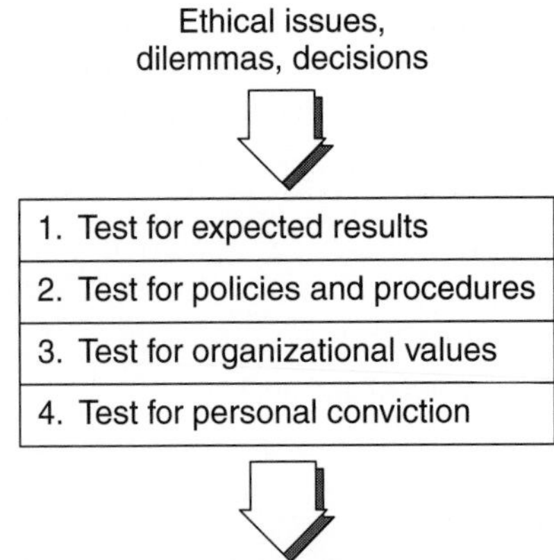

FIGURE 3.1. Four steps to an ethical decision (adapted from Hitt, 1990, p. 179)

But the actions called for require practical tools for making ethical decisions. One decision-making strategy that places ethics at the core is recommended by Hitt (1990). This strategy calls for a series of four tests: test for results, test for policies and procedures, test for organizational values, and test for personal conviction (p. 179).

Test one is **end-result ethics**. The decision we need to make is tested against expected consequences. We have to imagine the possible outcomes of a particular action. For example, in deciding the types of activities to use in a social event for delegates to a conference, the consequences of using a game requiring reams of colored paper might be that a lot of trash will be left to clean up after the event. The next test is about **rules ethics**. We consider the organization's relevant policies and procedures. For example, deciding who to hire for a new position in the organization might require attention to a policy that requires promotion from within the organization first.

The third test is more subjective and involves the organization's values. As distinct from written policies, the test for the **organization's values** is a kind of unwritten social contract among its members. For example, in determining the activities for the conference social event it would be important to know that the organization is an environmental advocacy group with strong feelings about environmental responsibility. Last is the test for **personal conviction**. This means that our decisions are guided by personal beliefs and convictions. Our commitment to affirmative action, for example, will lead us to appoint the qualified candidate from an underrepresented group for a new management position. In figure 3.1 we see a graphical representation of these four tests toward an ethical decision.

So, why are there recreation leaders? Those who lead in recreation, park, sport, and tourism organizations are vital contributors to the professional, performance, and ethical commitments of the profession.

ORGANIZATION GOALS

The recreation leader not only has a responsibility to society's goals and to the goals of the profession, but also has a duty to her employing organization's goals. Recreation, park, sport, and tourism organizations have specific results they desire to achieve.

Typically, for example, a corporate recreation department seeks to contribute to the health and well-being of employees, reduce absenteeism and the rate of accidents, and develop a sense of company loyalty. A therapeutic recreation institution is likely, on the other hand, to have goals that will contribute to the rehabilitation and normalization processes of its clients or patients.

Regardless of the specific type of recreation organization, the expressed intention is to provide varied options for meaningful and satisfying recreation. Beyond this foundational goal, many organizations also have specific objectives about how this will be achieved. For example, recreation leaders are responsible for working efficiently and assessing the success of their efforts.

Working Efficiently

Probably the most immediate challenge facing the leadership of recreation organizations today, and in the near future, is the need to develop creative ways of offering more service to constituents at less cost. Since the late 1970s, we have been working in an "era of limits." Thus, we must work efficiently by making the best use of available resources in providing recreation services.

So far, leaders in recreation organizations have striven to accomplish this efficiency by reorganizing departments, revising user fees and charges, developing self-sustaining facilities and programs, applying for grants, requesting gifts and bequests, contracting out for service provision, marketing more aggressively, and engaging in fund raising. The ultimate goal of these strategies is increased efficiency without sacrificing effectiveness.

To illustrate with a tourism organization, part of the success of Southwest Airlines is due to its efficiency. For example, the average time on the ground after landing and before taking off again, is about 39 minutes compared with 70 to 90 minutes for most other major airlines. Also, the number of passengers the airline carries per employee is more than double the figure for other major airlines. Part of the reason for these efficiencies is the company's emphasis on teamwork. For example, pilots might help out at the boarding gate when things are backed up or a ticket agent might pitch in with baggage loading when needed (Labich, 1995; Lippert, 1994).

Yet efficiency cannot be achieved at the expense of effectiveness. Effectiveness is the ability to achieve the organization's goals. Again, to illustrate with Southwest Airlines, the company has become a major player in the airline industry by focusing on friendly, no-frills service (no meals) between high-traffic cities for somewhat low fares. As a result it has built exceptionally loyal customers (Labich, 1995). This all illustrates that leaders in leisure service organizations must be both efficient and effective.

Assessing Success

In addition to working efficiently, recreation leaders must work effectively. Then measuring success of leadership means assessing both efficiency and effectiveness. Assessing success is a critically important organizational goal for recreation leaders. While the topic of evaluation and assessment is too broad for this book (see Riddick & Russell, 1999), we must spend enough time with it to substantiate its importance.

Leading without knowing impact is a lonely enterprise. Recreation leaders typically use a variety of monitoring techniques, such as opinion surveys, cost-benefit analysis, and social audits, to provide feedback on how well they are doing. An opinion survey provides information to the leader on the perceptions of the leader's success by constituents. A cost-benefit analysis calculates the ratio of the cost of a provided service relative to its benefits, and a social audit is a systematic study of the social, rather than the economic, performance of a leisure services organization. Techniques such as these help leaders determine the impact of program and facility services as well as unmet client needs.

There is another sense in which assessing success is important to the goals of a recreation agency. Evaluating leadership provides the basis for choosing from among candidates for leader and manager positions in the organization. It also provides useful information for the counseling and further professional development of incumbent leaders (Bass, 1990). The leisure services organization clearly benefits from a valid, assessment-based, selection of its leaders. Such techniques as performance appraisals are typical assessment tools. Performance appraisal means defining expectations for employee achievement, measuring and evaluating the performance against the organization's expectations, and providing feedback to the employee. While performance appraisals are done for a variety of reasons, including determining merit pay increases and the need for training, their major goal is to help leisure service organizations achieve best "fit" by successfully filling its leadership positions.

Recreation leaders are the "keepers of the flame" of organizational goals. Those who lead in recreation, park, sport, and tourism organizations have a responsibility to enable meaningful leisure experiences for constituents. Two expectations organizations have for carrying out this responsibility are efficiency and assessment.

PARTICIPANT GOALS

Regardless of the accuracy with which recreation leaders meet societal, professional, and organizational goals, all is lost if the participants' goals are not met. The benefit an individual intends to receive as a result of recreation involvement is paramount to the leader. The purpose of recreation leadership is the enabling of that benefit.

Who are the recreation participants? What are their goals for the recreation experience? Consider Reba Skaggs, a professor of chemistry at a state university with a recently developed interest in dancing. She is new in town and would like to meet other people. She is an inspired gourmet cook and good at fixing things. What goals might she have for involvement in the recreation services of her local agencies? Or consider Aaron Mann. A young telephone company operator, Aaron enjoys peace and quiet in his nonwork hours. He particularly likes to spend time outdoors, but his work schedule often requires working shifts on weekends. He lives in a large urban area. What expectations might Aaron have from the recreation leadership in his city?

The basic responsibility of recreation, park, sport, and tourism personnel is to provide, directly or indirectly, opportunities for people to behave recreationally. This means that the goals the participant seeks to satisfy and that the leader attempts to facilitate are manifested through recreation behavior. The participant is involved in recreation via her behavior. It follows then that those responsible for helping fulfill participant goals must have some understanding of participant behavior. We explore some of this behavior in terms of both individuals and groups.

Individual Recreation Behavior

Recreation behavior is rewarding. Recreation is pursued primarily for its own sake, not for a secondary or extrinsic value. In recreation, the "real" world is forgotten temporarily; everyday responsibilities, time, and roles are deemphasized. The participant tends to be deeply absorbed in the recreation experience and often loses track of the surroundings. There also appears to be a voluntary nature in recreation behavior; it is more likely to occur where constraints are fewest. Finally, the recreationist feels in control of the behavior and the outcomes. Recreation has been characterized by feelings of mastery, achievement, personal worth, and pleasure.

A great deal of research has been devoted to describing types of recreation behavior. Aerobic dancing, four-harness loom weaving, white water kayaking, and movie attending are recreation behaviors. But they are also different behaviors: the basic nature of the behavior varies. The range of recreation behaviors is diverse and broad.

Murphy, Williams, Niepoth, and Brown (1973) have developed a comprehensive categorization of the variety of recreation behaviors:

- **Socializing behaviors:** Some recreation behavior is oriented around getting to know and relating to other people. Such experiences as parties, visiting friends, and conversation would suggest the need for socializing behaviors.
- **Associative behaviors:** Another type of behavior is that in which people come together to pursue a common interest. Internet chat rooms, model railroad clubs, and rugby teams offer an outlet for associative behaviors.
- **Acquisitive behaviors:** Some recreation participation is manifested in collecting and saving behavior. The beer can collector, the miniature doll furniture collector, and the stamp collector exhibit acquisitive recreation behavior.
- **Competitive behaviors:** Competitive behavior is usually manifested in sports but is not limited to these activities. This behavior usually occurs within the context of set rules and procedures and includes either an actual or implied opponent. The essence of this behavior is to win against or defeat the opponent.
- **Testing behaviors:** Similar to competitive behaviors, testing behaviors are those in which an individual's skills are tested against some criterion or environmental condition. The hang glider pilot tests her skill and equipment; so does the video game player.
- **Risk-taking behaviors:** Many recreation experiences involve risk. In sky jumping and in casino gambling, for example, the participant measures the risk by assuming he has a reasonable chance for success or survival.
- **Explorative behaviors:** When a recreationist seeks to encounter new environments or to rediscover the finds of past adventures, explorative behavior is in evidence. Sightseeing, spelunking, and nature study are examples.
- **Vicarious experience behaviors:** Reading, television viewing, and spectator sports illustrate recreation behaviors that allow participants to encounter events or environments through the eyes of others.
- **Sensory stimulation behaviors:** Although all recreation behavior involves sensory stimulation to some degree, many experiences are more dependent on this behavior than others. The pleasure derived from sexual relationships and other experiences that appeal primarily to the senses are based on this behavior.

- **Physical expression behaviors:** Another facet of behavior that also seems to involve some sensory elements is physical expression. Movement through the use of the body in dance or in athletics is pleasurable.
- **Creative behaviors:** Expression in a creative sense—usually through the arts—is another behavior frequently called forth in a recreation experience. Playing the drums, painting, and miming usually require creative behavior.
- **Appreciative behaviors:** The results of creative behavior are observed and enjoyed by others. In appreciative behavior the participant usually responds to a product or an event rather than interacting directly. Visiting a sculpture gallery, attending a dance performance, and listening to the opera require appreciative behaviors.
- **Variety-seeking behaviors:** In this behavior participants seek a change from routine. Much of what individuals do in their free time probably involves an intention to change from life's normal pattern.
- **Anticipatory and recollective behaviors:** Recreation experiences usually include an anticipatory and recollective behavior in addition to the actual participation. These behaviors include looking forward to the experience, planning, gathering equipment, showing slides, and collecting souvenirs.

An individual participating in recreation may manifest several of these behaviors simultaneously. For example, playing volleyball may involve socializing behavior, competitive behavior, physical expression behavior, and variety-seeking behavior. The combination of behaviors will be unique for each individual. What is impressive about this list is the wide range of participant behaviors common to recreation experiences.

Other research reveals some other major insights about the nature of recreation and play behavior. These insights are important to your success as a recreation leader as well.

First, recreation behavior provides satisfaction to the participant. If asked, most people would declare that they engage in recreation for enjoyment or fun. Satisfaction is an emotional condition or feeling that is individually defined. It is a matter of reward.

Case in Point: Mentorship in Minneapolis

Implemented in 1991 by the Minneapolis Park and Recreation Board, the "Youthline Outreach Mentorship Program" targets the unstructured, unsupervised, and unproductive time of youth. Youthline's objective is to involve youth in wholesome recreation activities, introduce them to community resources, and create a sense of belonging. Based in 30 Minneapolis parks youth ages 12 to 16 are targeted in the six blocks surrounding each park. In the parks activities consist of developing a teen council, organizing community service projects, and identifying part-time job opportunities. An average of 50 youth per park spend an average of five hours a day, five days a week at the park. In addition, outreach activities include developing working relationships with youth workers at other agencies. Some comments from Youthline participants reported in a 1993 assessment are:

"I'm the new me. I used to get kicked out all the time because I was disrespectful. Now the little kids look up to me."

"I used to be very shy and a loner. Then I started comin' down here and got to know a lot of people. Now I help out every day."

"Here, you can talk to the staff and your friends about anything. Especially things you wouldn't talk to your parents about, like sex and relationships and stuff."

"It's kept me from learning how to kill somebody."

(Fisher, 1996, p. 63)

Persons participate in recreation because the positive rewards such as enjoyment, improved health, and new friends are satisfying. For some, satisfaction is derived from experiencing relaxation; for others, satisfaction is the result of adventure and challenge; and for others, satisfaction is brought about from a sense of success and achievement. People behave recreationally for different reasons; satisfaction is an individual matter (Tinsley, 1977).

As a recreation leader, you will note indications of the satisfaction that results from recreation behavior when you hear such phrases from your participants as "happy memories," "a chance to escape work pressures," "good time," "chance to meet new people," and "peace of mind." Recreation participants seek opportunities in sports, in crafts, and in drama because they seek a meaningful, positive, fulfilling emotional condition. Satisfaction from recreation involvement is an important concern for leaders because this is perhaps the ultimate participant goal. If the recreation leader is able to shape experiences so participants receive those rewards that are truly satisfying, then it has been a job well done.

Second, recreation behavior involves the participant at varying levels of intensity. How absorbed an individual is during recreation behavior ranges on a continuum from low or minimal to high or maximal. Compare for yourself, for example, how intensely involved you might become when climbing a rock face or when playing a game of chess. Answers to this reflection will differ for each of you. Yet as research has shown, chess can be as intense a behavior as rock climbing. For example, Csikszentmihalyi (1975) reported the following testimonies, the first about rock climbing and the second about playing chess:

> When I start on a climb, it is as if my memory input has been cut off. All I can remember is the last thirty seconds, and all I can think ahead is the next five minutes (p. 40).
>
> When the game is exciting, I don't seem to hear anything—the world seems to be cut off from me and all there is to think about is my game (p. 40).

Csikszentmihalyi (1990) has published some captivating research on the degree of involvement in recreation. He and his colleagues have developed a concept known as "flow." Flow is a dynamic condition that people feel when they act with total involvement. His studies of recreation behavior have found that individuals completely immersed in an activity lose their sense of time, themselves, and the world around them. They are said to experience an altered state of being. In this flow state a participant experiences a sensation that nothing else matters. Csikszentmihalyi also claims that one may experience flow in any activity, not just recreation. By this same logic, one may not be so intensely involved just because it is a recreation activity. Intensity of involvement, just as satisfaction, is an individual matter.

Third, recreation behavior includes participant interaction with the environment. The environment is the context within which the behavior occurs. It includes the physical elements (such as trees, rivers, chairs, kilns, and baseball mitts), as well as those other persons who are either directly or indirectly in contact. Participants in all recreation activity interact with and have an impact on their setting, and in many cases the circumstances of that setting can affect the characteristics of their behavior. The environment, then, is a stage on which recreation behavior is performed.

One way of conceptualizing how people interact with their environment while engaged in recreation can be studied in figure 3.2. A participant may enter a recreational

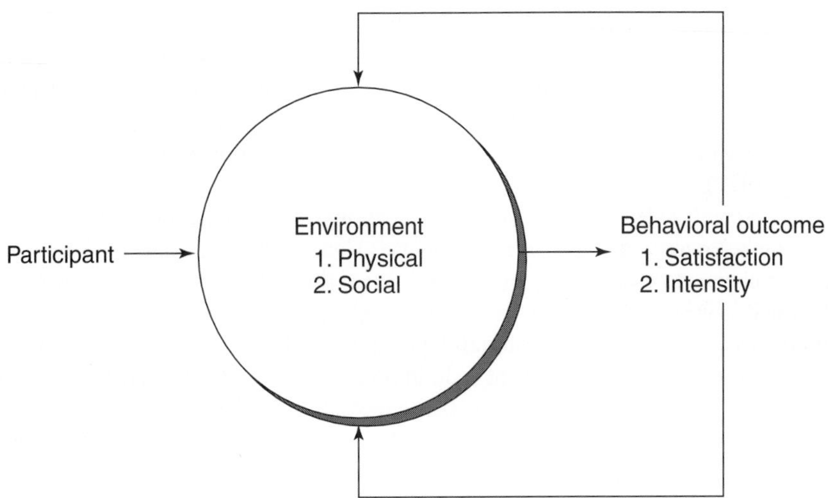

FIGURE 3.2. Participant's relationship with the environment

environment that has both physical and social characteristics within it. This participant behaves according to the complex influence of the physical and social components of the overall environment. At some point there is a behavioral outcome that can be translated into satisfaction and intensity of involvement. This outcome then feeds back into the environment, affecting both the physical and social aspects.

Consider a class in jazz dance. George Preston is the participant. He enters the environment of the class for a dance experience. This environment would include, perhaps, the hardwood floor, the wall mirrors, the dance posters, the jazz music, and the availability of good air circulation. This environment would also most likely include the leader, other dance participants, and perhaps some spectators sitting along one wall. Much to the displeasure of George, this environment could also include a pesky child who keeps crying and wanting his mom to pay attention to him. George's behavior in the dance class will be impinged by this total environment.

For instance, George may find the beat of the music inspiring but the intrusions of the child distracting. George's behavior in the class will also influence this environment. His inspired dancing could serve as a model for the other participants, and his complaints to the teacher about the child could mean that the child's mother must leave the class early.

The relationship between recreation behavior and the environment is therefore not unilateral. Behavior influences the environment, and the environment influences behavior. In a sense this relationship can be described as ecological.

Fourth, recreation behavior is governed by specific forces. The participant in recreation behaves according to the determining factors of her life experience. In a sense, then, the recreation participant is not truly free. What she chooses to be involved in, how this involvement is expressed, and the outcome from this involvement is subject to numerous conditions impinging on her. Broadly these controlling forces can be categorized as biological, demographical, psychological, and sociological (figure 3.3).

The biological forces dictating recreation behavior include such conditions as health, level of fitness, coordination, strength, and presence of disability. For example, the sports behavior of a hospitalized person will be different from the sports behavior of a college athlete.

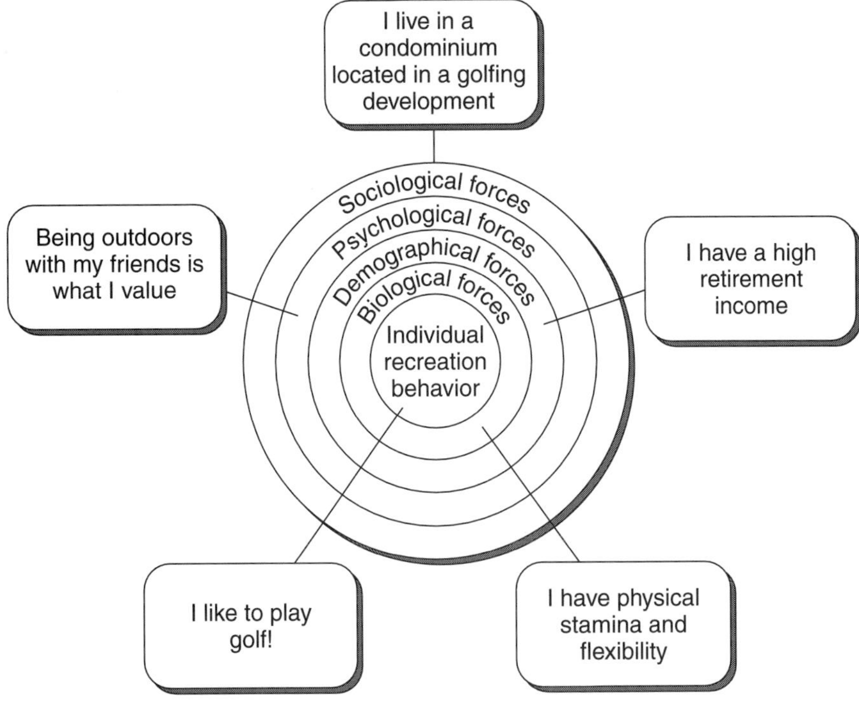

FIGURE 3.3. Recreation behavior is governed by specific forces

Demographical forces that shape recreation behavior include circumstances such as level of education, occupation, income level, type of residence, region of the country, age, gender, and so forth. Although age and gender are not the factors that most influence recreation behavior, they have been the ones most traditionally used when leading recreation participants. This may be a result of the ease with which this information can be known. Heavy reliance on demographic factors for leadership purposes, however, can lead to stereotypic services that may not adequately meet client goals.

Psychological factors governing recreation behavior include perceptions, attitudes, personal values, personality differences, and memory and learning capabilities. Attitudes and values in particular have been considered important influencers of recreation behavior—exactly how important an influencer remains an active concern of research. For instance, is it really possible for you to enjoy snowmobiling if you feel that snowmobiling is noisy and destroys the land? Is it possible that there are "snowmobile personalities" and "cross-country ski personalities"?

Finally, sociological factors dictating recreation behavior include those differences in family, peer group, neighborhood, community, and the mass media. All individuals are socialized by these factors to behave in certain ways. **Socialization** is the process by which people first acquire most recreation skills, interests, and values. A participant's recreation behavior becomes what it is within a social context. For most people, recreation is initially introduced in childhood family experiences and continues to be shaped in adulthood by friends, as well as the broader community.

To summarize (see figure 3.3), understanding individual recreation behavior is important to the effectiveness of recreation leaders. This is because leaders seek to enhance and maximize these behaviors. But not all recreation occurs on an individual basis. Thus, it is also vital that the recreation leader understand play that is group-based.

Group Recreation Behavior

There are many recreational pursuits that lend themselves best to group participation. Knowledge of group recreational behavior is important to the leader, because recreation, park, sport, and tourism personnel customarily work with a variety of groups. In some groups, recreation personnel will be the leaders. In other group settings, recreation leaders will relate as resource persons. Finally, in certain settings they will serve as group members.

Little is known of what influences a group specifically within the recreation context. However, what we do know about the uniqueness of the recreation group is interesting and useful to the leader's understanding of participant goals.

For example, there is the concept of "social worlds." Individuals tend to use recreation services because their families, friends, neighbors, or workmates use those services. As Cheek (1976, p. 132) indicated, "Social-psychological theory suggests that social worlds are becoming more important as reference groups in contemporary societies."

Social worlds tend to form around common participation in recreation activities. For example, card players, people who show dogs or cats, tournament bass fishing enthusiasts, and rock climbers form a subculture around the activity of joint interest (Kelly, 1996). In these social worlds people have similar skill levels, vocabularies, and social conventions.

The idea of social worlds is perhaps most visibly supported by the popularity of retirement communities. Retirees are more and more preferring to live in communities with other persons who have compatible ages, social status, and recreation interests. These communities provide a reference group that legitimizes certain recreation behaviors and choices.

We also know that recreation activities vary in their relative contributions to the group experience. For instance, some activities such as initiative games are better able to increase group communication, interaction, and cohesiveness. Outdoor activities,

Exercise: Hawser—A Game

Set-Up

You will need a thick rope, about twenty to twenty-five feet in length. Such a thick rope is called a "hawser" and its circumference is at least two inches. Rope this size is expensive so look for manufacturers remnants. This size of rope is also heavy, which is what you want.

The Game

A team of six players must move the hawser 100 feet without using hands and without maneuvering the rope onto their bodies. Only their feet can be used to move the hawser. The start position is standing within a circle made by the hawser. Finishing requires moving the hawser the 100 feet and then reestablishing the circle with all team members inside. This can be played as a timed event or as a relay with another team.

Discussion

How did the playing of this game affect your group? Do you think it may have increased group communication, interaction, or cohesiveness? Why or why not?

(From Rohnke & Butler, 1995, pp. 160–161)

particularly high adventure types, are also used in many recreation settings for their contribution to the group process. Television viewing, on the other hand, is a recreation activity that makes a low-level contribution to group communication and interaction.

So why are there recreation leaders? The essential answer to the question of this chapter is that the most important goal of recreation leadership is the facilitation of individual and group leisure expression.

Summary

Why are there recreation leaders? Recreation leaders exist to accomplish certain goals for their society, profession, employing organizations, and participants.

In the broadest sense, leadership in recreation has a responsibility to society. Recreation is not only an individual phenomenon but also a social phenomenon. As such the work that leaders do occupies a key role in modern societal life. The most important and challenging societal expectations on recreation leaders are (1) improvement of the quality of life, (2) promotion of social change, and (3) leisure education.

In addition to a social responsibility, leaders in recreation also have a responsibility to their profession. How successfully recreation leaders meet their challenges and opportunities depends not only on meeting expected service goals with competent skills and an enthusiastic attitude, but it also means performing according to honorable and appropriate standards and ethics. Often this involves attention to (1) professionalism, (2) performance standards, and (3) ethics.

As well, recreation leaders have a responsibility to their sponsoring organization. The recreation leader is the vehicle for transporting agency purposes into achievable goals. Critical organization purposes are (1) efficiency and (2) assessment of success.

Finally, leadership in recreation has a responsibility to the participant. This is perhaps the most difficult goal to achieve. The participant's expectations for recreation leadership are often diverse and at times contradictory. An understanding of the client's individual and group recreation behavior should be useful to the leader.

Meeting these four responsibilities is why there is recreation leadership. "How good a leader am I?" In subsequent chapters those skills and techniques that contribute to your success in these areas of responsibility will be taught. Yet success is not relevant—this question of how good a leader you are is not important—unless the question "What have I accomplished?" can also be answered.

Questions and Activities for Review and Discussion

1. Why should the recreation leader assume responsibility for social change? Defend why a recreation leader should not.
2. Compare two communities in which you have lived according to the quality of their physical-social environment. What specific aspects of these environments did you compare? What role did recreation have in this comparison?
3. What can the societal goal of leisure education mean to your work as a recreation leader? If you have a volunteer or paid position in a recreation organization, exactly what leisure education effort could you start right now?
4. What does it mean to you to be a professional? Does it mean the same thing to others in your course? To the recreation leaders working on your campus or in your community?

5. Visit a recreation or park organization (any type) in your community or on your campus. By interviewing a member of the staff find out what this agency chiefly wishes to accomplish. Return to class, form small discussion groups, and compare the various organization goals. How might these differences affect your leadership depending on the organization with which you are working?
6. Explain how efficiency and effectiveness are different goals.
7. Building on the interview results from question 5, how does the organization measure whether it is successful in achieving its goals? Can you think of additional ways of determining what the organization has accomplished?
8. Analyze your favorite recreation activity (e.g., jogging, reading, water skiing) according to Murphy et al's categorization of recreation behaviors. Which behaviors will most likely be found in your selected activity?
9. In retrospect, research does not know much about recreation behavior. In your own words summarize what we do know about this type of human behavior by discussing your example from the previous question.

References

Allen, L. R. (1991). Benefits of leisure service to community satisfaction. In B. L. Driver, P. J. Brown, & G. L. Peterson (Eds.), *Benefits of Leisure.* State College, PA: Venture Publishing.

Bartol, K. M., & Martin, D. C. (1998). *Management.* Boston: Irwin/McGraw-Hill.

Bass, B. M. (1990). *Bass & Stogdill's handbook of leadership: Theory, research, and managerial applications.* New York: The Free Press.

Cheek, N. H. (1976). Social groups and leisure settings. In N. H. Cheek, D. R. Field, & R. Burdge (Eds.), *Leisure and recreation places.* Ann Arbor: Ann Arbor Science.

Csikszentmihalyi, M. (1975). *Beyond boredom and anxiety.* San Francisco: Jossey-Bass.

Csikszentmihalyi, M. (1990). *Flow: The psychology of optimal experience.* New York: Harper & Row.

Eckersley, R. (1999, January, Vol. 34). Is life really getting better? *The Futurist*, 23–26.

Edginton, C. R. (1996). Perspectives toward the 21st century. In F. H. Fu, & P. P. C. Chan (Eds.), *Recreation, Sport, Culture, and Tourism for the 21st Century*. Hong Kong: Hong Kong Baptist University.

Fisher, D. (1996). An integrated approach to services for children and youth in Minneapolis, Minnesota. In P. A. Witt & J. L. Crompton (Eds.), *Recreation Programs That Work for At-Risk Youth: The Challenge of Shaping the Future.* State College, PA: Venture Publishing.

Hitt, W. D. (1990). *Ethics and leadership: Putting theory into practice.* Columbus, OH: Battelle Press.

Hyman, M. (1991). *Elderhostels: The students' choice.* Santa Fe, NM: John Muir Publications.

Jordan, D. J. (1996). *Leadership in leisure services: Making a difference.* State College, PA: Venture Publishing.

Kelly, J. R. (1996). *Leisure.* Boston: Allyn and Bacon.

Labich, K. (1995, May 2, Vol. 134). Is Herb Kelleher America's Best CEO? *Fortune*, 44–49.

Lippert, J. (1994, August 15). Wings of desire. *Detroit Free Press, Business Monday*, pp. 8F–9F.

Marans, R. W., & Mohai, P. (1991). Leisure resources, recreation activity, and the quality of life. In B. L. Driver, P. J. Brown, & G. L. Peterson (Eds.), *Benefits of Leisure.* State College, PA: Venture Publishing.

Mills, E. S. (1993). *The story of Elderhostel.* University of New Hampshire, Hanover: University Press of New England.

Mundy, J. (1998). *Leisure education: Theory and practice* (2nd Ed.). Champaign, IL: Sagamore.

Murphy, J. F., Williams, J. G., Niepoth, E. W., & Brown, P. D. (1973). *Leisure service delivery system: A modern perspective.* Philadelphia: Lea & Febiger.

Navar, N., & Tschumper, R. (January 1999). Leisure Lifestyle Center: A Combination of Teaching, Scholarship and Service. Society of Park and Recreation Educators–Teaching Institute. Myrtle Beach, SC.

Niepoth, E. W. (1983). *Leisure leadership: Working with people in recreation and park settings.* Englewood Cliffs, NJ: Prentice-Hall.

Otten, A. L. (1986, July 14). Ethics on the job: Companies alert employees to potential dilemmas. *The Wall Street Journal*, p. 21.

Riddick, C. C., & Russell, R. V. (1999). *Evaluative research in recreation, park, and sport settings: Searching for useful information.* Champaign, IL: Sagamore.

Rohnke, K., & Butler, S. (1995). *QuickSilver: Adventure games, initiative problems, trust activities and a guide to effective leadership.* Dubuque, IA: Kendall/Hunt.

Russell, B. (1946). *A history of western philosophy.* London: George Allen and Unwin.

Tinsley, H. E. A. (1977). The ubiquitous question of why. In D. J. Brademas (Ed.), *New thoughts on leisure: Selected papers from the Allen V. Sapora Symposium on Leisure and Recreation.* Urbana-Champaign: University of Illinois.

Web Resources

Benefits are Endless (NRPA): www.nrpa.org/beninfo.htm

Benefits Catalogue of the California Parks and Recreation Association: www.lin.ca/benefits.htm

Big Brothers/Big Sisters: www.bbbsa.org/

Center for the Study of Living Standards: www.csls.ca/overview.htm

Elderhostel: www.elderhostel.org

Fifty Plus Fitness Association: www.50plus.org/pages/directory.htm

LARNet: The Cyber Journal of Applied Leisure and Recreation Research: http://www/nccu.edu/larnet/larnet.htm

Leisure as Activity: www.als.uiuc.edu/leis/resources/definitions/activity.html

Leisure as Experience: www.als.uiuc.edu/leist/resources/definitions/experience.html

Leisure as Time: www.als.uiuc.edu/leist/resources/definitions/time.html

Quality of Life: www.QLMed.org/

Quality of Life and Leadership Resources Case: www.rcfdenver.org/

Quality of Life Research Journal: http://gort.ucsd.edu/newjour/q/msg01691.htm

Quality of Life Research Unit: www.utoronto.ca/chp/qlfintro.htm

Society for Park and Recreation Educators: http://www2.uncwil.edu/spre

Standard of Living: www.planif.com/eng.html

Standard of Living Index: www.webcom.com/retire/planning/soli.htm

State of Children's Play: http://www/geog.ualberta.ca/als/alswp6.html

World Bank's Living Standards: www.worldbank.org/html/prdph/lsms/lsmshome.htm

PART TWO

General Proficiencies

CHAPTER 4

Decision Making and Problem Solving

The winds and waves are always on the side of the ablest navigators.
—Gibbon, 1776, p. 1343.

LEARNING OBJECTIVES

All recreation leaders—whether they are youth activities specialists, fitness coordinators, rock climbing guides, aquatics supervisors, or the general manager of a resort—must be able to:

- make decisions
- solve problems

KEY TERMS

decision making p. 72
crisis p. 72
noncrisis p. 72
opportunities p. 73
programmed decisions p. 73
nonprogrammed decisions p. 73
preparation p. 74
incubation p. 74
illumination p. 74
verification p. 74
information exchange p. 75
groupthink p. 76
complacency p. 78
defensive avoidance p. 78
panic p. 78
framing p. 79
prospect theory p. 79
availability p. 79
problem solving p. 79
force-field analysis p. 81
brainstorming p. 83

Today numerous supervisors, administrators, executive directors, general managers, and presidents of recreation organizations are sitting at their desks attempting to write job descriptions for personnel vacancies on their staff. They are asking themselves the same question as they sit poised, pen in hand. What exactly is it that this recreation leader should be able to do? What proficiencies are necessary for this new employee to be effective? This part of the text is concerned with basic skill competency. To be competent is to be able to do something well. There is no doubt that leadership involves certain skills and capabilities that enable the leader to be of value to those led. For example, in commercial recreation some important skills might be verbal and written communication, public relations, sales, personnel management, and scheduling. For recreation leaders working in a therapeutic setting the basic skills competency list might include understanding rehabilitation and therapy, the group process, teaching, inter-agency relationships, referral processes, and legislation. Another example may be found in recreational sports management. Here an employer might expect the leader to have ability in sports programming, safety and first aid, sports officiating, coaching, and supervising skills.

Other lists of competencies found in recreation leader job descriptions are likely to include a wide range of skills such as ability to lead low organized games, conduct leisure counseling, evaluate programs, produce marketing surveys, play the piano, teach crafts, and develop multimedia presentations. The specific competencies required will vary from job description to job description.

Although no one individual can be competent in all the desirable skills for every recreation leadership position, certain basic or foundational skills are important to those who assume leadership roles in recreation, regardless of the specific setting. This chapter focuses on:

- Ability to make sound and timely decisions
- Ability to solve agency, participant, staff, and personal problems

This chapter, then, maintains that central to successful recreation leadership is a qualified and capable level of ability in the skills of decision making and problem solving. The ability to excel at these fundamental skills translates directly to more successful achievement of the recreation leader's reason for existing—the enabling of fulfilling recreation experiences for others. Subsequent chapters in this part of the text discuss such other general proficiencies as group management, communication, and participant motivation.

DECISION MAKING

Recreation leaders make many different decisions on a daily basis in the course of their work. **Decision making** is identifying problems and opportunities in an attempt for resolution. Some leadership decisions are simple and easy, while others are highly complex and difficult, requiring consideration of many factors. For the outdoor leader, for example, a "simple" choice between two hiking routes may require information about the terrain and elevations of each route, the predicted weather, the time of day, and the energy and skill levels of participants. As for all leaders, you may not always make the right decision, but you can use your knowledge of appropriate decision-making strategies to increase your odds.

As you see from the Fitness Machines "Case in Point," there are many reasons for making decisions. In this case, it was a matter of responding to trends. Leadership decision making typically centers on three types of reasons: crisis, noncrisis, and opportunity (Nutt, 1984). First, a **crisis** situation is a serious difficulty requiring immediate action. Examples of a crisis include the discovery of a severe cash-flow deficiency in the recreation organization, environmentalists protesting in front of the beach resort, or quickly rising water in a cave during a spelunking expedition. A **noncrisis** reason for decision making occurs when an issue requires resolution but does not simultaneously have the importance and immediacy characteristics of a crisis. Many of the decisions that recreation leaders make center on noncrisis reasons. For example, it may be an employee who is frequently late for work, an out-of-date organization mission statement, or a particular kind of insect that is slowly destroying the park trees.

Finally, we make decisions to take advantage of **opportunities**. Patricia's fitness center in the "Case in Point" demonstrated decision making when it took advantage of available trend data. Opportunities do not become successes unless they are chosen for action. An opportunity is a "situation that offers a strong potential for significant organizational gain if appropriate actions are taken" (Bartol & Martin, 1998, p. 140). Opportunities involve ideas that could be used, rather than difficulties that must be resolved. Ineffective leaders tend to focus on making decisions about crisis and noncrisis situations, and neglect the application of their decision-making skill to opportunities.

Leader Profile: The Present
Eileen Kilpatrick
Manager of Special Services, Minneapolis Park and Recreation Board. As a special event administrator, Eileen makes opportunity and programmed decisions on a daily basis.

In addition to facing three types of reasons for making decisions, recreation leaders also typically deal with different types of decisions. These are programmed and nonprogrammed decisions (Bartol & Martin, 1998). **Programmed decisions** are those made in routine and continual situations through the use of predetermined decision rules. These decision rules typically come from previous experience or professional knowledge about what works in a particular situation. For example, most recreation organizations have written procedures for handling participant injuries and for determining when supplies are reordered. **Nonprogrammed decisions** are those for which there are no previously determined rules or for which predetermined rules are impractical. For example, a city recreation agency may need to decide the location of a new softball complex or select a new evening program for teens.

Although programmed decisions are found in more everyday situations and nonprogrammed decisions are more specialized, both can be complex. To help, computers have enhanced our ability for making more sophisticated programmed and nonprogrammed decisions, because they can analyze large amounts of factors that inform the decision. There is one difference I haven't mentioned, however. Most of the decisions made by direct service leaders and many of those made by supervisory leaders are of the programmed type. At the other end, upper administrative leaders tend to make more nonprogrammed decisions. This phenomenon can be illustrated by figure 4.1.

There is a great deal of good advice about making good decisions. However, at the core of good decisions is rational thinking. Rationality is the condition of being able to reason soundly and logically. This kind of thinking is critical to the decision-making process, the decision maker, and the decision. As a decision maker, rationality means

Case in Point: Fitness Machines

To stay in shape Patricia Rich heads for the fitness center. Three times a week, she waits for a parking spot close to the entrance, and heads right to the strength and conditioning room. Patricia spends a few minutes on the treadmill, then works out on a circuit of strength-training machines. "I like the machines because you can tell what specific muscles you're working," says Patricia. Patricia's fitness center has 25 weight resistance machines, 5 rowers, 8 treadmills, and 15 recumbant cycles.

How did Patricia's gym make the decisions about how many and which kind of exercise machines to purchase? One way was from studying the fitness trend data available to them. When it comes to physical exercise, Patricia is a "muscle-flexing sign of the times" (Denny, 1999, p. D1). According to data that tracks the fitness movement "the '70s was the running decade and the '80s were typified by aerobic classes. But the '90s saw a shift to machines"—everything from muscle-building weight machines, to stair climbers, stationary bikes, total body stretchers, and sit-up machines (Denny, 1999, D1).

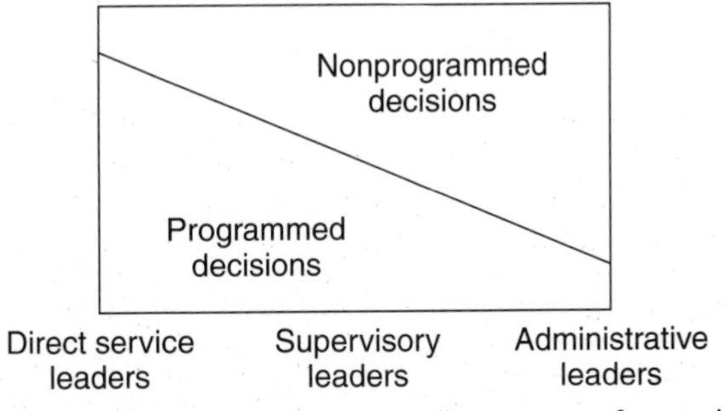

FIGURE 4.1. Types of decisions according to types of recreation leaders. Adapted from Bartol & Martin, 1998, p. 141

that you do the following:

- set optimal goals for the resulting decision
- engage as broadly as possible in a search of alternatives
- acquire adequate information and control of the factors influencing the outcome of the decision

How skillfully this rational thinking is carried out depends on many things. Circumstances and resources, for example, differ from decision to decision. In the next two sections we'll consider more specific advice for making good decisions. These are the importance of creativity in decision making and the role of group-made decisions.

Making Creative Decisions

To be effective decision makers recreation leaders must think creatively and rationally. The leader must have the ability to think of new options, to make unique thought connections, and to take on decisions that other people have passed up because they are difficult. Creative thinking involves four phases: preparation, incubation, illumination, and verification (Kelly, 1980).

Preparation is equipping your mind with the information and data necessary for making a decision. Preparation involves mulling over various concepts, conclusions, and facts and trying to get them to fit a variety of explanations. It is a matter of supplying the mind with all the possible ideas or circumstances involved in the decision. Once preparation has been accomplished, the next step in creative thinking is to relax, to enter a mental state of **incubation**. Creative decision makers have a thinking style that allows them to engage in other activities while their unconscious mind ruminates on the decision.

At this point it is not unusual for the best decision to become obvious. Most creative people can recall instances when a decision came to them, fresh and new. The effect is an **illumination**. The final phase is **verification**, in which the decision maker sets out to establish the validity and the usefulness of the selected decision.

Individual Versus Group Decision Making

One of the more interesting questions about decision making is whether individuals or groups make better decisions. Often the major decisions in recreation organizations are

Advantages
1. Information exchange
2. Higher motivation for better decisions
3. More security felt for the decision
4. Increased acceptance of the decision
5. Increased number and diversity of alternatives developed

Disadvantages
1. Lack of necessary maturity
2. Variety of motives
3. Failure to communicate
4. More time-consuming
5. Disagreements may delay decisions
6. Groupthink

FIGURE 4.2. Advantages and disadvantages of group decision making

made by more than one person because more perspectives are focused on the issue. But, group decision making also has disadvantages. Figure 4.2 summarizes the advantages and disadvantages of group decision making (Bartol & Martin, 1998; Johnson & Johnson, 1994).

There are several reasons why group decision making may be more effective than individual decision making. These can be summarized as follows.

First, in most decision-making groups, members with incomplete information interact with others who have different facts and perspectives relevant to the decision. Thus the quality of decision making in such a situation depends on the adequacy of **information exchange**. If a high-quality decision is to be made, the resources of each member must be coordinated or pooled. A group's knowledge should be greater than that of any one group member. A leader who is able to challenge another's thinking, enables a group decision that takes all viewpoints into account according to a workable compromise. In deciding which European cities to visit for this year's tour by the members of the older adult community center, group information exchange as a part of the group's decision-making process will yield a more successful decision.

Second, individuals working in groups often tend to have more motivation for making better decisions than do individuals working alone. Working in a group allows members to imitate the actions of more highly motivated members and to compare contributions with those of other members, both of which inspire greater efforts.

Third, groups seem to possess more security than individuals in making unique or different decisions. This means that a group discussion can polarize decisions by causing the group to adopt a position more extreme than those of the individual members alone. Thus this leads to an enhancement of participants' involvement with issues and their confidence that the selected decision is the correct one. An example of this is the preference for making group decisions about who to hire, particularly for top-level positions.

Fourth, by its very nature, group decision making may lead to increased acceptance of the decision by members and so yield more effective implementation of the results. Participants in a recreation setting who have a chance to influence their group's decision may have a greater commitment to the decision and even assume responsibility for making it work.

Finally, because good decisions depend on good choices, often group decision making benefits from the development of an increased number and diversity of alternatives. "Two heads are better than one" is the creative thinking aspect of decision making.

There are, on the other hand, a variety of factors that can hamper effective group decision making. (figure 4.2)

First, the group may lack the necessary maturity. Temporary, ad hoc groups do not usually have the time to develop enough maturity to function with full effectiveness; the group needs time and experience working together to be able to make effective decisions. Therefore group decision making in long-term recreation groups (such as teams, clubs, and staff) will be more successful than in short-term recreation groups (such as audiences, tour groups, and day-use visitors).

Also members bring into a group a variety of motives. When goals of a group are in conflict, members may be competing with one another in ways that reduce their effectiveness in decision making. For example, members of a gourmet cooking group may have different reasons for being in the group, therefore deciding how many times per month to get together for elaborate, time-consuming cooking could be difficult.

Another factor inhibiting effective group decisions is failure to communicate. That is, not all members participate equally in a group, and not all contributions are listened to carefully by all group members. Group effectiveness can also be reduced if one individual dominates the interactions through too much communication, persuasion, or persistence.

Group decision making is more time consuming, thus if there is insufficient time available to make the decision, an individual better make it. As well, disagreements may delay decisions and cause hard feelings.

Finally, **groupthink** may cause group members to overemphasize achieving agreement in the decision. Groupthink is the tendency in cohesive groups to seek agreement about an issue at the expense of realistically appraising the situation (Janis, 1982). The underlying theory of groupthink is that group members are so concerned about preserving the cohesion of the group that they are reluctant to bring up issues that may cause disagreements or to provide information that may prove unsettling to the discussion (Bartol & Martin, 1998). Here is a story told by a consultant of companies in the Silicon Valley that illustrates groupthink:

> In the late 1930s, Alfred Sloan was chairing a board meeting at General Motors. An idea was proposed and everyone present became very enthusiastic about it. One person said, "We'll make a lot of money with this proposal." Another said, "Let's implement it as soon as possible." After the discussion, a vote was taken on the idea. The vote went around the table, with each board member voting "yes," and when it came back to Sloan he too voted "yes." Then Sloan said, "That makes it unanimous, and for that reason I am going to table the proposal until next month. Seems we're getting locked into looking at this idea in just one way, and this is a dangerous way to make decisions. I want each of you to spend the next month studying the proposal from a different perspective." A month went by and the proposal was brought up again at the next board meeting. This time, however, it was voted down. The board members had had an opportunity to break through the effects of groupthink (von Oech, 1983, p. 113).

Are there other factors that hamper effective group decision making? There are quite a few such as egocentrism of group members, lack of sufficient heterogeneity among members, group size too large, members loafing, power or status differences, and distrust among members.

Methods of Group Decision Making

Think about the groups to which you belong. How do they make decisions? Do different groups use different methods? Does your family, your sport team, your sorority or fraternity, or your class use the same procedures for making decisions? Several methods can be reviewed (Johnson & Johnson, 1994).

Method 1: decision by authority without group discussion. The leader makes the decision without consulting the group members. The resulting decision is merely communicated back to the group.

Method 2: decision by expert. Group decisions can be made by letting the group member most expert on the issue decide what the group should do. The group does not discuss the issue, but rather allows the expert to decide on his own and then report the decision back to the group.

Method 3: decision by averaging individuals' opinions. Each group member is asked her opinion, and then the results are averaged. This procedure can be illustrated when a chairperson of a committee calls each member on the telephone, asks what the member's opinion is, and then takes the most popular opinion as the group's decision.

Method 4: decision by authority after group discussion. The group does originate ideas and hold discussions, but it is the designated leader who makes the final decision. Listening to a group discussion will usually improve the accuracy of a decision made by the group's leader.

Method 5: decision by minority. A minority of the group can make the group's decisions in several ways, some legitimate and some illegitimate. Legitimate methods include decisions made by executive committees or temporary, task force committees. Illegitimate methods include decisions made by railroading or by force.

Method 6: decisions by majority vote. Majority vote is the method of group decision making most commonly used in many recreation situations. The procedure is to discuss an issue only as long as it takes at least 51 percent of the members to decide on a course of action.

Method 7: decision by consensus. Perfect consensus means that everyone in the group agrees what the decision should be. Unanimity is often impossible to achieve. Therefore there are degrees of consensus, all of which bring about a higher level of member involvement than the other decision-making methods.

As this list indicates, there are many ways in which a recreation group can make a decision. Each group decision-making method is best used and appropriate for only certain circumstances. Each also has its particular consequences for the group's future operation. An effective leader is able to understand each method of decision making well enough to choose the method that is best for the following:

- Type of decision to be made
- Amount of time and resources available
- History of the group
- Kind of emotional climate within which the group is most comfortable
- Setting within which the group exists

Barriers to Decision Making

Recreation leaders face several barriers to effective decision making. Here we discuss not accepting the need to make a decision and then common decision-making biases (figure 4.3).

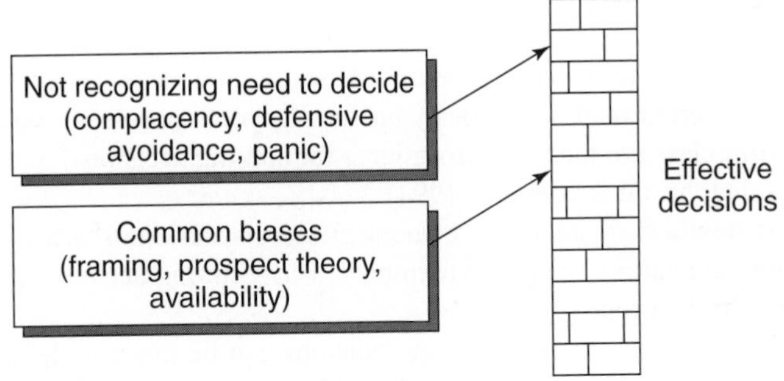

FIGURE 4.3. Barriers to decision making

When faced with the need to make a decision, there are four basic reaction patterns (Bartol & Martin, 1998). Complacency, defensive avoidance, and panic represent a nonacceptance of the need to make a decision. The fourth, deciding to decide, is the useful way to react. First, the **complacency** reaction occurs when an individual either does not see the problem or opportunity or ignores it. You might call this the "ostrich" reaction—putting your head in the sand and hoping the need to decide will go away. Complacency prohibits leaders and groups from accepting the need to make a decision. In **defensive avoidance** individuals either deny the importance of the problem or opportunity or deny any responsibility for a decision about it. If you've ever said or thought "It can't happen to me," "It can be taken care of later," or "It's someone else's problem" then you have engaged in the defensive avoidance of making a decision. Third, with **panic**-like reactions, individuals become so upset that they hastily make a decision that has not been thoroughly considered. Complacency, defensive avoidance, and panic are ways to avoid accepting the need to decide. **Deciding to decide**, on the other hand, is a productive response. In this response, the decision maker accepts the challenge of deciding what to do and follows an effective decision-making process.

Exercise: The Barrier of Framing in Decision Making

Consider this situation:

Threatened by a superior enemy force, the general faces a dilemma. His intelligence officers say his soldiers will be caught in an ambush in which 600 of them will die unless he leads them to safety by one of two available routes. If he takes the first route, 200 soldiers will be saved. If he takes the second, there's a one-third chance that 600 soldiers will be saved and a two-thirds chance that none will be saved. Which route should he take?

If you are like most people, you chose the first route, reasoning that the general should save the 200 rather than risk the higher losses. Suppose, on the other hand, this situation:

The general again has to choose between two escape routes. But this time his aides tell him that if he takes the first, 400 soldiers will die. If he takes the second, there's a one-third chance that no soldiers will die and a two-thirds chance that 600 soldiers will die. Which route should he take?

In this second situation, most people think the general should take the second route. Their reasoning is that with the first route 400 will certainly be dead. With the second route there is at least a one-third chance that no one will die, and casualties will only be 50 percent higher if the scheme fails.

But, take a much closer look. People make opposite decisions in the two situations even though the circumstances in them are exactly the same. They are just presented differently. The first situation is stated in terms of lives saved and the second in terms of lives lost.

(From Bartol & Martin, 1998, p. 152)

In addition to unproductive reactions to the need to make a decision, a second barrier is decision-making bias. Psychologists who have been investigating how decision makers operate, point out several biases that serve as blocks to decision making (see Dunegan, 1993 & Slovic, 1995). These include framing, prospect theory, and availability.

The tendency to make different decisions depending on how a problem is presented is called **framing**. As illustrated in the exercise "The Barrier of Framing in Decision Making," most people prefer to make those decisions they consider to result in a gain. To explain this decision pattern, psychologists (see Dunegan, 1993 & Slovic, 1995) have developed the prospect theory. Based on the assumption that decision makers tend to be "loss averse," the **prospect theory** claims that decision makers find the prospect of an actual loss more painful than giving up the possibility of a gain (Bartol & Martin, 1998, p. 152). For example, the director of a recreation department will be more willing to take a chance of saving money over loosing money in awarding construction company bids even though the potential of each is the same.

Finally, the decision making bias of **availability** is evident when the decision maker is overly influenced by the extent to which outcomes can easily be recalled. For example, "In a typical English text, does the letter "K" appear more often as the first letter in a word or as the third letter?" People generally judge that the letter "K" is more likely to be the first letter in a word even though the letter is almost twice as likely to appear in the third position. We do this because of the bias of availability. Recreation leaders can be affected by the availability bias in several ways. For example, they may base annual performance appraisals on the most recent and easily recalled performance of an employee or gauge client satisfaction with a program by relying on the views of those who telephoned the office.

PROBLEM SOLVING

Another basic skill needed by the recreation leader is problem solving. **Problem solving** is the decision making that occurs when something goes wrong. A problem arises when an undesirable situation exists or when hindrances to achieving a desired situation appear. In other words, a problem may be defined as a discrepancy or difference between an actual state of affairs and a desired or ideal state of affairs. Problem solving, then, is the process of changing this actual state of affairs until it matches the desired state of affairs.

According to many currently practicing recreation leaders, problem solving has been called the most important basic skill. It may be true. Professional leaders in recreation face a list of problems ranging from motivating a lethargic youth soccer team to finding ways to better publicize the zoo interpretive program.

The camp director wants something to be done about the decline in camper registrations for the summer resident camp program. The playground leader wants to be able to constructively control the behavior of a troublesome young participant. The interpretive naturalist in the state park wants to do a daily nature program without increasing the volunteer staff. The therapeutic recreation specialist wants to develop better ways of involving the room-bound patients in the ongoing social program. These are all problems to these recreation leaders; problems that need solutions.

There is really nothing difficult about problem solving. We do it every day: what to do about getting a loan for school or what to do about raising a midterm course grade. We will always have problems to solve. What is difficult about problem solving as we are considering it here is doing it well. Unfortunately, in solving personal problems, as well as professional problems, we are often tempted to act without getting all the facts, jump to premature conclusions, and ignore the potential consequences of our solution choice.

Theoretically, problem solving is a straightforward, specific process involving observation and sensitivity. To find solutions you must become aware of the factors influencing the problem situation, be sensitive to the possible courses of action that may be taken, and be critical in evaluating what the possible results of the action might be. Developing good analytical and observational skills is essential to effective problem solving.

Specific problem-solving techniques can help guide the recreation leader in the complexities often present in problem situations. This section of the chapter introduces some useful problem-solving practices. By also suggesting some recreation leadership situations in which they could be used, a better understanding of the problem-solving skills may be possible.

There are many valuable approaches to problem solving; the step-by-step approach described here represents a merger of several. The recreation leader can logically approach problem solutions by (1) recognizing that the problem exists, (2) defining the problem, (3) determining the objective for the problem's solution, (4) formulating solution alternatives, (5) deciding on and implementing a solution, and (6) evaluating the success of the solution.

Recognizing That the Problem Exists

Effective problem solvers agree that the first step is to identify the actual problem. You can only begin to solve a problem when you recognize that there is a departure from some preferred or desired situation. If this departure from a desired status is not recognized by anyone, then the problem cannot be solved.

Recreation leaders become initially aware of problems in a variety of ways: through program evaluations, through telephone complaints, or from supervisors. Many routine difficulties can be solved by the more or less automatic application of already existing organization policies or procedures. On the other hand, some problems persist, are more severe, are controversial, or are new and require specifically applied problem-solving attention.

For example, the recreation leaders at an air force base youth center might be confronted by any of the following types of problems:

- Problems with program participants such as attendance slumps, fighting, improper facility use, or alcohol abuse
- Problems with coworkers such as disagreements about responsibilities, cliques, unsatisfactory working relationships, or disagreements over center policies
- Problems with the broader community such as complaints from parents, difficulties in obtaining base support, poor volunteer recruitment, or interunit disagreements over jurisdiction rights
- Problems with staff supervision such as insubordination, lack of group unity, poor performances, or grievances

Defining the Problem

It is important to distinguish, however, that our first realization that "something is wrong" may only indicate the superficial symptoms of a more underlying problem. The problem must next be recognized for what it is. This step of defining the problem requires a careful analysis of the problem situation. Obtaining good information is essential.

Suppose that the air force base youth center is frequently vandalized. This is a problem. What are the facts? How did the problem develop? Who perceives it as a problem? Is the vandalism the problem, or is it a symptom for another underlying problem? To define the real problem in the youth center, we need to draw on as many relevant and accurate facts as we can that affect the problem situation.

Determining what factors are making an impact on a problem situation has been called **force-field analysis** (Johnson & Johnson, 1994). Diagnosing a problem according to force-field analysis is seeing the problem as a balance between "forces" working in opposite directions. According to force-field analysis, most problem situations can be understood in terms of the forces that push toward and against improvement. That is, the current situation is a result of opposing, helpful as well as restraining, forces.

It is useful to analyze a problem by making lists of those helping and restraining forces affecting a situation. Figure 4.4 illustrates the force-field analysis concept. The ideal situation toward which the problem solver is working is represented by the right side of this diagram. To solve the problem the current situation must move toward the right to come closer to the ideal or desired situation. As indicated in the diagram, this requires increasing or strengthening the helping forces while simultaneously reducing the restraining forces. On the other hand, if the restraining forces are increased, while the helping forces are reduced, then the situation will become worse.

An example of force-field analysis is possible by applying the youth center vandalism problem to figure 4.4. What might be the helping forces in this situation? The restraining forces? The recreation leader solving this problem might wish to increase such helping forces as a cooperative attitude of on-base residents, willingness by the basewide recreation director to budget more program money to the center, and increase in afterschool youth recreation programs at the schools. The restraining forces that the recreation leader solving this problem might seek to reduce are restrictive and punitive responses by base police, general disrepair of the center building, and lack of youth involvement in determining center programs.

FIGURE 4.4. Force-field analysis

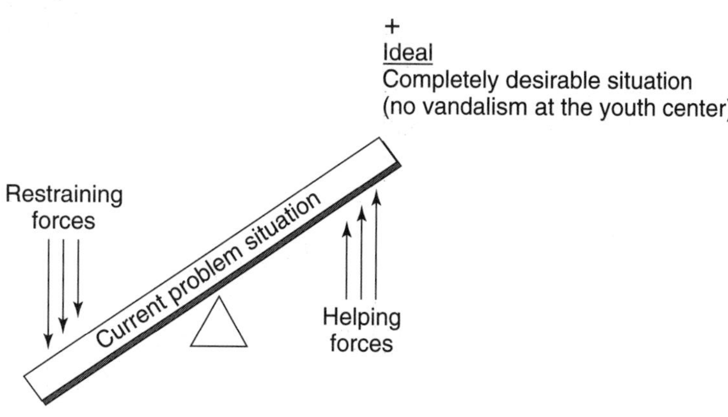

Determining the Objective

Now that the problem has been recognized and analyzed, the recreation leader can begin to move toward a solution. It is now a matter of determining what the "ideal" is and how far away the current situation is from the ideal. Objectives must at this point be set according to what is needed to be achieved for solution of the problem. In other words, in what positive way do we want the youth to relate to the center?

Ideals must be determined so that the recreation leader involved with solving the problem can measure the distance between the desired and the actual conditions. These ideals serve as standards of success or failure. Potential solutions to problems can be evaluated only by determining how effectively they meet previously determined objectives. This requires that the problem solver think of her task in terms of end results. Determining the desired end result helps the leader comprehend whether the later chosen solution is merely a temporary or a lasting solution to the problem.

Determining the objective is far from simple, if it is done well. The problem solver must have a clear idea of where he is attempting to go and what he hopes to achieve on arrival.

Formulating Alternatives

At this point in the problem-solving steps the recreation leader attempts to identify the possible courses of action or the alternative ways to solve the problem. Creativity, divergent thinking, and inventiveness are again essential.

For example, suppose we have determined that the problem we are concerned about is low attendance at the "Concerts in the Parks" program. What might be useful solution ideas or alternatives? Convert the program to an "Arts in the Parks" program? Provide free transportation to the concerts? Employ a marketing-publicity specialist? Reduce the amount of classical music programming? Increase the amount of jazz music programming? Print and distribute more promotional flyers? Make a personal appeal to potential participants by speaking at local civic groups? These represent alternative ways to solve the problem.

The problem solver's earlier efforts at force-field analysis are often a particularly useful tool for specifying possible solutions. Recall that according to this analysis, changes in the current situation will occur only as the helpful and restraining forces are changed so that the level where these forces are balancing is altered. There are two ways for changing this balance point between the two forces: increasing the strength or

Exercise: Air Hammer

1. Materials: A steel or wood twelve-inch ruler; a rubber or wood handled carpenter's hammer; a fourteen-inch section of cord (nylon or jute).
2. Task: Using only these materials, suspend all the objects in midair. Only the last inch of the ruler is allowed to touch another surface (such as a table). This means the ruler must be on top of the surface, not jammed into a drawer.

(Adapted from Rohnke & Butler, 1995, p. 160)

number of the helping forces or decreasing the strength or number of the restraining forces. Of the two, the preferable strategy is usually to reduce the restraining forces. Ideally, the problem solver would attempt to reduce restraining forces and at the same time increase helping forces. When this can be done, it is effective. This increase in helping forces becomes synonymous to developing problem solution alternatives.

Another useful tool for developing alternatives for this step in problem solving is brainstorming. **Brainstorming** is a technique that enables you to generate as many ideas as possible on a given issue without critiquing them. As either a group or individual activity, brainstorming works because the best way to get a good idea is to get a lot of ideas. The odds that any particular idea will help solve a problem isn't that high. But the more you get, the closer you are to reaching a useful solution. You will not be able to use all the solution alternatives that you generate in brainstorming. The idea is much like the approach of a professional photographer who takes hundreds of pictures when shooting an important subject. She'll change the exposure, the lighting, and the filters because she knows that out of all of the pictures she takes, only a few of them will be just right (von Oech, 1986).

There are four important principles in brainstorming. For the technique to be effective it must be approached this way:

1. Suspend judgment. Don't criticize ideas while generating them as possible solutions. Criticism during idea-generation inhibits creative thinking and the quantity of ideas.
2. Freewheel. Try to come up with outrageous ideas. Although these may never be used, they trigger other, perhaps more usable, ideas.
3. Go for quantity. As a reminder, "storm the brain" for as many ideas as possible.
4. Build on. Often the best solution ideas come from combining and improving on the ideas that have been offered.

Try your hand at the brainstorming exercise.

Exercise: Brainstorming

Instructions:

1. Divide into groups of four to five persons each and select a problem of common interest. If your group has trouble selecting a problem, try one of these:
   a. How can students be more involved in developing policies for your college or university?
   b. How can the campus reduce automobile traffic on campus?
   c. How can student binge-drinking be reduced?
   d. What could the department do to help seniors develop job leads?
   e. What can be done to help more students learn about your major?
2. Spend twenty minutes brainstorming alternative solutions to the problem. As each idea is suggested, one member of the group writes it down. Use the four principles of brainstorming presented previously. Even if you think you are running out of energy after ten or so minutes, keep going! Suggest even your wildest ideas and remember no judging of ideas now.
3. Go over the list and select the ten best ideas. Evaluate each according to its ability to solve the problem effectively and efficiently.
4. Narrow the list again to the three best ideas. Select the best idea.
5. Discuss your three best ideas and ultimate choice with other groups and/or classmates. Be prepared to explain why they are useful.

Deciding on and Implementing a Solution

Once all the possible solutions have been identified and formulated, the problem solver needs to select the best solution to be implemented. Now is the opportunity for action. In all problem-solving situations the end result is change. This action toward change involves two central efforts: decision making and decision implementation. Decision making will result in a choice among the previously determined alternative solutions. Decision implementation is the carrying out of the chosen decision.

How is this done? How does this action for change occur? The following checklist may be helpful to the problem solver deciding upon and implementing solutions for the problem of low attendance at "Concerts in the Parks."

__ Select the solution alternatives that seem best. List three positive values in adopting each alternative.

__ List the materials and other resources needed to implement each solution alternative. The cost of implementation in terms of time, people, and resources should be specified.

__ Evaluate how realistic each solution alternative is; necessary components should be within your power to influence.

__ Weigh the probabilities for success against the cost of implementation.

__ Select the best solution based on the results of the previous checklist items.

__ Try to anticipate all the barriers to implementation and how you will handle them.

__ Put the ideas and actions of each solution into a time sequence and estimate specific dates for the actions to occur.

__ Assign responsibilities to staff or other appropriate persons for implementing the solution.

__ Begin taking the first steps.

The skill of decision making, which is applied to problem solving, consists of choosing the most relevant and useful solution alternative based on the information at hand. In actuality no solution is likely to be absolutely the best. It will only be the best relative to the realistic constraints that the problem solver faces. Any solution will thus be a compromise between what the recreation leader would like to achieve ideally and no change or improvement in the problem situation. To be as effective as possible, a solution should (1) involve the least cost, (2) have the most positive values and the least disadvantages, (3) be the most realistic, and (4) have the greatest likelihood for successfully solving the problem.

Evaluating the Success of the Solution

The final effort is to evaluate the effectiveness of the implemented solution. To do this the recreation leader must determine whether the solution was correctly carried out and then what the effect or results were. The ultimate criterion in determining the success of a solution is whether the resulting state of affairs is closer to the desired state of affairs than it was before the solution was implemented.

The recreation leader in the "Concerts in the Parks" program, for instance, may discover that the solution has been successfully carried out but has failed to change the attendance problem. When this occurs, new solutions should be developed until one is found to be effective. The solution of one problem may, however, bring other problems into the forefront. Or in trying out different solutions the problem solver may discover that the effort has been addressing symptoms rather than the most critical or underlying problem.

The benefit of evaluation, then, is in showing the leader what problems have been solved, what problems still need to be solved, and what new problems have come up. Evaluation should result in the beginning of a new problem-solving sequence.

Blocks to Effective Problem Solving

Even the ablest of problem solvers will be unsuccessful at times. Problems can be complex and hidden and thus elude the arduous application of the problem-solving steps. There are blocks to problem-solving effectiveness. Overcoming these blocks will enhance your ability to solve problems but will not guarantee success.

Lack of clarity in stating the problem. Much of the initial effort of solving a problem is directed toward orienting to what the problem is. This is an extremely important phase of problem solving, and the recreation leader should devote sufficient time and effort to identifying the problem, defining it, and thereby getting others involved in and committed to solving it. Failure is guaranteed when the problem is inadequately defined.

Not getting the needed information. When information is minimal, the definition of the problem will be inadequate, fewer alternative solutions will be generated, and the potential effect of those solutions will not be properly explored. The result is relatively low-grade solutions. Great emphasis must be placed on fact finding if the problem is to be solved effectively.

Case in Point: "Doors"

The Problem: Because of economic factors, the length of stay in hospitals and clinical settings has been decreased and the amount of time allied professionals have to accomplish patient goals has also been decreased. Professionals have had to find new ways of meeting the needs of their patients, including arranging for the provision of services after the patients are discharged. While physical and occupational therapists are often able to offer home services for the continuation of treatment, these follow-up services are rare in the field of therapeutic recreation.

Many times, the patient is faced with obstacles that prevent him from implementing the therapy plan designed for him in the clinical setting. Such obstacles might include a lack of available and accessible transportation, no knowledge of local resources, absence of adapted equipment, and lack of funds.

The Solution: The Raymond Skinner Center, in Memphis, Tennessee, developed "Doors" as the answer to this problem. "Doors" is a transitional therapeutic recreation program for people with disabilities. Its objective is to provide a smooth recreational transition from a clinical/school/group home setting to a community setting. The transition program involves individual assessments, recreation plans, and one-on-one sessions with a therapeutic recreation specialist. Treatment goals that were not completed in the clinical setting are carried over into the community setting, with the help of a "Doors" transitional therapeutic recreation specialist. One-on-one "coaching" enables former patients to resume the activities they enjoyed before they became disabled—such activities as fishing, archery, swimming, painting, and sewing.

(Ardovino, 1997)

Premature testing of alternative solutions or premature choice. For most of us ideas are fragile creations, easily blighted by a chilly, or even indifferent reception. As you proceed in your problem-solving activities, you must avoid tendencies to evaluate each solution idea as it comes along. Instead there should be a pooling of a wide assortment of ideas, and then there should be a critical assessment of the worth of each.

A critical, evaluative, competitive climate. A supportive, trusting, cooperative atmosphere is necessary for solving problems successfully.

Pressures for conformity. Pressures for conformity and compliance slow the development of different ideas. Divergent thinking and convergent thinking are necessary for sound problem solving.

Summary

The recreation and park leader is expected to have a wide variety of skills. Indeed, to be a competent leader is to be able to do certain competencies well. Although no single individual can be an expert in all the desirable skills of a recreation leader, certain basic and foundational skills are important for those who assume leadership roles in recreation.

This chapter maintains that central to successful leadership is a capable level of ability in the skills of decision making and problem solving. The competence to do these fundamental skills well translates directly to more successful achievement of the recreation leader's main goal: to influence others in the meaningful expression of their recreational needs and interests.

Decision making is a skill required at all levels of leadership. Recreation leaders must continuously make creative and intelligent responses to routine situations or responsibilities. To make creative decisions the leader must have the ability to think in new ways and to make unique thought connections. In making intelligent decisions the leader must appreciate the evidence that claims small groups make better decisions than individuals working alone.

Another basic skill needed by the recreation leader is problem solving. Problem solving is decision making that occurs when something goes wrong. Theoretically, it is a straightforward process involving observation and sensitivity. When a leader is able to adequately solve problems consistently, a systematic technique has usually been employed. To do this the chapter suggests that the leader follow these steps:

- Recognize the problem
- Define the problem
- Determine the objective
- Formulate alternatives
- Decide on and implement a solution
- Evaluate the success of the solution

Questions and Activities for Review and Discussion

1. Explain the difference between programmed and nonprogrammed decision situations. Choose a recreation, park, sport, or tourism organization with which you are familiar and identify two programmed and two nonprogrammed decision situations.
2. Give an example of each of the common decision-making biases.

3. Assess the advantages and disadvantages of group decision making. Relate to classmates an example of one of the advantages and also one of the disadvantages that you have experienced.
4. Is there a difference between decision making and problem solving? In what ways are they different? In what ways are they similar?
5. Why is group decision making often more effective than individual decision making? Illustrate your answer by discussing a recreation group of which you are currently a part.
6. In the chapter seven methods of group decision making are presented. An effective leader is able to understand each method well enough to choose the most appropriate. What factors do you think determine the appropriateness of each group decision-making method?
7. Suppose you are the recreation leader responsible for a youth center on an Air Force base. Lately there has been significant vandalism (graffiti on exterior walls, trash can fires in the restrooms, and rock broken windows) at the center. Complete the following worksheet, determining which of the considerations listed would be included in each step of the problem solving process. Make a check in the appropriate problem-solving steps column for each consideration.

Steps in Problem Solving

Consideration	Recognize Problem Exists	Define Problem	Determine Objective	Formulate Alternatives	Decide & Implement Solution	Evaluate Success of Solution
1 A force-field analysis is conducted						
2 Staff cite such problems with participants as attendance slumps, fighting, and alcohol use						
3 Center director announces a staff meeting to discuss recent vandalism						
4 The staff gets together for brainstorming						
5 The solution to the vandalism problem also meant less use of the center						
6 Ideal standards of youth center success are developed						
7 Decision making						
8 Center director assesses potential costs of a new program						

(*continued*)

Steps in Problem Solving (*Continued*)

Consideration	Recognize Problem Exists	Define Problem	Determine Objective	Formulate Alternatives	Decide & Implement Solution	Evaluate Success of Solution
9 A list of helping and restraining forces affecting the situation at the center is made						
10 Hire more security guards? Change programs offered? Establish a youth advisory board? Search participants before they enter the center?						
11 A list of the materials and resources needed is drawn up						

8. Identify a specific and actual problem you are experiencing. Using the steps to problem solving from this chapter, develop and implement a solution. Write a brief evaluation analysis on how well the steps to problem solving worked for you.
9. In problem solving why is it so important that the problem be accurately defined?

References

Ardovino, P. (1997). Striking a balance in providing community therapeutic recreation services. In *Therapeutic recreation: Innovative programs in community recreation*. Arlington, VA: National Therapeutic Recreation Society, pp. 22–25.

Bartol, K. M., & Martin, D. C. (1998). *Management* (3rd ed.). Boston: McGraw-Hill.

Denny, D. (1999, January 21). New technology at the gym turns people into well-muscled fitness machines. *The Herald-Times*. Lifestyle Section.

Dunegan, K. J. (1993). Framing, cognitive modes, and image theory: Toward an understanding of a glass half full. *Journal of Applied Psychology, 78*, 491–503.

Gibbon, E. (1776). *Decline and fall of the Roman empire* (Vol. 2). New York, NY: Modern Library Giant.

Janis, I. L. (1982). *Groupthink* (2nd ed.). Boston: Houghton Mifflin.

Johnson, D. W., & Johnson, F. P. (1994). *Joining together: Group theory and group skills* (5th ed.). Boston: Allyn & Bacon.

Kelly, J. (1980). *How managers manage.* Englewood Cliffs, NJ: Prentice-Hall.

Nutt, P. C. (1984). Types of organizational decision processes. *Administrative Science Quarterly, 29*, 414–450.

Rohnke, K., & Butler, S. (1995). *QuickSilver: Adventure games, initiative problems, trust activities and a guide to effective leadership*. Dubuque, IA: Kendall/Hunt Publishing.

Slovic, P. (1995). The construction of preference. *American Psychologist, 50*, 364–371.

Von Oech, R. (1983). *A whack on the side of the head: How to unlock your mind for innovation.* New York: Warner Books.

Web Resources

Decision making: www.questtraining.com/library/decisionmaking.html

Decision making in teams: www.yorkteam.com/decis.htm

Decision-making skills: www.amcity.com/atlanta/stories/091696/smallb6.htm

Exercise equipment: www.heartrateinc.com/ClubEquipment.htm

Exercise equipment: www.lubbockonline.com/news/121397/UK8726.html

Future Problem-Solving Program: www.fpsp.org/overview.htm

Groupthink: www.dtic.mil/c3i/bprcd/6192.htm

Groupthink: www.cweb.com/doctor/risky.htm

Improve meetings through better problem solving and decision making: www.openthis.com

Project COPS (Challenging Outdoor Personal Experience): www.literati.com/cope

Raymond Skinner Center: http://hudson.idt.net/~kkps119/nonprofit/

Symptoms of groupthink: http://cadstudio.mae.cornell.edu/mae225/teamwork/gpthsymp.html

CHAPTER 5

Group Management

> Suppose that a football reformer observed the obvious fact that the object of the game is to make touchdowns. This would lead immediately to the important discovery that if the two teams would cooperate, hundreds of touchdowns would be made in a game, while only one or two of them are made when each opposes the other.
> —Thurman Arnold in CAPLOW, 1983, p. 158.

LEARNING OBJECTIVES

Recreation leadership often takes place in a group. Thus an important basic skill for leaders at all levels and in all settings is the capable management of groups. This chapter teaches this skill by exploring

- the nature of groups
- what makes groups effective
- the role of the leader in groups

KEY TERMS

participant groups p. 91
functional groups p. 91
group p. 91
forming p. 93
storming p. 93
norming p. 93
performing p. 93
adjourning p. 93
group cohesion p. 95
group morale p. 96
group norms p. 96
primacy p. 97
explicit statements p. 97
critical events p. 97
carry-over behaviors p. 97
group structure p. 97
centralization p. 98
decentralization p. 98
social specialists p. 100
stars p. 100
technical specialists p. 100
underchosen p. 100
goal-oriented behavior p. 100
maintenance behaviors p. 100
individual-oriented behaviors p. 100
synergy p. 104
teamwork p. 105

All day we interact in one group and then another. Our family life, our leisure time, and our careers are filled with groups. We learn, work, and play in groups. The inevitability of being in them makes groups one of the most important elements in our lives.

Recreation leaders are constantly dealing with groups. The existence of leadership is dependent on the existence of others to lead. To a large measure our leadership success is therefore dependent on our ability to manage groups. The 4-H Club, the water polo team, the bird song identification class, the lecture audience, the camp counseling staff, the advisory board, and the pool lifeguards are examples of groups found in recreation.

According to Niepoth (1983), the wide variety of groups that recreation and park leaders commonly relate to can be categorized into two general types: participant groups and functional groups. In **participant groups** the purpose is to engage in a recreation behavior. **Functional groups** exist to achieve some goal not directly associated with meeting the group member's own recreation needs. They exist primarily to accomplish tasks.

For example, let us consider a convalescent center. The patients who come down to the center's activity room every Wednesday afternoon for reminiscent therapy are a participant group. The volunteers who meet once a month to develop plans for the convalescent center's international dinners program are a functional group.

Leader Profile: The Present
Caryn Collopy
Caryn has been an integral force in promoting and hosting the US Nationals and World Championships of Underwater Hockey for several years. Her efforts demonstrate a recreation leadership's work with participant groups.

There are a wide variety of participant groups in recreation organizations. Some of these are focused on the expression of a particular recreation activity such as ski clubs, softball teams, poetry reading audiences, supper clubs, and tennis clubs. Other participant groups may be oriented toward the learning of a particular recreation skill such as folk dance classes, rock climbing clinics, loom weaving workshops, and leisure counseling groups. Participant groups exist because of a common interest in a recreation expression.

There are also a wide variety of functional groups in recreation organizations. The staff is a group. Recreation and park commissions, citizen advisory councils, boards of directors, task forces, interagency committees, volunteer associations, and treatment teams are examples. In a large recreation organization, numerous functional groups may exist. Functional groups are purposefully and deliberately formed. They are usually the result of organizational planning and conscious effort, but some functional groups such as citizen action groups emerge in recreation on the basis of a shared need by its members that they felt the organization overlooked.

Groups can have constructive or destructive effects on the quality of the recreation (or work) experience for individuals, depending on how they are managed. The more you understand the dynamics of groups, the more you will be able to adequately manage them so that destructive aspects are minimized and constructive aspects are maximized.

Yet knowledge of group dynamics alone is not sufficient to promote effective groups; leadership skills are also required. To promote effective group functioning you must know what an effective group is and have the skills necessary to actualize group success.

NATURE OF GROUPS

What is a group? What are some of the characteristic ways that groups act and react? How can one group such as a YMCA Step Fit class differ from another group such as a backpacking club? What is the role of the individual in groups? To answer these questions some background should be discussed.

Definition

If five strangers start playing basketball together just to pass a few spare minutes, do they constitute a group? If they do, is a group conceptualized differently when considering a basketball team? What defines a group? Just as there are many definitions of leadership, so too are there many conceptualizations of "**group.**" Commonly, any collection of people is thought of as a group. Thus the pick-up basketball situation can probably be considered a group. However, this is too general a specification for the purposes of studying the effective leadership of groups. We need to explore several more thorough definitions to understand how a group is conceptualized.

First, individuals must be aware of one another and consider themselves to be members of a group. This means that group members must perceive the existence of the group. This also suggests that, second, a group involves interaction, which leads to mutual influences between members. According to Shaw's definition (1981), " A group is defined as two or more persons who are interacting with one another in such a manner that each person influences and is influenced by each other person" (p. 8).

Another aspect of groups is the motivation that leads individuals to join a group. People are usually members of a group because they believe that it will satisfy some need. For example, an early definition proposed by Bass (1960) stated, "We define 'group' as a collection of individuals whose existence as a collection is rewarding to the individuals" (p. 39). This definition implies that groups failing to satisfy the needs of the members usually disintegrate.

Finally some authors define a group in terms of goals. This suggests that in terms of achieving certain needs a group is more productive than its individual members. This does not mean that a group and an organization are necessarily the same thing. Groups differ from organizations because organizations involve systematic efforts and the production of services or goods (Bartol & Martin, 1998). Groups typically do not engage in systematic efforts to the same extent and may not produce goods or services. Yet there is a link. Teamwork occurs when groups are able to work efficiently and effectively together to achieve organizational goals. More on this later in the chapter.

These and many other available definitions are all correct in that each identifies a unique and important aspect of the concept of "group." From the various definitions it can be summarized that if a group exists, then it is assumed that its members (1) are motivated to be in the group, (2) are aware of its existence, (3) receive satisfaction of some need, and (4) accomplish more than they could as individuals.

A definition by Johnson and Johnson (1994) offers a summary of the characteristics of a group:

> A group may be defined as two or more individuals who interact with each other, are interdependent, define themselves and are defined by others as belonging to the group, share norms concerning matters of common interest and participate in a system of interlocking roles, influence each other, find the group rewarding, and pursue common goals (p. 7).

According to this concept, a recreation group is characterized as a relational collection of people that meets members' needs through interaction. Each person within the group affects every other person so that attitudes and behavior patterns are modified. Every person in a group situation is significant to the life of a group. Every group member is part of a unitary effort toward a common interest or goal. Every person in the group is dependent on the group for interest or goal satisfaction as much as the group is dependent on every member for its existence.

Exercise: I Belong to Many Groups

List all the groups to which you belong. Be sure to include family groups, friendship and other social groups, activity groups, committees, teams, classroom groups, study groups, political action groups, interest groups, and every other group you can remember. After you've made your list share it with a classmate. As a result you will probably be able to think of even more groups to which you belong!

Group Development

Most of us belong to many groups. If we assume that people voluntarily join groups, a logical line of questioning follows: How exactly do groups form? Why do people join groups? How do groups stay together?

Groups go through phases, just as people do, as they develop (Galanes & Brilhart, 1997). Usually a new group is immature and does not function smoothly, whereas a long-standing group exhibits its maturity through its ability to get things accomplished. Researchers who have studied the group development process maintain that groups go through predictable developmental stages. One of the best known approaches to group development suggests the five stages of forming, storming, norming, performing, and adjourning (Tuckman, 1965; Tuckman & Jensen, 1977). Understanding these stages can help recreation leaders assist groups in achieving their leisure interests and needs.

Stage 1: **Forming**. When a group is forming, group members are busy assessing the situation. Members seek basic information about the goal or task, make a preliminary evaluation of how the group might interact to accomplish it, and begin to test the extent to which their input will be valued by the group (Bartol & Martin, 1998). In testing the group some members may try out various behaviors, such as making jokes or being sarcastic. Forming a new group is an uncertain stage as members try to make sense of the ground rules. Groups at the forming stage of development often need time to get acquainted with each other and the situation.

Stage 2: **Storming**. Often during the storming stage, groups experience conflict as they locate and attempt to resolve differences of opinions, personalities, and approaches. The conflict might revolve around differences in understanding of what is expected of them or around interpersonal relations. Sometimes at this stage there is a struggle for the leadership of the group if a leader has not been appointed externally (Bartol & Martin, 1998). Good listening and attempts to find mutually acceptable resolution of conflict issues are important at this stage, if the group is to develop. If the group cannot resolve this storming stage it will not be effective and may disband.

Stage 3: **Norming**. At the norming stage, groups begin to build cohesion and develop an understanding about norms for relating to each other and accomplishing the group goal. Now members begin to identify with the group as their roles also become clearer. The group also shows more ability to accomplish group problem solving. If there is no appointed leader or the appointed leader is weak, an informal leader will emerge (Bartol & Martin, 1998).

Stage 4: **Performing**. The performing stage of group development is that in which energy is channeled toward a group task or goal. There is teamwork. Solutions from the problem solving of the previous stage emerge. The roles of group members are clear and functional, and the group begins to achieve synergy. Not all groups reach this stage of development.

Stage 5: **Adjourning**. During the adjourning stage, group members prepare to disengage as the group reaches the successful completion of its goals. The adjourning stage applies more frequently to temporary task groups, such as committees, task forces, or teams. With ongoing or permanent groups, adjourning applies only when there is a disruption.

An entertaining illustration of these five stages can be seen in the movie *The Breakfast Club* (see "Case in Point"). This film illustrates how a group's energy and effort is focused during the developmental stages. As suggested in figure 5.1, goal and socioemotional efforts predominate at predictable periods in the group's development

(Galanes & Brilhart, 1997). At the beginning stages of development, the group focuses on interpersonal and socioemotional concerns. Group members apply their energy and effort to working out their relationships with each other. During these stages they form the group structure, processes, rules, roles, and leadership. They assess their own and others' strengths and weaknesses; they identify who can be counted on to do what.

As the group's development progresses, members begin to mesh into a coordinated whole that can function in a coordinated way. As the group moves into the later stages

FIGURE 5.1. Stages of group development and productivity focus

Case in Point: The Breakfast Club

In the movie *The Breakfast Club*, five high school students spend an entire Saturday in detention at their school. Claire, the prom queen, and Andy, the jock, are "cool" because they belong to the elite crowd. Brian, the scholar, is a nerd, and Alison, the artsy misfit, doesn't say anything for a long time. Bender, the tough guy, is loaded with resentment against the others because of what he assumes are their happy family situations. A more diverse collection of people would be hard to imagine, yet by the end of the movie these five students have developed into a cohesive group, if only for that one Saturday.

The detention teacher this day gives the students an assignment to complete an essay on "Who Am I?" Bored with watching them, after a while, he leaves for his office. At first, only Claire and Andy think they have anything in common, so they form a loose group by smiling at each other, nonverbally showing their mutual support. When one of the students calls the teacher a "brownie hound" the first common ground among the students is established—their shared dislike for the teacher. When Bender closes the door to the room in violation of the teacher's order, the teacher demands to know who did this. The rest of the students, even though they dislike Bender, refuse to betray him to their common "enemy."

As the plot of the movie continues the students realize that they have a lot of things in common. They all have problems with their parents, are worried they won't be liked by their peers, are afraid they are considered weird, and are generally insecure about growing up. As the Saturday goes on the students find things to do together (sneaking out), establish leadership and group norms, and become cohesive. By the end of the day, and the movie, even the antagonism between Claire and Bender that fueled much of the group's conflict, fades—as symbolized when Clair gives Bender her earring and he accepts.

(From Galanes & Brilhart, 1997)

of development, members are able to switch their focus to their assigned task or mutual goal. As the socioemotional concerns become resolved, the group is able to devote more energy and effort to the goal or task. Many groups do not have the opportunity to get to know each other before they have to start functioning as a group. Instead, they may be resolving their socioemotional concerns at the same time they are dealing with getting on with the accomplishment of the group's goals.

The precise sequence and experience of development varies with the kind of group, the situation in which the group functions, the goals of the group, and many other factors. Despite these differences, there are basic developmental similarities across groups. Most groups require some time for deciding what the group is about, experiencing a period of conflict regarding personal relations and authority, resolving these conflicts (or dissolving the group), and then achieving a productive state. Think about the groups with which you have been involved—a scout troop, a sport team, a choir. The developmental stages can be traced for many of these groups.

Group Characteristics

As is evident from even a brief inventory of recreation groups, the variety of groups with which the leader may work is endless. These groups will vary in many ways. They are different not only in their goals but also in the number of people, longevity of existence, degree of formalization, internal structure, importance or significance to their members, and in many other aspects.

A common way of thinking about a group's varied characteristics is by studying its essential properties. Regardless of the group's structure, complexity, or purpose, all groups possess the following characteristics: group cohesiveness, group morale, group norms, group structure, and group productivity.

1. Group cohesion. **Group cohesion** is the commitment group members make to each other and to the group. It is the degree to which members like being with each other. A group that is close and unified will behave differently, for better or worse, than one that is distant and fragmented. An indication of group cohesiveness is when members refer to themselves as "my team" or "our staff" or "our group." It is the force that holds a group together. If there is a sense of teamwork, of sticking together, and a "we" feeling, then group cohesiveness is high.

   The amount of cohesiveness in a group can have important consequences for the group experience. For example, people in relatively cohesive groups tend to communicate more frequently and more sensitively with one another. Group cohesiveness also influences the degree of aggression that one group exhibits toward another. Whether this is good or bad depends on the purpose of the group and other characteristics. That is, in a sport team, cohesiveness may be helpful when it leads to friendly competition among other teams. Yet aggressiveness can be an undesirable by-product of group cohesiveness, too. Another area affected by group cohesiveness is productivity. Highly cohesive groups tend to be more effective in reaching their goals. This is because members of such groups want to avoid letting the group down. Group cohesiveness can also affect a group's willingness to innovate and change (Bartol & Martin, 1998). Changes will be more difficult to implement when a highly cohesive group opposes them. But this can also work in reverse; a recreation leader's efforts to create organizational or community change will be greatly aided when backed by a cohesive group.

Exercise: Assessing Group Cohesiveness

Cohesiveness can be a useful characteristic of a recreation group. This exercise will help you assess the cohesiveness of a recreation group in which you are currently a member. Think of a sport team, social club, activity class, or other group. Alternatively, complete this exercise reflecting on a work-related group, such as a group preparing an assignment for a class or a group where you work.

Name of my group ________________

	No	Sometimes	Yes
1. Members respect each other.	1	2	3
2. Members enthusiastically support the group's goal.	1	2	3
3. Members are able to bring out the best in each other.	1	2	3
4. Communication within my group improves steadily.	1	2	3
5. A feeling of "we" rather than "I" prevails in my group.	1	2	3
6. My group pulls together.	1	2	3
7. My group checks with all members before making a decision.	1	2	3
8. If one member of my group needs help, other members are quick to respond.	1	2	3

Discuss with classmates (or your group) how each of the items in this exercise contributes to group cohesion.

2. Group morale. **Group morale** is the way members feel about the group. Good group morale is when the members have a positive and optimistic feeling about the group. When group members are in harmony, and the tone or atmosphere is one of warmth, the morale of the group is high. On the other hand, the tone of the group is low when group members display tension, competition, or conflict.

   One of the main concerns of leaders in recreation groups is the positiveness of group morale. Morale is heavily influenced by the nature of the group's goal; when the group's goal is satisfying recreation experiences, the degree of morale becomes a thermometer for the degree of recreation satisfaction. One of the most distinguishing characteristics of a recreation group (as opposed to a work group) is the social atmosphere, or tone. It is often up to the recreation leader to set an optimistic, friendly, and mutually positive group morale.
3. Group norms. **Group norms** are those values, standards, or traditions that characterize the behavior of the group. What behaviors are permitted, encouraged, or discouraged by the group members? Norms are unwritten rules; they are shared beliefs of most group members about what behavior is appropriate to be a member in good standing. For example, compare the behaviors encouraged by members of a rugby team versus a madrigal singing group.

   Norms are not always explicit; frequently the only way a norm is observable is by inadvertently breaking it to observe others' reactions. As a student, try brownnosing the teacher and watch the reaction of the other students. "Don't try to impress the person with authority" is a common student group norm. Group sanctions are usually the way in which groups enforce their norms. Sanctions vary and may range from a stern look to expulsion from the group. Some group sanctions may even involve a formal punishment by an outside authority, but most group sanctions are carried out by the group members.

Norms usually are not discussed openly, but still have a strong effect on the behavior of the group members. For example, in *The Breakfast Club*, the students do not discuss that their norm will be to protect each other against the teacher. So, how did the students come up with this norm? There are several ways norms are established in groups. These are: primacy, explicit statements, critical events, and carry-over behaviors (Galanes & Brilhart, 1997).

Group norms are developed through **primacy** when certain behaviors occur early in the group's history. When groups are first formed, members often feel uncertain. Thus, what first occurs in a group can easily become habit because it helped to reduce feelings of uncertainty (Galanes & Brilhart, 1997). Anything that reduces the uncertainty is welcomed by the group. This is why early group behaviors that become norms can cause problems for the group later. For example, excessive joking and teasing among group members may be useful in reducing early uncertainties in the group but may ultimately become hindrances to more mature interrelationships among group members.

Another way group norms are formed is through explicit statements. **Explicit statements** that a leader or member makes about what is and is not expected behavior often provide norms for a group (Galanes & Brilhart, 1997). For example, on the first day of class your instructor tells students that regular attendance is expected. Your instructor is attempting to establish this as a norm for the group. Explicit statements, like primacy behaviors, help reduce new member's uncertainty about appropriate behavior.

Some norms are established through critical events that occur in a group. Such **critical events** are important happenings that indicate what is or is not acceptable behavior (Galanes & Brilhart, 1997). For example, I was once on a softball team with people who came to trust each other, often revealing personal information to each other. One of the members told someone not on the team information about a team member. When other team members discovered this, they felt angry. At the next practice, team members expressed their feelings of betrayal. Before this critical incident, some team members thought it was all right to reveal team information to outsiders, but after this it was clear to all that such behavior was a serious violation of a group norm.

Finally, many norms are taken from the general situation in which the group exists. For example, you know a lot about how to behave at the beach, no matter where in the country it is located. True, beaches are somewhat unique, but certain standards of behavior (such as not sitting too close to strangers) carry over from beach to beach. Thus, many **carry-over behaviors** in a group are ones we have learned as members of a particular culture (Galanes & Brilhart, 1997). These provide a source for group norms. These carry-over behaviors can be specific to a particular culture, too. If you go to a beach in another country you may discover that the "allowed" distance between towels is much shorter than it is in the United States.

4. Group structure. **Group structure** involves the relative positions of the group members. These are the acknowledged positions of responsibility. Every group has both a formal and an informal structure. A formal group is officially created by an organization for a specific purpose. Formal groups can be a task force formed by

the department director to make recommendations for financing the afterschool program, as well as a painting class offered at the older adult center. Some groups such as the staff of a recreation organization are large and complex with numerous formal levels of responsibility and organizational charts to keep it all straight. The informal group, on the other hand, reflects the interaction patterns between group members; it is the group's communication network. It is established by the group members, often to serve members' social needs.

In some groups the formal and informal structures are the same, whereas in other groups they can be different. In either case both structures exert a powerful influence on the behavior of the members of the group.

For both formal and informal group structures, there are other structures that exist. This is the extent to which the group coordinates its actions and decisions in a centralized or a decentralized manner. **Centralization** is the extent to which power and authority are retained by members at the top of the group—that is, by the group leader, elected officers, adults, and so on. A centralized structure has several useful functions (Bartol & Martin, 1998). If all major decisions are made at the top levels, it is easier to coordinate the activities of various departments and individuals in the group. In addition, those at the top (leaders, for example) usually have the most experience and have a broader perspective, and therefore may make sounder decisions than individuals at lower levels in the group.

Decentralization, on the other hand, is the extent to which power and authority are shifted or delegated to group members at lower levels of the group. Decentralization also has several useful functions (Bartol & Martin, 1998). Encouraging decision making at lower levels tends to relieve the workloads and responsibilities of those at the top. Decentralization also enriches the experience for members at lower levels because it engages them directly in the goals of the group. Finally, decentralization often works well because people at the lower levels of a group (such as the lifeguards at the pool) tend to be closer to the "realities" or problems in a situation and, therefore, in a better position to make good decisions.

Think of centralization and decentralization as the anchors on a continuum. This means that there are many possible degrees of distribution of power and

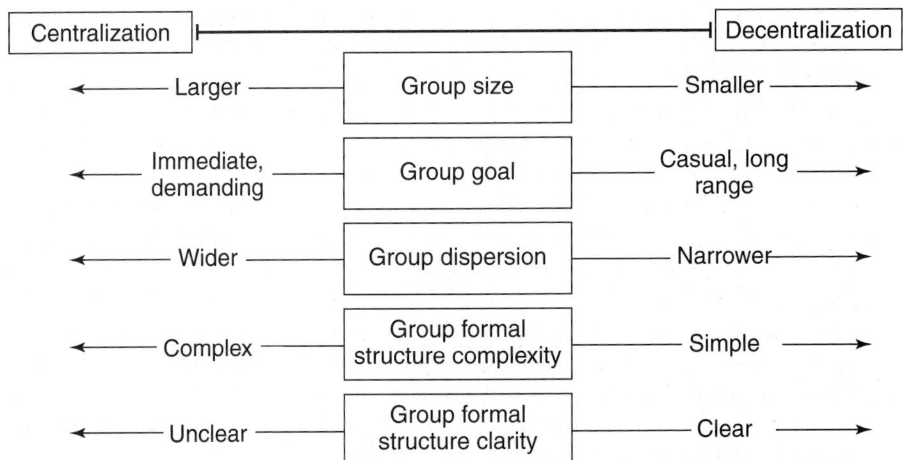

FIGURE 5.2. The centralization versus decentralization continuum (based on research cited by Bass, 1990)

Problem	Solution
Low group cohesion	Design group tasks that require greater frequency of interaction Implement activities that make the group more attractive
Extreme group cohesion (groupthink)	Encourage open expression of doubt Play "devil's advocate" Periodically divide into subgroups
Low group morale	Modify group goals to better reflect needs of individuals Ensure clearly established goals and clarify specific ways of achieving these goals
Low group productivity	Reexamine group goals for individual member resistance Enable group activities to match group goals

FIGURE 5.3. Facilitation of healthy group characteristics

authority in between. How a leader decides on the degree of centralization or decentralization for a group depends on many factors. The scale toward or away from centralization versus decentralization is based on such factors as group size, degree of dispersion of group members, and intensity of the group goal. That is, the larger the group, the wider the dispersion of group members (such as a recreation department that has offices across the city), and the more immediate and demanding the goal, the more likely is centralization to be appropriate. Other factors include the complexity and clarity of the group's formal structure (figure 5.2).

5. Group productivity. *Group productivity* refers to how well the group is able to achieve its goals. Recall that for a group to exist there must be a purpose; there must be a need-meeting function for the members. How well a group is able to satisfy this purpose is its productivity.

    Productivity depends on many things. If the group's goals are excessively difficult, too simple, or inappropriate, group productivity is likely to be low. For example, the making of Popsicle stick bird houses for members of an older adult social club may be too simplistic a goal for achieving any positive productivity. Similarly, if goals are unclear or not attractive, group members may not accept them, and this will also limit productivity.

    Productivity also depends on the resources available to a group. All the relevant skills, knowledge, and tools possessed by the group members and leader contribute to the group's ability to reach its goals. Finally, the way in which the group communicates, shares responsibilities, and resolves disagreements also determines its productivity.

    An appreciation of these five group characteristics—cohesion, morale, norms, structure, and productivity—can be useful to a recreation leader. When a group is unsuccessful as a result of a problem with cohesion, morale, or productivity, for instance, the leader is often able to influence a solution to these (figure 5.3). A leadership action "prescription" can be developed when problems emerge within these three group characteristics.

Individual Roles and Behaviors in Groups

Groups are composed of individuals, and therefore group experiences are the result of individual behaviors and contributions. However, group behavior is not merely the sum of individual behaviors. Evidence from research (Bass, 1990) indicates that people do behave differently in groups than when alone. Thus it is important to consider individuals in groups as a separate concern for leaders.

When joining a new group, it is common for people to experience feelings of tension or anxiety. Leaders can help new members with these emotional problems by minimizing their adjustment difficulties. By introducing new members to other group members, inviting them to do group activities, and chatting with them frequently in the beginning, leaders can help to create a sense of belonging.

Once individuals have become accepted members of a group, they usually take on different roles and exhibit different behaviors. From the research of Moment and Zalenznik (1963) and the interpretation of Hellriegel and Slocum (1982), four general individual role types in groups have been identified: social specialists, stars, technical specialists, and the underchosen.

Social specialists show a great deal of feeling and support for others. They are interested in keeping the group operating as "one happy family." **Stars** are actively involved group members. As a rule, stars are more likely to be satisfied with group decisions than are the other types. **Technical specialists** show great concern with group tasks and with using their expertise to enable them. As seen by others, they are neither supportive nor hostile to group members. The **underchosen** are uncommitted to the group and tend to show interest only in their personal needs. Their perceived lack of importance is more a result of ineffectiveness than invisibility.

The existence of these individual roles in groups has several implications for recreation leaders. First, it is unlikely all individuals can or will play the same role. Some prefer to be technical specialists, others to be social specialists. The role any group member plays is a function of his personality, communication abilities, and the leadership style of the leader.

Second, this classification of roles provides a useful diagnostic tool for leaders when their group is operating poorly. A leader can ask, "Is the group overbalanced with the underchosen, technical specialists, or social specialists?" Domination by any of these three roles may lead to an ineffective and unsatisfying group. A group is more effective as more members are capable of performing the star role.

Third, leaders may use this classification of group member roles to gain insight about their own behavior in groups. If you ever wondered why no one ever questions your decisions and your discussions are short lived, it could be that you are acting out the underchosen role.

Individuals and groups relate in another way. In addition to being attentive to the different roles individuals assume in groups, the recreation leader's success in leading a group can be enhanced by also understanding individual behaviors in groups. The behaviors of individual members of a group can be categorized according to their contribution to the group process. Some behaviors facilitate the group's goal, while others enable group maintenance. Still other individual behaviors focus on the individuals. A group **goal-oriented behavior** is one that contributes directly to the accomplishment of the group's task. Individuals who behave in ways that enable the group to accomplish its goals or tasks are vitally important to an effective group. Group **maintenance behaviors** are those that help the group maintain harmonious relationships and a cohesive interpersonal climate. Maintenance behaviors are also important to an effective group because they contribute to morale and cohesion. **Individual-oriented behaviors** consist of self-centered behaviors. A self-centered member places her needs ahead of the group's. These behaviors do not help the group in any way. Table 5.1 lists specific goal-related, maintenance, and individual behaviors.

TABLE 5.1. Goal-related, maintenance, and individual behaviors of members of groups

GOAL-RELATED BEHAVIORS

1. *Initiating and orienting*: Proposing goals, activities, or plans of action; defining the group's position in relation to the goal. "Let's get started by assigning ourselves different errands for preparing for the backpacking trip."
2. *Information giving*: Offering facts, information, evidence, or personal experience relevant to the group's goal. "Last year's group spent $100 on trail food."
3. *Information seeking*: Asking for facts, information, evidence, or relevant personal experience. "Tim, what does the U.S. Forest Service advise for our route?"
4. *Opinion giving*: Stating beliefs, values, interpretations, judgments. "I don't think that trail is open this time of year."
5. *Clarifying*: Making ambiguous statements clearer; interpreting issues. "I think our decision here boils down to what the weather is likely to be."
6. *Elaborating*: Developing an idea previously expressed by giving examples and explanations. "Another thing that this book recommends for emergency preparedness is . . . ."
7. *Summarizing*: Reviewing what has been said previously. "So, by next week, Karen will have the maps and Tim will have met with the equipment supplier."
8. *Coordinating*: Organizing the group's tasks. "How about if you, Karen, are responsible for getting the maps and, Tim, you meet with the equipment supplier?"
9. *Recording*: Keeping group records, preparing reports and minutes; serving as the group's memory. "I think we've already decided our budget; let me check my notes from last month's meeting."
10. *Suggesting procedure*: Suggesting a method to follow. "Why don't we try brainstorming to help us think of campfire activities?"
11. *Energizer*: Stimulating the group to higher levels of accomplishment. "Come on gang, we can get to that campsite by nightfall."

MAINTENANCE BEHAVIORS

1. *Establishing norms*: Suggesting ways to behave; calling attention to violations of norms. "Listen kids, it's not getting us anywhere when we call each other names."
2. *Gatekeeping*: Helping other members have their say. "Trish has been trying to get a word in here. What do you think, Trish?"
3. *Supporting*: Agreeing, supporting the ideas of others. "I think Billie is right about those game rules."
4. *Harmonizing*: Reconciling disagreement; suggesting compromise; calming. "Hey you two, I think you are both right. Here's how both of you can be 'it' in the game."
5. *Tension relieving*: Joking, making others feel at ease, encouraging informality. "We're all getting tired. Let's take a ten-minute break."
6. *Showing solidarity*: Reinforcing a sense of group unity and cohesiveness. "We're in this together."

INDIVIDUAL BEHAVIORS

1. *Withdrawing*: Giving no response to others; not taking a stand. "Do whatever you want, I don't care."
2. *Blocking*: Preventing group progress by constantly raising objections. "I don't care what the guidebook says, I keep telling you I think we should go this other way."
3. *Recognition seeking*: Boasting and calling attention on one's own expertise or experience when it isn't necessary; game playing to draw sympathy; switching the subject to one's self. "I think we should do it the way I did it last year. I've been in this club longer than you guys, you know."
4. *Acting helpless*: Pretending to not understand or be able to accomplish a group task. "I don't really know what you want me to do here. I've never put up this kind of tent before."
5. *Dominator*: Trying to assert control and manipulating the group through flattery, giving orders, or interrupting others. "Let me interrupt you again, Mary. You just don't understand what we're supposed to do here."

(Based on Allcorn, 1985)

Suppose you are leading a small young adult group on a tour of western national parks in the United States. Because some of the group's members have brought along more spending money than other members, a subgroup begins. Those persons with more spending money have begun to splinter off from the rest of the group for extra shopping and different restaurant choices. There has even been a discussion by some about leaving the tour group for a three-day independent side trip.

Or suppose you are coordinating a group of volunteers who lead recreation activities for children in an afterschool program. You have decided to encourage the volunteers to do their own program planning and have organized several meetings as a way of encouraging them. During these meetings, however, no one participates in discussions about future program ideas that you introduce, and no interest in working together in the planning is ignited.

What is happening in these two groups? Are they effective groups? Is there anything you could do as the leader to improve these groups? Group dynamics is a branch of social psychology that attempts to apply research findings to the improvement of group effectiveness. Recreation leaders are likewise concerned with the study and practice of group dynamics as a way of enhancing the effectiveness of those groups with recreation goals.

A successful softball team, tour group, playground staff, or chess club has the quality and kind of interaction among its members that enhances the experience. To be an effective softball team coach or chess club captain, you need an understanding of what group effectiveness is and how your behavior as a leader can contribute to this effectiveness.

A Model of Group Effectiveness

Several rules relate to effective groups, and together they make up a model that can be used to evaluate how well a group you are leading is functioning. An awareness of the difference between this ideal model and the way in which your group is functioning can assist you as the leader in improving the group's effectiveness:

- Group goals must be clearly understood, be relevant to the needs of group members, highlight the positive interdependence of members, and evoke from every member a high level of commitment to their accomplishment.
- Group members must communicate their ideas and feelings accurately and clearly. Effective, two-way communication is the basis of all functioning and interaction among members.
- Power and influence need to be approximately equal throughout the group. This should be based on expertise, ability, access to information, and not on authority alone.
- Group cohesion needs to be high. Cohesion is based on members liking each other; each member's desire to continue as part of the group; the satisfaction of members with their group membership; and the level of acceptance, support, and trust among the members. Group norms supporting psychological safety, individuality, creativeness, conflicts of ideas, and growth and change need to be encouraged.
- Problem-solving adequacy should be high. Problems must be resolved with minimal energy and in a way that eliminates them permanently. Procedures should exist

for sensing the presence of problems. When problems are dealt with adequately, the problem-solving ability of the group is increased, innovation is encouraged, and group effectiveness is improved.

- The interpersonal effectiveness of members needs to be high. Interpersonal effectiveness is a measure of how well the consequences of behavior match their intentions.
- Controversy and conflict need to be seen as a positive indication of the member's involvement. Conflicts arising from diverse ideas and opinions are to be encouraged. Controversies promote participation in the group's efforts and quality and innovation in decision making. These controversies must be negotiated in a way that is mutually satisfying and does not weaken the cooperative interdependence of group members.

How effective are the recreation groups to which you belong? How would you describe the group's goals? Are they clarified and formulated so that the best possible match between individual goals and the group's goals may be achieved? Is the group's cohesive spirit high? Do high levels of inclusion, acceptance, affection, support, and trust exist? How is controversy handled? Is it dealt with in a cooperative manner, or is it ignored and avoided? A summary comparison of effective and ineffective groups is discussed in figure 5.4.

How to Lead a Meeting

PREPARATION

Preparation is a key element in conducting effective meetings.

1. Make sure the meeting is necessary. People appreciate not having to attend meetings about routine matters that could be handled with a memo or over e-mail.
2. Define the meeting's objectives. Describe the objective in the memo that announces the meeting.
3. Identify the best meeting participants. Limit participation to those who are the decision makers, have needed expertise, and/or are affected by the outcome.
4. Prepare an agenda. If time, circulate the agenda early and obtain feedback.
5. Distribute needed background information ahead of time. Send only summaries of huge reports.

DURING THE MEETING

There are seven steps to running a good meeting.

1. Start on time.
2. Review the agenda and major objectives. Print them on a board or chart for groupwide reference.
3. Hear from individuals with preassigned tasks. Getting reports as early as possible ensures that presenters have adequate time and provides recognition for their premeeting work.
4. Encourage participant input. Be sure that the meeting is not dominated by one faction or a few members.
5. Keep the meeting on track. Refer to a point someone made just before the digression to get the discussion back on track.
6. Summarize and review assignments. Review what each person has agreed to do and make sure that deadlines are set.
7. End on time. No excuses, just do it.

FOLLOW-UP AFTER THE MEETING

Leading a good meeting also includes some follow-up tasks.

1. Send out a memo summarizing the meeting.
2. Follow up on assignments where appropriate.

(Bartol & Martin, 1998, p. 493)

Effective Groups	Ineffective Groups
Goals are clarified and cooperatively structured	Goals are unclear; members accept imposed goals
Open and accurate expression of ideas and feelings is emphasized	Only ideas are expressed; feelings are ignored
Ability and information determine influence and power; power is equalized and shared	Position determines influence and power
Individuality is endorsed	Rigid conformity is promoted
Problems are innovatively and effectively solved	Problems are not adequately solved
Interpersonal effectiveness and self-actualization are encouraged	Order, stability, and structure are encouraged
Constructive controversy is encouraged	Controversy is avoided

FIGURE 5.4. Comparison of effective and ineffective groups

Synergy

In encouraging effective recreation groups, synergy is of concern to recreation leaders. In an example from sports it is known that every leader's job in a team sport is to mold the individual talents and skills of players into a synergistic effect. When a group of players are working together and focusing their energy on a common goal, they are said to be synergistic and the quality they are displaying is synergy. Through the interrelationships of the individuals on the team, a total effect (synergy) is achieved that is greater than the sum of the effect of the skills of all the players and leaders functioning in an unrelated, independent way (Fuoss & Troppmann, 1981). **Synergy** is the ability of the whole to equal more than the sum of its parts. In essence, synergy is the "team" concept.

Synergy can be encouraged by leadership for any group. It means that the leader fosters a united spirit. To do this the leader needs to be charismatic and the group members need to perceive themselves as a psychological whole. Since each person is different, effecting psychological bonding does take specific leadership skill.

Fuoss and Troppmann (1981) have described synergy as being the result of the circular interaction of the elements of cohesiveness, productivity, and morale. That is, the greater the group's productivity, the greater is the morale, which increases group cohesiveness, which comes full circle to foster greater group productivity. Figure 5.5 graphically expresses this relationship. In a performing modern dance group, for example, the more cohesive the group, the more successful the performance, and the more successful the performance, the greater the morale expressed by the dancers. Greater morale in turn leads to higher levels of cohesiveness, thus maintaining a cause-and-effect circular connection.

Fostering synergy among a group of recreation participants is not as simple as this suggests. Many other important factors may also influence this sequence. The ability of a leader to get every participant to optimize her individual potential requires sensitivity

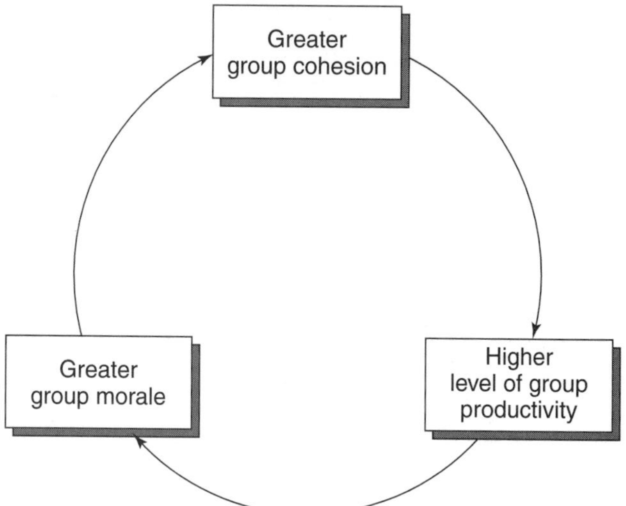

FIGURE 5.5. Model of synergy

to the "team" or "we" concept, rather than the "I" concept. However, the rewards and benefits derived through a synergetic effort are greater than those a participant can attain individually.

Developing Teamwork and Trust

One of the most important functions of a recreation leader in enabling effective groups is establishing a climate of *trust* and promoting **teamwork**. The group experience is more effective when members trust and support one another. The following suggestions can help you establish a climate of trust (Galanes & Brilhart, 1997).

1. *Establish norms that build trust.* Many leaders are far too slow to speak to group members who exhibit individual-oriented, self-centered behaviors. Norms that build trust encourage respectful listening, cooperation, and confidentiality.
2. *Be a coordinator rather than a dictator.* Trust can be developed when the leader acts as though her job is to serve the needs of the group, not to order people around. Members can then feel free to express themselves. Ask for volunteers to do jobs for the group rather than ordering someone.
3. *Enable group members to get to know each other.* People trust each other and feel safe in a group if they know each other as individuals. Leaders should build into the group experience unstructured time for members to get acquainted more thoroughly. This can be accomplished through social gatherings, such as staff picnics.

Additionally, the development of teamwork can help the group be effective and achieve its goals. Here are some suggestions (Galanes & Brilhart, 1997):

1. *Speak of "us" and "we," rather than "I" and "you."* Referring to the group and its members as "we" communicates your commitment to the group and its values.

Leader Profile: The Past
Joseph Bannon
Former Chair, Department of Leisure Studies, University of Illinois-Urbana-Champaign. This photo was taken at the beginning of his career. Today he uses team building skills to manage a consulting firm that advises recreation and park organizations world-wide.

Case in Point: Math Magic

In 1994, *Money* magazine described Raleigh, North Carolina, as the "best place to live in America." Yet, like most towns and cities all is not perfect. Raleigh has its share of substance abuse, violent crime, academic drop-outs, and teen pregnancy problems. To respond, several of the city's social service agencies developed a comprehensive summer program. One of the elements in this program is Math Magic. Math Magic is studying math on the playground. Math is presented to playground participants through everyday situations to emphasize its relevance, and through challenge games that build each child's confidence in math. "At first I thought, 'Math on the Playground'?" commented one administrator from the Raleigh Parks and Recreation Department. "But, it worked! It really did, and the children have great fun with it."

(Witt & Crompton, 1996)

2. *Develop a name or another symbol of group identification.* We do this continually in recreation groups, but perhaps you've not realized its important role in building teamwork. Shared identification can be displayed by T-shirts, logos, "inside" jokes, and slogans.
3. *Watch for hidden agendas that conflict with group goals.* Promptly bring to the attention of the group any hidden agendas you suspect are interfering with the group's goals. Avoiding such problems makes them worse, not better.
4. *Manage conflict in the group.* Conflict does not have to hurt teamwork in a group, but if it is allowed to go on too long or to become personal, it can cause lasting damage.
5. *Share rewards with the group.* Leaders often receive praise from supervisors. To enhance teamwork in the group, leaders should in turn give credit to the group. Your public acknowledgment of the good things accomplished by group members fosters cohesiveness and team spirit.
6. *Lighten up.* Share a laugh with the group. Humor helps reduce tensions and makes people feel good about each other.

Summary

Recreation leadership often occurs within the context of a group. Thus an important skill for leaders is the capable management of groups. The wide variety of groups that recreation, park, sport, tourism, and therapeutic recreation leaders commonly relate to can be categorized into the two general types of participant groups and functional groups. The effective management of both of these group types depends to a large degree on the practice and mastery of certain skills. For example, it is important to know how groups form, how they develop, what their essential characteristics are, and essentially what a group is.

Group effectiveness is of prime concern to the recreation leader. Many recreation experiences occur maximally within a group. If the group is operating poorly, the opportunity for realizing the recreation goal is greatly diminished and perhaps impossible. Although the ultimate responsibility for an effective group rests with each group member, the leader can have a role. A review of the other sections in this chapter provide the leader with some generalizations about helping groups become more effective. To summarize this chapter, we collect into two categories of leader roles: group-building roles and group task roles. The group-building roles are those leadership behaviors that contribute to the group's maintenance. Group task roles are those leadership behaviors that help groups achieve their goals.

The following are among the major group-building roles:

- Tone setting: encouraging group members to participate by praising performance, being fair in response to others, and encouraging and accepting others' opinions
- Harmonizing: mediating and conciliating differences of viewpoint, smoothing troubled waters, and working toward a group feeling of "we-ness"
- Standard setting: making sure that all members adhere to the agreed rules of conduct and ethical standards and preventing "cheap shots" and special interest pleading
- Tension reducing: encouraging stroking and other forms of expression that relieve tension and drain off negative feelings and accentuating positive rather than negative viewpoints

The following are among the group task roles:

- Opinion seeking and opinion giving: asking for or stating one's view about something the group is considering
- Information seeking and giving: asking for or providing relevant facts or critical information pertinent to the group's task
- Clarifying and elaborating: asking for and building on previous comments by restating what has been said and expanding on it so that the issues become clearer and better understood
- Coordinating: putting together the ideas and suggestions of various members so that a unified view can be established and demonstrating the relationship of various ideas in such a manner that unity is encouraged or achieved
- Testing: checking with the group to see if it is ready to take some action or make a decision
- Initiating: asking for new ideas or ways of acting, being the first to introduce a concept or begin a discussion that has relevance to the goals achieved, and proposing new actions or activity
- Summarizing: restating the highlights of a discussion, identifying the points developed by the group, and verbalizing the consensus reached or decision made by the group

These roles are essential to good group functioning. If they are inappropriately performed or are nonexistent, the group's success will be endangered. Although leaders may exhibit all or several of these, it is not necessary that they perform all of them. It is necessary, however, for the leader to make sure that someone in the group assumes each of these behaviors. The group's effectiveness, its health, and its success depend on this.

Recreation leaders are not born with the leadership skills necessary for working with groups. Like other leadership skills, these skills are learned. Learning how to manage a group is no different from learning how to dance. To learn group skills you must do the following:

- Understand why group leadership skills are important and how they will be of value to you
- Understand what group leadership skills are and what component behaviors you must engage in to perform the skills

- Find situations in which you can practice these skills
- Get someone to watch you and tell you how well you are performing
- Keep practicing

Questions and Activities for Review and Discussion

1. Identify one recreation participant group and one functional group to which you currently belong. Using the characteristics of an effective group discussed in this chapter, evaluate the two groups.
2. How do groups differ one from another? In what ways might one group be different from another?
3. Explain the significance of norms in group functioning. Think of a group to which you belong. What are four important norms in the group? How did they develop?
4. Explain the significance of cohesiveness in group functioning. Assess the level of cohesiveness and its consequences in a group to which you belong.
5. Explain how groups develop. Trace the development of a group in which you have participated.
6. As a group member, what roles do you tend to assume?
7. Why does the leader want recreation groups to be effective?
8. Observe a recreation participant group over an extended time. Analyze and describe the group according to the five stages of group development.

References

Allcorn, S. (1985, September, vol. 63). What makes groups tick. *Personnel*, 52–58.

Bartol, K. M., & Martin, D. C. (1998). *Management.* Boston, MA: McGraw-Hill.

Bass, B. M. (1960). *Leadership, psychology, and organizational behavior.* New York: Harper & Row.

Bass, B. M. (1990). *Bass & Stogdill's handbook of leadership: Theory, research, and managerial applications (3rd ed.).* New York: The Free Press.

Caplow, T. (1983). *Managing an organization.* New York: CBS College Publishing.

Fuoss, D. E., & Troppmann, R. J. (1981). *Effective coaching: A psychological approach.* New York: John Wiley & Sons.

Galanes, G. J., & Brilhart, J. K. (1997). *Communicating in groups: Applications and skills.* Boston, MA: McGraw-Hill.

Hellriegel, D., & Slocum, J. W. (1982). *Management* (3rd ed.). Reading, MA: Addison-Wesley Publishing.

Johnson, D. W., & Johnson, F. P. (1994). *Joining together: Group theory and group skills* (5th ed.). Boston: Allyn & Bacon.

Moment, D., & Zalenznik, A. (1963). *Role development and interpersonal competence: An experimental study of role performance in problem-solving groups.* Boston: Division of Research, Graduate School of Business Administration, Harvard University.

Niepoth, E. W. (1983). *Leisure leadership: Working with people in recreation and park settings.* Englewood Cliffs, NJ: Prentice-Hall.

Shaw, M. E. (1981). *Group dynamics: The psychology of small group behavior* (3rd ed.). New York: McGraw-Hill Book.

Tuckman, B. W. (1965). Developmental sequence in small groups. *Psychological Bulletin, 63,* 384–399.

Tuckman, B. W., & Jensen, M. A. C. (1977). Stages of small-group development revisited. *Group and Organization Studies, 2,* 419–427.

Witt, P. A., & Crompton, J. L. (eds.). (1996). *Programs that work: Public recreation in high risk environments.* Arlington, VA: National Recreation and Park Association.

Web Resources

American Psychologist (readings on group dynamics):
www.vcu.edu/hasweb/psy/psy633/read.old

The Breakfast Club (movie): www.geocities.com/Hollywood/Bungalow/8821
And: www.fortunecity.com/meltingpot/regent/827/tbc.html

Group dynamics and interpersonal communication: http://earth.colstate.edu/empathy/

Group dynamics workshops: www.mohicanresort.com/wrkshops.htm

Groups and outdoor leadership: www.princeton.edu/~oa/manual/sect9.html

Groups (introduction): www.nwmissouri.edu/nwcourses/martin/socialpsycho/GR

Groups, teams, and corporate culture:
www.sbe.csuhayward.edu/~lmasters/MKTG/MGMT/Groups1

Marketing through groups: www.msearch.com/cgt.html

Raleigh, North Carolina:
http://dir.yahoo.com/Regional/U_S_States/North_Carolina/Cities/Raleigh/

Raleigh Parks and Recreation Department: www.raleighcvb.org/parks.htm

CHAPTER 6

Communication and Interpersonal Processes

I'm willing to discuss it; I just don't want to talk about it.
—Mr. Fairy Bear, a Shari Lewis puppet, in Cohen, Fink, Gadon, & Willits, 1980.

Learning Objectives

Communication is foundational to all effective leadership. It is perhaps the most important ability needed by recreation leaders. This chapter will help you understand:

• the communication process • communication skills (nonverbal, listening, feedback) • organizational communication systems • influences on effective communication • developing interpersonal relationships

Key Terms

communication p. 111
information p. 112
life space p. 112
two-way interchange p. 113
communication relationship p. 113
informational sign p. 113
communication act p. 113
message p. 113
feedback p. 113
oral communication p. 116
exposition p. 116
entertainment p. 117
facilitation p. 117
persuasion p. 118
bypassing p. 119
e-mail communication p. 120
nonverbal communication p. 120
listening p. 124
written communication p. 126
jargon p. 127
wordiness p. 127
networks p. 129

"Hi." "Hi, how's it going?"
A dancer turns slowly and bows.
The bird chirps from high in the tree.
The air conditioner clicks on.
The telephone rings.
Two people sit down to watch the six o'clock evening news.
The husband reaches across the kitchen table and takes his wife's hand.

These incidents are the events of normal, everyday life. These events are communication. Most of our daily activities involve communication. Communication is a pervasive activity; it is basic to the existence of life. It includes the job interview, accepting (or refusing) an invitation, ringing a doorbell, quarreling, not attending a class, and chewing fingernails. Just "being" is, in a sense, communicating.

It is hard to fully appreciate how long it has taken human beings to develop communicative skills to their present level. Communication involves a complex background of habits, information, attitudes, biases, and knowledge that interrelates to determine what we will say and how we will react to what is said. The way to understand communication is to appreciate the complexity of its processes because understanding the nature of communication gives us a tool that helps us understand one another more easily. Such knowledge enables us to become better communicators.

There are many definitions for communication. Perhaps most broadly defined, **communication** is any information-sharing activity. For our purposes we shall restrict the definition to interpersonal communication—meaning that interaction between and among people. A rather comprehensive definition of interpersonal communication from Andersen (1972, p. 17) will be useful as a foundation for later discussion: "Communication is a dynamic process in which we consciously or unconsciously affect the thinking of another through materials used in symbolic ways." This means that communication is the exchange of messages between people for the purpose of achieving common meanings (Baskin & Aronoff, 1980).

From the communicator's point of view, communication is the process by which we seek to influence the thinking of another person in desired ways through the use of symbols. From the receiver's point of view, it is a process by which we perceive, interpret, and respond in some way to a stimulus provided by a source.

We do not really have to study the previous definition too carefully: we already know it. Communication is an integral part of our lives. Some of us may tend to assume that there is really nothing to communication; we do it almost automatically. But does having communicated all our lives confirm that we are effective communicators? The truth is that interacting with others effectively is not automatic. Bad, as well as good, habits become a part of our communication behavior. "Mere interaction with others, without knowledge and without insight, will not of itself guarantee the development of good interpersonal communication skills or the correction of counterproductive communication behaviors" (Brooks & Emmert, 1980, p. 4).

To mention that being able to effectively communicate is important to the recreation leader appears redundant. Certainly, communication is critical to the excellence of recreation leadership. Consider the following illustrative case:

> The recreation director of a small, suburban community interviewed and selected 16 leaders for the summer day camp program. She notified them in mid-April that they had been hired. However, several of these newly hired leaders continued to "shop around" for other jobs and informed the director just a week before the day camp program began that they would not be working for her. This left the director short of staff and without sufficient time to interview and select other leaders (adapted from Kraus, Carpenter, & Bates, 1981, p. 352).

What went wrong in this situation? Were any of the problems a result of difficulties or errors in communication by the camp director or by the leaders? Are any of the possible solutions a matter of more effective communication? This chapter relates what is known about communication to the typical responsibilities and settings of a recreation leader.

THE PROCESS OF COMMUNICATING

How does human communication work? An excellent analogy from Schramm and Porter (1982) stated that studying communication behavior is like studying the ocean. It may be done at any level and beyond a certain depth must be done in darkness. Yet what happens in the communication process does not have to be completely mysterious. Let us begin with a simple discussion and build to a more complex model.

A Basic Discussion

What is common about the communication that exists between you the reader and me the writer this instant, between you and your friends yesterday, and between the recreation leader and participants tomorrow? These are communication incidents. What is common to them is information, a communication relationship, and the special kind of behavior that handles the information and takes place only in communication relationships (Schramm & Porter, 1982).

Information is the stuff of communication. Communication exists for the purpose of conveying, sharing, or processing information. Information is what distinguishes communication from other behaviors. The information that persons seek from most communication is whatever will help them structure or organize a situation in which they must act. Information makes existing in situations and the accompanying decisions easier. Information reduces the uncertainty of the situation. For example, if you have information about what sections in this chapter are most important for an upcoming examination, the uncertainty of the examination situation is most likely reduced.

The relationship in which communication takes place involves two or more people interacting with information that is of mutual interest to them. Into the communication relationship all involved persons bring a well-filled **life space**, containing a unique storage of experiences, against which they interpret and respond to the information that comes to them. If people are going to communicate effectively, their stored experiences must have some overlap of common interest. In figure 6.1 the circles represent the life

FIGURE 6.1. Life spaces: The setting of communication

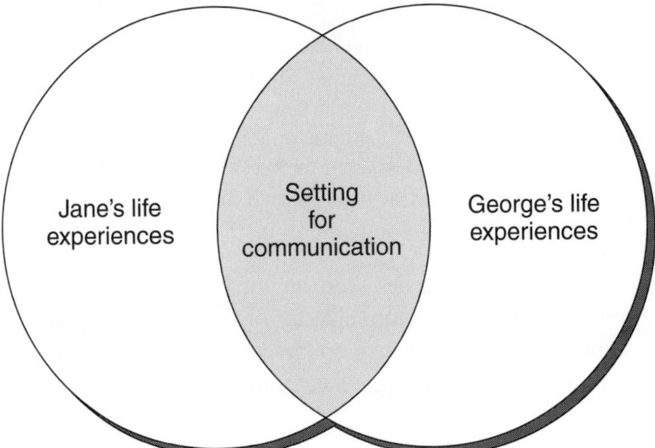

spaces of two persons, Jane and George, with the overlapping area being the setting for their communication.

Life spaces are never perfectly congruent. No two people ever have identical experiences or learn identical values. It is amazing that communication relationships work as well as they do!

Most communication is two way. It is hard to think of any communication that is completely one way. Even watching television involves some two-way communication. Turning on the set and selecting the station is a response to the television network. Viewer responses are seriously measured by networks, and future program decisions are made based on this response.

Leader Profile: The Present
Betty Jo Gaines
Director, Department of Recreation and Parks, Washington D.C. As a chief administrator, Gaines establishes and maintains communication relationships with staff, participants, citizens, and government officials.

The most typical and frequent pattern of a communication relationship is an extended **two-way interchange**, usually with those involved taking uneven roles in the exchange. It is a relationship in which information is shared, although not exactly precisely. The result is that the understanding between the communication participants is likely to grow closer as the exchange continues. It never becomes, however, a completely congruent set of meanings because no two people are ever completely alike. As the communication exchange continues, new points of difference between the participants almost certainly appear, and these should be resolved by further exchange. So communication is best understood as a relationship—a relationship that involves sharing information that leads to an understanding.

What happens inside the **communication relationship**? It includes communication acts and informational signs. An **informational sign** is the tool of communication. It is a sound, a printed word, or a picture that represents information. In essence, what happens inside the communication relationship is that one individual puts out the signs and another makes some use of them. The process is the same whether it is a two-person conversation, a lecture, a discussion group, or a message carried by mass media. Figure 6.2 graphically represents what basically occurs in the communication relationship.

At the minimum there are three components: a **communication act**, a set of signs, and a second communication act. The second communication act has often been referred to as feedback. It means a return flow from the first communication act, which has likewise been referred to as the **message**. **Feedback** is a most powerful tool. When it does not exist or is delayed—such as when a scuba diving class is required to listen to a lecture on decompression without responding—doubt and concern in the communicator who sent the message and frustration in the audience is engendered. Feedback operates like any other communication process. It is a reversal of the flow.

In summary, the process of communication requires at least two people who interact in an information-sharing relationship bound by a set of informational signs. The purpose of the relationship (e.g., persuasion, instruction, or entertainment) determines the roles these persons play. Whatever the roles, one person—drawing on her cognitive

FIGURE 6.2. A diagram of what happens in a communication relationship

needs, resources, and communication skills—encodes the informational signs and offers them to the other person. The second person—also drawing on his cognitive needs, resources, and communication skills—decides whether to accept the signs. If he accepts the signs, they are processed according to his understanding. If the situation calls for it, he may then formally (and also informally through indications such as facial expressions) encode some signs and carry out a communication act back to the first person.

A Model

We are ready for a model of the communication process. Studying a model is useful to understanding communication because it deliberately oversimplifies by leaving out some details and highlighting others. The model shown in figure 6.3 attempts to represent the communication process as inclusively as possible. It stresses the major elements involved and suggests some of the interrelationships of these elements, which were just discussed.

Whether a person is identified as a sender or a receiver is frequently a matter of time or perspective. We act as a sender and a receiver in an interchanging way and can even be both at the same time. Studying the model we see that the sender is the person who initiates the communication relationship. The sender places the message in the channel. The sender has a vast store of information, beliefs about the nature of things, and values. He has many habits, interests, needs, and desires. The sender is influenced by these factors and the ways in which they are interpreted. The sender's store of knowledge and ideas can be regarded as resources or as liabilities.

As the model indicates, the receiver is the individual who perceives a message. Although the receiver is often regarded as passive, this is not the case. A sender can only encode a message; the receiver must act to give meaning to this message. At times the receiver may formally respond to the sender by encoding a message of her own. The receiver brings the same resources to the communication relationship as the sender. The receiver brings experiences, biases, needs, wants, and desires that are unique and individual. These resources help determine the meaning the receiver derives from the message and any response made to it. The response the receiver makes is called feedback. Feedback can be interpreted, you may recall, as indicating the impact the message has on the receiver.

The message is the constellation of information that the sender places in the communication channels. The message is not what the sender intended to communicate; nor

FIGURE 6.3. A general communication model. - - -➤ , Informal message channels; ◄- - - , informal feedback channels; ⟶ , formal message channels; ⟵ , formal feedback channels. *Modified from Andersen, K.E. (1972).* Introduction to communication: Theory and Practice. *Menlo Park, CA: Cummings Publishing*

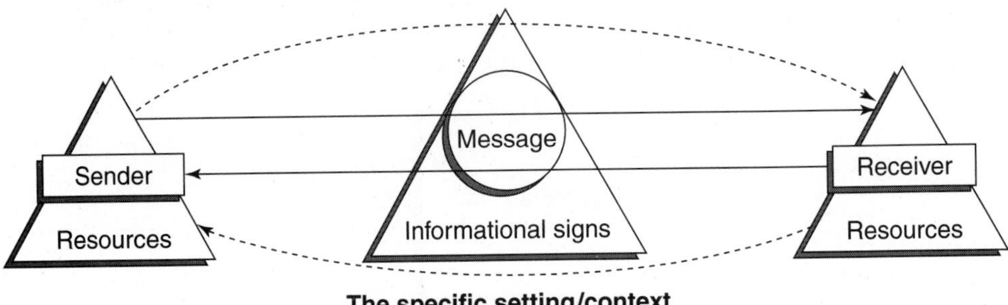

is it what the receiver thinks was communicated. This signifies that meanings do not exist in messages. Instead, they exist in the minds of those individuals involved in the communication relationship. The meaning one person assigns to a message may differ a great deal from those others assign to it. Also the meanings assigned to the message today may not be the same as those assigned next week.

The informational signs are the medium in which the message exists. Technically, the informational signs may be any physical matter that can affect the sensory mechanisms of a receiver. The signs most often used affect the senses of sight and hearing. A television, a radio, a memo, a letter, a telephone, a picture, a cheering voice, a musical note, a smile, a frown—these are informational signs. Signs are employed by the sender and the receiver as representatives of the information collected together in the message. The appropriate or most useful informational signs are dependent on the specific setting or context of the relationship. Certain settings may require the use of certain signs.

The channels in the communication model indicate the flow, or the exchange nature, of the process. Messages that are "packaged" as information signs are exchanged, usually over and over. This exchange can be either formal such as a speech or a performance or informal such as a raised eyebrow or a yawn.

The specific setting, or context component, in the model refers to the conditions or circumstances within which the communication takes place. A specific setting might be a pancake restaurant late at night. It could be a classroom, a pup tent, a rock face, a dressing room, or a dance floor. The specific context is also used to refer to the "total environment" that may affect the communication process. The size of the audience and the amount of available time are also factors that would interact and affect the communication process. It is this concept of specific setting and context that emphasizes the dynamic quality and the process nature of communication. All these factors interrelate, and an understanding of these interrelationships can help in comprehending the reasons for communication successes or failures in recreation leadership.

Exercise: One-Way, Two-Way Communication

Instructions: Independently and in secret draw a diagram containing five squares of the same size. The squares can be oriented in any way, but there can be no more than five. Here is the idea:

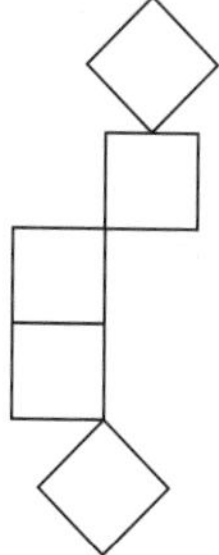

Now, pair off with a classmate, still keeping your squares diagram a secret. The first round demonstrates one-way communication. One of you in the pair turns your back and verbally explains your diagram to the other person. While the diagram is being explained, the second person draws what she/he understands about the diagram on a spare sheet of paper. The drawing person may neither ask questions nor give verbal responses to the explaining person. Afterward, compare the original diagram with the drawn diagram. How accurate is it? Now, reverse roles. The other one in the pair faces his/her partner and explains his/her diagram to the other person. As an illustration of two-way communication, this time the drawing person may ask questions of the explainer, and request reexplanations if needed. No hand motions are allowed, however. Afterward, compare the original diagram with the drawn diagram. How accurate is it? What have you learned from this exercise about the differences between one-way and two-way communication? Which took more time? Which yielded more accuracy? In which experience was there more confidence in the communication?

The quality of your communication makes a difference in your success as a recreation leader. In study after study, it has been clearly demonstrated that the quality of communication is more important than the quantity (Bass, 1990). As the sender and the receiver of communication as expressed in the model (figure 6.3), you must be able to convey accurate and persuasive meaning in the message, by ably using informational signs. In this section of the chapter, we explore the communication skills that you need to capably implement the communication process model. These skills include oral, nonverbal, written, listening, and giving feedback.

ORAL COMMUNICATION SKILLS

The recreation leader must be able to effectively use verbal communication. The fitness leader is interviewed on a local radio show. The recreation director of the retirement apartment complex addresses the monthly meeting of the residents association. The cultural arts coordinator makes a verbal request to the community arts council for additional funding for a summer children's theater camp. The director of beach activities welcomes new guests to the resort at the weekly newcomers' dinner. The naturalist talks to park visitors about the local bear population while showing slides. The camp counselor tells a ghost story around the camp fire. The therapeutic recreation specialist presents information on a patient at a hospital team meeting. In these and many other situations, the recreation leader must have some competence in making oral presentations.

Oral communication, or the spoken word, takes place mostly through face-to-face conversation with another individual, meetings with several individuals, and telephone conversations. Oral communication is the most frequently used skill because it is fast, usually more personal, and provides immediate feedback from others involved in the conversation. But there are disadvantages. Oral communication can be time-consuming; more difficult to terminate; and additional effort is required to document what is said, if necessary (Bartol & Martin, 1998).

Types of Oral Communication

There are numerous oral communication situations for the recreation leader. Basically, these situations can be categorized into four types: exposition, entertainment, facilitation, and persuasion (Andersen, 1972). Distinguishing these types is only a matter of convenience rather than of clear difference.

When a recreation leader is speaking to share or give information, he is involved in the **exposition** type of oral presentation. Expository communication seeks to cause comprehension of information. This may be data, feelings, judgments, or instructions. The information can be controversial such as the announcement of the closing of a community lake to swimming. As an oral communication technique, exposition is one of the most important methods.

Many of the elements in the communication process described earlier in this chapter are highly relevant to the oral transmission of information. The receiver's motivations, the state of current knowledge, and the extent to which that understanding is consistent with the new information are central. If the receiver has little previous understanding of the information communicated (such as centering clay on a potter's wheel), there are limitations on what can be accomplished. Also if the receivers assume that they have accurate knowledge and if the information to be transmitted (such as ways to reduce the site impact by camping) contradicts this view, problems in comprehension and attention should be anticipated.

Circumstances on the sender's side of the communication process are also important in the adequacy of expository oral communication. The depth of your understanding of the material and of your resources are involved. If your knowledge of CPR is partial, incomplete, or inaccurate, for example, sharing CPR technique information with others becomes more difficult.

All this is critical for the recreation leader in the preparation of expository oral communication. In exposition the leader should:

- Evaluate the receivers' motivations, the receivers' current understanding of the material, and the level of certainty with which they hold that information.
- Make a definite decision of where to begin. Usually you will begin with the recall and confirmation of what is already understood and build from there.
- Make use of such communication supports as explanation, definition, illustration, analogy, testimony, repetition, and restatement.
- Try to overcome knowledge limitations through further preparation such as reading or talking with good resources.

In thinking of **entertainment** in oral communication situations in recreation, you might initially think of the "stand-up" comic. Yet much of the communication in any setting involves entertainment either as an end in itself or as a means to accomplishing other ends. The verb *to entertain* is defined as to hold attention agreeably, to amuse, to divert. Often people who entertain also have a message beyond the entertainment. The point made with wit and humor can often hold attention and instruct better than any other form of oral communication.

Entertainment can be a travelogue, a ghost story, a joke, or an exaggerated tale. Humor is perhaps entertainment's main technique. It can be the most obvious slapstick or a more sophisticated play on words. Most of us are not professional humorists; yet there are many situations in which we wish to entertain. A joke or anecdote that evokes a laugh may end an argument or smooth a misunderstanding.

You as a recreation leader will more frequently use entertainment as a means to another end. It will probably be spontaneous and occur in small group settings. When more formal efforts at entertainment are demanded, as where an audience is gathered for an evening lodge program in a state park, the following suggestions may be helpful to the leader:

- Analyze the audience and the material to know where the entertainment value lies. Entertainment must be appropriate to the particular people, subject, and occasion.
- Put people at ease, have confidence and mastery of the situation, and enjoy the process along with the audience. An audience is unlikely to enjoy itself if the leader is nervous and insecure.
- Know in which forms of entertainment you are most competent. Some people are highly skilled in storytelling with children, whereas others may bore children and make adults grin time after time at their dry wit.

The term **facilitation** suggests ease and assistance. Being a chairperson, a master of ceremonies, or a toastmaster are roles that demand the communicator be a facilitator.

Speeches of welcome, tributes or dedications, and guest introductions are also forms of facilitation. Oral communication that facilitates does not seek a goal in its own right as much as it supports the accomplishment of other goals.

Facilitation is highly patterned. Specific rituals are common. Analyzing the factors affecting the situation will dictate what patterns of facilitation should be used. In some instances the master of ceremonies needs to be a dominant figure who carefully and powerfully controls the proceedings. When chairing a debate followed by a public forum on a controversial recreation policy issue, the facilitator may need to stress the rules and ensure that they are observed.

In general, the best facilitator is one who takes only as much spotlight as necessary. For example, in a speech of introduction it is best to introduce the person by first identifying her; briefly indicating certain abilities, qualities, or achievements; and finally remarking on your own favorable impression. The long, florid, overembellished introduction is becoming less in vogue. What constitutes the best introduction is again a matter of appropriateness to the introducer, to the receivers, and to the person being introduced.

In developing competency as a facilitator the leader should remember the following:

- Be direct, sincere, and somewhat spontaneous.
- Avoid being excessive and showy.
- Seek only to facilitate, to focus attention on the other individuals or subjects that are at issue.
- Perform the rituals of facilitation with a sense of novelty, excitement, and the unusual.

There is a close relationship between persuasion and the other forms of oral communication. A persuasion effort can be informative, it can entertain, and it can facilitate. We can think of the entire communication process as an effort of some to influence others. Persuasion as a distinctly considered and prepared oral communication type can range from the hard sell before the city council for a county and city recreation management merger to an extended campaign for election into an office in a professional recreation and park association. Persuasion can even be seen as the effort of a day-care leader to use the teaching of a new game to distract the children from disruptive behavior.

Persuasion is a communication situation in which the sender wishes to affect the thinking, attitude, or action of the receivers. A persuasion effort may be a single, isolated phenomenon or part of an ongoing series of efforts by many people. In essence, persuasive communication is clearly goal directed. As a persuader, your desire is to have impact on others. Unlike its reputation, persuasion is not necessarily bad. When professionally used, it is a useful means of accomplishing better recreation and park services.

In persuasion, your approach must be adjusted as specifically as possible to your target receivers. For this reason you must know your audience. Persuasion can have negative results, it can be boring, and it can have a reverse impact. This means that receiver beliefs and attitudes must be analyzed before the persuasive communication begins.

Some persuasion strategies are acceptable to use:

- Identify yourself with the receivers. Establish common experiences and common identifications.
- State your purpose openly.
- Use strong motivational appeals. An audience will normally be receptive to them.

- Direct the energy of a group to specific actions. Let them commit themselves by making specific responses.
- Use the common interests and commitment of audience members to reinforce one another. Slogans can prove effective. Group participation can unite them and enhance persuasion.
- Be professional but human too.

The Symbolic Nature of Language

Recreation leaders who use words effectively are keenly aware of their symbolic nature. They know that words do not have meanings in and of themselves, so they use words carefully to enable the message receivers to understand their meaning, rather than the meaning of the words per se (Galanes & Brilhart, 1997). That is, as receivers of a spoken message we are trying to understand what the speaker means rather than what the words mean. For example, the leader as oral communicator is trying to guard against bypassing.

Bypassing occurs when two or more people have different meanings for a word but do not realize it. When this happens the conversation leads either to a false agreement or false disagreement (Galanes & Brilhart, 1997). Bypassing is rather commonplace because the various meanings and shades of meanings that individuals attach to words depends on many factors, including background, experience, and status differences.

Many words, especially abstract ones, are likely to be interpreted differently by different people. Words vary from highly concrete to highly abstract. For example, the words in the following list become more abstract (more vague) as you move down the list, therefore the likelihood increases that people will understand them differently.

Kenneth Louis

director of guest services

certified leisure professional

young adult

man

human being

Such words as effective, efficient, excellent, and enjoyable are abstract and likely to be understood differently by different people. The level of abstractness matters a lot during conversations, particularly because having a meaningful conversation without abstract

Bypassing

What the leader said	*What the leader meant*	*What the participant heard*
We'll need to complete this project as soon as we can.	The crafts room will close next week for renovation.	The instructor is getting impatient with my slow progress.
Your performance at the swim meet last week was below your usual; I really expected more out of you.	You're going to have to try harder, but I know you can do it.	If you screw up one more time, you're off the team.

Case in Point: Saying What You Mean with Electronic and Voice Mail

For electronic mail: How would we get things done these days without e-mail? It is fast and easy, but without some attention to the opportunities for misunderstanding, **e-mail communication** can be troublesome. Here are some hints:

- Do not use all capital letters. This is the same as shouting in a person's ear.
- Use very short paragraphs.
- Generally keep messages short.
- Don't use e-mail for controversial or confidential matters or for communications that can be readily misunderstood.
- End your message with your name, otherwise the message ends abruptly.
- Copy others on messages sparingly.
- Always proofread the message before sending it to reduce misunderstandings due to typos, and so on.
- Never send an e-mail message when angry. Wait until you are calm.
- Before sending a message, ask yourself "Would I say this in person?"

For voice mail: Voice mail is today's answering machine. It is an efficient way to communicate, as it is estimated that only 50 percent of phone calls are completed on the first try. Here are some tips to help you leave effective voice mail messages:

- Keep messages short and to the point.
- Never leave a harsh or negative message on voice mail.
- Don't record anything that is confidential.
- Always be prepared to leave a message.
- Avoid flippant messages, even as a joke.
- Don't leave messages from noisy restaurants, parties, bars, and so on. Background noise can be heard clearly over the phone.

words would be impossible. So, what can you do to reduce misunderstanding when using highly abstract words?

1. Speak as concretely and specifically as possible to express what you mean. Don't use jargon or doublespeak to show off.
2. When using a highly abstract word that may be confusing to many people, use concrete examples of what you mean as well. For example, "The meeting was energizing (abstract word) for the group because it left everyone clear on what they were expected to do next."
3. You can sometimes define highly abstract terms by using synonyms or descriptors. For example, "The program next week will take place at the recreation center located in midtown."
4. Quantify when possible. For example, "That budget has a 75 percent chance of being passed by the board." (Galanes & Brilhart, 1997)

NONVERBAL COMMUNICATION

In a sense it is impossible not to communicate. In silence, and in speech, we are constantly communicating with each other. Through gesture and posture, sound and distance, glance and blush, frown and smile, we are in a perpetual process of communication.

The implications of this principle to recreation leadership are far reaching. To lead people, to understand people, to help people achieve fulfillment in leisure experiences, we need to explore the other processes by which we come to influence one another. These processes have been labeled nonverbal communication.

Nonverbal communication includes how and when we look at each other and what happens when our eyes meet. Nonverbal communication involves how far apart we stand and how directly we face each other. Nonverbal communication is also our movements, strength, expressions, and gestures. Even when people talk, more is communicated than just speech. The term nonverbal is commonly used to describe human communication that transcends spoken or written words.

For the recreation leader, nonverbal communication should be seen as an inseparable part of the total communication process. Oral communication needs the support of nonverbal communication. Nonverbal behavior can repeat, contradict, substitute for, complement, accent, or regulate verbal behavior (Knapp, 1980).

For example, if you told a young camper to go to the tent and bring back a compass and then pointed in the direction of the tent, this nonverbal hand motion would be a repetition of what you said. Or when a tired and downtrodden tennis instructor walks into the pro shop, the body movement and facial expression substitute for the statement, "What a rotten afternoon!"

Because of the contribution to your overall communication ability, proficiency in sending and receiving accurate nonverbal signals is important to your skill as a recreation leader. You must be able to correctly interpret the nonverbal expressions of feelings and attitudes from your participants and colleagues. Likewise, you must be able to accurately send nonverbal expressions of feelings and attitudes to them. It is essentially a matter of developing social competence; it is what enables some people to be more effective on the playground, in the office, or at the board meeting.

In essence, we learn nonverbal skills by imitating and modeling others and by adapting our responses to the feedback from others. You can practice nonverbal sending and receiving communication skills; but without accurate feedback from others, you may not improve your ability.

Body Movement and Proximity

The heart of human nonverbal communication is the human body and the movement it makes during interpersonal contacts. In other words, the way your body moves is not random; it is inextricably linked to what you say. Most of the research on body movement and body posture has been devoted to their relationship to communicating liking and disliking, status and power, and deception (Knapp, 1980).

A recreation leader indicates a liking for someone by a more forward lean, a closer proximity, more eye contact, more openness of arms and body, more face-to-face body orientation, more touching, and more postural relaxation. The use of a hands-on-hips position by a standing leader is indicative of interacting with disliked persons more than liked persons. Leaders in therapeutic recreation have reported the use of matching their posture with the posture of clients as a means of promoting greater client-therapist rapport.

Body movements and body proximity also communicate status and power. Research has shown that persons relate to powerful, high-status persons with less eye contact, less relaxed posture, greater voice loudness, more expansive movements and postures, and more distance. People tend to raise their heads more when speaking to a high-status person and will use the hands-on-hips position more often when talking to a person considered to have a lower status (Galanes & Brilhart, 1997).

Culture is an important factor in this, and much of the attention on cultural differences has focused on the use of space (Heslin and Patterson, 1982). For example, Arabic, southern Mediterranean, and Latin American societies tend to relate to each other in close spatial proximity. At the other extreme, the English and northern Europeans are "noncontact" societies and relate to each other more comfortably with more spatial distance in between. Americans apparently fall somewhere within these two extremes.

Touching

Touch is an important aspect of some recreation leader and participant relationships. It plays a role in giving encouragement, expressing tenderness, and showing emotional support. The act of touching is like any other message we communicate—it may result in negative reactions, as well as positive ones, depending on the circumstances.

There are many explanations for differences in reactions to touch. Some children grow up learning "not to touch." Certain situations will have a facilitating or inhibiting effect on touching behavior as well. The research reported by Henley (1977) suggests that people may be more likely to touch others when (1) giving information or advice rather than asking for it; (2) giving an order rather than responding to it; (3) asking a favor rather than agreeing to do one; (4) trying to persuade rather than being persuaded; (5) participating in "deep" rather than casual conversation; (6) attending a party rather than working; (7) communicating excitement rather than receiving it from another; and (8) receiving disturbing news from another rather than sending such messages.

Touching has also been classified according to the different types of messages communicated. The categorization reflects a continuum from impersonal to personal. These more impersonal types are appropriate in certain leadership settings in recreation:

- *Functional-professional*: The communicative intent of this impersonal businesslike touching is to accomplish some task. The receiver is considered to be an object or vehicle for accomplishing this task. Examples of such situations may include a swimming instructor gently nudging a young child to enter the water and a golf pro moving the hands on the club grip of a new golf player.
- *Social-polite*: The purpose of this type of touching is to affirm the other person's identity. Although the other person is treated as a "person," there is still little genuine involvement between them. The business handshake is perhaps the best example of this type of touching.
- *Friendship-warmth*: This kind of touching behavior begins to recognize more of the other person's uniqueness and expresses a genuine liking for that person. This type of touching considers the other person as a friend, such as a "pat on the back" and a "high-five."

The exact meaning of any touching message will vary according to the context within which it occurs, its intensity, and its duration. The meanings we attach to touching behavior vary according to what part of the body is touched (shoulder or knee), how long the touch lasts (a fleeting second or a couple of minutes), the strength of the touch (soft or hard), the method of the touch (open or closed fisted), and the frequency of the touch (rarely or often). Yet in some recreation leadership cases, touching can be an effective method for communicating. It must be used with professional caution, however.

In an inappropriate context or by an inappropriate person, touching can be misunderstood and as a result the wrong message communicated.

Facial Expressions

A poker player draws her fourth ace in a game with no wild cards. Her face, however, leads the other players to believe the card she drew is worth nothing.

As illustrated in this example, the face is rich in communicative potential. It is the primary location for the communication of emotions and attitudes, and some say that next to speech it is the primary source of information (Knapp, 1980). We frequently place considerable reliance on facial cues when we make important interpersonal judgments. The face is used as a conversational regulator, opening and closing communication channels, complementing and qualifying other behaviors, and even replacing spoken messages. The way you position your eyelids, forehead, eyebrows, jaw, and lips and how wide you open your eyes tell others exactly how you feel about yourself and them (or how you want them to think you feel, as when you play poker!)

Eye Contact

"We're seeing eye to eye now." "She could look right through you." "He has shifty eyes."

These and many other common expressions illustrate how much is communicated with our eyes. Downward glances are associated with modesty; wide eyes are said to mean frankness, terror, or naiveté; immobile facial expressions with a constant stare are associated with coldness; and eyes rolled upward suggest disgust with another person's behavior. We use our eyes to get attention, to reveal thoughts and feelings about ourselves and others, and to close or stop a communication interaction.

Visual contact occurs usually when we want to signal that the communication channel is open. In some instances eye gaze can almost insist on an obligation to interact.

Factors That Influence the Amount and Duration of Eye Contact

More eye contact is predicted when at least one of the following applies to the leader:	*Less eye contact is predicted when at least one of the following applies to the leader:*
Physically distant from the other person	Physically closer to the other person
Discussing easy, impersonal topics	Discussing difficult topics
Nothing else to look at	Other relevant objects or people to look at
Interested in the other person's reactions	Not interested in the other person's reactions
Interested in the other person	Talking rather than listening
Perceives self as a lower status person than the other	Not interested in the other person
Trying to influence the other person	Perceives self as a higher status person than the other
Extravert	Introvert
High affiliative or inclusion needs	Low affiliative or inclusion needs
Listening rather than talking	Embarrassed, ashamed, sorrowful, sad, submissive, or trying to hide something.
Female	

Modified from Knapp, M.L. (1980). *Essentials of nonverbal communication.* New York: Holt, Rinehart & Winston.

Likewise, when you want to stop social contact, your eye gaze will likely diminish. In addition to opening and closing the channel of communication, eye behavior regulates the flow of communication by providing turn-taking signals (Knapp, 1980). Speakers do seem to glance at listeners at the end of an idea or thought. This can signal that the other person may now assume the speaking role. Similarly we use these glances to obtain feedback, to see how we are being received, and to see if the other person will let us continue. Also we seem to gaze more at people we like and at people we perceive as liking us.

A variety of research studies have attempted to determine what factors or circumstances influence the amount and duration of eye contact in human encounters. Knapp (1980) has summarized this research to indicate that spatial distance, physical characteristics, personal and personality characteristics, nature of tasks, and cultural backgrounds determine eye contact behavior. This summary as applied to a recreation leader is presented in the boxed material.

LISTENING

Leader Profile: The Present
Steve Fiala
A trail developer for East Bay, California—working on the Regional Park District's Master Plan for Regional Trails. The development of recreational trails requires accurate listening to the needs and interests of potential users.

Philosopher-novelist Gide once opened a lecture by noting, "All this has been said before, but since nobody listened, it must be said again" (Walsh, 1982). **Listening** has been romantically labeled an art; but as an important ingredient to good communication, it is perhaps more accurately described as a skill. It is a skill that requires knowledge and effort. It is a mental skill that is developed primarily through training and practice.

"Nobody listened" can result in waste, and waste costs money. No one can estimate how much recreation and park budgets suffer as a result of missed appointments, misunderstood information, and inaccurate printed materials. But the bottom line can be diminished services and even a tarnished reputation for the organization. Poor listening has been blamed for both major and minor losses; and as losses accumulate, poor listening can affect everyone in the agency.

Researchers tell us that we spend 80 percent of our awake hours communicating, and about 45 percent of that time is spent listening (Walsh, 1982). With training, practice, and genuine interest you can become an effective listener. All it takes is an awareness that listening requires effort. Yet when mastered, it is perhaps the most perfect gift we can give those with whom we work and live.

The Basics of Productive Listening

For listening to be effective, we must be active participants in the entire communication process. This means not only working with just our ears, but also responding with our full capacity and inner perceptions. Good listening entails being fully attentive and awake; it means being active in thought and feeling; and it means being open and receptive to others. It demands of us an enhanced vitality and a firm desire to relate to others. To achieve all this there are at least three main ingredients: discipline, concentration, and comprehension.

First, the development of good listening requires discipline. It is imperative that we practice listening regularly to the point of missing it if we stop practicing. We must train ourselves to be in the mood to want to listen.

Concentration is a second prerequisite of good listening. To concentrate fully when listening, we need to be patient with ourselves. We must remove distractions from the

Exercise: Listening Self-Assessment

How well do you listen? Complete the following questionnaire, thinking of your behavior in recent meetings, conversations, and class discussions.

	Yes	No
1. I frequently attempt to listen to several conversations at the same time.	_______	_______
2. I sometimes pretend to pay attention to people.	_______	_______
3. I usually know what another person is going to say before he or she says it.	_______	_______
4. I usually end conversations that don't interest me by diverting my attention from the speaker.	_______	_______
5. I frequently nod, frown, or whatever to let the speaker know how I feel about what is being said.	_______	_______
6. I usually respond immediately when someone has finished talking.	_______	_______
7. I evaluate what is being said while it is being said.	_______	_______
8. I usually prepare a response while the other person is still talking.	_______	_______
9. I usually ask people to clarify what is being said rather than guess at the meaning.	_______	_______
10. Most people feel that I have understood their point of view when we disagree.	_______	_______

Which of these behaviors do you think make for good listening? Read the next section of the chapter and discuss with your classmates.

path of our listening. By concentrating, we can be curious and alert, without confusion or interference. In listening, it is essential that full attention be given to the situation at hand. In so doing, we learn to live more fully in the present and to evaluate things as they are. Good listening demands active participation. It involves keeping one's mind in a state of relaxed alertness—open and flexible to all relevant changes in a given situation.

A third factor contributing to the effectiveness of listening is comprehension, the understanding of the true meaning of what is heard. Comprehension in any given situation is to be found not in the words that are spoken but in the meaning given by both the sender and the receiver. To do so you must break through the barriers of intellectualization. As human beings, we may desire to hear only what we want to hear. This interferes with good listening. It can be overcome by more objectivity, learning to see people and things as they really are. We must "hear the other person out" without imposing our preconceived notions or opinions. Since the goal is to comprehend what the speaker is saying, we must learn to hold back our judgments and decisions until after he has finished. Having listened to our fullest capacity, we can now digest and evaluate what is important to us and the situation.

Checklist for Good Listening

Listening is an important communication skill for recreation leaders. Listening effectively to participants, to supervisors, to other staff, to dissatisfied clients, or to interested citizens requires practiced skill. The following are ways you can enhance your listening skills (Walsh, 1982; Bartol & Martin, 1998; Galanes & Brilhart, 1997):

- Look for areas of interest instead of tuning out dry speakers. Ask, "What's in it for me. How can I use this information?"
- Listen patiently, even if you disagree with what is being said.
- Indicate acceptance (not necessarily agreement) by nodding or commenting with "Yes" or "I see."
- Focus on content, not delivery. Pay attention to what the speaker is saying, not on how he is saying it.
- Do not be distracted. Noises, machines, and people talking tend to make the mind wander. The outcome can be sidetracking the conversation.
- Be alert. Daydreaming is a common listening fault. If you find your thoughts are running ahead of the speaker's words, use the time to evaluate what's been said or review her key comments.
- Learn to take good notes. Depending on the situation, take many or just a few. Do not rely on a single system.
- Be objective, not argumentative. Avoid silent arguing. Get the full picture accurately before jumping to conclusions and planning a rebuttal to the speaker's remarks.
- Identify the speaker's purpose. Is he trying to inform, persuade, or entertain? Maybe there is more than one aim involved.
- Ask questions whenever possible, especially open-ended ones. "What would you have done?" "Could you give me examples?" "What do you think about that?"
- Try not to interrupt a speaker. Hear her out before interjecting your own comments. "We never listen when we are planning to speak," noted La Rochefoucauld, a seventeenth-century French writer.

Giving Feedback: A Special Form of Listening

Feedback is the receiver's response to the sender's message in the communication process. Feedback results in a reversal of the communication process in that the receiver becomes the sender and the sender becomes the receiver. Feedback provides information to the sender about the success of the communication process (Bartol & Martin, 1998), thus it is an important communication skill for the recreation leader.

Effective feedback has several main characteristics (Kaplan, Drath, & Kofodimos, 1984). It focuses on the relevant outcomes of the communication, rather than on the person. It deals with specifics rather than generalities. Perceptions, reactions, and opinions are labeled as such, rather than presented as facts. As well, feedback spells out what individuals can do or cannot do. Upholding these important characteristics is the task of both giving and receiving feedback. Typically we have no difficulty receiving positive feedback. Receiving feedback that is negative is usually more difficult, however. When you are receiving negative feedback, it is useful to paraphrase what is being said (so that you can check your perceptions), ask for clarification and examples, and avoid reacting defensively.

Leisure service organizations have learned that it is important to obtain feedback from clients, customers, and participants—particularly dissatisfied ones. As discovered by many after it is too late, only one dissatisfied client in fifty complains; the rest simply switch to another recreation service provider or product. Yet when a complaint is redressed, not only is the dissatisfied client likely to remain, but others with similar, yet silent, complaints remain as well. As a result park and recreation agencies use a variety of methods to encourage feedback, such as suggestion boxes in centers, 1–800 telephone numbers, or convened focus groups.

COMMUNICATING IN WRITING

As the model of the communication process in figure 6.3 symbolizes, the informational signs are the medium in which the message exists. The signs most often used in our society are oral and written. Let us now look at **written communication**.

First, the recreation leader communicates in writing in many ways during a typical day. As a part of your responsibilities, you may write, for example, copy for a program brochure, a memo to your supervisor, a letter to a colleague, a meeting agenda, an evaluation summary on a special event, a vandalism report, a request and justification for additional funds, a philosophy statement, additions for an operations manual, and a news release. Writing well is an important responsibility for persons in recreation and park leadership situations.

It is important for the leader to recognize that written communication not only represents the individual writer but also reflects on the worth of the sponsoring recreation organization. Thus it is important that your written communication be accurate, complete, and carry the intended meaning.

Effective written communication is hard work. It requires attention to some basic but not so easy to achieve qualities. Good writing does not come naturally. It is a matter of practicing. You learn to write by writing. All writing is ultimately a question of solving a problem. It may be a problem of where to obtain the facts or how to organize the material. It may be a problem of approach, tone, or style. You must learn to use written tools in a way that will achieve the greatest accuracy and the greatest impact. In its truest form, good written communication is not a strategy or a gimmick; it is an honest and clear use of carefully selected and arranged language.

How does this happen? Good written communication is a matter of thinking and writing clearly, developing an appropriate writing style, knowing your audience, achieving unity, looking up corrections, and presenting ideas orderly.

Thinking and Writing Clearly

Clutter is the disease of most written communication. The secret to good writing is to strip every sentence to its cleanest components.

Select words carefully. Eliminate those words that serve no function; convert long words to short words; and use adverbs only when the verb does not carry the same meaning. Short words and short sentences are easier to understand. Get the litter out of your sentence. Say only what needs to be said. Select only those words that most precisely fit what you want to say. Simplify.

The main culprits of uneconomical writing are jargon and wordiness. **Jargon** is the substitution of a euphemistic phrase for a familiar term (e.g., "monetary felt scarcity" for "poverty"). Jargon should be avoided. Furthermore, wordiness is every bit as irritating and wasteful as jargon. It too can impede good written communication. **Wordiness** is the use of several words when one word will do. Use no more words than are necessary to convey the meaning. Embellishment is not writing style; it is bad writing.

To clear your writing of clutter you must clear your head of clutter. Muddy thinkers write muddy communication. Think before you start every sentence; think about every word. This means that you must constantly ask yourself: What am I trying to say? Then you must look at what you have written and ask: Have I said it? All your writing must meet the standard of being clear to someone encountering the subject for the first time. A clearly written memo, letter, or program evaluation report is no accident.

Know Your Audience

Your writing must mirror your reader. Important to good written communication is knowing for whom you are writing. As a recreation leader, you will be writing to numerous audiences. Members of governing boards, supervisors, association officers, participants, the general public, prospective customers, colleagues, volunteers, and fellow staff are different readers and require different writing styles.

Successful writers have the ability to adopt their readers' viewpoint, whatever their writing project. Consider the background of your readers. What can you expect them to know about your subject already? What reading and vocabulary skills can you take for granted? How will they use the information they read?

The types of written communication that you might use in a recreation setting range from memos to grant applications. Doing a good job at these requires using the right style for the purpose you want to achieve and for the audience for whom you are writing. Language and form must match. Your organization may even have standard formats to follow for each purpose and audience.

Unity

Before you begin to write, you must make certain decisions about what tone you want to adopt. This is called the development of unity. It keeps you and your message receivers from straggling off in all directions.

One decision you must make is the choice of pronoun. Are you going to write in the first person (as a participant in the action) or in the third person (as an observer of the action)? Unity of tense is another choice. Sometimes you will write in the past tense, at other times you will write in the present or future tense. What is not permissible is to switch back and forth within the same written piece.

Another choice is mood. Are you going to write in a chatty and casual way, or would it be better to approach the communication with more formality? All tones are acceptable, but select the most useful for your specific purpose and then stick with it.

Look It Up

Good writing is also dependent on good language. You must properly use paragraphs; you must spell correctly; and you must use accurate sentence structure, punctuation, and grammar. Errors in these aspects of writing detract from the message. Errors can create an unfavorable impression that decreases your credibility. Worse, errors in spelling and grammar can cause inaccurate and misunderstood communication.

With attentive practice you can rid your written communication of faulty language, but consulting dictionaries, grammar handbooks, spellers, style manuals, and other references is always good advice. Use a dictionary to check words you are unsure of. Check a handbook on style and usage for punctuation and grammar. To avoid weak verbs such

Basic Outline Formats

The number-letter format

I. Under . . . .
  A. Under . . . .
    1. Under . . . .
      a. Under . . . .
        (1) Under . . . .
          (a) Under . . . .
            i) Under . . . .
            ii) Under . . . .
          (b) Under
        (2) Under . . . .
      b. Under . . . .
    2. Under . . . .
  B. Under . . . .
II. Under

The decimal format

1. Under . . . .
  1.1 Under . . . .
    1.1.1. Under . . . .
      1.1.1.1 Under . . . .
        1.1.1.1.1 Under . . . .
        1.1.1.1.2 Under . . . .
      1.1.1.2 Under . . . .
    1.1.2 Under . . . .
  1.2 Under . . . .
2. Under . . . .

as "Joe runs the ski program," consult a thesaurus for more specific verbs such as "Joe manages the ski program."

Orderly Presentation of Ideas

"Thought units"— whether single words, a sentence, a paragraph, or a longer section— must have order. So that you communicate well, you must aim for a logical flow of words, ideas, and themes. Such continuity can be achieved in many ways.

Perhaps the most useful way is to outline. Writing from an outline helps develop and preserve the logic of what you are communicating. It identifies main ideas, defines subordinate ideas, disciplines your writing, maintains the continuity and pacing, discourages digressions, and points out omissions. Even an outline for a letter is useful. To be of real value, an outline is prepared before the writing begins.

Your working outline may consist of casual jottings, or it may be more formal and consistently developed. You may choose either a topic outline or a sentence outline, depending on your preference. The entries in a topic outline are words, phrases, or clauses; whereas the entries in a sentence outline are complete sentences. You will also need to choose the format for an outline. The two basic formats for an outline are the number-letter sequence and the decimal pattern. The examples in the boxed material above compare these two forms.

ORGANIZATIONAL COMMUNICATION

When communication occurs in groups, such as organizations, recreation leaders need to be able to develop and work productively with communication networks. **Networks**, or communication systems, are the patterns of information flow among group members (Bartol & Martin, 1998). Most typically groups have one of the network structures shown in figure 6.4.

Three of the networks operate as a centralized scheme; that is, most messages flow through a particular person. This could be someone official, such as a director or supervisor, but could also be a popular member of the group. For example, in the wheel

FIGURE 6.4. Common communication networks

	Y	Wheel	Chain
Centralized networks			
	Circle	**Star**	
Decentralized networks			

network, which is the most centralized structure, all messages flow through the person at the center. Two of the networks are considered decentralized structures because messages flow more freely among the various group members. For example, in the star network all members can communicate with any other member.

For relatively simple and routine tasks, the centralized networks are usually faster and more accurate. This is because in each of the centralized networks the person in the central position (marked by an "x" in figure 6.4) becomes the coordinator, thereby enabling the completion of the tasks (Bartol & Martin, 1998). On the other hand, more complex group tasks respond better to the decentralized networks. Under these circumstances the circle or the star communication networks are faster and provide for greater performance in accomplishing the tasks. This is because with complex tasks, the free exchange of information in the circle and the star facilitates the process and encourages creativity (Bartol & Martin, 1998).

Research shows, however, that regardless of the complexity of the group's task, group morale tends to be higher in the decentralized networks (Shaw, 1981). This creates a dilemma for the leader. Which to use? Centralized networks are better for achieving accurate performance on simple tasks, especially under a time restraint. However, morale may suffer. For more complex tasks, decentralized networks provide both high performance and high morale.

Regardless of the communication network, making communication work in groups takes work. The communication principles described throughout this chapter have particular implications for groups. As adapted from Galanes & Brilhart (1997), these are:

1. Making group communication productive is the responsibility of every member. In any organization there is a great tendency to blame others when there are communication problems. If you don't understand something, you should say so. If you can't hear, you should ask the others to talk louder. Everyone must constantly monitor how the communication process is working and correct problems as needed.
2. Perfect understanding among group members is impossible. There are many ways that the communication process can break down or be confusing, thus maintaining a "pure" system of organizational communication is not possible. We all have different words in our vocabularies and different experiences with words, thus we inevitably differ in what meaning we ascribe. Therefore, some difference in

understanding always exists between two or more people. In a group, we need only to communicate well enough to coordinate our actions toward a common goal.

3. Disagreement is not necessarily a sign of a breakdown in group communication. People often say that conflicts could be avoided if people would communicate better. This is not necessarily true. While it is true that some group conflicts are due to misunderstandings resulting from poor communication, many conflicts are the result of differing values, goals, and beliefs among group members. So it is possible for disagreeing persons to understand each other's position. Nonetheless, resolving the conflict calls for hard work and skill by all in the group.

Summary

Recreation leaders dare not neglect the skill of communication. We are in the "people business," so communication is top priority. It is an essential skill in teaching swimming, organizing teams for rugby, decorating the lounge, recruiting volunteers, demonstrating loom weaving, conducting a leisure values clarification discussion, and almost everything else that a recreation leader does. This chapter discusses the dynamic and complex process of communication.

Communication exists for the purpose of conveying, sharing, or processing information in some way. Into the communication relationship all involved persons bring a well-filled life space, containing a unique storage of experiences, against which they interpret and respond to the information signals that come to them. This is ideally a two-way relationship that leads to a clearer understanding.

In conclusion, the recreation leader must be grounded in the following basic understandings:

- Good communicators are made, not born.
- Good communication is the responsibility of both the sender and the receiver.

Case in Point: Lake Area Wellness Council

The Lake Area Wellness Council is a nonprofit organization of people interested in alternatives to traditional Western medicine. Each month, the council sponsors a seminar, open to everyone, where the featured speaker is a practitioner of some form of alternative medicine. The council operates with a small budget and usually relies on volunteers to present the seminars; volunteers are given a token gift, such as a T-shirt with the council's logo. At one meeting of the council's executive committee, committee member Rhea suggested that the group schedule Chief Robert, a Cherokee medicine man, to speak and that the group buy Chief Robert a piece of equipment he needed as compensation for giving the seminar. Members agreed that Chief Robert, a prominent local healer, deserved a substantial gift, but the equipment was expensive ($200) and paying him would set a precedent for future speakers, which the council could not afford. Norm, the chair of the executive committee, said "I don't know how we'll be able to afford something like that, though I agree that he's certainly worth the money," whereupon Rhea said, "Okay, that sounds good to me." At the next council meeting, Sonya reported that publicity for Chief Robert's seminar was proceeding well, and noted how pleased she was that the council had agreed to buy the chief his equipment, and especially how grateful he was for their generosity. At that point, the meeting exploded into cries of "What? What do you mean pay him? We didn't agree to pay him!" Committee members had misunderstood each other, and as a result Rhea had obligated them to a $200 gift that would come close to wiping out their funds.

- Good communication requires effort and hard work.
- Degrees of good communication vary.
- Participation in the communication process is a means to an end and an end in itself.
- Breakdowns in communication are inevitable but solvable.

Questions and Activities for Review and Discussion

1. How would you define communication?
2. Consider the case on p. 131. What went wrong in this situation? Based on the material presented in the chapter, what recommendations would you make for avoiding such problems?
3. What role does a person's life space have in the communication process?
4. Develop a topic outline, using the number-letter sequence, for a fictional newsletter to the summer part-time workers for a beach resort. Or locate a need for written material for an organization and write the outline for this.
5. Write a brief self-evaluation of your current competency in the four types of oral communication. Discuss with colleagues or friends ways in which you might practice those types in which you need more work.
6. Define nonverbal communication. What is its role in the total communication process for the recreation leader?
7. In your opinion based on your experience, what is the appropriate role of touching in a recreation leader's communication? What should it be in working with nursing home patients? Children at camp? Participants in a folk dance club? Coed intramural volleyball at a college? Discuss these roles with other class members.
8. What are the main ingredients of good listening? What specific things do you need to practice to improve your own listening effectiveness?
9. Table 6.1 is a list of nonverbal communication behaviors. Pick a day on which you will pay attention to these and the messages they indicate. At the end of the day think back and record how you responded to each of these messages. If it helps, think of specific people who used these and record how you responded to them. Also identify those messages that had the greatest and least effect on your behavior.
10. Outline the major types of centralized and decentralized group communication networks. Explain the conditions under which each type is likely to result in the best performance.

TABLE 6.1. Nonverbal communication behaviors

Behavior	What Was the Message?	How Did You Respond?	How Did It Affect Your Behavior?
Handshake	----	----	----
Facial expressions	----	----	----
Voice tones	----	----	----
Voice volume	----	----	----
Smiles	----	----	----
Eye expressions	----	----	----
Posture	----	----	----
Stance	----	----	----
Distance	----	----	----

References

Andersen, K. E. (1972). *Introduction to communication: Theory and practice*. Menlo Park, CA: Cummings Publishing.

Bartol, K. M., & Martin, D. C. (1998). *Management* (3rd ed.). New York: McGraw-Hill.

Baskin, O. W., & Aronoff, C. E. (1980). *Interpersonal communication in organizations*. Santa Monica, CA: Scott, Foresman.

Bass, B. M. (1990). *Bass & Stogdill's handbook of leadership: Theory, research, and managerial applications* (3rd ed.). New York: The Free Press.

Brooks, D., & Emmert, P. (1980). *Interpersonal communication*. Dubuque, IA.: W. C. Brown.

Cohen, A. R., Fink, S. L., Gadon, H., & Willits, R. D. (1980). *Effective behavior in organizations: Learning from the interplay of cases, concepts, and student experiences*. Homewood, IL: Richard D. Irwin.

Galanes, G. J., & Brilhart, J. K. (1997). *Communicating in groups: Applications and skills*. Boston, MA: McGraw-Hill.

Henley, N. M. (1977). *Body Politics: Power, sex and nonverbal communication*. Englewood Cliffs, NJ: Prentice-Hall.

Heslin, R., & Patterson, M. L. (1982). *Nonverbal behavior and social psychology*. New York: Plenum Publishing.

Kaplan, R. E., Drath, W. H., & Kofodimos, J. R. (1984, August). Power and getting criticism. *Center for Creative Leadership Issues and Observations*, 1–8.

Knapp, M. L. (1980). *Essentials of nonverbal communication*. New York: Holt, Rinehart & Winston.

Kraus, R. G., Carpenter, G., & Bates, B. J. (1981). *Recreation leadership and supervision: Guidelines for professional development*. Philadelphia: Saunders College Publishing.

Schramm, W., & Porter, W. E. (1982). *Men, women, messages, and media: Understanding human communication*. New York: Harper & Row.

Shaw, M. E. (1981). *Group dynamics: The psychology of small group behavior*. New York: McGraw-Hill.

Walsh, E. (1982). Listen here. *Parks and Recreation, 17*(7): 38–39.

Web Resources

Communication (general): www.csuchico.edu/cmas/webpages/whatcom.htm

Interpersonal communication: www.mediachallenge.com/products/interp.htm
www.ndirect.co.uk/~cultsock/MUHome/cshtml/psy/db self.htm
www.coled.mankato.msus.edu/dept/labdist/mentor/interpersonal/index.a
www.lewisu.edu/~culleema/tsld073.htr

Interpersonal communication exercise:
http://phil.winona.msus.edu/lorihw/Assign/perceptioncheck.htm

Nonverbal communication internet links: http://zen.sund.ac.uk/~hb5jma/lstbersn.htm

Oral communication: http://144.16.72.150/~raja/teaching/oral.htm

Oral presentations: www.commerce.concordia.ca/COMM212/howoral.htm

Persuasion: www.trinity.edu/~mkearl/prsuasn.htm
www.21bet.cin/shared/shop/rdawson/shopday persua.htm

Verbal and nonverbal communication: www.artoftravel.com/02communication.htm

CHAPTER 7

Leading Change and Innovation

"I take this world and my city and all that therein is and has come to pass, as I find it, and although it be a good city as cities go, I do my best to make it go better, as an abiding place for its people."
—**Charles Doell, 1979.**

Learning Objectives

At no time since the Industrial Revolution has the world faced so many opportunities. Yet, the world's greatest resource, the mind, still goes untapped. Imagination, conceptual thinking, and creative ability are the cerebral skills recreation leaders need to practice and advocate.

In this chapter, you will learn:

- innovative change
- innovative organizational change
- innovative change leadership
- managing resistance to change

Key Terms

change p. 135
innovation p. 135
uncertainty p. 135
knowledge-intensive p. 135
controversial p. 136
crossing organizational boundaries p. 136
external forces p. 136
internal forces p. 136
creative thinking p. 136
mental blocks p. 137
germinal phase p. 138
practical phase p. 138
groupthink p. 140
alignment p. 142
self-initiated activity p. 142
unofficial activity p. 143
serendipity p. 144
diverse stimuli p. 144
within-organization communication p. 144
self-interest p. 148
misunderstanding and lack of trust p. 148
different assessments p. 148
low tolerance for change p. 148
education and communication p. 149
participation and involvement p. 149
facilitation and support p. 149
negotiation and agreement p. 149
explicit and implicit coercion p. 149

A recent issue of a management magazine (reported in Smith, 1997) outlined major challenges to today's leaders. At the top of the list was how to manage change. Contemporary challenges require a new style of leadership. This new leader is a change agent—someone who creates an environment that unleashes the natural creativity and potential of others (Smith, 1997). As a change agent, the new leader removes barriers and obstacles built up over years of bureaucracy in an organization. The new leader provides direction and looks out for the needs of people. In this chapter we discuss what it takes to be a new leader. First, let's look at the nature of change and innovation.

THINKING CREATIVELY ABOUT CHANGE AND INNOVATION

When Dr. Rene Laennec was looking for a way to help him diagnose the health of his patients, what incident provided the inspiration for his invention of the stethoscope?

__ Children sending signals to each other by tapping on either end of a log?
__ A medical colleague chewing his lunch loudly with his mouth wide open?
__ A woodpecker pecking on a tree outside the hospital?

Rudolf Diesel got the idea for the design of his diesel engine from looking at

__ a typewriter.
__ a daVinci drawing of the human lungs.
__ an Aztec spear.

For Dr. Laennec it was children playing at sending signals to each other by tapping on a log, and for Diesel it was an Aztec spear. For both, such inspiration led to significant inventions that changed the course of human history. In this section our goal is to clarify what we mean by change and innovation and to think about the essential ingredient to both—creative thinking.

Distinguishing Change and Innovation

In considering more closely the concepts of change and innovation, we first must distinguish between them. **Change** is any alteration of the status quo. On the other hand, innovation is a more specialized kind of change. **Innovation** is a new idea applied to initiating or improving a process or service (Kanter, 1983). All innovations imply change, but not all changes are innovations because some types of changes may not involve new ideas or lead to significant improvements in a service or organization. For example, a change to a landscape is produced from a tornado, but it is certainly not an innovation for those in the tornado's path.

Innovations in recreation organizations can range from radical new breakthroughs (such as registering city softball teams via the Internet) to small, incremental improvements (such as extending the softball registration deadline by one day). Both types of innovations can be useful.

Innovation's Characteristics and Forces

Innovation in recreation organizations encompasses a combination of characteristics (Kanter, 1983; Bartol & Martin, 1998). For one thing, innovation involves considerable **uncertainty**, because progress and success outcomes may be difficult to predict. For another, the process tends to be **knowledge-intensive** in that those close to the development of the innovation may possess most of the knowledge about the situation, at least during the early stages. A third characteristic is that the innovation process is typically

controversial, because innovation requires resources that some may not be willing to allocate or reallocate. Finally, the innovation process often **crosses organizational boundaries** because the implementation of innovation often involves more than one unit within the organization. This makes it a complex effort. The point is, therefore, that because of these characteristics, leaders need to understand how change and innovation are accomplished and plan purposively for managing them. Increasingly, greater pressure for constituents and clients, as well as wider and more global forces, mandate that the recreation organization be nimble and proactive.

A variety of forces influence change and innovation in recreation organizations. Some of these forces are external, while others arise internally. **External forces** for change and innovation on organizations can include such things as environmental forces (the effects of a hurricane on a coastal state park system) and increased government regulatory pressures (new insurance coverage laws for high-risk recreation services companies). As well, upgraded national agency accreditation standards might force a city recreation organization to change and innovate. So, while some external forces may pressure organizations to change in ways that are less than desirable, such forces often do open opportunities for applications of innovative ideas (Haveman, 1992).

Internal forces for change and innovation develop from a variety of sources. Some of these include organizational leadership shifts, reorganizations, and technological advances. For instance, a new emphasis on quality of services as inspired by the faculty advisory council for the college student union is an internal force for change and innovation. Many internal forces ultimately can be traced to external factors (the new emphasis on quality of services might be motivated by upgraded accreditation standards), yet some internal forces are inherent within the organization as it naturally develops through its life cycle.

Leader Profile: The Past
Mel Miller (1961)
He worked his way up from professional clown to circus publicist to the curator of the Ringling Museum of the Circus at Sarasota, Florida. As a form of entertainment, the circus has based its success on innovation.

Nature of Creative Thinking

But, even with all this said about characteristics of and forces for change and innovation—what is the kind of thinking required here? It is called creative thinking. **Creative thinking** requires an attitude or outlook that allows you to search for ideas and manipulate your knowledge and experience (von Oech, 1983). With this outlook, you try various approaches, first one, then another. You use crazy ideas as stepping-stones to practical new ideas. You break the rules occasionally, and hunt for ideas in unusual places. In creative thinking you open yourself up to both new possibilities and to change.

Exercise: Naming a New Soft Drink

Suppose a major soft drink company has asked you to name a new sugar-free soft drink that will soon be marketed around the world. There are many ways to come up with possible names, but try this one:

In either order, combine one of the word roots on the left side with one of the beverage-specific words on the right. Form at least ten names for the new soft drink.

The left side:		*The right side:*	
dec	hemi	ade	ola
aero	oid	pop	sip
quas	ix	soda	nutr
tri	digi	vim	swig
equ	plus	x-tra	gulp
max	visi	flow	drink
ast	dyna	squirt	cool
nutra	tex	pep	wet

Nutragulp, Vimplus, and so on. You get the idea!

Creative thinking is transforming one idea into another. By changing perspective and playing with our knowledge and experience, we can make the ordinary extraordinary and the unusual common place. It is a discovery process—the discovery that comes from looking at the same thing as everyone else and thinking something different. Why don't we "think something different" more often? There are two reasons. First, we don't need to be creative for most of what we do (von Oech, 1983). We don't need to be creative when we fill our car with gas, eat lunch, ride an elevator, or wait in the cashier's line at the grocery store. Most of our daily lives are filled with routines. These routines are important to us. Without them our lives would be too chaotic. But, too much reliance on them retards our ability to generate new ways to accomplish our goals. Second, we are restricted in thinking differently by mental blocks. **Mental blocks** are our belief systems that keep us thinking in ways of sameness rather than differentness. There are many sources of mental blocks; here are ten (von Oech, 1983):

1. *The right answer.* One source of mental block is, unfortunately, our system of education. We are taught from the earliest of ages to look for the one right answer. By the time the average person finishes college, she will have taken over 2,600 tests, quizzes, and exams for which she was rewarded (or punished) for getting the right answers (von Oech, 1983, p. 21). While this may be fine for some information and problems of learning, it is not a useful way of thinking and learning for everyday life. Life is much more ambiguous; there are many right answers. It depends on the situation and what you want and need. If you think there is only one right answer, then you will stop looking for the other right answers. This is a mental block to creativity.
2. *To err is wrong.* We are taught to try to always be right. From an early age we are taught that right answers are good and wrong answers are bad. Adhering too often to "to err is wrong" can undermine your ability to generate new ideas. Errors are useful to creative thinking in three ways:
   - Serve as stepping-stones to another new idea. The whole history of invention is filled with people who used failed ideas as stepping-stones to new ideas. Remember Columbus who thought he was finding a shorter route to India?
   - Tell us when to change direction. When things are going smoothly, we usually don't think about them. It is only when things begin to fail that they get our attention. Negative feedback means that the current direction or approach is not working and we need to figure out a new one.
   - Trial and error is a fundamental tool for progress. The rate of making errors is a function of familiarity with that activity. If you are doing things that have no history in your experience, then you will be making mistakes. Only when you leave

Case in Point: The Chalk Dot

One day my college instructor put a small chalk dot like the one here on the board. *

She asked us what it was. A few seconds passed and then someone said, "A chalk dot on the board." We were all relieved that the right answer had been provided, and no one else had anything more to say. "My how you've changed," she said. "Yesterday I asked a group of children and they thought of fifty different things that this could be: an owl's eye, a cigar butt, the top of a telephone pole, a star, a rock, a squashed bug, a rotten egg."

(from von Oech, 1983, p. 22)

that which is familiar, and thus make mistakes, will you improve your performance as a recreation leader.

3. *That's not logical.* To understand this mental block we first have to distinguish between two main phases in the development of new ideas: a germinal phase and a practical phase (von Oech, 1983). In the **germinal phase**, ideas are generated and manipulated; in the **practical phase**, generated ideas are evaluated and executed. Both types of thinking play an important role in the creative process, yet logical thinking is a necessary tool for only the practical phase of carrying out new ideas. Logical thinking in the germinal phase can prematurely narrow your thinking of good ideas. Thinking "that's not logical" to ideas developed early in the creative process is a mental block.
4. *Follow the rules.* Suppose you have the following list:

   painted eggs

   fireworks

   champagne

   candy canes

   shamrocks

   jack-o'-lanterns

   More than likely, you quickly recognized the pattern in this list. These are all symbols of American holidays. You were able to notice what the items in this list had in common because the human mind is good at searching for patterns. Much of what we call "intelligence" is our ability to recognize patterns (von Oech, 1983). We see patterns everywhere—even in the clouds and stars. Finding patterns is important because it helps us understand the world around us. Patterns become the rules by which we live. But seeing only the obvious patterns is not useful to us in creative thinking. Creative thinking is not only constructive, it's also destructive. This means that we break out of one pattern to create a new one. Thus, challenging the rules is an effective creative thinking strategy.

Case in Point: The Keyboard

QWERTYUIOP

Do you recognize this configuration of letters? I know you have seen this pattern many times. It is the top row of letters on your computer keyboard.

Back in the 1870s, Sholes & Co., the leading manufacturer of typewriters at the time, received many complaints from users about the typewriter keys sticking together if the typist went too fast. In response, top management asked its engineers to figure out a way to fix the keyboard to prevent the sticking of the keys. The engineers discussed the problem until one of them said, "What if we slowed the typist down instead? If we did that, the keys wouldn't jam together nearly as much. So, how can we slow the typist down?" One answer was to have an inefficient keyboard configuration. For example, the letters "A" and "O" are the first and third most frequently used letters in the English alphabet, and yet the engineers positioned them on the keyboard so that the relative weaker ring and little fingers had to depress them. Check it out! This logic was a brilliant idea that solved the problem. It involved breaking the pattern of lining up the letters in alphabetical order.

(from von Oech, 1983, p. 51)

5. *Be practical.* Always seeking practical solutions to problems is a mental block to creative thinking too. A fun way to practice not being practical is to ask yourself a series of "what if" questions. For example, what if gravity stopped for one second every day? Or, what if human life expectancy was two-hundred years? What if everybody in your organization played a musical instrument, and you had a jam session every Friday afternoon? The key to asking "what if" is allowing you to probe the impossible. While impossible ideas are not always creative, they are often provocative in stimulating us to think about other ideas. The value of impractical ideas is where they lead your thinking. While it is unlikely that any given "what if" answer will produce a useful creative idea, a few eventually will. How many "what if" questions did Einstein ask before he invented the concept of relativity? He eventually got one good idea that he probably wouldn't have gotten had he stayed in the practical realm. Practicality alone will not generate new ideas. You need to break this mental block.
6. *Avoid ambiguity.* An ambiguous situation is one that can be interpreted in more than one way. Most people don't like ambiguous situations. They're confusing and they cause communication problems. As a result, people try to avoid ambiguity. This is a good idea for most everyday situations, such as giving instructions, documenting programs, or drawing up contracts. In these situations it is important to be clear, precise, and specific in order to be accurate. There are other situations, however, when ambiguity can be a powerful stimulant to your creative thinking. Too much specificity can stifle your imagination. What if a recreation leader asked a group of teens to paint a mural on the side of the community center? What might be the result? What if the teens are told exactly what the mural is to look like right down to the last detail? Might the resulting mural be different? There is a place for ambiguity when you are searching for new ideas.
7. *Play is frivolous.* Play is one of the major avenues through which people develop. Some people, however, think that if you're playing at something, then you're not working on it. They see work and play as two mutually exclusive spheres. But what is missed in this perspective is that one of play's outcomes—fun—is one of the most powerful motivators around. People who are having fun in their work will come up with more ideas.

Exercise: Where do you hunt for ideas?

Where do you hunt for ideas? What people, places, activities, and situations outside of your usual stomping grounds do you use? Check those that apply to you and give an example of each.

- ☐ Magic =
- ☐ Vacations and trips =
- ☐ Junk yards =
- ☐ Walking through the mall =
- ☐ People who are different =
- ☐ Listening to music =
- ☐ Browsing titles at a bookstore =
- ☐ Flea markets =
- ☐ Magazines =
- ☐ Sports =
- ☐ Want ads =
- ☐ Meetings I'm not supposed to attend =
- ☐ Reading at a shallow level
- ☐ Other ____________________

8. *That's not my area.* It is one thing to be open to new ideas; it's another to actively hunt for them. In this hunt you will often want to search outside your area. Specialization is a fact of modern life. For example, our occupations have become more narrowed. Succeeding often means that we have limited our field of view. Yet when you are trying to generate new ideas, such narrowness can be troublesome. To counteract this mental block, make it a habit to keep on the lookout for ideas that others in other areas or fields have used successfully. Your idea will be original in its adaptation to the problem you are working on.
9. *Don't be foolish.* Conformity serves at least two practical purposes. First, to live in a society requires cooperation among its members. Second, in many situations we can find out what to do by looking around and noticing how others are behaving. New ideas, however, are not produced in a conforming environment. Pressure to be like everyone else can inhibit originality. When everyone thinks alike, no one is doing much thinking. We discussed this in an earlier chapter as **groupthink**. All creative thinkers have to overcome conformity and groupthink. But how? One idea is the device used by royalty in the Renaissance (von Oech, 1983). The king's advisers were often "yes-people"—they told the king whatever he wanted to hear. The king knew this wasn't always useful in making decisions so he kept a fool on hand. It was the fool's job to parody any proposal under discussion. The fool's jokes whacked the king's thinking and forced him to examine his assumptions. In this way, the king protected himself from conformity and groupthink and could make better decisions.
10. *I'm not creative.* Let's discuss this mental block through an exercise and a parable (von Oech, 1983).

    Exercise: Are you creative? (check the appropriate box)

    ☐ yes ☐ no

    Parable: Once upon a time, two frogs fell into a bucket of cream. The first frog, seeing that there was no way to get any footing in the white liquid, accepted his fate and drowned. The second frog was unhappy with his plight so started thrashing around in the cream and doing whatever he could to stay afloat. After a while, all of his churning turned the cream into butter, and he was able to hop out.

    The moral of both the exercise and the parable is that if you think you are creative then you will be creative. What you think has a way of becoming true. If you want to be more creative, believe in the worth of your ideas, and have the persistence to continue to work on them.

FRAMEWORK FOR AN INNOVATIVE ORGANIZATION ENVIRONMENT

While it is fun to learn about and practice creative thinking, there is a desperately serious purpose to it. Cutting-edge technology, a burgeoning global economy, and ever persistent and novel social problems all feed into an environment that is fast changing. To survive, incremental improvements by an organization are not enough. Dramatic change is often necessary. No organization can sit on its laurels. The days of secure niches for a state park system or a summer resort, supported by government protection, geographic location, or weak competition, are gone. To add to the ever-changing dilemmas, there are growing complexities in organizations. Fewer are designed around neatly defined functions. Instead, a web of joint ventures and alliances characterize many organizational charts (Conger, Spreitzer & Lawler, 1999).

Thus, it is important that recreation, park, sport, and tourism organizations are able to change in innovative ways. To do this there must be an environment for creative change within the organization. By adapting the ideas on how this can be done from the arena of corporate creativity, we learn that managing creative change in an organization is about raising probabilities (Robinson & Stern, 1997). While the organization cannot know where specific efforts at creative change by employees will come from or what they will be, they can take action to increase the frequency with which creative changes occur. Following are some of the elements needed for an organizational environment that increases the probability for creative change (Robinson & Stern, 1997).

Leader Profile: The Past
Jane Addams
Founder of The Hull House, Chicago, Illinois. Study the story of the Hull House to learn of Jane's ability to develop and communicate a vision for an organization.

Alignment

The first element, **alignment**, is about ensuring that the interests and actions of all staff are directed toward an organization's key goals so that any staff member will recognize and respond positively to a potentially useful idea. Organizations can function with poor alignment, but they cannot be consistently and wholeheartedly creative unless they are strongly aligned. Solid organizational alignment is difficult to achieve, yet when it exists, it affects how everyone in the organization makes decisions, big and small (Robinson & Stern, 1997, p. 122).

Case in Point: Disney and the Pirates

There is a wonderful anecdote about Walt Disney that illustrates several of his unique strategies for creativity. Just before opening the Pirates of the Caribbean ride at Disneyland, Disney was touring the ride and felt strangely dissatisfied. He felt that something was missing, but couldn't put his finger on it. He gathered as many employees as he could find—including the maintenance and food service personnel—and asked them questions.

"Does it look right?" he asked. Yes, the costumes and shrubbery were authentic, and the buildings had been copied from the New Orleans French Quarter.

"Does it sound right?" The latest in audio equipment had been installed to accurately reproduce the sounds of music, voices, boats, and even the animals of the Caribbean.

"Does it feel right?" Disney engineers had controlled the temperature and humidity to exactly match that of a sultry Caribbean night.

"Does it smell right?" An elaborate smell-producing system had been created that could combine the smells of Cajun food with gunpowder, and moss.

The ride looked, sounded, felt, and smelled right. Yet something was still missing. "What is it?" Disney asked.

Finally, one of the young men who had been sweeping the floors said, "Well, Mr. Disney, I grew up in the South, and what strikes me is that on a summer night like this there ought to be lightning bugs." That was it! Disney had live lightning bugs shipped in until he could figure out a way to imitate them mechanically.

Attention to detail? Following your intuition? Integrating diverse points of view? Getting the best out of your people? Using all of the senses? Breaking large tasks down into smaller manageable pieces? Adopting the view of "the other"? Disney was an innovation role model.

(from Mattimore, 1994)

Strong alignment in an organization requires three things:

1. Clarity about the key goals of the organization. For creative change to come from any staff member, an organization has to ensure that all staff members are clear about what the organization stands for.
2. Commitment to initiatives that promote the key goals. For creative change to come from any staff member, an organization has to ensure that all staff members are deeply committed to its key goals.
3. Accountability for actions that affect the key goals. Organizations must hold their staff and managers accountable for decisions that affect the organization's key goals. Corrective action has to be taken when these decisions are out of alignment.

Self-Initiated Activity

The second element, **self-initiated activity**, describes an organizational climate where a single staff member is permitted—even encouraged—to pick a problem, come up with an idea for its solution, and make it happen. It allows staff to own ideas that might be possible, take hold of them, and make them work. This means that staff intrinsic motivation is much higher than it would be if the project had been planned or picked for them by someone else. People have a natural drive to explore—a drive that leads them to initiate new activity (Koestler, 1964). While organizations can plan for change, this takes the organization only in the direction it has already anticipated. What about leading the organization into unanticipated places? Unexpected creative change—the ones organizations tend to ignore—will result only from self-initiated activity.

It is rather straightforward to promote self-initiated activity in an organization. The desire to be creative is already present in most people, so the organization only has to unleash it. All that is needed is an effective system for responding to staff ideas (Robinson & Stern, 1997):

1. The system must reach everyone. There is no way to predict who will be involved in a self-initiated creative change effort, therefore everyone in the organization must know about the system for contributing ideas and have ready access to it.
2. The system must be easy to use. Few staff members will participate in a system for contributing ideas if it is difficult to use.
3. The system must have strong follow-through. Few people will send in ideas to a system that does not give them immediate and serious attention.
4. The system must document ideas. Good systems require that employees write down their ideas and that records are kept of what happens to them. The reason for this is accountability. Also the act of putting ideas down on paper forces people to clarify their thinking.
5. The system must be based on intrinsic motivation. In general, the less an organization uses rewards and recognition, the greater its creativity will be.

Unofficial Activity

Unofficial activity is activity that occurs in the absence of direct official support and with the intent of doing something new and useful. Every unanticipated creative change begins with a period of unofficial activity, when it is worked on without direct and official support. Sometimes this unofficial period lasts for minutes and sometimes it can last for years. When an idea is new to an organization, it is often resisted and opposed. Unofficial activity gives ideas a safe haven where they have the chance to develop until they are strong enough to overcome that resistance. Giving an idea official status can raise barriers that might kill it prematurely. Unless an organization makes the space for unofficial activity, it cannot be receptive to unanticipated new and useful ideas.

It is important, therefore, for an organization to legitimize unofficial activity, so that official activity does not squeeze it out. Essentially, this is accomplished by getting the message out that the organization wants everyone on the staff to work unofficially when an opportunity arises to do something new and potentially useful. For example,

1. Establish a policy that specifies the portion of time staff should spend on unofficial activity. It needs to be a large enough portion to carry the message that unofficial activity is worth paying attention to. Some organizations have found that 15 percent is about right.
2. Allow organizational supplies and equipment to be used for unofficial activity.
3. When internal publications (such as newsletters) describe the good work of employees, they should also stress the role that unofficial activity played.

Serendipity

The fourth element in creating an organizational climate for creative change is serendipity. A **serendipitous** discovery is one made "by a fortunate accident in the presence of keenness of insight" (Robinson & Stern, 1997, p. 14). Such fortunate accidents arise when people interact with each other and their work, and take notice of the significance of the combination. Think of it as ideas bumping into each other—ideas that in the beginning don't have anything in common, realizing this only later. Serendipity can be promoted through organizational strategies that provoke and exploit accidents:

1. Increase the frequency of accidents that could turn out to be fortunate by creating a bias for tinkering and experimenting.

Case in Point: The U.S. Forest Service

In 1985 the Department of Agriculture criticized the U.S. Forest Service for its lack of creativity and bureaucratic ways. This prompted them to formulate a new "people-oriented" management philosophy, aimed at fostering innovation. One of the first initiatives under this new philosophy in the Eastern Region of the organization was to reinvent the suggestion system. The old system had required employees to fill out a four-page form. In the previous four years, the Eastern Region's twenty-five hundred employees had sent in only 252 ideas, a rate amounting to one idea from each employee every forty years. Now, the revamped system required only a simple form, which employees could fill out on their computers and submit locally or e-mail directly to the regional office. One other change in the suggestion system attested to the new commitment. If an idea was submitted and the suggester received no response within thirty days, then as long as the idea did not break any laws and fell within the Forest Service's domain of activity, it was automatically approved and had to be immediately implemented. There were no rewards given for ideas that were approved (only a silver sticker with a picture of a skunk on it with its tail down; rejected ideas also got skunk stickers—with the tail up). Almost at once came a rush of new ideas. Over the next three years, the Eastern Region received more than twelve thousand ideas, of which about 75 percent were implemented.

(from McKenna, 1993)

2. Increase awareness of the accidents that do occur; don't overlook the exceptions.
3. Encourage staff to learn about subjects and skills not directly related to their work by going to conferences where they are not making a presentation and by taking study leaves or sabbaticals.

Diverse Stimuli

The fifth element needed by organizations able to make creative changes is **diverse stimuli**. A stimulus may provide fresh insight into something a person has already set out to do, or it may bump that person into something different. While most stimuli arise in connection with daily life or with the work itself, it is important for an organization to provide opportunities for its staff to at least tell others about the diverse stimuli they have received and the possibilities these stimuli suggest to them.

While organizations should do everything they can to identify and provide diverse stimuli to their staff, it should be recognized that such efforts will have relatively little impact (Robinson & Stern, 1997). Programs of visiting lecturers, libraries, and newsletters may well stimulate new thinking, and will certainly create a positive climate for creative change, but most will not lead to an improvement or an innovation. This is because it is impossible to predict how anyone will react to a particular stimulus. Another may not even notice what inspires one person. Here's how organizations might increase opportunities through diverse stimuli:

1. Identify stimuli and provide them to staff (guest lectures, special events, libraries, interesting newsletters, study or sabbatical leaves, etc.).
2. Rotate staff into every job they are capable of doing; often they notice stimuli that others before them had not.
3. Arrange for opportunities for staff to bring into the organization stimuli they get on their own. This means that you must create regular opportunities for staff to bring up ideas for informal discussion even when the ideas have no bearing on anything else under consideration.

Within-Organization Communication

The final element is within-organization communication. Unanticipated **within-organization communication** seems to happen naturally in smaller organizations but not so automatically at larger ones. Every organization carries out planned activities, and communication channels are necessary for these activities. But it is the unanticipated exchanges between staff who normally do not communicate with each other that often enable projects that have to be planned to self-organize and move forward. Here are some strategies for accomplishing this:

1. Provide opportunities to meet for persons on the staff who do not usually interact with each other. Plan joint meetings or retreats across divisions; take trips to visit other sites.
2. Ensure that every staff member has a sufficient understanding of the organization's activities to be able to tap its resources and expertise.
3. Create an organizational priority that stresses the importance of being responsive to requests for information or help from other staff.

Recreation leaders will be more effective in bringing about change and innovation for their organizations and the services they provide if they follow the process outlined in figure 7.1. To manage creative change the leader follows these eight basic steps (Kotter, 1999):

FIGURE 7.1. Steps to leading change and innovation

1. Recognize an opportunity or problem –>
2. Line up a powerful coalition –>
3. Develop and communicate a vision –>
4. Empower others to act on the vision –>
5. Plan for and create short-term wins –>
6. Prepare to overcome resistance –>
7. Facilitate more change –>
8. Institutionalize changes –>

Identify a Problem or Opportunity

Most change and innovation begins when someone identifies a problem or opportunity. Making major (and in some cases minor) changes in any organization requires a leader who sees the need for change. This means that major change often occurs best when there is a new leader. Without a new leader, a great leader, or other change champions in the recreation organization, this first step will be a huge challenge. Additionally, there needs to be something to change. It is usually easier to recognize problems when things aren't going well. But true innovative leaders are able to make change when there do not appear to be any immediate and urgent problems to solve. Noted management consultant Peter Drucker argues there is a tendency to focus on immediate problems and to ignore opportunities. To help overcome this, Drucker recommends that leaders and their staff report to each other at meetings not only what is not going well, but also what is succeeding, which others might adopt too (Drucker, 1985).

However, even when change is inspired by opportunities, the leader must at this first step establish a sense of urgency for the change. Crises, potential crises, and great opportunities that are timely must be communicated vigorously, otherwise people won't be motivated to help with the change. When is the sense of urgency high enough? From my experience, the answer is when about 75 percent of the organization's staff are convinced that the current situation is unacceptable.

Line Up a Powerful Coalition

Change and innovation do not usually occur without the full commitment of individuals who are powerful enough to influence others to support the new approach. Likewise the support of those responsible for the resources needed to enable the change must be secured. In actuality most change programs start with just one or two people. When the transformation of the organization or service is successful, it is because these few people have also been successful in growing a leadership coalition around the change program. In the most successful cases, the coalition is always pretty powerful in terms of titles, information and expertise, reputations, and relationships.

Because this coalition usually includes members who are not part of the senior management, by definition it tends to operate outside the normal organizational hierarchy. This is a good thing. While at times this can create awkwardness, this kind of coalition is necessary because if the existing hierarchy was working well, there would be no need for change. Nonetheless a sense of urgency within the senior management levels helps enormously in putting a guiding coalition together. But when it comes right down to it, someone needs to get these people together, help them develop a shared assessment of their organization's problems and opportunities, and create a supportive level of trust and communication. Off-site retreats for two or three days are one popular vehicle for accomplishing this task.

Leader Profile: The Present
Christopher K. Jarvi
President of the National Recreation and Park Association (NRPA), 1998–1999. Jarvi led NRPA's comprehensive self-assessment and futures design program that resulted in "Vision 2000"—NRPA's strategic plan.

Develop and Communicate a Vision

To bring about change and innovation, it is important to be able to develop a picture of the future that is easy to communicate and has appeal to those who must change or support change. A vision goes beyond the statistics typically reported in strategic plans. A vision says something that helps clarify the direction in which a recreation organization or service needs to move. Sometimes the first draft of the vision comes from a single individual. It is typically blurry. But after the coalition works at it for three, five, or even twelve months, something that is much better emerges through their combined thinking and dreaming.

Without a central vision, a change effort can easily dissolve into a list of confusing and incompatible projects that can take the organization in the wrong direction or nowhere. In a failed change program you often find plenty of plans and directives, but no vision. A useful rule of thumb: if you can't communicate the vision to someone in five minutes or less and get a reaction that signifies understanding and interest, you are not yet ready to move on to the next step.

Empower Others to Act on the Vision

Leaders need to embolden staff and service clients to take actions in behalf of the vision. This step is what the previous section was devoted to—creating an organizational climate for change. Staff and clients are encouraged to try new approaches, to develop new ideas, and to provide leadership. The only constraint is that their actions fit within the broad parameters of the overall vision. The more people involved, the better the outcome.

Leaders also need to remove obstacles that preclude staff and clients from doing so. Sometimes the obstacle is the organizational structure. For example, narrow job categories can seriously undermine efforts to make innovative changes. Sometimes a compensation or performance-appraisal system makes people choose between the new vision and their own self-interest. Perhaps the worst, are leaders who refuse to change. At this stage of a major change, no organization has the momentum, power, or time to get rid of all obstacles. But the big ones must be confronted and removed. If the blocker is a person, it is important that he be treated fairly and in a way that is consistent with appropriate personnel policies. But action is essential to empower others and to maintain the credibility of the change effort.

Plan for and Create Short-Term Wins

Major changes and innovations can take time, risking that those involved will lose focus or give up. One way of maintaining the momentum is to include some projects or phases that are likely to be successful within a short time, such as several months. As these successes are realized it is important to provide celebrations, recognition, and other rewards that keep the focus on the vision. Most people won't join a lengthy change process unless they see compelling evidence within twelve months that the effort is producing the expected results. Without short-term wins, too many people give up or actively join the ranks of those people who have been resisting the change.

Creating short-term wins is different from hoping for short-term wins. The former is active. To be successful as an innovative change manager, recreation leaders must actively look for ways to obtain clear recreation service improvements or achieved organizational objectives. For example, suppose the guiding coalition in a fitness center operation developed a highly visible and successful new fitness service for corporate executives. The new service had the short-term win advantages of: launched within one month, relatively low cost, production of sizable new revenues, use of existing staff and other resources, and minimal resistance by the governing board.

Prepare to Overcome Resistance

Just because you decide to make a change in a recreation service or organization, or even that a group (even top management) supports a change, does not mean that others will readily go along with it. Resistance to change is inevitable so you must purposively prepare how you will manage it. Until changes sink deeply into your organization's culture, a process that can take many years, new approaches are fragile and subject to erosion. Later in this chapter an entire section is devoted to managing resistance to change.

Facilitate More Change

When you are feeling victorious in the changes and innovations you have made, it is too easy to stop and sit back on your laurels. It is tempting to declare victory with the first clear indications of service or organizational improvements. But it is the premature victory celebration that kills the momentum. Then the powerful forces associated with tradition retake the territory.

Instead of declaring victory too soon, leaders of successful efforts use the credibility afforded by short-term wins to tackle even bigger problems. This is sort of a round two in the innovation effort. It moves more deeply—to changing basic systems, structures and policies that don't fit the vision. For a recreation organization this means hiring, promoting, and developing staff who can implement the vision. It also means reinvigorating the process with new projects, themes, and change agents.

Institutionalize Changes

The final step in the innovation process is to institutionalize the new approaches. Unfortunately, strides toward innovation can reverse themselves quickly unless they become part of the organization's culture. There are two factors that are particularly important in institutionalizing change. The first is articulating the connections of the changes with service or organizational success. This means that you purposively show people how the new approaches, behaviors, and attitudes have helped improve performance. This requires lots of communication. One way to do this is to spend time at every staff meeting discussing why things are improving. The second factor important to establishing changes in the organization's culture is making sure that the next generation of upper-management leaders endorses the new approaches. An overnight change in leadership can wipe out years of hard work.

MANAGING RESISTANCE TO CHANGE

One of the reasons an entire chapter has been devoted to leading creative change is that it is difficult to do, in large part because people are often resistant. Sometimes people oppose a change even when it appears to others that the change is in the best interests of those affected. Anthropological research has concluded that groups (such as organizations) naturally resist change, and sociological and psychological theories underscore that groups particularly hate change that's forced on them (O'Toole, 1995).

Why are people so against change? Although we could list many reasons, a few of the major ones follow (Kotter & Schlesinger, 1979). One reason is **self-interest**. When people hear about an upcoming change, they have a natural and first tendency to ask how the change will affect them. If a person perceives the answer to be "adversely," the person will resist the change. Another reason for resisting change is **misunderstanding and lack of trust**. People are usually against change when they don't understand it. As well, low levels of trust between employees and management can contribute to misunderstanding a change. Resistance can result as well from **different assessments** of the benefits of a change. Because innovations in particular involve new concepts, their value is not always obvious to others. A final reason is **low tolerance for change**. People differ in their ability to adjust to new situations. Some fear that they will not be able to learn the new skills or perform the new behaviors a change might entail.

There are several methods that leaders can adopt to help overcome at least some of the resistance to change (Kotter & Schlesinger, 1979). One technique for overcoming

Case in Point: The Wet-Tongued Napkin

Several years ago Henry Arias and Denise Heimrich founded their Chicago-based company Thinking Heads to invent and license new toys and games. They went out to lunch one day, and in a playful mood, Denise, as a child might, picked up a paper napkin and stuck her wet tongue through it at her partner. She started laughing, but her partner Henry suggested, "We might have something here." For some time they had been trying to invent a very low cost, simple action game for young kids. Until Denise put her tongue through the napkin, they had been coming up somewhat dry. Her childlike spontaneity was the creative spark that inspired them to invent the successful game Thin Ice. Thin Ice is ingeniously simple. Kids spread a tissue over a raised platform to form the "ice." Below the "ice" is a water-filled reservoir with marbles in it. Kids pick up the wet marbles with "ice tongs" and place them, one by one, on the tissue. The first kid to add the marble that "breaks through the thin ice" loses.

(from Mattimore, 1994)

resistance to change is **education and communication**. This means the leader provides adequate information and makes sure that the change is clearly communicated to those it will affect. Another way to help people overcome their resistance to change is **participation and involvement**. Resistance tends to lessen when the people who will be affected by a change are allowed to participate in planning and implementing it. Typically leaders tend to underuse participation as a means of overcoming resistance to change. The use of **facilitation and support** might also be useful to overcoming change resistance. When people react to impending changes with fear and anxiety, encouragement and help from the leader often lower their resistance. Other ways to provide facilitation and support are through training and the provision of the proper equipment and materials.

Negotiation and agreement is another approach to reducing resistance to change. Negotiation can be a particularly useful strategy when a group perceives that it will be hurt by the change and is in a position to cause the change initiative to fail. If other strategies, such as participation and education, fail, it may be necessary to negotiate in order to gain support for the change program. Finally, **explicit and implicit coercion** might be tried to overcome resistance to change. This involves the direct or indirect use of power to pressure those who resist the change to join. Tactics such as threatening loss of job, promotion, pay, recommendations, and so forth are examples. With coercion individuals may be fired or transferred. The fallout, of course, is that the recipients of the pressure will be resentful even if they succumb. It can also backfire if the coercion escalates the resistance. Even with these dangers, if a change is relatively unpopular but must be implemented quickly, a leader may be forced to use this strategy. Use it as a last resort.

Summary

Contemporary challenges require a new style of leadership. This new leader is a change agent—someone who envisions better ways of doing things and creates an organizational environment that unleashes the creativity of staff and constituents to accomplish them. In this chapter we discussed what it takes to be a change agent.

The subject was first introduced by distinguishing change as any alteration from the status quo and innovation as a type of change that improves a process or service. Innovation in recreation organizations is sparked by both external and internal forces and can be characterized as uncertainty, knowledge-intensity, controversial, and crossing organizational boundaries. These become a dynamic medium for leading creative change, but what really fuels it is the creative thinking of the organization's leaders, staff, and constituents.

In becoming a creative thinker mental blocks that are grounded in our belief systems must be overcome. These mental blocks include these admonishments: the right answer, to err is wrong, that's not logical, follow the rules, be practical, avoid ambiguity, play is frivolous, that's not my area, don't be foolish, and I'm not creative.

In being a change agent a recreation leader has essentially two responsibilities. First, is establishing a framework for an innovative organizational environment. Techniques for accomplishing this are ensuring that the interests and actions of the staff are aligned with the organization's key goals and permitting staff to self-initiate problem solutions, unofficially tinker with new ideas, and take advantage of serendipity. Also, you'll need to regularly expose staff to diverse external stimuli and provide opportunities for staff to communicate informally.

As a change agent your second responsibility is to lead innovative change. To accomplish this we studied an eight-step process:

1. identify a problem or opportunity
2. line up a powerful coalition
3. develop and communicate a vision
4. empower others to act on the vision
5. plan for and create short-term wins
6. prepare to overcome resistance
7. facilitate more change
8. institutionalize changes

Finally, in the chapter special focus was devoted to managing resistance to change. Leading creative innovation is difficult because people are often resistant. Their reasons include self-interest, misunderstanding and lack of trust, different assessments of the benefits of a change, and low tolerance for change. To help remedy resistance such methods as education and communication, participation and involvement, facilitation and support, negotiation and agreement, and explicit and implicit coercion were advocated.

Questions and Activities for Review and Discussion

1. When was the last time you came up with a creative idea? This morning? Yesterday? Last week? Last month? Last year? What was it? What inspires you to be creative?

2. What is your creative thinking style? Answer these questions to determine:

   a. How frequently do you ask "what if" questions or use impractical ideas as stepping-stones to practical new ones?
      __ never __ seldom __ sometimes __ often

   b. How frequently do you question assumptions, challenge the rules, or discard obsolete ideas?
      __ never __ seldom __ sometimes __ often

   c. How frequently do you use soft-thinking tools such as the metaphor and ambiguity to generate ideas?
      __ never __ seldom __ sometimes __ often

   d. How frequently do you hunt for ideas in outside areas?
      __ never __ seldom __ sometimes __ often

   e. How frequently do you break up potential "groupthink" situations?
      __ never __ seldom __ sometimes __ often

3. What is the difference between change and innovation? What is the recreation leader's responsibility for innovation?

4. Interview a leader in a recreation organization in your town. Use as the outline for your interview the framework for an innovative organizational environment discussed in the chapter. Find out how supported the leader you interview feels in proposing new ways of doing things in that organization. Ask him or her to elaborate on what could be done to feel even more supported in this.

5. As a group assignment, develop a case example for a recreation organization of interest that illustrates the eight steps in bringing about innovation. The case can be either factual or fictional.

References

Bartol, K. M., & Martin, D. C. (1998). *Management* (3rd ed.). Boston, MA: McGraw-Hill.

Conger, J. A., Spreitzer, G. M., & Lawler, E. E. (eds.). (1999). *The leader's change handbook: An essential guide to setting direction and taking action*. San Francisco: Jossey-Bass.

Doell, C. E., & Twardzik, L. F. (1979). *Elements of Park and Recreation Administration.* (4th ed.). Minneapolis, MN: Burgess.

Drucker, P. F. (1985, April 29, vol. 182). A prescription for entrepreneurial management. *Industry Week*, 33–34.

Haveman, H. A. (1992). Between a rock and a hard place: Organizational change and performance under conditions of fundamental environmental transformation. *Administrative Science Quarterly, 37*, 48–75.

Kanter, R. M. (1983). *The change masters*. New York: Simon and Schuster.

Koestler, A. (1964). *The act of creation*. London: Penguin Books.

Kotter, J. P. (1999). Leading change: The eight steps to transformation. In J. A. Conger, G. M. Spreitzer, & E. E. Lawler (eds.), *The leader's change handbook: An essential guide to setting direction and taking action*. San Francisco: Jossey-Bass.

Kotter, J. P., & Schlesinger, L. A. (1979, March-April, vol. 56). Choosing strategies for change. *Harvard Business Review*, 106–114.

Mattimore, B. W. (1994). *99% inspiration: Tips, tales, & techniques for liberating your business creativity*. New York: Amacom: American Management Association.

McKenna, J. F. (1993, April 5, vol. 191). Empowerment thins a forest of bureaucracy. *Industry Week*, 64.

O'Toole, J. (1995). *Leading change: Overcoming the ideology of comfort and the tyranny of custom.* San Francisco: Jossey-Bass.

Robinson, A. G., & Stern, S. (1997). *Corporate creativity: How innovation and improvement actually happen.* San Francisco: Berrett-Koehler.

Smith, G. P. (1997). *The new leader: Bringing creativity and innovation to the workplace.* Delray Beach, FL: St. Lucie Press.

von Oech, R. (1983). *A whack on the side of the head: How to unlock your mind for innovation.* New York: Warner Books.

Web Resources

About Peter Drucker: www.forbes.com/forbes/97/0310/5905122a.htm
www.theatlantic.com/unbound/bookauth/jb6.htm
www.pathfinder.com/fortune/1998/980928/dru.html

American Recreation Coalition: www.funoutdoors.com

Barriers to change: www.well.com/user/bbear/psych.html

Center for Creativity and Innovation: www.uccs.edu~creative/index.html

Change and organizational development:
www.onu.edu/user/FS/mgovekar/Crs2Mat/333C16/index.htm

Change resources: http://cor-ex.com/sites/bestchng/Sites/Chane-Sites.htm

Creative management: www.bemorecreative.com/cm/index.html

Creative thinking skills: www.tiac.net/users/seeker/creathink.html

Creativity and what blocks it: www.deoxy.org/creative.htm

Creativity Journal: www.erlbaum.com/977.htm

Innovation and recreation: www.seattletraders.com/outdoors.htm

Innovation Network: www.thinksmart.com/

Leading organizational change: www.lionhrt.com/loc.html

Organizational change and stress management:
http://mars.wnec.edu/~achelte/ob1/lprob17/index.htm

Organizational change, innovation, & stress:
http://voltaire.is.tcu.edu/~stephens/teaching/mana3153/Change/index.htm

Peter F. Drucker Foundation for Nonprofit Management: www.pfdf.org

Resources for creativity and Innovation: www.ozemail.com/au/~caveman/creative/

Technical Museum of Innovation: www.thetech.org/

Walt Disney Imagineering: www.opengroup.com/open/stbooks/078686246.shtml
www.character-shop.com/anmtrnfx.html
www.disney.com/investors/annual97/imaginee.htm

CHAPTER 8

Participant Motivation

The urban problems of Dade County were taking their toll. For example, an estimated 3,000 to 5,000 youth and young adults aged 11–24 were involved in over 80 active gangs. Of these individuals, 91 percent had prior arrest records and 80 percent were high school dropouts. An alarmingly high 94 percent reported that they were bored, with nowhere to go and nothing to do.

—Witt & Crompton, 1996, p. 72.

Learning Objectives

An important proficiency for recreation leaders is energizing, giving direction, and helping sustain behavior. For the direct service leader, the focus is on recreation behavior. For the top management and supervisory leaders, the focus is on the work behaviors of the organization's staff. To achieve both recreational and organizational goals, individuals must be sufficiently stimulated and willing to commit their energy to realize their aim. In this chapter we explore this through the concept of motivation. You will learn about:

- the nature of motivation
- how to harness intrinsic motivation
- other motivation strategies

Key Terms

primary motives p. 154
secondary motives p. 154
motivation p. 154
direction of effort p. 154
intensity of effort p. 154
motivation process p. 155
Maslow's hierarchy of needs p. 156
goal-setting theory p. 156
behaviorism p. 156
intrinsic motivation p. 157
extrinsic motivation p. 157
situational and personal factors p. 158
multiple motives p. 159
competing motives p. 159
unique motives p. 159
motives change p. 160
leaders influence motivation p. 160
readiness p. 161
environmental stimulus p. 161
status p. 161
planned progression p. 161
competition p. 162
peer pressure p. 162
prizes and rewards p. 163
behavior modification p. 163

Somewhere in the Cascades the elderly man and woman move slowly along the trail upward toward the notch in the ridge. At 8,000 feet, their progress is labored. Their packs are heavy and their clothes sweat-drenched. At the crest, they slip out from under their loads and lean back against a rock.

Three hundred miles away the ten-year-old kills twenty more aliens on his video game with a measured and confident force of vengeance. Behind, in the garage, his mother with matching measure and confidence bends over a table saw and carefully cuts the oak board. Soon it will be ready as the last piece in the coffee table she has been working on all year.

Meanwhile, downtown, the director of the city park and recreation department interviews the sixth candidate today for the position of coordinator of the summer arts-in-the-parks program.

All of these situations illustrate behavior. Three are recreation behaviors, and one is work behavior. Why do these people behave in these ways?

One of the more basic questions for all time has been, "What determines the way in which people act?" Two people stand on the edge of the shore—one goes into the water for a swim, the other remains on shore to sunbathe. Why? The study of motivation is the study of the causes of human behavior. The concept of motivation usually refers to those factors or motives that initiate, sustain, and stop behavior.

Usually we distinguish between primary and secondary motives. **Primary motives** are concerned mainly with physiological drives such as hunger, thirst, sleep, pain avoidance, and so forth. These motives are thought to be innate. **Secondary motives**, on the other hand, reflect social demands on the individual and include the need for affiliation, recognition, autonomy, acceptance, and dominance. These motives are thought to be learned. However, all motives may be modified by learning. For instance, money may become a valued and learned goal if an individual is motivated to obtain money because it helps him satisfy either primary or secondary motives.

In this chapter, we explore the basic nature of motivation, drawing a distinction between intrinsic and extrinsic motivation. Further, we consider specific strategies useful to the recreation leader for inspiring both the recreation behaviors of clients and constituents and the work behaviors of recreation organization staff.

THE NATURE OF MOTIVATION

Motivation is a psychological explanation of why we behave in the ways we do. It helps us understand why we go out on Saturday night instead of doing the laundry or why we study after midnight instead of going to bed. Motivation is any internal condition within us that appears to produce our goal-directed behavior. Whether it is motivating a volleyball player to "give 110 percent" or a client to stay with a rehabilitation program, motivation is critical to the success of recreation professionals. Frequently it is not a technical knowledge of leadership, but the ability to motivate people that separate the good recreation leaders from the average ones.

Defining Motivation

A simple way to define **motivation** is as the direction and intensity of one's effort (Weinberg & Gould, 1995). The **direction of effort** refers to whether an individual seeks out, approaches, or is attracted to certain situations. For example, the elderly couple we glimpsed on the rock ledge is attracted to mountain wilderness environments, and the ten-year-old seeks out video games. **Intensity of effort** means how much effort a person puts forth in a particular situation. For instance, the ten-year-old plays video games with a "vengeance." While for our discussion it is useful to separate the direction from the intensity of effort, for most people direction and intensity of effort are linked (Weinberg & Gould, 1995). That is, it is possible for two people to be attracted to the same activity, but approach their participation with widely differing intensities. Take playing golf, for example. Two people could play a round of golf together and one may want to make a winning putt so badly that she tightens up and misses the shot. Meanwhile the other approaches the endeavor more casually and with a lazy swing of the club makes the lucky break on the green and sinks the putt. As a result, the intense golfer who lost the round may feel less attracted to the game and the casual golfer who won may feel more attracted to it. And so it goes in a symbiotic relationship between motivation intensity and direction.

The Motivation Process

Because motivation is something within a person, we cannot measure the motivation of others directly. Instead, we typically guess whether an individual is motivated by watching her behavior. But our guess is not a wild one. As the result of a great deal of research, guessing about people's motivation can be based on an understanding of the major motivational theories. In a nutshell, there are three categories of theories: need, cognitive, and reinforcement. When combined these three theoretical perspectives can be labeled the motivation process.

Leader Profile: The Present
Girls on Wagon Train Sesquicentennial of the Mormon Trail. People are motivated differently for different forms of leisure. Leaders must understand participant motivation for a wide array of leisure expressions.

To state it another way, the **motivation process** is composed of three main elements. These are shown in figure 8.1. As the diagram indicates, our inner needs (such as for food, friendship, and self-fulfillment) and our cognitions (such as knowledge and thoughts about efforts that we might expend and rewards that we might receive) lead to various behaviors. Assuming that the behaviors are appropriate to the situation, they may result in rewards. These rewards in turn help reinforce our behaviors by fulfilling our needs and confirming our knowledge. The process can also work in reverse. A lack of rewards may lead to unfulfilled needs, leave behaviors unreinforced, and influence our thinking about where not to expend our efforts in the future (Bartol & Martin, 1998).

In support of each of these three elements of the motivation process, there are numerous theories. For example, need theories argue that we behave the way we do because of internal needs we are attempting to fulfill. Need theories include Maslow's hierarchy of needs, Herzberg's two-factor theory, the ERG theory, and the acquired-needs theory. What these theories have in common is that the fulfillment of higher-level

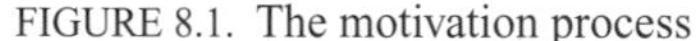
FIGURE 8.1. The motivation process

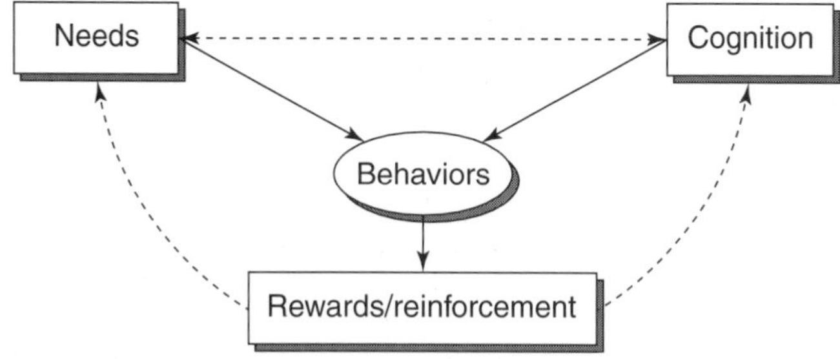

FIGURE 8.2. Maslow's hierarchy of needs

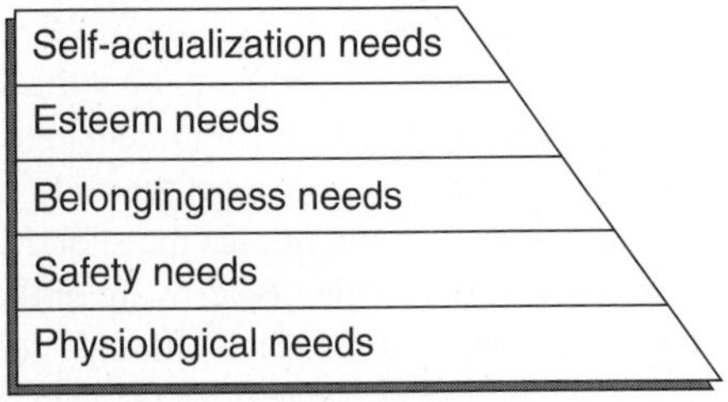

needs is an important source of motivation. To illustrate this point, let's review **Maslow's hierarchy of needs** (figure 8.2).

According to this hierarchy, our first need is for survival so we concentrate on basic physiological needs such as food, water, and shelter. Next, we concern ourselves with safety needs—those that help us feel secure and free from threats. Once survival and safety needs have been met, we can turn our attention to relationships with others in order to fulfill our need for belonging. Here we try to satisfy our desire to affiliate with and be accepted by others. Once achieved we are able to focus on esteem needs, such as the desire to have a positive self-image and to have our contributions valued and appreciated by others. Finally, we reach the highest level, self-actualization needs. Here we are concerned for testing our creativity, seeing our ideas implemented, developing our talents, and trying new things.

Need theories, such as Maslow's hierarchy, try to identify the internal desires that influence our behavior, but they do not explain how we think about and rationalize our behavior. This is the point of the cognitive element in the motivation process and there are also numerous theories that support this. Cognitive theories attempt to isolate the thinking patterns that we use in deciding whether to behave in a certain way (Bartol & Martin, 1998). Some of the cognitive theories are expectancy, equity, and goal setting.

To illustrate, the basis of the **goal-setting theory** is that setting goals is motivating because it directs our attention and action, increases our persistence, and encourages us to figure out ways to achieve the goals. Feedback on how well we achieved our goals is also an essential element (Locke & Latham, 1990). According to the theory, some goals are better motivators than others. For maximum motivation the goals participants and employees set for themselves should be specific, challenging, attainable, relevant, and achievable within a defined period. Also, those goals in which we are more committed and attached to will provide more motivation for our behavior. We are more likely to be committed to attaining a goal when we have high expectations of success in reaching it and truly value the rewards that accompany reaching it. The usefulness of goal setting in enhancing motivation has strong research support. Therefore, recreation leaders are likely to find it a helpful tool.

Finally, the motivation process of reinforcement also has theoretical support. Noted psychologist B. F. Skinner developed the idea of a reinforcing approach to motivation, which he labeled **behaviorism**. Opposite of the cognitive theories, in behaviorism an individual's thought processes have nothing to do with shaping behavior. According to the reinforcement theories, our behavior can be explained by consequences in the environment. Behaviors having pleasant or positive consequences are more likely to be repeated and behaviors having unpleasant or negative consequences are less likely to be repeated.

Exercise: Positive Reinforcement

Positive reinforcement can be a powerful motivator. Rank order from most important (with a "1") to least important (with a "10") the potential of the following positive reinforcements for you in an employment situation. Afterwards, compare your results with other class members and discuss the differences.

- ☐ monthly pay check
- ☐ pay check every two weeks
- ☐ a free trip for two after achieving a major goal
- ☐ the organization's president stopping by your office several times every month to let you know your efforts are appreciated
- ☐ certificate and pin for twenty-five years of service
- ☐ monthly perfect attendance award
- ☐ refreshment break every morning and afternoon
- ☐ baseball tickets given to employees for achieving particular goals
- ☐ your supervisor brings in doughnuts an average of every two or three weeks to treat everyone in the office
- ☐ a feature article about the success of one of your projects in the organization's newsletter

In the reinforcement process, a stimulus provides a cue for a response or behavior that is then followed by a consequence (Bartol & Martin, 1998). If we find the consequence rewarding, we are more likely to repeat the behavior when the same stimulus occurs later. If we do not find it rewarding, we are less likely to repeat the behavior. For example, assume that you are the manager of the campus student union. One day the student government president asks for your help in developing a proposal to the state legislature for increased funding for student activity services (the stimulus). You say you will, pull some of your staff from other priorities, and stay late to produce the proposal report (the behavior). Throughout the next weeks while the proposal is being considered, the student body president and other officers continually recognize you and your staff for your efforts (consequence). As a result, are you likely to put extra effort into helping the student government in the future? Probably, you will because the positive consequences from your behavior will reinforce a repeat of this behavior. The motivation strategy of behavior modification that is discussed later in the chapter relies on the concept of reinforcement.

INTRINSIC AND EXTRINSIC MOTIVATION

Another way of conceptualizing motivation is to say there are two broad classes: intrinsic and extrinsic motivation. **Intrinsic motivation** means that the behavior itself is rewarding. It is not pursued primarily for some other benefit. Intrinsic motivation comes from within the individual. Ideally, all recreation activity participation should be intrinsically motivated. Many writers such as Levy (1978) and Iso-Ahola (1982) maintain that the experience can only be considered recreational if it is intrinsically motivated. As Iso-Ahola explains, the participant chooses the recreation activity with the expectation that the activity will be successful. This promotes a sense of intrinsic reward—a feeling of freedom of choice and competence.

Extrinsic motivation is that which comes from the outside. The reward is established artificially. The motivation is created by these rewards. External motivators give no direct satisfaction at the time the behavior is performed. The principle behind using extrinsic motivation is that the individual is given a reward in the belief that this will cause the person to behave in a certain way.

Many people in leadership roles in the recreation and park fields put emphasis on extrinsic motivators. "Win that prize" is a common message coming across to many participants, and "earn that salary raise" is the common motivator to many employees. The recreation leader is perhaps most knowledgeable about extrinsic motivation. We should, however, also be concerned with intrinsic motivation. Typically the extrinsic reasons for participating in recreation or doing a good job are not as enduring or long lasting as the intrinsic reasons.

Leader Profile: The Past
Edgar C. Lindgren
Former Senior Gardener, Los Angeles City Recreation Department.
Lindgren's many years of service to the gardens remind us of the leader qualities of dedication and commitment.

Let's consider some examples of this in the area of sports by looking at how competitive success and failure can affect intrinsic motivation. We tend to focus on who won or lost a sport competition. This is the objective outcome of the contest. But the subjective outcome from competition is also important. We can lose at a particular competition but still feel terrific because we think we played well against a superior opponent, or the flip side is that we can win but be disappointed in playing poorly against a weak opponent. Thus the perceived or subjective outcome from sport competition is more likely to influence intrinsic motivation.

Usually people who perceive that they performed well show higher levels of intrinsic motivation than those with lower perceptions of success (McAuley & Tammen, 1989). To illustrate, by manipulating players' perceived success and failure on a motor task one group of researchers noted that people have higher levels of intrinsic motivation after success than after failure (Weinberg & Gould, 1995). As well, a study on young hockey players performing a balance task also showed that positive feedback from adults increased feelings of competence, which in turn increased intrinsic motivation, whereas the reverse proved true for negative feedback (Vallerand & Reid, 1984).

Case in Point: The Intrinsic Motivation of Recreation

At Original Copy Centers, Inc., a corporate and legal copy service in Cleveland, Ohio, the intrinsic motivation of recreation is used to motivate the more than 145 employees. The workers perform relatively mundane and repetitious tasks, such as operating copy machines and delivering materials. Noting that the average age of employees was under thirty and that many were single, owners Nancy Vetrone and Robert Bieniek came up with a well-appreciated reason to come to work. At the center they installed a laundry room, a six-person sauna, locker rooms and showers, a minitheater, a video library, a game room with a billiards table, an exercise room, computers for employee use, various arcade games, a kitchen, and free coffee.

(from Bartol & Martin, 1998)

MANAGING MOTIVATION

There are some fundamental guidelines for leaders in building motivation in recreation activity participants and organizational staff.

1. When trying to enhance motivation, consider both **situational and personal factors**. Often when leaders work with clients or staff who seem to lack motivation, they immediately attribute the cause to be the person's lack of personal character-

istics: "These kids don't care about learning the rules of the game." At other times problems in the situation are singularly blamed for poor motivation: "This activity must be boring." In reality, low motivation is usually the result of a combination of personal and situational factors (Weinberg & Gould, 1995). Both personal and situational factors interact to cause people to lack motivation. The key for the leader is to focus on both factors and either change both or make a change in the easier one.

2. Realize that people have **multiple motives** for involvement. People participate in a particular activity usually for more than one reason. For example, you might lift weights because you want to tone your body and also because your friends are avid weight lifters and you enjoy the camaraderie. There is a great deal of research on the motives for involvement in various activities. For example, from studies on exercise participation, the major motives cited include (Wankel, 1980):

   For beginning an exercise program: Improve poor health
   Weight loss
   Fitness
   Self-challenge
   Feel better

   For continuing an exercise program: Enjoyment of program
   Leadership
   Activity type
   Social enjoyment

3. As well, people often have **competing motives** for involvement. Tonight you might want to both lift weights at a fitness club and study for tomorrow's exam. There aren't enough hours in the evening to do both, so which will you choose? As a recreation leader you will need to be aware of such conflicting interests as they can have an important influence on participation.
4. Another guideline to remember is that people have **unique motives**. Motives for recreation participation vary greatly and can be unique to each individual (Weinberg & Gould, 1995). For example, in addition to the more typical motives for exercise listed, there are also some rather idiosyncratic ones discovered by research, such as extra attention, critical comments from others, achieving control of mind over body, and habit (Gauron, 1984).

Case in Point: The Coaching of Vince Lombardi

Experienced sport coaches have known about athletes' unique motives for participating for years. Legendary football coach Vince Lombardi, for example, structured his coaching environment to meet individual athlete needs (Kramer & Schaap, 1968). With one player—all-pro guard Jerry Kramer—Lombardi was constantly on his back. Kramer claims that Lombardi always yelled at him. (But Lombardi would also provide some positive reinforcement just when Kramer was discouraged enough to quit.) For all-pro quarterback Bart Starr, who was not as thick-skinned as Kramer, Lombardi treated him much more positively. Lombardi understood that these two players' different personalities and needs required a coaching environment flexible enough for both.

5. Next, **motives change** over time. The recreation leader should remain alert and monitor motives for participation. A motivation for participation in recreation is not static, but can be altered as a result of the participation. Notice, for example, that from the list of exercise motives, motives for staying with a program are different from those that motivated participation in the first place.
6. Finally, **leaders influence motivation**. This guideline is perhaps the most important. The rationale for this chapter is that as a recreation leader you have a critical role in influencing participant motivation. At times your influence may be indirect and you might not even recognize the importance of your actions. For example, a playground leader who is energetic and enthusiastic about the games will, based on this kind of personality alone, influence the participants' interest in playing them. On the other hand, on the day the playground leader has a headache and is not as bubbly, participants will likely be less motivated to play the games.

Increasing Intrinsic Motivation

Ideally, recreation leaders seek to encourage particular recreation behaviors by increasing intrinsic motivation. Based on our earlier discussion on the importance of perceived success in intrinsic motivation, this means the leader works to increase perceptions of success in participants. Here are some suggestions for creating perceptions of success (based on Weinberg & Gould, 1995):

1. *Provide for successful experiences.* For example, lowering the basket for young basketball players or traveling to higher class whitewater rivers for experienced boaters will more likely lead to successful experiences with basketball and kayaking, which in turn will more likely increase intrinsic motivation for participating in these activities. Even in instructional classes or practice sessions, leaders need to watch for creating successful experiences. For example, an exercise class can get tedious and boring unless the leader varies the content, pace, and sequence of the exercises. The point is that you and the participants set realistic performance goals. Performance goals based on a personal level of performance (e.g., to improve your time in the mile run by five seconds) leave participants in control of their experience and make success more likely.
2. *Use verbal and nonverbal praise.* Leaders and managers sometimes forget how powerful praise can be. Praise provides positive feedback and helps participants (and employees) continue to strive to improve. This is especially important for participants who are "second string" or not particularly skilled in an activity and get little recognition otherwise.
3. *Involve participants in decision making.* Allow participants and staff members more responsibility for making decisions. This will increase their perception of control and lead to feelings of personal accomplishment. Let the youth baseball players organize a practice session, encourage those working on a quilt at the convalescent center to determine the recipient of the finished quilt. People perceive that they have greater competency when they are active in the decision-making process. This, in turn, increases intrinsic motivation.

Other Motivation Strategies for the Recreation Leader

Recreation behavior, like all behavior, is purposeful and goal directed. Yet, uniquely, recreation behavior is chiefly motivated by the rewards inherent in the experience. It is more often engaged in for its own sake rather than for a secondary reward. Many theorists view recreation behavior as intrinsically motivated because of its ability to meet certain needs such as enjoyment, belonging, achievement, and relaxation.

There are circumstances in recreation, however, where initial participation or involvement must also be externally encouraged. At least at first, recreation leaders may need to employ those techniques that have been found useful in energizing or motivating people for participation. For instance, the members of the Junior High Spanish Club have arrived for the dance and the band has begun playing. Yet no one is dancing. What can the leader do to help encourage the club members to dance? Or a middle-aged male patient in the cardiac unit of the hospital has been unresponsive to the therapeutic recreation program that is offered. When asked, he claims he is not interested in doing anything, but he always watches the other patients during their participation. Can the leader help encourage this patient to join in? Or a park nature center has extremely poor attendance at programmed activities for older adults. Not enough people attend the programs to make them worthwhile. Yet the older adults in the community continue to complain that there is nothing for them at the nature center. What can the leader do to solve this? It is toward the resolution of these and other similar situations that the following motivational techniques are suggested.

1. **Readiness.** People are often involved and committed to a particular recreation pursuit because they are interested, excited, driven, or ready. Your task as the recreation leader is to take people who are on the brink of active involvement and accurately determine their interest or ripeness for a particular activity. It can be a matter of combining the right people with the right recreation. This means that you must first know who your participants are and what their interests and needs are.
2. **Environmental stimulus**. If you lead people to a polluted pond, you will have to push them in to get them to swim. If you lead them to a crystal clear, cool, and calm sweet water spring, they will probably waste no time at diving in head first on a hot summer day. The physical properties of the environment in which the recreation activity takes place can produce an almost automatic motivational response. Consider the lighting at a dance. No one would brightly light up the gymnasium like a holiday living room and wonder why people do not get up and dance.

   The environment can indeed affect the participant's motivation for a recreation experience. Set the atmosphere, set the "stage"—create a feeling for the behavior expected by the way you arrange the room, the way you set the intensity and color of the lighting or the volume on the stereo, the decorations you choose, and the way you hang them.
3. **Status**. Participants in recreation can be motivated by the status of the activity. It has something to do with the human need to belong and to be recognized. We constantly adorn ourselves with the symbols, badges, and uniforms of our recreation. We do this because by associating ourselves with an activity that we feel impresses the people whose positive opinion we desire, we will increase our stature with these people. Many recreation activities require distinctive equipment such as surfboards, skis, dancer warmup leggings, jogging suits, and others. Because of the motivating influence to participate that can be caused by status, recreation leaders are able to put this to use. Badges, membership cards, mugs, uniforms, patches, T-shirts, well-maintained equipment, and other symbols can serve as motivators to participation.
4. **Planned progression.** Historically, planned progression systems have served recreation leaders rather well as motivators. The merit badge system has been a

useful motivational technique for Scout leaders for many years. When planned progression is used as a motivator, a hierarchy of ranks or titles, each a little more difficult to attain or achieve, is presented to participants as a way to mark their involvement or progress in a recreation activity. This approach to motivation could be considered a form of structured growth—step-by-step growth that can be tangibly observed by the participant. Some common examples include A, B, and C teams in sports; all-league, all-city, all-state, and all-nation athletes; first, second, and third seats in orchestras; beginner, intermediate, and advanced swimmers; and white, brown, and black belts in karate.

5. **Competition.** Well-planned and well-controlled competition can serve as a participation motivator. Competition has the capacity to create artificial yet exciting challenges that make participation interesting and unpredictable. Competition runs throughout our lives, and people should be prepared to face it and respond to it. Yet the recreation program is not the place to condition people for life's competition. It should be used by the leader as an interest builder, adding zest to experiences, not as an end in itself.

   It takes trained, insightful, sensitive leaders to keep competition from becoming demotivating. If not handled well, competition loses its motivational potential. You may find the following guidelines to be helpful in appropriately using the motivational potential of competition:

   - Analyze individual personalities with special attention to stress thresholds in activities in which competition is used.
   - See that the reinforcements provided are not only for winning but for effort, performance, sportsmanship, and cooperation.
   - Adjust the competitive situation so that participants strive against those with equal ability, thereby making competition more satisfactory to both losers and winners.
   - Distribute the possibility of winning. The more classes or plateaus separating the abilities for competition the better, as long as sufficient numbers exist to create a meaningful contest.
   - Avoid working only with the skilled few.
   - Handicap those who have achieved mastery and championship status, or they will drop out.
   - Arrange the program so that, despite the necessity of a winner in competition, many can experience success. One approach is to expand the number of winners. This can be done by finding other achievements to recognize besides the total on the scoreboard.

   The best approach to using competition is to provide a broad program of recreation experiences where there are equal opportunities to select from both competitive and cooperative activities.

6. **Peer pressure.** Recognize and employ the power of peer pressure as a motivator to recreation participation. The human need to be a part of the group, to interact with and be accepted by the others can be a strong factor in energizing people to join in the fun. Identify those persons within your group who are the extraverts, who are popular, and use them as the starter people—the "snowballers." Once the act of participation by a peer member happens, those persons who are borderline holdouts will begin to join in and there is a chain reaction. Peer pressure is a motivator in much the same way as announcing, "Limited seating available!"

7. **Prizes and rewards.** Blue ribbons, door prizes, gold stars, free gifts, coupons, and certificates are examples of the motivational power of extrinsic reward. Extrinsic rewards are a crutch—but a useful crutch in some leadership situations—when the intrinsic rewards of the activity are not adequate. The major danger of extrinsic rewards is that they will replace an interest in the activity with an interest in the award. So as with competition, the use of awards as motivation must be handled with care and expertise. The best advice is to keep the award directly associated with the activity such as by engraving an inscription about the event on the award. This will help to keep the emphasis on the activity rather than the award.
8. **Behavior modification.** Sometimes people are motivated to participate in recreation for the wrong reasons. For example, I once conducted a volleyball program for young prison inmates who were motivated to play hard in order to inflict injury on their opponents. As well, sometimes people have weak motives for participation in recreation. For example, a cardiac rehabilitation patient beginning a fitness program under doctor's orders may not really care about the health outcomes from the program. Thus it is sometimes necessary for the recreation leader to use behavior modification techniques to change undesirable motives and strengthen weak motives. Behavioral techniques can produce positive change in a variety of behaviors. *Behavior modification* techniques are behavioral interventions based on the concept of reinforcement. Usually these steps are followed (Weinberg & Gould, 1995):
   - Target the behaviors—Identify a couple of specific behaviors to work with, such as trying to hurt others in volleyball.
   - Define targeted behaviors—Try to define behaviors in a way that makes them readily observable and easy to record. For example, number of times the volleyball hits someone, number of jogged laps, craft class attendance, and so on. People need to know specifically what behaviors are expected of them so they can modify their behavior accordingly.
   - Record the behaviors—Record defined behaviors on a checklist to give participants feedback.
   - Provide meaningful feedback—Detailed feedback will enhance motivation. If a participant can see a simple set of checkmarks or stars on an easy-to-read graph that clearly displays his progress, it encourages praise, attention, and knowledge of improvement that helps in motivation. Public display of this feedback can also stimulate peer interaction that could possibly reinforce the desired behavior.
   - State the outcomes clearly—Behavior modification requires that participants are clear on what behaviors are expected and what will be the result of their performing or not performing these behaviors.
   - Tailor the reward system—Rewards given to participants who perform the expected behaviors should be appropriately matched. The larger the behavioral change, the larger the reward and vice versa.

Summary

An important proficiency for recreation leaders at all levels is energizing, giving direction to, and helping sustain behavior. For the direct service leader the focus is on recreation behavior. For the top management and supervisory leaders the focus is on the work behaviors of the organization's staff. To achieve both recreational and organizational goals, individuals must be sufficiently stimulated and willing to commit their energy to realize their aim. In this chapter we explored this through the concept of motivation.

Motivation was defined as the direction and intensity of one's effort, and the process of motivation was discussed as fulfilling our inner needs and confirming our knowledge, that in turn results in rewards that help reinforce our behavior. Each of these elements in the motivation process is supported by theories. For example, there is a hierarchy of need, cognitive, and reinforcement theories.

Motivation is also described by two broad types: intrinsic and extrinsic. Accordingly, there are motivation strategies that are useful to recreation leaders. Such strategies are based on the fundamental guidelines for leaders in building motivation in recreation activity participants and organizational staff:

1. Consider both situational and personal factors.
2. Realize that people have multiple motives for involvement.
3. People often have competing motives for involvement.
4. People have unique motives.
5. Motives can change over time.
6. Leaders can influence motivation.

Questions and Activities for Review and Discussion

1. Briefly describe the concept of motivation and explain the motivation process. Describe a situation that illustrates the concepts of direction of effort and intensity of effort.
2. Explain the hierarchy of needs theories. Assume that you are the manager of the youth sports program for an Air Force base. How could this theoretical approach help you motivate the participants?
3. Explain the cognitive theories of motivation. Assume that you are a leader in an older adults community center. How could this theoretical approach help you motivate the participants?
4. Explain the reinforcement theories of motivation. Assume that you are the director of an aquatics center. How could this theoretical approach help you motivate the center staff?
5. What is the difference between intrinsic and extrinsic motivation? Illustrate your answer by describing recreation experiences for which you are intrinsically motivated and those for which you are extrinsically motivated.
6. In a recreation leadership situation in which you are involved or are able to observe, which of the suggested motivational techniques for increasing intrinsic motivation are being used? Judge their success in encouraging greater participation.
7. Does the leader in the situation in question 6 use other motivation strategies? How are these strategies different than those used for increasing intrinsic motivation in terms of the fundamental guidelines for building motivation?

References

Bartol, K. M., & Martin, D. C. (1998). *Management* (3rd ed.). Boston, MA: McGraw-Hill.

Gauron, E. (1984). *Mental training for peak performance.* Lansing, NY: Sport Science Associates.

Kramer, J., & Schaap, D. (1968). *Instant replay: The Green Bay diary of Jerry Kramer.* New York: Signet.

Iso-Ahola, S. E. (1982). Intrinsic motivation: An overlooked basis for evaluation. *Parks and Recreation, 17*(2), 32–33.

Levy, J. (1978). *Play behavior.* New York: John Wiley & Sons.

Locke, E. A., & Latham, G. P. (1990). *A theory of goal setting & task performance.* Englewood Cliffs, NJ: Prentice-Hall.

McAuley, E., & Tammen, V. V. (1989). The effects of subjective and objective competitive outcomes on intrinsic motivation. *Journal of Sport & Exercise Psychology, 11*, 84–93.

Vallerand, R. J., & Reid, G. (1984). On the causal effects of perceived competence on intrinsic motivation: A test of cognitive evaluation theory. *Journal of Sport Psychology, 6*, 94–102.

Wankel, L. M. (1980). Involvement in vigorous physical activity: Considerations for enhancing self-motivation. In R. R. Danielson & K. F. Danielson (eds.), *Fitness Motivation: Proceedings of the Geneva Park Workshop.* Toronto: Ontario Research Council on Leisure.

Weinberg, R. S., & Gould, D. (1995). *Foundations of sport and exercise psychology.* Champaign, IL: Human Kinetics.

Web Resources

Extrinsic motivation: www.ils.nwu.edu/

Intrinsic motivation in learning: http://seamonkey.ed.asu.edu/

Motivation: http://cw.prenhall.com/

Motivation and children: http://transitivity.freeservers.com/

Motivation and goal-setting worksheet: www.coun.uvic.ca/

Motivation and work needs: www.mgarrison.com/

Motivation in the workplace: www.nursing.oouhsc.edu/

Motivation theories: www.churcher.com/

CHAPTER 9

Facilitating Recreation Behavior

"Leisure activity has the potential of liberating women by offering freedom and integrity."
—Henderson, Bialeschki, Shaw & Freysinger, 1989, p. 115.

LEARNING OBJECTIVES

Recreation experiences result in specific educational, developmental, or therapeutic outcomes for participants. Therefore, recreation leaders employ a variety of facilitation techniques to help participants maximally attain these desired outcomes. In this chapter we discuss:

- reasons for facilitating the recreation experience
- guidelines for facilitation
- facilitation techniques
- reducing constraints to participation

KEY TERMS

facilitation p. 167
transfer of learning p. 167
specific transfer p. 167
nonspecific transfer p. 167
metaphoric transfer p. 167
group position p. 168
time p. 168
single speaking p. 169
participation p. 169
role clarity p. 169
confidentiality p. 169
diagnose p. 170
design p. 170
delivery p. 170
debriefing p. 170
detachment p. 170
discussion p. 170
fishbowling p. 171
funneling p. 172
filters p. 172
frontloading p. 174
feedback p. 174
constraints p. 176

An increasingly important skill for recreation leaders in every type of leisure services organization is activity facilitation. This is a fairly new leader skill having its origins in the 1960s through adventure recreation programs. At that time, as more teachers, counselors, therapists, and other human service professionals became involved in conducting these experiences, techniques were imported from their fields to heighten the experience. In this chapter these facilitation techniques are presented and their use is encouraged.

WHY FACILITATE RECREATION EXPERIENCES?

While our first thought is always for the intrinsic "fun" of a recreation experience, today's recreation leader is also expected to provide clients with leisure experiences that achieve other goals that enhance their lives in developmental or therapeutic ways. For example, an Outward Bound instructor was overheard saying "let the mountains speak for themselves" (Priest & Gass, 1997, p. 174). We know that he was talking about the intrinsic power and majesty of the mountains and the profound effect they can have on people. This will always be the case, and Outward Bound leaders depend on this when they take people to the mountains. But from research we know that not everyone who goes to the mountains will experience the mountains positively. Some—especially first-time visitors—will find them frightening and full of hardship. Therefore, the Outward Bound leader also relies on facilitation techniques to closely ensure that people will learn, grow, and change in positive ways through mountain experiences. Certainly, without facilitation, people learn, grow, and change on their own, but often not as effectively as with the aid of a leader's facilitation.

Leader Profile: The Past
Aldo Leopold. Outdoor philosopher and activist. Would Leopold have agreed with the idea of facilitation of recreational experiences? Research his life and writings to find out.

When a recreation leader facilitates an experience what is she doing? **Facilitation** helps recreation participants:

- reflect on their experience
- evaluate the good and the bad about their experience
- analyze mistakes, failures, or successes in the experience
- consider the impact of their actions and decisions during the experience
- anticipate consequences from the experience
- understand how they have learned, grown, or changed as a result of the experience

Thus in using facilitation techniques, the recreation leader is guiding people through these reflections and analyses.

How do these reflections and analyses enhance the recreation experience? Most agree that facilitation works because of the concept of transfer of learning (Priest & Gass, 1997). **Transfer of learning** refers to the integration of learning from a recreation experience into the participant's real life. According to Gass (1985), there are three types of learning transfers from recreational experiences:

1. **Specific transfer** involves the learning of particular skills for use in a related situation (Gass, 1985). For example, when a participant transfers what he's learned from swinging a bat in baseball to swinging a bat in softball, or when she ties knots for rock climbing based on her previously learned skill of tying knots in boating, specific transfer of learning has occurred. The bat swings and the knots serve similar purposes, even though the specific activities are different.
2. **Nonspecific transfer** refers to the learning of more general principles or skills and applying them to a different situation. For example in adventure recreation programs, the general principle of trust developed through "trust games" can translate to trusting one another for support when belaying down a rock face (or when sharing secrets with friends or suggesting new ideas at work) (Priest & Gass, 1997).
3. **Metaphoric transfer** is a more specialized form of transfer of learning. Recall that a metaphor is an idea or object used in place of a different idea or object in order to draw attention to the similarity between the two (Gass, 1985). This kind of transfer of learning can occur between many recreational activities too. For example, someone who learns to express his feelings through his watercolor paintings may see the parallel when meeting with a therapist to deal with a troublesome personal relationship. Or, taking the first step into a cave on a spelunking outing may represent to a participant the same courage needed to leave home and start four years of college. The ability of a recreation experience to make such a metaphoric transfer to

real life depends on the strength of the connection. The greater the power of the parallels, and the clearer the parallels, the better the metaphor of the recreation experience is in transferring to a real-life situation.

Case in Point: Trust Fall

"Probably lots of you think that this exercise has something to do with trusting others, or with knowing that people will support you if you let them. And that's a fine meaning to get out of this activity. But our purpose in choosing this exercise is actually pretty different; we picked it because we feel there is an even more important lesson here. And that lesson concerns letting go of an old lifestyle. Let me tell you a bit more about what I mean.

"Each of you will be getting up here and holding on to this tree before falling backwards. Before you fall, I'm going to ask you to close your eyes and imagine that the tree is that part of your personality—that piece of you—most responsible for your drinking and drugging. I don't want you to think of this as a tree anymore; I want you to think of it as the most powerful factor responsible for your using. And I want you to hug it like you love it—like it's all you've got.

"Because after you hold on to it for awhile, for 30 seconds, I'm going to ask you to let go—to give up and let go of whatever it is that keeps you drinking and drugging. You'll just lie back and fall toward these people.

"And don't be surprised if you feel a little nervous. All alcoholics/addicts have at least some love for their old lifestyle, no matter how much they really want to change it. And there's always some degree of hesitation toward committing to a drug-free life. 'Cause you don't know what it is like. So I'd be surprised if you didn't feel some kind of nervousness about falling."

(from Bacon, 1991, pp. 11–12)

GUIDELINES FOR FACILITATION

Before we delve into the discussion of activity facilitation techniques, let's set some additional foundation by mentioning the ground rules for facilitation and presenting the facilitation process.

The Ground Rules

There are some ground rules that you can implement to help you become a good recreation activity facilitator (Hammel, 1986; Knapp, 1990, 1993; Nadler & Luckner, 1992; Priest & Gass, 1997).

1. **Group position** is important for effective communication. When a leader uses any of the facilitation techniques (see the discussion later in this chapter) group members must be in an appropriate physical configuration. This means that they must be able to see the leader and each other make eye contact, and see facial expressions and body language. The setting should be relaxed. For example, after the softball game a discussion of how the game went might be best situated with the coach and players sitting in a circle under a shade tree.
2. **Time** is also important. For example, a lengthy group discussion after the softball game might cause discomfort for the players because they are anxious to go home, shower, and see their families and friends. In reflecting on a recreation experience it is necessary to schedule the right amount of time for it. The timing should match the maturity and needs of the participants and the intensity of the experience. In some high-risk activities, for example, the time allocated to debrief an experience may need to be as long as the experience.

3. **Single speaking** means that only one person speaks at a time. This is a sign of group respect and ensures an opportunity for each person to equally hear others and be heard by others.
4. The rule regarding **participation** refers to the client's right to participate in any facilitation techniques used by the leader as well as to not participate. Participants should be able to select their ways of getting involved in the experiences. Similarly, violence, whether physical or emotional, is never accepted or tolerated by participants in an experience.
5. **Role clarity** is also an important ground rule in activity facilitation. It means that the leader proactively establishes his role and the group's responsibilities. The leader needs to be clear with participants about what is expected for their commitment to and responsibility for the experience. For example if this rule is followed, the leader will not hear "Why didn't you let us know we were going in the wrong direction five miles ago?!" (Priest & Gass, 1997, p. 178). As the leader you need to be clear about what you are there to do and what you are not there to do.
6. In some activity facilitation situations, the leader and the participants must have a mutually clear understanding about **confidentiality**. Make sure everyone knows whether information can be shared outside the group. Promise confidentiality carefully because in some situations laws may mandate that you report certain issues that arise in the process of facilitating an activity. For example, you may be required to report to the police illegal actions by participants that are confessed within a postactivity discussion.

The Process

The process of facilitating recreation activity experiences can be ordered into five phases: diagnosis, design, delivery, debriefing, and detachment (Priest & Gass, 1997). (figure 9.1.)

FIGURE 9.1. The five phases of facilitating recreation activity

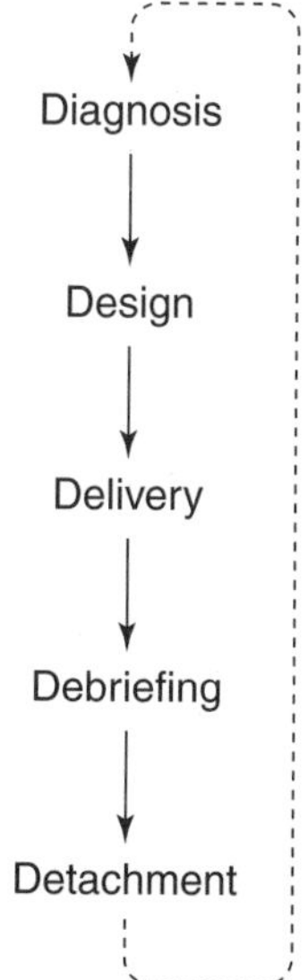

To **diagnose**, the leader seeks information about the goals and needs people bring to the recreation activity experience. In the **design** phase, the leader plans the best experiences to meet these goals. In the **delivery** phase, the leader presents the experience in as safe and educationally effective manner as possible, and in the **debriefing** phase the leader guides a reflective discussion or analysis of the experience to help people get the most out of it. Finally, in the **detachment** phase, the leader provides follow-up and ongoing support to continue the benefits people obtained from participating in the activity (Priest & Gass, 1997). This may sound like the program planning steps to you, but there is a difference. In the facilitation process the recreation activity or program is accomplished so that participants are intentional about their experience. That is, the leader calls participants' attention to the nature of the experience and its meaning for them.

To illustrate the process, suppose your clients are interested in learning the skills of white-water kayaking. Before the trip you interview all participants to determine their personal goals for the experience and what they might fear about learning this new recreational skill (diagnosis). Based on their input, you then plan a white-water "experience." This could be a trip or a series of lessons in a swimming pool, or both. In preparing for the trip, you take care to select the river and its degree of difficulty, the length of the trip, and the type of equipment according to the needs of the participants (design). Then, you conduct the trip—using good judgment about safety and a developmental approach to teaching the paddling skills (delivery). As a part of this "experience delivery" you may have conducted several paddling technique sessions in a swimming pool before the trip. At the end of each day of the trip (or between each set of rapids) you gather the group around on the shore or near the campfire to discuss the experience. Together you talk about what has been learned and its meaning for individual participants (debriefing). After the trip you provide a list of resources to help people practice and improve their new kayaking skills on their own (detachment).

While figure 9.1 presented the facilitation process as linear, or a straight line, depending on the nature of the recreation activity it could also be viewed as a cyclical process. The model you follow depends on the type of program you are leading. The linear process seems to work best with recreational activities for which the usual purpose is to have fun, to learn a new skill, or to be entertained (Priest & Gass, 1997). A cyclical process, whereby the detachment phase leads right into the diagnosis phase and the process repeats itself, seems to work best with more developmentally focused activities (Priest & Gass). That is, facilitation is a circular process when the purpose is to improve some behavior or train in new or different behaviors, such as in a therapeutic recreation situation.

FACILITATION TECHNIQUES

There are many ways the recreation leader might facilitate an activity. Some are done before the activity or program, some during, and some afterward. Here we discuss four facilitation techniques: discussions, debriefing, frontloading, and feedback.

Discussions

Most often used after the activity, **discussion** is an unstructured form of facilitation that encourages participants to analyze a past experience and to transfer learning from that experience to their lives. It is a group verbalization of reactions to the activity. It can serve to reinforce participants' perceptions and enable them to see the activity experience from an alternative perspective. As well, when participants know that a discussion will follow an activity, they are often more attentive to the experience while they are engaged in it.

The leader who uses discussion as an activity facilitation technique, guides the discussion using a number of strategies to make the discussion content and format valuable to participants (Priest & Gass, 1997). For example, for a facilitating discussion to succeed, participants must feel they are in an atmosphere of trust, respect, equality, acceptance, and flexibility (Priest & Gass, 1997). Only if participants are psychologically comfortable can they take the risks of experimenting with new thoughts and feelings. To establish this atmosphere, as the leader you need to be sure that the discussion follows the ground rules previously discussed. Therefore, it is best to arrange participants for the discussion in a circle. All should be on equal height levels—(i.e., either all standing or all sitting). The leader should also be part of the circle in order to guide the discussion, read body language, and make eye contact with the participants.

As well, you must guide the group in evolving its own ground rules. These may include speaking for oneself; listening and talking in the here and now, instead of dwelling on the past; welcoming all points of view; agreeing or disagreeing with the idea, not the person; and avoiding put-downs (Priest & Gass, 1997).

The discussion content should proceed from positive topics to dealing with negative issues, and then end on a positive note. Create a balance in the topics of discussion. You shouldn't always focus on mistakes or failures. Also discuss strengths, successes, and achievements.

Ask open-ended questions (figure 9.2) and for each question allow plenty of time for participants to think and answer fully. Acknowledge and validate all responses with a verbal thank you or a nonverbal signal such as a nod. Frequently paraphrase participant responses to be sure everyone is understood. Invite quiet participants to contribute without putting them on the spot. For example, call them by name, make gentle eye contact, lean forward, or smile. Listen to overbearing participants, but be aware of the need to move on to others. Redirect tangential speakers back to the topic of discussion without sounding critical. Stop lengthy speakers with a polite interruption.

A discussion technique that you might like to use is the fishbowl. **Fishbowling** calls for splitting the discussion group in two and organizing them into two concentric circles (sitting or standing). For the discussion the outer circle observes the inner circle's discussion and takes notes about what is said. Afterward the outer circle reports their findings to the inner circle, and then the two groups change places.

Another strategy for enabling participation in the discussion is to have participants toss a ball of string, with the tail unraveling, from speaker to speaker (Priest & Gass, 1997). This enables the group to identify a pattern of the more active versus passive participants. Participants might also pass a "talking stick" around the group. Only the person with the stick may talk.

Debriefing

As a facilitator your role in debriefing is to guide activity participants through reflective processes so they discover their own learning (Priest & Gass, 1997). This can take place

For enhancing group communication:
- How many different ways were used by the group to communicate messages?
- Which ways seemed most effective? Why?
- Did you learn something about communication that will be helpful later? What was it?
- Can anyone give an example of when you thought you communicated effectively?

For drawing out feelings:
- Can you name a feeling you had at any point in this activity?
- What was your main thought behind the feeling?
- What did you do with the feeling?
- Did you express that feeling to others?
- What feelings were expressed nonverbally by the group during the activity?

For recognizing group leadership:
- Who assumed leadership roles during the activity?
- What were the behaviors that showed this leadership?
- How did the group respond to these leadership behaviors?
- Did the leadership role shift to other people during the activity?
- Why didn't some of you take a leadership role with this group?

For calling attention to diversity:
- How are you different from some of the others in the group?
- How do these differences strengthen the group as a whole?
- What would this activity have been like if there were few differences in people?
- How are you like some of the others in the group?
- Did these common traits help or hinder the group's experience of the activity?
- How did this setting help you discover how you are similar to others?

For recognizing cooperation:
- Can you think of specific examples of group cooperation?
- How did it feel to cooperate?
- What were the rewards of cooperating?
- Were there any problems associated with cooperation?
- How can you cooperate in other areas of your life?

For evaluating the activity itself:
- In what ways did you enjoy this activity?
- In what ways did this activity bring out the best in you? And the worst?
- Did you feel you were a "natural" for this activity? Why or why not?
- Would you do anything differently if you were starting the activity again?

FIGURE 9.2. Open-ended questions for the discussion facilitation technique

periodically during an activity and afterward. The discussion technique previously discussed is one way of conducting a debriefing, but there are several others also.

For example, in a **funneling** approach you guide the participants through a series of steps that "funnel" their attention from the experience toward making beneficial changes in their lives. During the funnel process you consider the experience through a series of six "filters" (Priest & Gass, 1997). **Filters** are questions that "distill" learning through client reflection on and answers to these questions. The idea of a funnel means that the reflections called for in the earlier filters are broader than in the later filters. (figure 9.3.)

For example, the first filter poses review questions. Your goal in this part of the debriefing is to focus the participants on the topic or issue of interest, based on their needs and your objectives for the program (Priest & Gass, 1997). You want the group to focus on a single topic. To help, you can ask the group to replay the experience in their minds or to describe it out loud to refresh everyone's memories. The next filter poses questions

Recreational experience

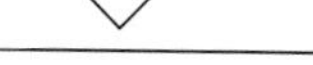

1. The review filter:

Can you review the last activity?
Let's talk about your experience in this activity a bit.

2. The recall and remember filter:

Do you remember an example of an excellent (issue or topic) during the activity?
Can you recall a particular moment or event that was good?

3. The affect and effect filter:

What emotion did you experience?
How did this make you feel?
How did your emotion affect the rest of the group?

4. The summation filter:

What did you learn from all of this?
Can you sum up what you have gained from our reflections here?

5. The application filter:

Do you see a connection between what you learned or gained in the activity and your life (at school, work, home)?
Can you apply this to your job?
To your family?

6. The commitment filter:

What will you do differently next time?
How will you commit to change?
Complete this: "I will . . ."

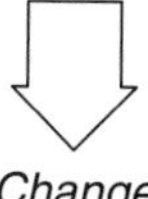

Change

FIGURE 9.3. Filter questions for the funneling debriefing technique

that enable the participants to more specifically remember the designated topic or issue through the experience. Your goal is to enable the participants to take ownership of the topic. In the effect and affect filter questions address emotions and their causes. These questions in the debriefing focus on the emotional impact of the recreation experience. At this level, discussion is about sharing feelings and noting concerns about what happened (Priest & Gass, 1997). The summation questions in the next filter help highlight new learning as a result of the recreation experience. So far, participants have identified a topic from the experience and noted its impact on them. Now they have the opportunity to think about what this has meant to them. The next filter poses application questions that help participants establish connections between what they have learned from the recreation experience and their lives. These questions help to establish links. Finally, the commitment filter directs the focus to the future—toward changes in participants' behaviors or attitudes as a result of the recreation experience. Here the leader ends the debriefing by inviting a plan of action.

Debriefing recreation activity experiences requires that you remain flexible in what is discussed, what questions you ask, and the manner in which you ask them. You must use your best judgment in "customizing" the session (Priest & Gass, 1997).

Leader Profile: The Present
Carolyn Love
Associate Professor, Department of Parks, Recreation, and Tourism Management, College of Forest Resources, North Carolina State University, Raleigh. When Dr. Love facilitates a group of students in a discussion she provides an excellent demonstration on the qualities of appropriate feedback.

Frontloading

Using the **frontloading** approach means you have the discussion before the recreational program or event. The facilitation takes place "up front" and it is "loaded" because the learning hoped for from the experience is "preloaded." Frontloading means punctuating the key learning points in advance of the recreation experience (Priest & Gass, 1997), rather than debriefing or discussing any learning after the fact.

In frontloading the aims of the activity and what can be learned or gained from it are discussed. You could also ask participants motivation questions that ask them to think about why they want to experience the activity. In other words, this facilitation technique is a briefing rather than a debriefing.

Giving Feedback

A critical technique in activity facilitation is providing appropriate feedback from the leader to clients and between clients. **Feedback** is the "exchange of verbal and nonverbal responses based on commonly observed behavior" (Upcraft, 1982, p. 80). The qualities of appropriate feedback are (Upcraft):

1. Good feedback is descriptive, rather than evaluative. This means that the sender of the feedback offers observations of the event, rather than a personal reaction to it. When descriptive, feedback allows the recipient to use the information in a way that works best for her.

Case in Point: The Wall

The activity called "The Wall" includes a 12- to 14-foot high wooden structure with a platform ledge on the back side. The group is challenged to pass its members up the front and over the top, using no additional props. The two most difficult aspects of this activity are getting the first person up and over and getting the last person up. In frontloading this activity, the leader could mention the group goal (getting everyone over the wall), constraints (you cannot hold onto the edges of the wall), and safety rules (remove all jewelry). The leader could also alert participants to what groups typically learn from this experience and how to recognize it as the group works through the task.

2. Appropriate feedback is specific, rather than general. Instead of saying that a particular action or decision was "stupid" try "I didn't understand why you took off your life jacket."
3. Good feedback is well intended. Remember that the purpose of feedback is to produce positive changes in individuals or to make them or a group more functional. This means that you take their safety and enjoyment to heart, and in giving them feedback you take their needs into account. When the motivation becomes destructive, such as to make another person feel inferior, the feedback will not be appropriate.
4. This brings us to the next quality of appropriate feedback. It is directed toward change. It is a response to a participant's action that can become the basis for follow-up or improvement or enhanced appreciation. Presenting feedback about a shortcoming that the receiver has no control over only makes for frustration.
5. Good feedback is solicited rather than imposed. Feedback is most appreciated when participants are seeking it, rather than when it is forced on them. Asking if the person would like to receive feedback on her golf swing, for example, will improve the chances that the feedback will be received and followed.
6. Feedback works best when it is well timed. Feedback that immediately follows the experience reduces any confusion that can develop when the action and its feedback are separated by a lengthy period. While this may not always be possible, due to logistical constraints or the person is not immediately ready to hear it, timing remains an important quality of good feedback.

Exercise: Feedback

Try this activity with your classmates. The goal is to experience giving and receiving positive feedback in a nonthreatening way.

It is often possible to enjoy a small gift more than a large one. Yet, we sometimes become so concerned about not being able to do great things for each other that we neglect to do the little things that can also be meaningful.

1. Divide yourselves up into groups of six to ten participants who have had some experience already working as a group. Everyone will need a pen or pencil and paper.
2. Write on a piece of paper a message to each member of the group. The messages are intended to make that person feel positive about her/himself.
3. Here are some guidelines for the messages:
   a. Try to be specific: say, "I like the way you smile at everyone when you arrive," rather than, "I like your attitude."
   b. Write a special message to fit each person rather than a comment that could apply to several persons.
   c. Include every participant, even if you are not too well acquainted with them. Choose whatever it is about the person that you respond to most positively.
   d. When trying to think of things to say, consider what you think is the person's real strength or notable success, why you would like to know him/her better, why he/she makes you happy, or why you are glad to be in the group with him/her.
   e. In writing your message, use the other person's name and state your message in the first person ("I like . . .").
   f. You are encouraged to sign your messages, but you do have the option of leaving them unsigned.
4. After each message is finished, fold it over once and place the name of the recipient on the outside. Distribute your messages to a place designated by each participant as her/his "mailbox."
5. When all messages have been delivered and read, share the feedback that was most meaningful to you with the rest of the class. Also use some time to clarify any ambiguous messages and to express the feelings you experienced during the exercise.

(from Pfeiffer & Jones, 1973)

7. Feedback on feedback is periodically needed. While giving feedback, check in with the recipient periodically to be sure your message was understood as you intended. Also, from time to time appropriate feedback is checked out with the group. When possible and appropriate, invite other participants to provide a sounding board for your feedback. They can tell you what is valid from their point of view. Be careful, though, that there are no negative consequences that result from this.

REDUCING CONSTRAINTS TO PARTICIPATION

Leader Profile: The Present
Peg Smith
National Executive Director, American Camping Association. Smith believes that camp is a unique space in which amid the lessons of nature, it is possible to find one's self and understand one's place in the world. She works to reduce constraints on more children participating in camping.

The other side of the facilitation "coin" is the idea of constraints against recreation activity participation. Within the past five years recreation leaders have become more interested in factors that constrain recreation participation and enjoyment—including those that limit participation in desired activities, explain the decision to cease participating in an activity, or account for failure to achieve desired levels of enjoyment in an activity (Jackson, 1994). What are constraints? Many are possible. They could include programs held at inconvenient times for the target participants, a facility that is not accessible to wheelchair users, poor physical health, lack of transportation to the activity site, fear of crime, and so on.

This focus suggests that one way to facilitate recreation is to remove or reduce constraints against it (Hultsman, 1993), because often it is possible to modify the activity, its delivery, or even aspects of people's lives. One way to do this is to consider that there are two main ways in which the effects of **constraints** can be alleviated (Scott & Jackson, 1996). On the one hand, individuals can be encouraged to modify their behavior and attitudes. This is because some constraints are fairly consistent according to age and gender. For example, we know that due to disproportionate responsibilities for child care, women experience a sense of not "earning" the right to participate in recreation (Henderson, Bialeschki, Shaw, and Freysinger, 1989). Thus the removal of this constraint would require that women begin to think of themselves as deserving and needing abundant amounts of recreation in their lives. This would require a personal attitudinal change.

On the other hand, recreation leaders can develop, deliver, and market their programs and services in ways that take into account the constraints that people encounter and institute strategies to alleviate or reduce them. The following is a research study that illustrates this perspective.

Cleveland Metroparks in cooperation with the University of Akron (Scott & Jackson, 1996) conducted the research. Over 1,000 people in the greater Cleveland area were interviewed by telephone about their use of city parks. The respondents were asked how frequently they used the parks. Nonusers and infrequent users were also asked to indicate the extent to which fifteen different constraints factors limited their use of parks. Then these nonusers and infrequent users were asked whether ten changes in park operations or programming might result in their using public parks more often. These changes represented possible ways of removing the constraints that limit people's use of the parks.

From the results, the leaders of the Cleveland Metroparks organization learned that the two largest constraints were "lack of time" and "being too busy with other activities." The older women in the sample were found to be particularly constrained by safety issues, lack of companionship, and poor health. Those factors that represented the lowest constraint on using parks were "parks are overdeveloped," "park facilities and programs cost too much," "no way to get to the parks," and "public transportation."

The analyses also indicated to the leaders that improved programming and promotion were the favored strategies for encouraging more park use in the future. For example, three-fourths of the sample felt that efforts should be made to "make the parks safe" and "provide more information about existing parks and programs." About half of the respondents wanted officials to "provide more activities" and "develop parks closer to home." In other words, while reducing personal barriers to participation was important to respondents, they were less likely to view them as potentially successful strategies for increasing their participation. The researchers in this study believe that the results suggest that park districts do not necessarily need to develop more parks, but may attract nonusers and infrequent users to existing facilities via better programming and promotion and creating an image that parks are a safe place to visit.

Summary

In addition to enabling people to have a good time, today's recreation leader is expected to provide clients with leisure experiences that achieve other goals that enhance their lives in developmental or therapeutic ways. To assist with this expectation, leaders often use facilitation techniques.

In using facilitation techniques the recreation leader is guiding people through reflections and analyses about the recreation experience and its meaning to them. How do these reflections and analyses enhance the recreation experience? Facilitation is based on the concept of transfer of learning. Transfer of learning refers to the integration of learning from a recreation experience into the participant's life.

The process of facilitating recreation activity experiences can be ordered into five phases: diagnosis, design, delivery, debriefing, and detachment. There are many ways the recreation leader might facilitate an activity throughout this process. Some are done before the activity or program, some during, and some afterward. In this chapter we discussed four facilitation techniques: discussions, debriefing, frontloading, and feedback. Most often used after the activity, discussion is an unstructured form of facilitation that encourages participants to analyze a past experience and to transfer learning from that experience to their lives. It is a group verbalization of reactions to the activity. It can serve to reinforce participants' perceptions and enable them to see the activity experience from an alternative perspective. As a facilitator your role in debriefing is to guide activity participants through reflective processes so they discover their learning (Priest & Gass, 1997). This can take place periodically during an activity as well as afterward. The discussion technique discussed is one way of conducting a debriefing, but there are several others also. For example, in a funneling approach you guide the participants through a series of steps that "funnel" their attention from the experience toward making beneficial changes in their lives.

Using the frontloading facilitation technique means you have the discussion before the recreational program or event instead of afterward. Here the facilitation takes place "up front" and it is "loaded" because the learning hoped for from the experience is previewed. Finally, a critical technique in activity facilitation is providing appropriate feedback from the leader to clients and between clients. Feedback is the exchange of verbal and nonverbal responses based on commonly observed behavior.

The other side of the facilitation "coin" is the idea of constraints against recreation activity participation. Within the past five years recreation leaders have become more interested in factors that constrain recreation participation and enjoyment—including those that limit participation in desired activities, explain the decision to cease participating in an activity, or account for failure to achieve desired levels of enjoyment in an activity (Jackson, 1994).

Questions and Activities for Discussion and Review

1. Differentiate the three types of learning transfer. From your own learning experiences, give examples of each. What has been a powerful life metaphor for you from your own recreational background?
2. Why is it so important to obey the ground rules of facilitation outlined in the chapter? Cite several examples from your experiences of what can happen when they are not followed.
3. What distinguishes debriefing from frontloading? Also, how are they similar?
4. To practice the funneling approach to debriefing, choose a partner, develop questions for each of the filters, and practice asking them as a way of debriefing today's class session. Give each other feedback (review these guidelines from the chapter) on how well each of you conducted the debriefing.
5. Read the Scott and Jackson (1996) study cited in the chapter, paying particular attention to the content and format of the questions. Then "mimic" this study with one of yours by researching the constraints to participation and their solution for students at your campus recreational sports center or program.

References

Bacon, S. B. (1991). Using the ropes course to help alcoholics resist temptation. In M.A. Gass and C.H. Dobkin (Eds.), *Book of metaphors: Volume I.* Durham, NH: University of New Hampshire.

Gass, M. A. (1985). Programming the transfer of learning in adventure education. *Journal of Experiential Education 8*(3), 18–24.

Hammel, H. (1986). How to design a debriefing session. *Journal of Experiential Education, 9*(3), 20–25.

Henderson, K. A., Bialeschki, M. D., Shaw, S. M., & Freysinger, V. J. (1989). *A leisure of one's own: A feminist perspective on women's leisure.* State College, PA: Venture.

Hultsman, W. (1993). Is constrained leisure an internally homogeneous concept? An extension. *Journal of Leisure Research, 25*, 319–334.

Jackson, E. L. (1994). Activity-specific constraints on leisure. *Journal of Park and Recreation Administration, 12*, 33–49.

Knapp, C. (1990). Processing experiences. In J. C. Miles & S. Priest (Eds.), *Adventure education.* State College, PA: Venture.

Knapp, C. (1993). Processing experiences. In M. A. Gass (Ed.), *Adventure therapy: Therapeutic applications of adventure programming in therapeutic settings.* Dubuque, IA: Kendall/Hunt.

Nadler, R., & Luckner, J. (1992). *Processing the adventure experience: Theory and practice.* Dubuque, IA: Kendall/Hunt.

Pfeiffer, J. W., & Jones, J. E. (1973). *A handbook of structured experiences for human relations training—Volume IV.* La Jolla, CA: University Associates.

Priest, S., & Gass, M. A. (1997). *Effective leadership in adventure programming.* Champaign, IL: Human Kinetics.

Scott, D., & Jackson, E. L. (1996). Factors that limit and strategies that might encourage people's use of public parks. *Journal of Park and Recreation Administration. 14*(1), 1–17.

Upcraft, M. L. (1982). *Learning to be a resident assistant.* San Francisco: Jossey-Bass.

Web Resources

Experience based learning: www.ebl.org/

Feedback on golf skills—personal game analysis: www.shotbyshot.com/

Mediation services: www.just-solutions.org/

Online photographic image critique: http://w3.one.net/~davev/photo/

Online resource guide to facilitating change in managing natural resources: wysiwyg://22/http://nrm.massey.ac.nz/changelinks/

Outward Bound: www.outwardbound.org/

CHAPTER 10

Managing Participant Behavior

There is only one success—to be able to spend your life in your own way.
—Christopher Morley, *Where the Blue Begins*, 1922.

LEARNING OBJECTIVES

The underlying premise of this chapter is that recreation leaders can function successfully only if they have a manageable grasp on the behavior of participants. Here we discuss:

- preventive behavior management
- discipline
- conflict resolution
- safety management

KEY TERMS

primary reinforcers p. 186
secondary reinforcers p. 186
privilege reinforcers p. 186
activity reinforcers p. 186
social reinforcers p. 186
discipline p. 188
positive discipline p. 188
conflict p. 189
conflict resolution p. 189
task interdependence p. 190
sequential task interdependence p. 190
reciprocal task interdependence p. 190
scarce resources p. 190
goal incompatibility p. 190
communication failures p. 190
individual differences p. 190
poorly designed reward systems p. 190
change situational factors p. 191
superordinate goals p. 191
interpersonal conflict-handling approach p. 191
safety management p. 192
accident potential p. 192
general supervision p. 192
specific supervision p. 193

The behavioral management skills that enable recreation leaders to work effectively with participants can be difficult to learn. Yet they are among the most important competencies you will use in recreation leadership situations.

For example, for the following excerpts of participant conversations, which response would you as the leader make?

CAMPER: "Why do I have to clean up the tent? I wasn't the one who messed it up. I always get stuck doing everything!"

a. "You think I'm picking on you just because I asked you to clean up the tent."
b. "You feel angry because you don't feel you should have to clean up the tent."

c. "I know you feel angry about having to clean up the tent, but I'll help you, and we'll get done faster."*

CAMPER: "I can't do it; I just can't do it. I'm never any good at sports."

a. "Sure you can do it if you just try."
b. "Why do you think you can't do it?"
c. "You sound frightened to try."*

As another type of example, what would you do as the leader in the following situations?

> You are explaining how to play a game when the camper next to you begins making an annoying noise. The noise is not affecting the other campers but is bothering you.*
>
> You are leading an arts and crafts program, and you notice Frank put your felt marking pen in his pocket. To avoid embarrassing him, you say, "Frank, would you please pass me the pen, I need to help Lance with his project." Frank responds with, "I haven't got your pen; I don't know where it is."*

The choice of best leader response or action for these situations is not an easy one, yet these choices come from everyday conversations and everyday situations in recreation settings. Because of this common occurrence, this chapter conveys the basic principles of behavior management.

The underlying premise is that recreation leadership can function effectively only if it has a manageable grasp on the behavior of participants. Two distinct limitations must, however, be recognized. First, there is no general agreement in the literature or in practice about many aspects of human behavior. Exactly why people behave as they do is the subject of continual research and debate. Second, a solid understanding of behavior requires more study and practice than is available in a single chapter or a single text. This means that you will most likely spend much of your entire career seeking to improve your behavior management skills—regardless of the setting.

The recreation participant behaves in a wide variety of ways. Leaders work with children who fight and children who are afraid to fight, persons who seek the limelight and those who are withdrawn, persons who possess a sense of dignity and worth and those who have no self-confidence, and also persons who lose their head in softball and others to whom defeat is a matter of relative unimportance.

The recreation leader is someone who, because of position and role, influences the behavior of others. The extent of this influence is measured in large degree by the breadth and depth of the leader's understanding of human nature and her ability to respond appropriately.

Preventing problem behaviors and encouraging positive behaviors is the goal. It is preferable to prevent problem behavior rather than to correct it. This is especially important when you realize that problem behaviors tend to encourage other problem behaviors, whereas good behaviors tend to create more desirable behaviors.

The basic idea underlying behavior management is that much behavior is outcome directed. That is, many times you choose behaviors that get you what you want or need. If you decide to try a recreational activity that you have never tried, whether you will do

* These examples were adapted from an excellent resource on dealing with camper behavior by Vinton and Farley (1979). It is one module in a camp staff training series and is packaged as a competency-based manual.

it again depends on how well you enjoyed it. By depending on how things work out, we settle on patterns of behavior that are most appropriate for us.

Behavior can result in many outcomes. Outcomes are specific events that follow specific behavior and influence other behaviors. Outcomes can be desirable, undesirable, or neutral. When you award blue, red, and white ribbons to artists, you are providing a desirable outcome. When you evict a player from a game, you are providing an undesirable or punishing outcome. When you ignore a young camper's outbursts, you are providing a neutral outcome.

To make a useful application of this central idea of behavior management, specific advice is offered in this chapter. First, approaches to behavior management are discussed as both preventive and disciplinary. Then, conflict management and safety management are presented as two special skills in behavior management needed by the recreation leader.

Case in Point: Youth Golf

Young people have been coming to the game of golf more enthusiastically than ever, and many leisure service organizations have begun to take notice. In Peoria, Illinois, the Peoria Park District is leading the way. It developed a multidimensional golf program to fit a community in which 57 percent of the children in the public school system live below the poverty level. The program's rationale is that golf is a wholesome lifetime activity, and when people are introduced to the game at a young age, they will generally return to the sport as adults, whether or not they continued to play throughout their formative years.

So the Peoria Park District set out to increase the skill level and diversity of its customers and to encourage play from new target groups, including youth, minorities, those with physical disabilities, and the financially disadvantaged. The staff contacted the United States Golf Association Foundation, and together they built an outstanding and unique facility and program. Programs such as Hook a Kid on Golf, First Swing, Detweiller Drivers children's golf club, and lessons were implemented at the Golf Peoria Learning Center and Academy. The center includes all-weather indoor and outdoor playing facilities, a large outdoor putting green, and practice sand bunkers. A nine-hole pitch and putt course is ideal for junior play with movable tees and no holes longer than 100 yards. One of the programs, Hook a Kid on Golf, especially demonstrates the mission of the Center. The participating youngsters come from the Peoria Housing Authority's low-income housing complex, and receive, at no cost to them, golf clubs and bag, balls, shirts, visors, and an instructional video to keep. They take four two-hour lessons from park district PGA professionals and finish the program with a tournament at nine-hole Detweiller Golf Course.

At Peoria, the golf program never ends, and the park district staff know that youth education is the future of the game.

(Woolard & Zucco, 1999)

APPROACHES TO BEHAVIOR MANAGEMENT

Leaders are not so much interested in controlling other's behaviors (although at times this may be necessary), but rather try to guide people's actions. Why? Because we know that certain behaviors and actions maximize the benefits people can derive from recreational activities. Children on the playground develop better social skills and have more fun when no one is fighting. Members of the city basketball league experience more physical fitness and have more fun if they don't have to stand around during the game waiting for officials to correct abusive behaviors by spectators.

There are numerous approaches to behavior management. Many of the methods originate in the teachings of sociology and psychology. For example, behavior modification, which we mentioned in a previous chapter, is based on the branch of psychology known as behaviorism. In this section of the chapter, two approaches to behavior management are presented. These are preventive methods and discipline.

Preventive Methods

The idea of preventive behavior management is to minimize or prevent behavioral difficulties. As a basis for preventing problems before they occur, the leader frequently monitors and responds to participants' behaviors. This enables the leader to respond appropriately—such as giving praise for an achievement—and in a timely way. Through frequent monitoring, the leader can also be sure that the rules are clear so they can be followed. Preventive behavior management is good leadership. For example, you can avoid arguing among game participants if you see that there is enough equipment for everyone, and that the boundaries are clearly marked and understood.

One of the most important skills for the leader in managing participants' behavior is responding to their actions and words appropriately. For example, if the leader uses understanding responses, the participant will be encouraged to go on exploring his feelings. If the leader uses responses that are judgmental or interpretive, the participant's resulting behavior will be different. Listening is the first and most important step. The type of responses you make will be either hindered or enhanced by how well you listen. As well, knowing how to respond is to a large degree dependent on an accurate assessment of the situation. According to Vinton and Farley (1979), there are some major types of responses.

1. *Judging response.* A judging response implies placing a judgment or evaluation on the person, on the statement, or on the feeling behind the statement. The leader may respond to participant behavior with a positive judgment, a negative judgment, or a moralizing judgment. Negative and moralizing judging responses usually cause a person to feel "put down."

   Example— "Now listen here, that's a rotten thing to say. You're no worse off than anyone else. I don't want to hear you talk that way again."
2. *Topping response.* A topping response is a form of "one-upmanship." When the leader uses this response, it immediately shifts the focus away from the person who is exhibiting the "listen-to-me" behavior. As a result, the person then often feels deflated and unimportant.

   Example— "You think you have it bad. Think about me with two parents in a nursing home. Can't you just imagine what I've been going through!"
3. *Advice-giving response.* An advice-giving response suggests what possible action or steps can be taken to deal with or solve a problem. It is easy for a leader to give but is often not helpful in an emotional situation. Advice is usually ignored if the person does not first feel accepted and understood.

   Example— "I think you should look at what you're doing to make the others pick on you. You'll no doubt find that you're a part of this problem. Why don't you count to ten before you act so you won't get so angry?"
4. *Interpretive response.* An interpretive response gives facts and opinions intended to give insights or understandings to the situation. In giving this response the leader may help the participant understand that her behavior is typical for the situation.

   Example— "Well, what happened this time? Did you get the worst of it? Do you think you should stay away from them for a while?"

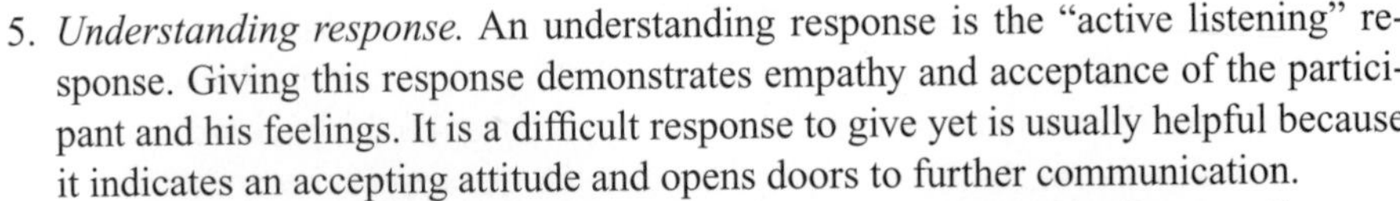

5. *Understanding response.* An understanding response is the "active listening" response. Giving this response demonstrates empathy and acceptance of the participant and his feelings. It is a difficult response to give yet is usually helpful because it indicates an accepting attitude and opens doors to further communication.
   Example— "It sounds like you are really hurt and you're really angry."

Giving the best possible response to a participant is often important to the management of her resulting behavior. From your own daily conversations and interactions, you know that certain responses can lead to certain behaviors. Some make you feel angry, some defensive, and some appreciated. These resulting feelings are responded to with behavior such as silence, fighting, pouting, friendliness, or confidence. In most situations, recreation leaders will find interpretive, questioning, and understanding responses to be most effective.

With the ability to respond to participant actions appropriately as the basis, what are some specific preventive behavior management techniques? There are many and which you use when depends on your abilities with and beliefs about people. Despite the oceans of textbooks, articles, and advice on the subject, no one can provide you with a "formula" that will work for every participant in every situation. There are, however, some suggestions that have been effective in many recreation situations.

Leader Profile: The Past
Coastal Pleasure Grounds
1924 Pacific Beach, Washington. The physical environment can be manipulated to manage participant behavior. How do you think this early campground environment was reflected in participants' behaviors at the time?

Structure the physical environment. Arranging the space and time wisely can enhance the likelihood of positive or desired behaviors. Chairs in a circle for group discussion, providing locker space to assure property rights, brief activity periods for short attention spans, removal of dangerous objects, proper lighting, and adequate room size for the number of persons can do a great deal toward encouraging appropriate behaviors. The physical environment can also be manipulated through different room colors and wall decoration. For example, the color red increases heart rate and respiration, which serves to excite people. Most blue tones, on the other hand, act as a calming influence. Music also has differing affects on people—establishing various moods (Jordan, 1996).

Clearly state privileges and rules. Think positively by letting participants know what they may do and what is necessary for them not to do for safety and efficiency. If participants clearly understand what the acceptable behavior limits are, they will not need to test you to determine these acceptable limits. Too many "don'ts" or rules communicated in a negative or hostile way will often encourage undesirable, rebellious behavior. Do attempt to involve the participants in the establishment of their privileges and rules. People are more likely to internalize rules that they have helped establish. Also explain to participants the need for rules. If you cannot offer a reason, perhaps the rule is not needed.

Clarify benefits of desirable behavior. Continually point out the benefits, rewards, or positive consequences of desirable and acceptable behavior. A person who clearly understands what the behavior will do for him, and who wants this benefit, will likely behave accordingly. Be sure that the positive consequences are genuine and reasonable. People can tell when you are making positive comments for the sake of influencing them to act in a certain way. You must be authentic. When the behavior is accordingly positive, give praise.

Modeling. Consistently display behaviors that you expect others to exhibit—in words and in actions. For example, acting in a friendly and respectful manner, letting others know where you stand in a positive way, playing fair, and being generous, are leader behaviors that help promote the desired behavioral norm. By demonstrating productive behaviors and then allowing individuals to practice them, they will better understand the leader's expectations.

Reinforce desirable behavior. Provide clear, direct, and valued responses following the occurrence of behavior that is considered to be desirable. A sincere smile, praising gesture, or reward is often all that is necessary to encourage a person to maintain or increase acceptable actions. This strategy of "positive reinforcement" works particularly well with skill development. Your response, which should closely follow the behavior, must not be ambiguous and must be perceived by the participant as positive and wanted.

Exercise: Responding

These are instructions for a class activity that demonstrates the impact of different reactions to helping responses.

1. One person serves as the facilitator. Select two to three people to be the problem solvers. Then select six to be the helpers with the rest of the group serving as observers.
2. The problem solvers are seated at the table, and the helpers leave the room. The observers are spread around the room so that they can observe the action at the table.
3. The facilitator joins the six helpers outside the room. She/he briefs the helpers by explaining that they will each have one-half minute to help the problem solvers solve a puzzle. The facilitator assigns each of the helpers a specific helping response. (It might be useful to write each response on a card for the helper.) These responses are:
   a. *Referent*: As you try to help, show empathy, warmth, familiarity, and liking for the problem solver.
   b. *Expert*: As you try to help, act like an expert.
   c. *Reward*: As you try to help, offer encouragement and some reward for a successful solution. Promise something good.
   d. *Coercive*: As you try to help, urge work at the puzzle through threats if it is not completed in time.
   e. *Legitimate*: As you try to help, make it clear that you are responsible to your teacher (or other supervisor) for the others' effective work.
   f. *Charismatic*: As you try to help become "personality plus," and hope your enthusiasm and confidence catch hold.
4. The facilitator returns to the room and presents the puzzle to the problem solvers. Here are two ideas for the kind of puzzles that work in this activity, but you may want to select some others if the problem solvers already know these.

Problem: Take away eight toothpicks so that there are only two squares left.*

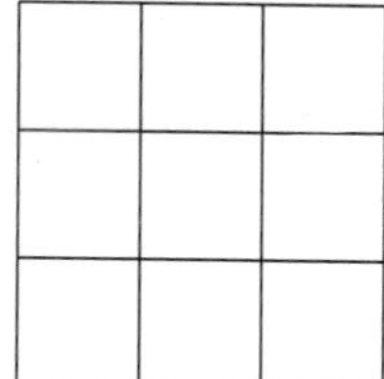

Problem: Connect all nine dots with four straight lines.*

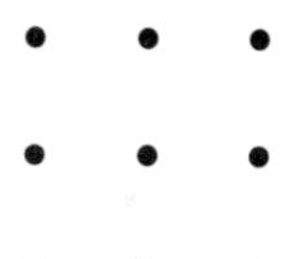

* Solutions are at the end of the chapter.

5. Before the problem solvers begin to work on the puzzle, bring one of the helpers into the room. This helper, according to her/his assigned response, has one-half minute to help. Then bring in another helper who uses his/her assigned response to help, and so forth. Continue until the puzzle is solved. If it is solved before all six helpers have entered the room, have a second puzzle ready.
6. After the sixth trial to solve the puzzle, the facilitator leads the class in a debriefing of the experience. First, the problem solvers report the effect of the various helping styles on accomplishing the task. Also, the observers report how they saw the effects of the various helping responses. How were the six helping styles different in how the problem solvers felt? Their motivation to solve the puzzle, and so on?

(adapted from Pfeiffer & Jones, 1973)

There are several types of positive reinforcements. **Primary reinforcers** include edible and sensory reinforcers (e.g., a candy bar or pat on the back). **Secondary reinforcers** include such items as trophies and certificates. Secondary reinforcers can also be grouped according to type: **privilege reinforcers** (e.g., being first), **activity reinforcers** (e.g., getting to choose the activity), and **social reinforcers** (e.g., a verbal "nice job") (Wolfgang & Wolfgang, 1995). As a social reinforcer, praise is a frequently used form of positive reinforcement. Because praise is a feeling, value, or thought of the leader, it is best to phrase it as an "I" statement, rather than a "you" statement (Jordan, 1996). For example: "I appreciate you helping Mark clean up the cabin" rather than "you did a good job helping Mark clean up the cabin." Using the "I" praise statement shows that the praise remains with the person who owns it.

Contracting. In some situations it might be useful to establish a written or verbal agreement with the participant. This agreement explicitly states the expected behavior and the resulting reward when this behavior is exhibited. Although contracting often involves the reinforcement of desirable behaviors, it adds a component of mutual goal setting and negotiation. Behavioral contracts are most successful (for any age) when they are a shared effort. This is because effective contracts outline what is expected of both the participant and the leader. Usually the leader is expected to help the participant achieve his behavioral goals by being supportive, giving reminders, and aiding in ways that reinforce the desired behaviors. When contracts fail, it is often because the leader was not available to give out reinforcers when needed.

A contract is a rather formal (often written) agreement that the participant will behave in a specified way. The desired behaviors are identified as are the consequences for failing to meet the contract (Jordan, 1996). To work, contracts should also be drawn up privately and in a positive way. Reasons are given for the need for the contract.

Regulated permission. In other situations it may be appropriate to provide socially acceptable opportunities for behavioral expressions that are usually manifested in unacceptable ways. For example, allowing a child to punch a boxing bag when the child feels like hitting someone or organizing a controlled competition or debate when participants want to assert their power over each other may be effective. Many group initiative games are valuable as forms of regulated permission.

Tolerate some undesirable behavior. Too much attention given to annoying behavior may not only interfere with your leadership effectiveness, but it may also serve to encourage undesirable behavior. Certain undesirable behaviors may be typical for the participant's developmental stage such as for a child. Also for those situations where the undesirable behavior is minor and situational, planned ignoring could be useful. For example, if the undesirable behaviors are not causing difficulties for others or presenting a safety concern, it might be useful to ignore them. When people are in groups they expect children to fidget, whisper, and move about.

Use nonverbal cues. Some undesirable behavior, however, cannot and should not be ignored. Before responding verbally, it may be possible to eliminate the inappropriate behavior by making clear, nonverbal responses. Eye contact, completed with a frown or gesture, may enable you to avoid the possibility of embarrassing the participant. Also positioning yourself near or in front of the offending participant may also encourage her to suppress undesirable behavior.

Redirect or change the activity. Sometimes undesirable behaviors result from dissatisfaction or boredom with the activity. The challenges of recreation activities should match the participant's ability level. Activities that are either too difficult or lack sufficient challenge for an individual or a group may result in negative or even disruptive behavior. In such situations a change to another activity or a modification in the current activity may be in order.

Develop, state, and enforce consequences of unacceptable behavior. Participants should clearly understand the alternatives available to them. This is particularly important to establish during the beginning of the program. For example, "If you continue pushing Billy, the following will happen . . ." may be useful in some situations. In other situations you may want to encourage the participant to develop the consequences of his behavior. Be sure to avoid the use of a threatening tone of voice when clarifying consequences. Above all, be prepared to follow through if the undesirable behavior continues. The enforcement of consequences should be immediate, nonpunitive, and consistent, and should attempt to foster participant responsibility.

Use time-out procedures. It may be advisable to temporarily remove a disruptive participant from the situation in which the undesirable behavior is occurring. Follow this by placing her in a different location where little or no positive reinforcement is received. Once removed, however, the participant should be allowed to return after a short time, but the return should be contingent on acceptable behavior.

A special word on rules. As a recreation leader, in a variety of settings and organizations, you will frequently manage participant behavior through rules. Without rules of some kind, few people would have an enjoyable and satisfying recreational experience. Yet, while rules are necessary, you do not have to be overly constraining with rules. The following principles will help you to use rules successfully (Jordan, 1996):

- *Rules should have reasons.* Arbitrary rules serve no purpose other than to enforce the leader's power. Have good reasons for rules and share those reasons with participants. The basis of rules is to keep participants, leaders, equipment, and facilities safe from harm and destruction. When participants realize that the rules don't relate to this, the leader can lose respect and authority.
- *Negotiate rules with participants.* When possible, and as much as possible, develop rules with those whom the rules affect. When rules are developed jointly by participants and leaders, participants (and leaders!) are much more likely to understand and thereby follow the rules.
- *Express the rules in positive language.* Above all else, avoid a long list of "no" statements. You have seen the signs as you enter the hotel swimming pool, the public lake, and the gym. "No gum. No glass containers. No running. No feeding the ducks." Haven't you wondered what it is that you are allowed to do there? Such statements establish a negative tone, which suggests that the leader is always expecting for people to break the rules. "Please protect the flower beds by walking only on the sidewalk" establishes a more positive and inviting tone (Jordan, 1996).
- *Keep rules short and clear.* The clearer and more succinct the rule, the easier it is to understand. Be concise and unambiguous.
- *Rules should define responsible behaviors.* If participants do not know what behaviors are expected, they will not likely be able to comply with the rules.
- *Clarify, practice, and monitor rules continuously.* Participants often need practice in following the rules. Both participants and leaders can monitor the progress.
- *Rules must be appropriate for participants.* Be sure that the rules match participant developmental levels. Expecting too much from participants can set them up for failure.

- *Rules should be fair.* Rules should be developed so that they affect all participants in a similar fashion and can be enforced equitably. A rule of "No containers in the football stadium" shouldn't be applied only to the student spectators at the college game.
- *Rules must be enforceable.* When rules are not enforced they are no longer rules—they are merely threats. To be effective, rules should be developed with an eye on their enforceability.
- *Have only a few rules.* If participants feel overwhelmed by the sheer quantity of rules they will not only feel that they are not trusted, but also that obeying the rules is impossible. Have as few of rules as possible.

Discipline

Undesirable behavior is not inevitable. In some recreation and park leadership situations it is less of a problem than it can be in other situations, because recreation participants usually are more motivated and voluntarily involved in the program. Also well-planned and well-led recreation programs that appeal to the needs and interests of participants can help to minimize the probability of behavioral problems. However, behavior problems requiring **discipline** can occur.

Disruptive behavior in any recreation setting, if not adequately dealt with, can ultimately diminish the value of the experience for the participants—not to mention the resulting frustration for the leader. If the behavior disrupts the program so that the enjoyment by other participants is lessened, if the behavior detracts from your ability as a leader to meet your responsibilities, and if the behavior is contrary to the best interests of the participant, it should be disciplined.

Discipline is a set of assertive methods used in behavior management to maintain orderly behaviors. Discipline can include direct instruction, the use of punishment, and an overall tone of leader control to force compliance in others. Like all forms of behavior management, positive discipline is preferred. **Positive discipline** helps to move the sense of control from the leader to the participant. There are some critically important points to keep in mind if you are to use positive discipline (Jordan, 1996):

- actively listen to participants
- show genuine respect for individual differences
- accept failures as a part of learning
- provide structured choices
- be flexible
- incorporate encouragement
- be systematic
- give second chances
- be honest

The ultimate goal of positive discipline is that participants will learn to depend more on their own self-discipline.

Positive discipline can be contrasted with punishment. Punishment is anything that decreases a particular behavior. It has a negative connotation and usually involves taking away privileges or reinforcements (Sherrill, 1993). Many leaders are opposed to the use of punishment because they do not think it teaches about the more desirable behaviors. At times it can lead to resentment, rebellion, retreat, and revenge by participants (Windell, 1991). Also, punishment has been shown to inhibit learning.

Use punishment with caution. Use it only as a last resort when the suggestions in the previous section for managing behavior fail to be effective. However, in situations involving risk to personal safety or rule violations, the use of punishment should be immediate and direct.

Punishment is a predefined penalty a participant must take when an important rule is broken or when disruptive behavior becomes a major problem. Its purpose is to ensure that the same behavior will not continue; as such it rarely solves the cause or origin of the discipline problem.

Many recreation and park organizations provide specific guidelines for their staff members that outline procedures to be followed in cases requiring punishment. Usually, these departmental procedures specify when parents should be called, when the police should be called, and what reports to write. In some circumstances, specific departmental procedures are available for dealing with certain types of problems such as drug abuse, drunkenness, abusive language, and fighting.

CONFLICT RESOLUTION

Whenever we have relationships with other people, we create potentials for conflict. Every relationship contains elements of disagreement and opposed interests. A **conflict** exists whenever an action by one person prevents, obstructs, or interferes with the actions of another person. Even though conflict is inevitable when people work and play together, people tend to consider conflicts to be bad—that a good relationship is one without conflict. We well know some of the destructive consequences of conflict. For example, conflict can cause people to become hostile. It can delay programs, drive up costs, cause valued employees and participants to leave, and even start world wars. But, as Johnson (1981) maintains, it is the failure to handle conflicts in constructive ways rather than the mere presence of conflict that leads to the destruction of relationships among people. When conflict is dealt with constructively, it can lead to a higher quality relationship. It can promote change, enhance morale and cohesion, and stimulate creativity and innovation.

Thus, the recreation leader must develop the skill of conflict resolution. **Conflict resolution** involves methods of reducing and resolving conflict. Accordingly, leaders need to understand the causes of conflict and know how to convert their destructive potential to opportunities for constructive resolve.

Causes of Conflict

Several controllable things contribute to conflicts among people. These are:

1. **Task interdependence.** First, there is **sequential task interdependence** in which one individual or group is heavily dependent on another (Bartol & Martin, 1998). For example, a Little League coach must usually rely on the city parks maintenance crew to prepare the field to play the game. Second, **reciprocal task interdependence** is when individuals or groups are mutually interdependent (Bartol & Martin, 1998). For example, getting participants over "the wall" in an adventure challenge

Exercise: Conflict Resolution

Develop a list of all possible triads in your class. Within each triad, two persons are to be designated similar to each other and different from the third. After completing your triads list, review it and make a second list of the qualities of people or situational reasons that governed your thinking as you formed the triads. Are these qualities or reasons conducive to conflicts within the triads? How? How can these potentials for conflict be "managed" so they become sources of growth and productivity for the triads? If you were the leader of the class and needed to form students into study groups of three each, upon what basis would you form the groups? Why?

program requires reliance by everyone on everyone if the goal is to be achieved. Sometimes such task interdependence creates situations of conflict.

2. **Scarce resources.** The possibility of conflict expands when there are limited resources, such as equipment, funds, training, time, office space, parking space, and so forth. (Bartol & Martin, 1998). For example, if a group of cross-country skiers and a group using snowmobiles require the same trails in the park, there will be conflict. Each group will feel more entitled to the trails, that their needs are more important, and likely be unwilling to compromise.
3. **Goal incompatibility**. It is common in a recreation setting that participants pursue goals that can be somewhat different from one another, setting the stage for potential conflicts (Bartol & Martin, 1998). A group of hikers may each have a unique goal, for example, on how many miles to hike on the first day of the trip.
4. **Communication failures**. Effective and continued communication is of vital and perhaps primary importance in relationships. Communication breakdowns can easily occur, such as when one person dislikes, distrusts, or feels angry toward another person.
5. **Individual differences.** Conflict can also arise because of differences in personality, experience, and values. (Bartol & Martin, 1998).
6. **Poorly designed reward systems.** Without intending to, reward systems can lead to destructive conflict when they reward competition in situations that require cooperation (Bartol & Martin, 1998). For example, conflict arising from too much "team spirit" can spoil sport activities, and often it is the leader's reward system that creates this.

Resolving Conflict

Leaders can rely on a number of methods to reduce or resolve conflict. Such methods are typically aimed at minimizing the destructive impact of conflict (Bartol & Martin, 1998).

1. **Change situational factors**. One way to reduce conflict is to eliminate or change the factors in the situation creating the conflict. For example, you could increase the available resources, reorganize so that task interdependency is reduced, take steps to improve communication, or redesign the reward system.
2. Focus the group on superordinate goals. If a situation is causing excessive conflict, and it is difficult to change it, leaders are sometimes able to refocus the group on major common goals that require the support and effort of everyone (Bartol &

Case in Point: Spectator Sports

A useful example of reward systems creating a forum for conflict is in spectator sports. In the United States, spectator sports are big entertainment. And no wonder—with major league baseball attracting over 55.5 million in attendance each year and men's college basketball reveling in over 33.5 million fans who attend games each year. But something has gone wrong! With greater frequency we read about rioting and violence in the crowd at sporting events. Fires have been started in the stands and property destroyed; fans have crossed barricades to attack and sometimes kill the fans of the other team or an athlete; referees have been assaulted.

Researchers and essayists have wondered why spectators have become so violent. Some suggest that it is the violence in the game—aggression breeds aggression. For example Eitzen's observations (1984) suggest that when athletes are violent on the field or court, there is a greater likelihood for violence by the fans. Another possible answer is that of self-selection. Hostile spectators may gravitate toward the more aggressive games. Or perhaps, it is a matter of out-of-line reward systems.

1. Can you offer a possible rationale for this latter hunch?
2. How might poorly designed reward systems by society, by professional and college league sport organizations, and even by your local city sports program, lead to such spectator conflicts?

Martin, 1998). These are called **superordinate goals.** The secret to conflict resolution in this case is determining a goal that is equally important to all parties. For example, superordinate goals might be beating a significant competitor in a tournament for a sport team or saving a forest from development for an environmental conservation club.

3. Use an **interpersonal conflict-handling approach.** If you the leader are involved in a conflict, there are ways you can attempt to resolve it (Reitz, 1987; Rahim & Magner, 1995; Bartol & Martin, 1998).
   - Avoiding involves suppressing a conflict in the hope that it will either go away or not become too disruptive.
   - Accommodating focuses on solving conflicts by allowing the desires of the other party to prevail. As the leader you let the other person have her way rather than continue the conflict.
   - Competing involves attempting to win a conflict at the other person's expense.
   - Compromising tries to solve conflict by having each party give up some desired outcomes to get other desired outcomes. Compromising requires a situation that offers both sides the chance to be in a better position or at least in no worse position after the conflict is resolved. With compromise both positions lose some and win some.
   - Collaborating strives to resolve conflicts by developing solutions that allow both sides to obtain their desired outcomes. That is, both parties win at least on their major issues.
4. **Bring in a third-party.** When you are not involved in the conflict, as the leader you could serve as a neutral and objective "third-party" and directly attempt to resolve it. To accomplish this you will need to establish a positive working relationship with each of the conflicting sides. Then proceed to obtain adequate enough and substantive enough knowledge about the conflict issues, encourage a problem-solving attitude among the conflicting parties, and facilitate a creative joint solution (Deutsch, 1990).

Leader Profile: The Present
Penny Wagoner
Portland, Oregon Skate Patrol. Wagoner demonstrates stopping techniques for some young participants at Oregon Safe Kids Coalition gear up games.

SAFETY MANAGEMENT

As our final consideration in the management of participant behavior, we discuss safety management. Every time you lead a group or individual participants in a recreation activity, there is the potential for an accident. **Safety management** refers to those procedures you put into effect to reduce the possibility of accidents (Priest & Gass, 1997).

Usually, most accidents occur when two types of dangers—human and environmental—combine and interact to create an accident potential. An **accident potential** is the risk, or likelihood, that an accident will occur. It does not automatically mean that an accident will occur. Thus the point of safety management is to see that both the human and environmental dangers are under control, and thus reduce the accident potential. For example, when there is horseplay on a slippery pool deck, the conditions are conducive to an accident. If you don't stop the horseplay (human danger) and/or lay down a nonslip deck surface (environmental danger) the accident potential will remain quite high.

Activity Supervision

Supervising participants as they engage in recreation activities is an important element in managing safety. When a recreation, park, sport, or tourism organization sponsors and conducts leisure activity, supervision is required. A direct-service recreation leader usually performs activity supervision.

There are various elements of a recreation activity that help to determine the required nature of the supervision (Jordan, 1996). The chart in figure 10.1 indicates the specificity of supervision according to participant, activity, and environment factors. For example, suppose you take the children, ages seven through eleven, who are participating in a summer day camp program, on a trip to a nearby state park. At the park you visit two areas: the swimming beach on the lake and the historical interpretation village where craftspeople demonstrate pioneer customs. Will there be a difference in the degree of your supervision of the children between the lake and the village? Most likely, yes. Why? Because the environments are different and the activities performed at each are different. The lake beach poses more inherent risk and the activity of swimming is more difficult than is the setting of the village and the activity of walking around and watching craftspeople spin yarn and make apple butter. Thus the supervision at the beach will be more specific and that at the village will be more general.

Let us consider both types of supervision: general and specific. **General supervision** describes where a leader oversees a broad area of activity. For example, the leader on the day camp trip to the state park might stand in the center of the village and keep an eye out for the children as they enter and leave each of the craft cabins on their own. You might provide general supervision of the entire gym while adult league volleyball is underway. Under general supervision you would notice if a thunderstorm approached quickly or if someone played too aggressively, and would also be visibly available for participant questions and problems. Under general supervision, visual and voice contact are easily maintained with participants in the area being supervised.

Recreation leaders must engage in **specific supervision** when there is skill instruction involved, participants are low skilled or young, and when the activity has inherent risk (Jordan, 1996). Specific supervision is where there is direct and close

Factors	Highest specificity of ⟵⟶ supervision	Lowest specificity of supervision
Participants		
Age	Very young	Adult
Skill level	Low	Advanced
Previous experience	None	Lots
Activity		
Complexity	High	Low
Difficulty	High	Low
Inherent risk	High	Low
Environment		
Condition	Poor	Excellent
Participant familiarity with space	None	Lots

FIGURE 10.1. Specificity of supervision (adapted from Jordan, 1996)

visual and voice contact with participants. Examples include spotting in gymnastics, coaching a sport team in skill development, or giving instructions to novice rock climbers.

Leader Duties

Beyond correctly matching the degree of leader supervision to the activity, participant, and environmental conditions, there are other ways recreation leaders should manage safety. These will help you reduce the potential that accidents will happen, or if one does, minimize its consequences.

1. *Plan ahead.* Admit that an accident can happen even under your supervision. Sometime in your career as a recreation leader, there is a likelihood that an accident will occur despite your best efforts. The key is being ready to deal with it. Know what you will do for each potential accident before it happens. Know your organization's accident policies and procedures. Know and be current in first aid and CPR.
2. *Render first aid care.* Should something go wrong and a participant require emergency care, provide it yourself or see that it is provided by an emergency care professional in as timely and efficient a manner as possible.
3. *Search for dangerous situations and conditions.* Maintain a continuous vigilance for dangers in any situation. Train your mind to imagine what might happen at any time. When there are numerous dangers present (crashing thunderstorm, muddy trail, after dark), be extra alert and cautious.
4. *Point out potential dangers.* Once you have identified dangers, draw the attention of participants to them. Alert the hikers to be extra careful because of the muddy trail.
5. *When possible remove factors that contribute to dangerous situations.* For example, remove the glass bottle from the softball field. If leaving the tent equipment at the site enables the group to reach safety more quickly during a weather emergency, do so. You can go back for the gear at another less life-threatening time.

6. *Enforce rules.* Establish, communicate, and enforce all rules equitably and consistently.
7. *Have a solid knowledge of your participants.* To conduct an activity safely you must understand the skills, previous experience, and the physical and emotional condition and capabilities of your clients. Once you have this information you can make good decisions about leading them in the activity. For example, should you use a regulation softball? How explicit do your directions need to be? What is the optimal group size? Answers to these questions should come directly from your knowledge about your participants.
8. *Have a solid knowledge of the activity.* Know what equipment is appropriate, the activity's rules, and the best sequencing and progression. For example, the game "Red Rover" can be dangerous for players (children and adults) and perhaps shouldn't be allowed when there is a wide mix of player sizes and weights.

Summary

The behavioral management skills that enable recreation leaders to work effectively with participants can be difficult to learn. Yet they are among the most important competencies you will use in recreation leadership situations. In this chapter we discussed these competencies as preventive behavior management, discipline, conflict resolution, and safety management.

The idea of preventive behavior management is to minimize or prevent behavioral difficulties. As a basis for preventing problems before they occur, the leader frequently monitors and responds to participants' behaviors. One of the most important skills for the leader in managing participants' behavior is responding to their actions and words appropriately. Listening is the first and most important step. The type of responses that you make will be either hindered or enhanced by how well you listen.

When preventive behavior management doesn't work, behavior problems requiring discipline can occur. Discipline is a set of assertive methods used to maintain orderly behaviors. Discipline can include direct instruction, the use of punishment, and an overall tone of leader control to force compliance in others. Like all forms of behavior management, positive discipline is preferred.

The recreation leader must also develop the skill of conflict resolution. Conflict resolution involves methods of reducing and resolving conflict. Accordingly, leaders need to understand the causes of conflict and know how to convert their destructive potential to opportunities for constructive resolve. And finally, we considered safety management in this chapter. Every time you lead a group or individual participants in a recreation activity, there is the potential for an accident. Safety management refers to those procedures you put into effect to reduce the possibility of accidents.

Questions and Activities for Review and Discussion

1. Discuss with classmates the response options to the two camper scenarios posed on the opening page of this chapter. Which ones better manage participant behavior? In what way?
2. Develop your own case study (real or fictional) that demonstrates at least two (out of thirteen) of the suggestions for managing participant behavior.
3. From your experiences in leader-led recreation activities, which of the advice about rules seems most important to you? Why, in terms of your experiences?

4. What is positive discipline, and why is it recommended?
5. Explain the causes of conflict in recreation groups. Describe a conflict situation in a recreation group of which you are aware and trace its causes.
6. Describe several ways to reduce or resolve conflict. Recall the conflict situation example from question 5 and indicate what approaches you could have taken to reduce or resolve the conflict.
7. What is accident potential? Name at least five ways it can be reduced.

References

Bartol, K. M., & Martin, D. C. (1998). Management (3rd ed.). Boston, MA: Irwin McGraw-Hill.

Deutsch, M. (1990). Sixty years of conflict. *The International Journal of Conflict Management, 1*, 237–263.

Eitzen, D. S. (1984). *Sport in contemporary society.* New York: St. Martin's Press.

Johnson, D. W. (1981). *Reaching out: Interpersonal effectiveness and self-actualization.* Englewood Cliffs, NJ: Prentice-Hall.

Jordan, D. J. (1996). *Leadership in leisure services: Making a difference*. State College, PA: Venture.

Pfeiffer, J. W., & Jones, J. E. (1973). *A handbook of structured experiences for human relations training: vol. iv*. La Jolla, CA: University Associates.

Priest, S., & Gass, M. A. (1997). *Effective leadership in adventure programming.* Champaign, IL: Human Kinetics.

Rahim, M. A., & Magner, N. R. (1995). Confirmatory factor analysis of the styles of handling interpersonal conflict: First-order factor model and its invariance across groups. *Journal of Applied Psychology, 80*, 122–132.

Reitz, H. J. (1987). *Behavior in organizations* (3rd ed.). Homewood, IL: Irwin.

Sherrill, C. (1993). *Adapted physical activity, recreation, and sport.* Dubuque, IA: Brown & Benchmark.

Vinton, D. A., & Farley, E. M. (1979). *Camp training series: Module 5. Dealing with camper behavior.* Lexington, KY: University of Kentucky, The American Camping Association, & Hawkins & Associates.

Windell, J. (1991). *Discipline: A sourcebook of 50 failsafe techniques for parents.* New York, NY: Macmillan.

Wolfgang, C., & Wolfgang, M. (1995). *The three faces of discipline for early childhood.* Boston, MA: Allyn & Bacon.

Woolard, W. P., & Zucco, M. L. (June 1999, vol. 34, no. 6). Golf Peoria's youth movement. *Parks and Recreation*, 64–71.

Web Resources

Accelerated communication training: Leadership development programs: www.rollcast.com/ACTleadership.htm

Behavior Modification—MIR Glossary of Terms—Mentalhealth Internet Resources: http://mirconnect.com/glossary/behaviormodification.html

Behavior modification therapy: www.plgrm.com/health/B/Behavior Modification.htm

Classroom management: www.csrnet.org/csrnet/management.html

Conflict management resources: www.mediationworks.com/indxconm.htm

Parenting tool box: www.parentingtoolbox.com/hand.html

Performance management: www.behavior.org/performanceMgmt/performance welcome.html

Safety Store: www.safetystore.com/

Solutions to "Responding" exercise

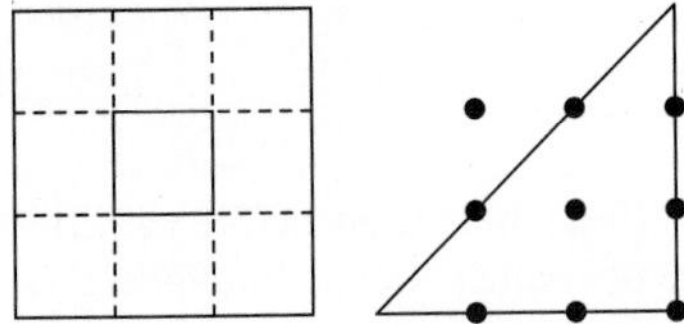

CHAPTER 11

Teaching

In a classical perspective, leisure is the cultivation of the mind, spirit, and character.
—Bammel and Burrus-Bammel, 1996, p. 19.

Learning Objectives

Another important skill for recreation leaders is teaching. Teaching enables the leader to give participants the skills, knowledge, and attitudes required to satisfyingly experience recreation. In this chapter you will learn about teaching according to:

- types of learning
- range of learning
- how learning happens
- teacher roles
- designing effective lessons
- teaching strategies

Key Terms

direct service approach p. 198
indirect service approach p. 198
knowledge p. 199
skill p. 200
attitude p. 200
memorization p. 200
comprehension p. 200
application p. 200
generalization p. 201
systemization p. 201
learning gradient p. 201
individual differences p. 202
personal meaning p. 202
learning by doing p. 202
existing knowledge p. 202
feedback p. 202
motivation p. 202
dictated role p. 203
prescribed role p. 203
directed role p. 203
consulted role p. 203
interpreted role p. 204
automated role p. 204
shared role p. 204
lesson plan p. 205
full value contract p. 205
learning objectives p. 206
lecture p. 207
discussion p. 207
drill and practice p. 208
group investigation p. 209
learning center p. 210
demonstration p. 211
simulation p. 211
independent study p. 212

The recreation leader does many things. Yet working within the context of even a wide diversity of settings, the recreation leader's primary function is the provision of opportunities for others to experience satisfying recreation. One of the ways that recreation leaders provide this opportunity is through the selection and leading of recreation activities. The successful leadership of activities in music, sports, crafts, drama, nature, dance, games, and other areas requires specific techniques. This chapter addresses the basic concept of another of these important activity leadership abilities: teaching. But first we take a short diversion.

The recreation or park organization provides opportunities for recreation through activities in two ways. These organizations can provide recreation activity services (and facility and administrative services) by either a direct approach or an indirect approach.

Recreation activities provided by the **direct service approach** are preplanned, organized, promoted, and implemented by the staff and "delivered" to the participants. With this approach, recreation activities are considered the "product" that is created and then distributed.

The relationship between the participant and the leader using the direct service approach is one of provider and consumer. This assumes that the recreation leader is the expert who has the knowledge and skill needed to acquire the resources and transform them into specific activity opportunities.

On the other hand, recreation activities offered by the **indirect service approach** are focused on helping participants do for themselves. Instead of being oriented toward the creation and distribution of recreation activities, the leader in this approach assists other individuals in attaining the appropriate skills, attitudes, or materials. The participants are encouraged to help themselves, to experience recreation activities independent of an organization's preorganized program.

This indirect, or enabling, approach suggests a different relationship between the leader and the participant. It requires the development of a cooperative relationship. The leader works with participants to help them acquire the knowledge, skills, and attitudes necessary to provide their own recreation experiences. This approach is based on the assumption that the recreation leader is not the only member of society who has the ability to plan and implement recreation activities. It presumes that this ability can be taught to other individuals by the professional. The professional recreation leader then becomes the enabler, the catalyst, and the facilitator.

The organization of sports activities can serve as an example of how these two approaches are used. Using the direct service approach, what would be the work of the recreation leader? According to this approach, the leader would plan and carry out programs of athletic activities. This might involve establishing the rules; determining the number and composition of the teams; scheduling a tournament; hiring and training officials, scorekeepers, timers, and coaches; advertising the activity; lining and preparing the field; and leading the players in lead-up drills and practice sessions. The leader of the sports program acts as the provider. The details of the program's organization, promotion, and implementation are taken care of and the participant is the recipient.

Using the indirect service approach applied to this same example, the work of the recreation leader would be different. Rather than planning *for* the participant, the role of the leader is to plan *with* the participant. The participant assumes responsibility for the organization, promotion, and implementation of the sports program. This means that the leader might help interested individuals form an independent and nonprofit sports association, provide consultant services on the fundamentals of fund-raising, provide sport groups with information on the latest sports equipment or national rule modifications, or offer sport facilities for games. The recreation leader would therefore not plan and implement a swim meet, for example; rather this would be the responsibility of those persons interested in competitive swimming. The organization's leadership may instead only provide the swimming pool and advice on the ordering and scheduling of each event.

Both the direct and indirect service approaches are employed in recreation and park organizations. In some situations both approaches are used simultaneously, according to the type of activity. For example, an organization may assume the direct service approach for the provision of craft activities for children and the indirect service approach for dramatic activities for adults.

The assumption of this chapter (as well as the previous chapter on facilitation and the others in this part of the book) is that persons who work in the recreation fields as leaders will spend a great deal of their energies providing recreation activity opportunities through the direct service approach. One ability that is important in direct activity leadership is teaching.

A basic truism operates in recreation activity participation. It goes something like this: To gain full enjoyment and satisfaction from a recreation activity, the participant must possess at least a minimal amount of skill and knowledge about that activity. For example, to enjoy wind surfing, the participant must be able to stay fairly well balanced on the board while in the water and be able to handle the sail to catch the wind (at least some of the time!). To make a pair of copper-enameled earrings, the participant must know how to copper enamel. This is why many recreation activity programs include instruction in the activity.

LEARNING

Recreation leaders teach. The most common teaching situation is as just described, where participants desire to learn about a specific recreation activity such as the use of poling in downhill skiing, the translation of international codes in orienteering, the proper phrasing and timing in madrigal singing, or steps in folk dancing. Also recreation leaders are often teachers in nonactivity specific situations such as in-service training sessions for other staff in the organization or job orienting for new workers. In both staff training and specific activity situations the recreation leader attempts to create environments and circumstances for learning to occur.

Leader Profile: The Present
Buffalo Tiger
Chief of the Miccosukees in Southern Florida from 1952–1985. Buffalo Tiger attempts to use cultural tourism as a way to educate others about his people's way of life. What role in teaching does this illustrate?

Types of Learning

In recreation learning situations, and in most other learning situations, there are three types or categories of learning: knowledge, skill, and attitude. These three concepts should be taught to recreation participants learning an activity or to staff members learning a new job.

Knowledge, or cognitive learning, refers to "knowing" something. It includes those concepts, information, or abstractions necessary to perform an activity. Knowledge of the loom in weaving, knowledge of different grades of wax in cross-country skiing, knowledge of bird songs in the hobby of ornithology, and knowledge of rules in wallyball are examples. From the learner's standpoint mental or intellectual processes are involved.

Exercise: My Teachers

Throughout your life teachers have influenced you. Perhaps one or two of them stand out in your mind. Think about them for a moment by completing the following:

1. The teacher I remember best is:
2. I think I learned a great deal from this teacher because she/he:
3. The reason this was so effective in helping me learn was:
4. This impacted me in this way:

In most recreation situations the concern is with the practical application of knowledge. The participant needs the knowledge of the loom so that he is better able to weave a set of place mats; or knowledge of different grades of ski wax so that she can ski to the hot springs without backsliding or icing up.

Skill, or psychomotor learning, on the other hand, refers to the ability to perform or engage in an activity. Recreation leaders are frequently involved in the teaching of activity skills. We teach participants how to strum a guitar, how to roll in kayaking, how to run in a triathlon, and how to develop a snapshot into a print.

Learning a recreation activity skill usually requires learning a movement, a coordination, or an action sequence. For example, in learning the golf swing the participant must learn to hold the club, position the wrists, swing the club back and then forward, position the feet, focus the eyes, and numerous other things. The full movement must be learned as a coordinated sequence.

In recreational learning situations, leaders often conceptualize skill teaching according to different levels. Beginning, intermediate, and advanced skill performance levels are common, with teaching at the beginner's skill level being most common.

Attitude, or affective learning, is the third type of learning and refers to feelings. An attitude is an emotional condition that usually affects other things such as behavior or preference. An individual who has the attitude that going fast is dangerous will probably not be interested in bicycle road racing. To enjoy a recreation activity the participant not only needs to learn the skills and knowledge required for the activity but also to learn the activity's compatible attitude. Recreation leaders frequently attempt to teach attitudes.

Attitudes may vary in intensity and in direction (Niepoth, 1983). Some attitudes are held more intensely than others, and some attitudes are more favorable than others. This means that people may hold strongly positive or strongly negative attitudes. For example, an avid backpacker would be likely to have strong positive feelings about the setting aside of wilderness areas and strong negative feelings about commercial development in backcountry areas.

Range of Learning

In addition to viewing learning from the perspective of categories, we can also consider it as having depths, ranging from shallow to deep or basic to complex. According to Priest and Gass (1997) there are five progressively deeper levels: memorization, comprehension, application, generalization, and systemization.

At the most basic and shallow level is **memorization,** where the learner memorizes by repeating factual information and by identifying right and wrong answers. For example, a memorizing learner in a painting class will be able to list the primary and secondary colors. The memorizing learner can also identify right and wrong ways to belay, such as not keeping the "breaking" hand on the rope at all times (Priest & Gass, 1997).

At the second, or **comprehension,** level, the learner is able to explain how processes work and why, as well as when or where the learning can be applied. In the painting class, for example, the learner can explain how pigment is mixed and what happens when you mix particular proportions of particular pigments. In belaying a comprehending learner is able to describe the step-by-step sequence of hand movements and describe rock climbing situations in which belaying may or may not be needed (Priest & Gass, 1997).

At the **application** range of learning, the learner is able to apply his comprehension by practicing or demonstrating the skill or knowledge in a specific situation. For example, the art student is able to take the leader's instructions about portraying sunlight in a landscape painting and accomplish it during a painting field trip to the park. In belaying the learning climber is able to set up and handle a horizontal belay in the classroom and transpose this to setting up and operating a vertical belay on the rock face (Priest & Gass, 1997).

The fourth level of learning is **generalization.** When generalizing the learner is able to carry over the technique learned to a new situation. The art learner can use the technique to paint sunlight and shadows on a landscape out of doors to paint incandescent lighting and shadows on a still life indoors. The generalizing learner is able to vary the technique from belaying on a river crossing to belaying during a rappel to belaying a lead rock climber. Each situation is different, requiring correct modifications to adapt to the new situation.

At the deepest, most complex level of learning, the learner creates new knowledge from her base of existing knowledge. This is **systemization.** The accomplished painter is able to develop new ways to mix pigments or create light and shadow on a painting, and the expert rock climber is able to find a new and perhaps better way to belay.

Another way of looking at range of learning is as a gradient. Called by Priest and Hammerman (1990) the **learning gradient,** this is a continuum of how much information is typically retained by learners according to four methods of teaching: telling, showing, doing, and questioning. (figure 11.1). As the learner progresses along the continuum from being told, to being shown, to doing, and to questioning, the amount of information she is able to recall, process, and apply increases.

In teaching a recreation skill, for example, you might begin by telling, progress to showing and having the learner practice, and finally to asking if there are any questions and asking the learner questions. Suppose you are trying to teach how to knit. People forget most of what they hear, so your participants will not learn how to knit only by being told. Similarly, watching you knit a few rows is also usually insufficient for learning how to knit, although the demonstration will have greater learning impact than simply hearing about it. Your learners must also have practice at knitting under your guidance and an opportunity to test their understanding. It is the old Confucius adage: "I hear and I forget, I see and I remember, I do and I understand," to which we add "you ask me and I know."

Leader Profile: The Past
Pat Nixon
Recreational bowler and wife of former president of the United States, Richard Nixon. Like every recreational participant, Pat must have at least a basic skill level to enjoy the activity.

How Does Learning Happen?

In the past several years a vast amount of research on learning has been produced. Researchers have investigated how people learn and what causes them to learn. As a result,

FIGURE 11.1. The learning gradient

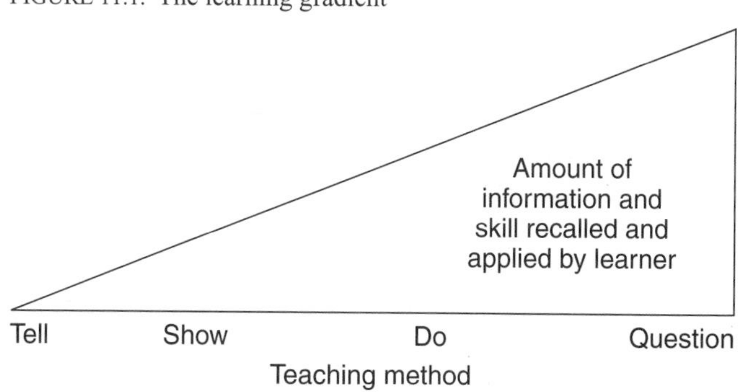

there is available certain widely accepted principles important for the teaching done by recreation leaders.

1. **Individual differences.** It is essential that the recreation leader be aware that each learner is an individual and thus learns in unique ways. Different people benefit from different teaching methods, value different concepts or skills more highly, prefer different learning settings, and remember different things. This suggests that leaders should attempt to avoid standardized teaching approaches and standardized expectations of what participants can learn. The leader should be attentive to each individual.
2. **Personal meaning.** Learners interpret new skills or knowledge according to their own perceptions and reference points because each learner is motivated by his self-concept, biases, and needs. To help individuals to more effectively learn a recreation activity, the leader should help them discover their personal meaning in the activity. Research has indicated that people learn only that which has, or comes to have, personal meaning to them. Leaders should thus help participants realize how the recreational skill or knowledge being taught is related to them. What are the personal benefits of learning it?
3. **Learning by doing.** People learn better by doing. Trying an activity skill is more productive than being told about an activity. The best learning occurs during involvement. The leader must be aware of this principle and get people involved in the dance step or craft procedure as rapidly and as meaningfully as possible. In teaching loom weaving, for instance, it would be important to encourage participants to begin working with the loom and the yarn on simple projects near the beginning of the instructional program.
4. **Existing knowledge.** New information will make more sense to learners if it is related to their existing knowledge. If the new knowledge makes sense, the learner will not only have an informational head start but will also approach the new learning task with greater self-confidence. This principle requires that the leader know what the participants have already learned about an activity.
5. **Feedback.** Reinforcing learning with appropriate feedback gives the learner an idea of how well she is progressing. It informs the learner of needed corrections. As in the shooting of an arrow into a target, the feedback is immediately valuable to improving the accuracy of the shot. Yet there are many other activities where the results of performance are not so easily or readily perceived. The feedback in learning to dance, for instance, may not be easily determined by the learner. It is thus necessary for the leader to monitor the participant's progress and provide this information for the learner.
6. **Motivation.** Unless participants are ready to learn, learning will not be successful. Motivation is necessary. This refers to a general level of interest or eagerness to learn an activity. There must exist a psychological and physiological foundation that makes the individual ready to learn. Many teaching devices can be employed to help set this readiness.

TEACHING ROLES

Just as there are many different ways your clients learn recreation skills, knowledge, and attitudes, there are many different roles you can have when you teach. As you follow this discussion, keep in mind that no particular role is the best—each is appropriate for certain learning situations and goals. The teaching roles we consider here are: dictated, prescribed, directed, consulted, interpreted, automated, and shared (Priest & Gass, 1997).

Dictated

In the **dictated role,** the leader controls for the clients how, what, when, where, and who is taught. The teacher dictates at all phases of the learning situation: preplans, implements, and evaluates. This is an "I'm in command" teaching role, which may seem too overbearing for a recreation learning situation, but it does have an appropriate place. In dangerous or risky learning conditions—where it is important to do things the correct way to avoid injury—a dictated role may be necessary. For example, in teaching the handling of a pocketknife to children, you will want to dictate that everyone hold the knife exactly the same way so that you can easily survey the group and immediately spot a potentially dangerous action by a child.

Prescribed

The **prescribed role** is the same as the dictated role with one exception. As in the dictated role the leader controls how, what, where, and who is taught, as well as why, but there is a difference in when. In a prescribed teaching situation you let the clients determine how they will integrate and use what you have taught them (Priest & Gass, 1997). For example, you can dictate in your teaching of how to ride a bike, paddle a canoe, or cross-country ski, but allow participants to practice what you've taught under different circumstances—learning from the consequences of their actions. Let's use cross-country skiing instruction as an example. As a teacher using the prescribed role you control every aspect of the first hour of instruction, which is held out on the flat meadow. In the second hour you allow the participants to make their own decisions about whether to continue practicing on their own on the flat meadow or trying out some of the nearby trails. You've taught them how to turn on the flat surface, but leave it up to them to learn how what you've taught them applies when turning while going up hill.

Directed

In the **directed role** you control how, what, when, where, who, and why to teach, and you control how the skill is practiced and applied. What is different is that you let the clients have authority to go at their own pace during the learning experience. You allow them to make their own decision on such as how fast to go, which direction to take, when to rest or stop, and what pieces to repeat (Priest & Gass, 1997). The directed role is useful at times when participant control to choose is important, yet your control over their safety is equally important. Teaching knot tying is a good example. Most knots can be tied in many variations. Some of these variations can appear correct to the novice, but can fail under certain circumstances. In using the directed role, you allow participants to try their own variations while you are teaching them, but when it comes to applying their knots in a boating or belaying situation, you assume full control over their action.

Consulted

The **consulted role,** unlike the prescribed role, which allows participants freedom of choice in the application of what is learned, and the directed role, which allows participants freedom of choice in learning at their own pace, allows participants freedom in both learning at their own pace and in the application of what is learned. As the leader you plan the experience by selecting the learning objectives, content, methods, locations, schedules, and so on. Once the experience begins, however, you step back and let participants determine how the experience will proceed and how they will apply their learning. This is an effective teaching role when safety is not critical, yet achieving the objectives of the learning is. In employing the consultative role you do not provide feedback to the learners—you allow the natural consequences of their experience to do that. For example, if they do not pitch their tent correctly, and it rains and they get wet, they've learned the lesson. In other words, the participants are experiencing consequential learning.

Interpreted

In the **interpreted role** the leader has responsibility and control over the application of the learning only. Here the clients plan and execute the learning experience, making their own choices about how, what, when, where, and why to learn. Afterward, you guide their interpretation of what they learned by directing the evaluation, feedback, and follow-up. Service learning situations can benefit from an interpreted teacher role. Suppose, for example, that you are the leader of a Girl Scout troop and you want the troop members to learn the importance of community service. You allow them to completely plan where they'll provide the service, what the service will be, its duration, and so on. Afterward you direct them in interpreting what they learned and how what they learned could be carried over into other aspects of the community.

Automated

In the **automated role** the leader allows the clients to make choices and have authority over all aspects of the learning situation. Clients make the choices about planning, executing, and interpreting their learning. As the leader, your role is to support their efforts to implement their choices (Priest & Gass, 1997). The automated role is appropriate for participants who have mastered all or most of the fundamentals of a skill and are in the final stages of applying their learning. Again, in a service learning situation, the troop members may be taking older adults on a bicycle trip. This follows a biking clinic for the older adults the troop members conducted earlier—a learning experience that used the prescribed or consulted teaching roles. Based on this previous learning experience, the troop members are able to finalize their learning. For this, the automated teaching role is useful.

Shared

As the label suggests, the **shared role** is a mix of two or more roles at a time. This may mean that you and your participants work together to shape the how, what, when, where, and who of the learning experience, but then you shift to the dictated role during the instruction phase and return to a sharing of control over the evaluation of what was learned. The shared role could also mean that you switch teaching roles on the spur of the moment when safety, for example, suddenly becomes an issue or when participants become frustrated with the role you have been using. For example, in the previous illustration of the prescribed role, you might choose to switch to a dictated role if the cross-country skiing novices are having too much trouble trying out their newly acquired skills on the trails. So, you call them back to the flat meadow where they can apply their skills under your direct supervision.

DESIGNING EFFECTIVE LESSONS

In several of the teaching roles we have discussed, the leader's role is in directly preparing the how, what, when, where, and who of the learning experience. How can we best accomplish such preparations for instruction? There are a number of tips that can improve your ability to do this. These include lesson planning, establishing a teaching environment, and setting learning objectives.

Lesson Planning

Preparing for a teaching experience often means preparing a **lesson plan.** The key to effective lesson planning is keeping the learner's perspective in mind. Continually ask yourself as you plan the lesson: "what might the learner think of this lesson?" (Priest & Gass, 1997). To help you do this, try these steps:

1. List the skills, concepts, and attitudes you want the learners to achieve from the teaching session.
2. Organize this list into a logical flow, or sequence, of learning. Most of the time you will organize the list linearly, such as from the observed to the abstract, from the whole to pieces, from simple to complex, from the general to the particular, and so forth. This logical flow becomes the main body of the lesson.
3. Once you have organized the skills and concepts into the lesson's main body, add a conclusion that summarizes what the lesson was about. This should include a review of the main points and some suggestions for applying what was learned.

Case in Point: Full Value Contract

Sometimes in a recreation learning situation it is important to prepare people in advance. Particularly if participants have some fears or reticence about their ability to learn the new skill, the teaching leader should help ready them for learning. One way of accomplishing this is the full value contract. Adapted from the ideas of Medrick (1979), the **full value contract** asks participants to agree to certain "terms" for the learning experience. Imagine the leader who is readying a group of middle-aged nonathletes for a distance running clinic saying,

"Because we want each of you to get what you came for, we are asking each of you to agree to abide by what we call the full value contract while you participate in this running clinic. There are two parts to this contract. The first is that you agree to fully value, respect, and consider yourself during our activities as a group. This includes your reactions to all physical and emotional issues that may arise. Treat yourself as you want to be treated by the group, and let the group know, as well, how you want to be treated. The second part of the contract is to fully value, respect, and consider others during our activities as a group. If you see another group member who may not be valued, agreeing to this contract also means that you will address this.

"Fully valuing yourself and others is a serious undertaking, but a condition that we've found to be extremely helpful in making sure our learning situation together is productive and valuable. Is this contract clear to everyone? If it is, we'd like everyone to verbally agree that they are willing to work by these two principles while we are together."

4. Finally, prepare an introduction that overviews what the lesson will be about and that motivates and readies participants for learning. Be sure to mention the purpose of the lesson and its connection to past learning.

Establishing the Teaching Environment

In recreation learning situations we have both the indoors and the outdoors as our classroom. In both situations you'll need to consider the participants' safety and comfort if learning is to be maximized. For example, in terms of temperature in the outdoors, you may need to ask them to wear layers of clothing so that they can add or subtract clothes as temperatures rise and fall. Also outdoors, have participants stand facing away from the sun while you explain a skill or procedure. Pay attention to seating as well. Even outdoors have participants sit so that eye contact can be maintained for everyone. Sitting in circles and semicircles works well, even when lecturing.

Setting Learning Objectives

Learning objectives form the foundation for teaching (Priest & Gass, 1997). You will use them to define the direction of the learning and to prepare and organize for the learning experience. Writing down objectives can enable the teaching process for you, the teacher, and for participants, the learners, because learning objectives are specific target declarations. For example, perhaps the learning objective of your focus is to teach the mechanics of long distance running to enhance the self-concept of a group of nonathletes.

The learning objectives that you set should be fairly detailed. They should establish precisely what behaviors or actions indicate that participants have learned. For example, in the long distance running clinic you might write these down as learning objectives.

Participants will show:

- commitment to running by completing the final distance run event without aid
- an understanding of proper training by not becoming injured during the clinic program
- higher self-concept by scoring higher on a self-concept questionnaire after the clinic

These objectives specify the learning goals, participants' targeted behaviors, and the conditions under which these behaviors are to occur. That is, the goals for those in the running program are "commitment to running," "understanding of proper training," and "higher self-concept." To determine that these goals were accomplished, participants are to demonstrate the behaviors of "completing the run," "not becoming injured," and "scoring higher." The conditions under which these are expected are "without aid," "during the clinic program," and "on the self-concept questionnaire."

This reminds us of another purpose of learning objectives. In addition to defining the direction of learning and providing a structure for preparing and organizing the learning situation, learning objectives enable us to evaluate the effectiveness of the learning experience. Thus the more appropriate the learning objectives, the more accurate is our evaluation of the learning achieved.

Teaching Strategies

Ways of teaching that help participants attain instructional goals are discussed here as strategies. Several are presented because no one best teaching method fits all learning situations.

Lecture

Telling learners or reading to learners is a teaching strategy best used when instructions need to be given, an issue is to be clarified, a pertinent personal experience is shared, or the leader's expertise is needed. The definition of **lecture** is that it is a method of teaching by which the leader gives an oral presentation of facts or principles.

The leader who uses the lecture teaching strategy, then, needs to both cope with the limitations of the method and use its strengths to best advantage. Lecturing is an economical use of time and allows the leader to work with larger numbers of participants and to cover larger amounts of material. The strategy is also helpful for introducing new skills or knowledge, particularly where background material is needed. On the other hand, lecturing is a one-way process with the learner usually assuming a passive role. In using the lecture strategy the learning progresses at the pace of the leader rather than that of the participant.

The lecture teaching strategy is most useful to the recreation leader when recreation activity knowledge or information is to be taught, such as safety rules in candle making or the history of the novel in a great books club. It is often inadequate for teaching recreation activity skills and attitudes.

The "Competency Checklist for the Lecture Teaching Strategy" summarizes those teaching behaviors that are desirable when using the lecture method.

Discussion

Learners in recreation activities can profit from contact with the thinking and know-how of leaders and with that of other participants. The **discussion** teaching strategy helps

Competency Checklist for the Lecture Teaching Strategy

When using the lecture strategy, the leader usually performs the following behaviors:

_____ Obtaining the attention of the audience at the start
_____ Making clear the purpose of the lecture
_____ Making periodic checks to determine where the listeners "are" in regard to the material presented
_____ Defining the time limit in advance for the audience
_____ Accompanying the lecture with multisensory aids
_____ Talking with sufficient volume to reach all listeners
_____ Projecting warmth, friendliness, confidence, and interest in the subject
_____ Repeating the main ideas
_____ Highlighting main ideas verbally so the audience may take notes
_____ Varying voice intonation and emphasis
_____ Pacing ideas and verbal delivery with some variety
_____ Incorporating examples
_____ Using humor to relieve tension, refocus attention, and create a mutual bond
_____ Allowing for audience feedback through paraphrases and questions

Modified from Gilstrap, R. L., & Martin, W. R. (1975). *Current strategies for teachers: A resource for personalizing instruction.* Pacific Palisades, CA: Goodyear Publishing.

provide for both. Common sense suggests that the more learners contribute, the more involved they become, and the more they learn.

There are three uses of the discussion method in a teaching context that the recreation leader can employ. First, in the problem-solving discussion the participants attempt to share the responsibility for learning by together resolving learning problems such as the best way to apply the wax in batiking. Second, is the open-ended discussion, in which participants are asked to discuss any thought-provoking questions related to their lives such as their management of leisure time as an aid in stress reduction. Third, the diagnostic discussion is directly related to what the group is learning. Its purpose is to assess whether the participants understand the lesson by getting an idea of what they know and do not know, such as emergency procedures while winter camping.

The main advantage of the discussion method is that it involves the participant more directly in the learning process and provides an avenue for involvement by everyone. The pooling of the discussion group's information may also result in new insights for participants. On the other hand, the outcome of a discussion is unpredictable, even when carefully organized. This strategy usually does not function well unless participants have a common background of knowledge.

The "Competency Checklist for the Discussion Teaching Strategy" summarizes those teaching behaviors that are desirable when using the discussion method.

Drill and Practice

Teachers have always emphasized that skills worth learning should be mastered accurately. The teaching strategy of **drill and practice** is valuable in bringing about skill accuracy, speed, and use. Remember multiplication table flash cards? Learning to make a light, flaky croissant requires practice—so does learning to throw the javelin. To be most effective the drilling and practicing of motor skills or mental skills must be indi-

Competency Checklist for the Discussion Teaching Strategy

When using the discussion strategy, the leader usually performs the following behaviors:

- _____ Providing an initial "jumping off" activity; e.g., a field trip, reading assignment, movie
- _____ Organizing the physical facilities to enhance discussion; e.g., arranging chairs in a tight circle
- _____ Providing sufficient and appropriate multimedia materials
- _____ Encouraging persons to participate in responding, interacting, challenging, and conducting the discussion
- _____ Referring questions back to the group or to individuals in the group
- _____ Using probing questions, especially those of the "why" and "how" type
- _____ Generally refraining from judging their answers or responses as "right" or "wrong"
- _____ Being supportive; for example, by giving credit for perceptive contributions and by providing ample time for participants to develop ideas and responses
- _____ Enabling the discussion to move toward some positive end or purpose

Modified from Gilstrap, R. L., & Martin, W. R. (1975). *Current strategies for teachers: A resource for personalizing instruction.* Pacific Palisades, CA: Goodyear Publishing.

vidualized. The strategy is an individual problem-solving process. It must include initial learnings, varied contact, and repetition.

This teaching method is able to provide opportunities for "overlearning" specific skills, which tends to enhance retention. It focuses on specific components of a learning task, such as hand positions when centering clay on a potter's wheel, so that participants can concentrate on learning one thing at a time. Without careful supervision by the leader, however, drill and practice experiences may permit participants to practice an incorrect skill. Mere repetition is not the same as drill and practice. Additionally, if incorrectly led, drill and practice can be boring; thus it requires careful preparation according to the needs of individual learners. Because of the individualized nature of practice, it is difficult to apply to a group setting. How does the leader determine, for example, whether a group is ready for its first ocean scuba dive? The method is also inappropriate for the development of activity values.

The "Competency Checklist for the Drill and Practice Teaching Strategy" summarizes those teaching behaviors that are desirable when using the drill and practice method.

Group Investigation

Group investigation is a learning activity for a small group. Its function is to work cooperatively together toward answers and solutions to learning concerns or problems. The focus of the group's investigation can be related to a larger topic or can be a topic of interest only to the group conducting the investigation. Usually the intention is for the group to clarify its objectives, plan procedures, gather information, analyze findings, draw conclusions, and report its findings to a larger group or to the leader.

Competency Checklist for the Drill and Practice Teaching Strategy

When using the drill and practice strategy, the leader usually performs the following behaviors:

_____ Planning for a progression in the session; for example, include a "warm-up" or a demonstration before the start of the drill and move from relatively simple to more complex operations as the session proceeds

_____ Providing "real life" conditions for the drill and practice that resemble as much as possible those in which the skill will be used

_____ Providing a variety of drill and practice situations until the objectives are achieved

_____ Using positive verbal reinforcement

_____ Using positive nonverbal reinforcement

_____ Assessing participant level of progress; for example, walking around the area observing and letting them know how well they are doing

_____ Providing careful supervision, especially for those who are having trouble

_____ Encouraging participants who show sufficient competency to proceed with drill and practice independent of the leader

Modified from Gilstrap, R. L., & Martin, W. R. (1975). *Current strategies for teachers: A resource for personalizing instruction.* Pacific Palisades, CA: Goodyear Publishing.

Competency Checklist for the Group Investigation Teaching Strategy

When using the group investigation strategy, the leader usually performs the following behaviors:

_____ Identifying the skills needed by the group in accomplishing its investigation
_____ Reviewing the basic procedures for group investigation with the participants
_____ Helping participants identify the topics or problems to be explored
_____ Providing guidance to participants as they organize into groups and select leaders
_____ Serving as a resource to the groups as they make initial plans and survey available resources
_____ Judging whether or not the plans made by the participants are within their range of abilities
_____ Supervising carefully the participants' activities so that assistance is available when needed
_____ Closing out activities tactfully if progress is not proceeding in a positive direction
_____ Assisting the participants in analyzing and drawing conclusions from their findings
_____ Assisting the groups in evaluating the effectiveness of their efforts

Modified from Gilstrap, R. H., & Martin, W. R. (1975). *Current strategies for teachers: A resource for personalizing instruction.* Pacific Palisades, CA: Goodyear Publishing.

Group investigation is often used with children and young participants and is particularly suited to subjects in outdoor education. Along with learning the knowledge under investigation, participants in the group investigation teaching strategy also have an opportunity to learn cooperative group skills. Such skills, like other skills, are learned through practice. The important rule to remember in using this teaching method is that the participants plan their own learning through open-ended tasks rather than just carrying out the leader's assignment for them.

As with the other methods, there are advantages and disadvantages to the group investigation method. It allows learners to use their inquiry skills, provides opportunities for more intensive study of a subject, is conducive to developing participant leadership, and allows learners to become more actively involved in their learning. The major disadvantage, on the other hand, is that the success of the method depends on the ability of the participants to lead themselves and to work independently with minimal leader direction.

What does the leader do when using the group investigation method? The "Competency Checklist for the Group Investigation Teaching Strategy" overviews the necessary leader teaching behaviors.

Learning Center

An attempt at individualizing instruction resulted in the teaching strategy of the **learning center.** This is a loose term for an area in the organization's facility (such as the library at camp, the lounge at the older adult center, or the nature center in the park) where a wide assortment of resources for learning is available. The emphasis is on making observable learning gains by individualized interaction with books, pictures, computers, objects, multimedia materials, and other resources.

This teaching strategy is perhaps most productively used in recreation learning situations when the concern is for skill or knowledge development. It allows participants to proceed at their own pace and ability level and according to their own learning style. The leader serves as a learning facilitator and consultant.

The method should be selected with care as it encourages an active learning environment that may be unfamiliar and even uncomfortable for some participants. It may be difficult for those learners who have not developed such skills because it stresses independent work skills. Also it requires a greater amount of initial preparation time and energy for the leader.

Case in Point: The Indianapolis Children's Museum

The Children's Museum of Indianapolis, the largest children's museum in the world, is considered an innovator in the museum and education fields. As interpreted by this museum the concept of a children's museum departs from the standard museum in four ways:

1. Education justifies every object, activity, and event. There is an educational purpose behind each display, a story to tell.
2. Bright, vivid colors and dramatic lighting effects are used to capture attention. Labels are written in easily understood, contemporary language.
3. Exhibits are placed carefully to afford even the youngest a good look. Whenever possible, exhibits are "hands-on" or participatory.
4. No matter how sophisticated the exhibit, human contact remains the most important source of learning.

The Children's Museum of Indianapolis houses more than 105,000 artifacts in ten galleries, or "learning environments," that explore science, history, foreign cultures, space, and the arts. In the galleries signs read, "Please touch!" Visitors can get their hands dirty at an archaeological dig, pace the platform of a Victorian railway depot, ride a turn-of-the-century carousel, barter for goods in a French fur trading post, sit in the driver's seat of an Indianapolis race car, and pet a snake. There is a separate hands-on gallery especially for preschoolers and another gallery that encourages self-expression and creativity by providing experiences in dance, song, literature, and art. As well, several thousand programs are offered annually as classes, workshops, gallery demonstrations and interpretation, live performances, field trips, parent/child activities, adult programs, special interest clubs, and fairs.

The "Competency Checklist for the Learning Center Teaching Strategy" outlines those teaching competencies necessary for the success of the learning center teaching strategy.

Other Teaching Strategies

Many more methods of teaching recreation activity skills, knowledge, and attitudes are available to the leader. These include demonstration, simulation, and independent study.

In many recreation learning situations the component parts of an activity skill are initially taught by **demonstration**. This is often done by the leader or a selected group of participants showing the computer game, the racquetball swing, or the kite construction. A verbal description of the skill and audiovisual aids are also useful in supporting a demonstration. The demonstration technique is usually not singularly used but is a component of other teaching strategies, such as the lecture or drill and practice.

The simulation teaching technique asks participants to pretend to be someone else to better understand what the other person's situation might feel like. In the most general

Competency Checklist for the Learning Center Teaching Strategy

When using the learning center strategy, the leader usually performs the following behaviors:

_____ Identifying the objectives to be accomplished through the learning center, with consideration given to participant needs, interests, and abilities

_____ Selecting an appropriate format for the center; for example, three-paneled carrel, bulletin board, or poster

_____ Selecting materials needed to accomplish the objectives and procedures for evaluating each participant's attainment of these objectives, using multimedia equipment whenever possible

_____ Devising an eye-catching, thought-provoking title that will motivate the participant to use the center

_____ Preparing directions for the center that are easy to locate, understand, and follow

_____ Orienting people to the use of the center

_____ Developing guiding questions for inclusion at the center that are open-ended and varied so that each participant can achieve success at her own ability level; for example, "List as many as you can of _____________."

_____ Serving as a resource to the center users as they need assistance in completing the projects

Modified from Gilstrap, R. L., & Martin, W. R. (1975). *Current strategies for teachers: A resource for personalizing instruction.* Pacific Palisades, CA: Goodyear Publishing.

terms **simulation** is defined as obtaining the essence of something without reproducing all aspects of reality. This is customarily accomplished through such methods as role playing, sociodramas, and simulation games. Simulation can be a particularly useful teaching strategy to in-service training or staff meetings.

Independent study can be interpreted in many ways. Broadly defined, it can include anything the learner does independently—from studying postage stamps at home to taking a trip to the Grand Canyon National Park to study nature photography. Independent study can take place in any setting and does not require special equipment or staff. This method may also be organized into formal steps or in an informal manner. The leader's major effort is in locating materials and learning experiences that correspond to the needs of the participant's interests and abilities.

Summary

Those of us who work in the recreation fields as leaders will spend a great deal of our energies providing recreation opportunities through the direct service approach. One ability that is important in direct activity leadership is teaching. In this chapter, highlights about how people learn and ways we might teach them were presented.

First, we considered types of learning. That is, recreation leaders typically teach the knowledge, skill, and attitude needed by participants to experience satisfying recreational activities. In addition to viewing learning as types, we also considered it as having depths, ranging from shallow to deep or basic to complex. We discussed the five progressively deeper levels of memorization, comprehension, application, generalization, and systemization. Another way of looking at range of learning is as a gradient. Called the learning gradient, this is a continuum of how much information is typically retained by learners according to four methods of teaching: telling, showing, doing, and questioning.

In the past several decades researchers have investigated how people learn. As a result, there is available certain widely accepted principles that are important for teaching recreation participants. These include paying attention to individual differences and the personal meaning individuals ascribe to a learning situation, the importance of learning by doing and relying on a foundation of existing knowledge, and the appropriate use of feedback and motivation.

Just as there are many different ways your clients learn recreation skills and knowledge, there are many different roles you can have when you teach them. The teaching roles are: dictated, prescribed, directed, consulted, interpreted, automated, and shared. What is most important about this is that each role is useful and appropriate according to specific learning situations. In several of the teaching roles the leader directly prepares all aspects of the learning experience; therefore tips for lesson planning, establishing a teaching environment, and setting learning objectives were also offered in the chapter.

Finally, ways of teaching that help participants attain instructional goals were discussed as teaching strategies. These included lecture, discussion, drill and practice, group investigation, and learning centers.

Questions and Activities for Review and Discussion

1. What is the difference between the direct and indirect service approaches in recreation? Under which approach is the leader skill of teaching more likely to be useful? Why?
2. Compare the six roles of teaching with the learning gradient (figure 11.1). That is, which roles might be more and less appropriate in terms of particular locations on the learning gradient?
3. Now, compare the five ranges of learning with the learning gradient. That is, in what ways is the same learning phenomena being explained by both?
4. Recall the last time you taught a skill or concept to someone. What teaching strategy did you use? Why did you select it and how effective do you think it was in teaching in this situation?
5. Plan a lesson for teaching a specific skill or concept. Present your lesson to the rest of your class, pointing out how the information in this chapter was helpful to you.
6. Write two learning objectives for your lesson plan.

References

Bammel, G., & Burrus-Bammel, L. L. (1996). *Leisure & Human Behavior* (3rd ed.). Madison, WI: Brown & Benchmark.

Gilstrap, R. L., & Martin, W. R. (1975). *Current strategies for teachers: A resource for personalizing instruction.* Pacific Palisades, CA: Goodyear Publishing.

Medrick, R. (1979). *Confronting passive behavior through outdoor experience: A TA approach to experiential learning.* Denver: Outdoor Leadership Training Seminars.

Niepoth, E. W. (1983). *Leisure leadership: Working with people in recreation and park settings.* Englewood Cliffs, NJ: Prentice-Hall.

Priest, S., & Gass, M. A. (1997). *Effective leadership in adventure programming.* Champaign, IL: Human Kinetics.

Priest, S., & Hammerman, D. (1990). Teaching outdoor adventure skills. *The Journal of Adventure Education and Outdoor Leadership, 6*(4), 16–18.

Web Resources

Children's Museum of Indianapolis: www.childrensmuseum.org/

Cooperative learning: www.petech.ac.za/robert/cooplearning/fslide3.htm

Lesson planning resources on the web: wysiwyg://385/http://members.aye.n . . . socialstudies/lesson/resource.html

Sport educators: http://strip.colorado.edu/~hooverj/sported.html

Teaching strategies online: www.teachingstrategies.com/

Teaching wilderness living skills to all ages and abilities: wysiwyg://375/http://biznet.maximizer.com/windigo/

The Learning Company: www.learningco.com/

PART THREE

Other Leader Skills

CHAPTER 12

Using Resources

To do two things at once is to do neither.
—Publilius Syrus, circa 42 BC, in *Bartlett*, 1953.

Learning Objectives

The recreation leader's skill in using resources is important to the full application of leadership responsibility. In this chapter you will become familiar with the resources of:

• staff • volunteers • public relations • other organizations • technology

Key Terms

job analysis p. 219
job description p. 219
job specification p. 219
affirmative action p. 219
recruitment p. 221
two-factor theory of worker motivation p. 228
maintenance factors p. 228
motivator factors p. 228
preventive discipline p. 229
punitive discipline p. 229
positive discipline p. 229
volunteers p. 230
direct services p. 230
clerical or administrative tasks p. 231
public relations p. 231
fund-raising p. 231
policy making p. 231
publics p. 234
participants p. 234
colleagues p. 235
supervisors p. 235
general public p. 235
persuasion tools p. 235
band wagon approach p. 235
card stacking p. 236
loaded words p. 236
testimonial p. 236
repetition p. 236
planned publicity p. 236
logos and slogans p. 236
public service announcements p. 236
advertising p. 236
corporate image advertising p. 237
advertorials p. 237
interorganization coordination p. 237
colocation p. 238
information technology p. 239
records management p. 240
Internet p. 240
Intranet system p. 240
electronic messaging p. 240
e-mail p. 240
geographic information system (GIS) p. 241

The recreation, park, sport, and tourism leader is a multiple-skilled professional. Not only is competence in the basic skills of decision making, problem solving, and communication essential, but also added is the necessity of quality performance in group management, change and innovation management, and motivation.

This does not suggest that the leader must function independently of assistance. Being able to manage other resources that will benefit the achievement of recreation leadership goals is in itself a desirable skill.

Befriending resources is not an automatic occurrence. Resources, to be useful, must be actively identified, recruited, supervised, and evaluated. Recreation leaders should be able to develop and use resources both from within and from outside their organizations. They cannot do it all, all by themselves, and do it well. Regardless of whether your focus as a recreation leader is the direct or the indirect service approach, employing resources will enable you to better achieve the targets of your leadership aim.

Consider the following situation:

> The director of recreation services for a large apartment complex drove the usual six miles to his office earlier than usual this morning. It was going to be an extra busy day, and he was enthusiastic to begin. While hanging his coat up he glanced at the day's agenda that he had written down before leaving for home last night. First was a meeting with his three part-time staff assistants to complete the plans for the new after-school program. Then he had scheduled an appearance before a university recreation class to speak on the general topic of private recreation. While with the students, he hoped he could interest some of them in volunteering to help with the weekend sports program.
>
> After lunch, representatives from the community mental health agency would be coming over to discuss the wellness program that he hoped they together could sponsor for the apartment complex's adult residents. Later he had planned to reserve some time to work the "bugs" out of the new computer reservation program. If he could get it running, it would make the reservation system for the many meeting and social rooms located in the complex much more efficient. Then tonight he would be returning to work to run the weekly filmfest program. As he sat down to begin preparing for the staff meeting, the phone rang. It was Penny Stowe from the shopping mall. She wanted to know if he would like to reserve exhibit space for the upcoming "This is Our Community" day.

Leader Profile: The Present
Ed Merritt
Supervisor of the Kettering, Ohio, Ice Arena, and a recent graduate of Bowling Green State University. Merritt is responsible for the operation and programming of the arena and therefore must manage both the presence and absence of important resources.

This recreation leader is using available resources to expand on what he is able to accomplish. Without these resources his success in meeting the recreation needs of the apartment complex residents would be greatly reduced. First, by working with other staff and with volunteers he is making use of valuable human resources. Also public relations and interorganization cooperation are important resources. Finally, the computer is a resource to recreation service provision that is absolutely necessary.

STAFF SUPERVISION

To direct the functioning of other staff or agency employees toward greater fulfillment of your own leadership objectives, you need to have competency in supervision skills. The goal of such skills is to make the agency's services more effective by helping staff work more effectively. As Niepoth (1983) emphasized, supervision is an enabling process. It is a process in which you help staff make the best use of their knowledge and skill so that they do their jobs more capably.

When you hire others to help you with your leadership functions, you become dependent on these persons for the achievement of your objectives. Therefore whatever you can do to help them do a better job will contribute to your overall effectiveness in providing recreation services. This means that supervision is primarily an educational process. Your goal is to help staff learn to be more proficient.

Staff supervision is a relevant endeavor in recreation organizations, particularly when you consider the large numbers of part-time and seasonal employees. As a recreation professional, you will have many opportunities to supervise other employees.

When you are supervising staff, you will need to perform a wide range of functions. Endless books have been written about what supervisors should do. Many writers agree that the activities of those who supervise may be grouped into separate yet related functions (Carrell & Kuzmits, 1982; Christenson, Johnson, & Stinson, 1982). These are planning, organizing, staffing, directing, and controlling.

Planning

Human resource planning is the process of determining future staff needs relative to an organization's strategic plan and devising the steps necessary to meet those needs (Bartol & Martin, 1998). As a supervisor you will have to consider demand and supply issues and potential steps for addressing any imbalances. Such planning often relies on a job analysis as a way of understanding the nature of jobs under consideration in the planning.

Job analysis is the systematic collection and recording of information concerning the purpose of a job, its major duties, the conditions under which it is performed, the contacts with others the job requires, and the knowledge and skills necessary to perform the job effectively (Bartol & Martin, 1998). As a supervisor you can conduct a job analysis in various ways. You could observe people as they do their jobs, conduct interviews with them and their superiors, have them keep diaries of job-related activities, and distribute questionnaires for them to complete (Milkovich & Boudreau, 1988). The results of a job analysis are often used to develop job descriptions.

A **job description** is a statement of the duties, working conditions, and other significant requirements associated with a particular job. Job descriptions are frequently combined with job specifications. A **job specification** is a statement of the skills, abilities, education, and previous work experience required to perform a particular job. Formats for job descriptions and job specifications tend to vary among organizations, but figure 12.1 offers one example.

Another important aspect of human resource planning is considering the affirmative action implications. **Affirmative action** is any special activity undertaken by an

Exercise: Linking Specific Activities in Managing Staff

Several important components of the human resource managing process are listed here. Match these components with the specific activities shown.

Human Resource Managing Components

A. Selection
B. Training and development
C. Compensation
D. Recruitment
E. Human resource planning
F. Performance appraisal

Specific Activities

☐ orientation

☐ job descriptions

☐ interview

☐ skills inventory

☐ job posting

☐ needs analysis

☐ management by objectives

☐ decertification

☐ replacement planning

☐ affirmative action plan

Some of these activities were not discussed in the text. If you have trouble matching them, do some independent study to discover what they mean.

(from Garcia, 1997, p. 44)

Position title: Assistant Director of Fitness/Wellness

General information: The assistant director of Fitness/Wellness supervises the group exercise leaders who conduct activity sessions for students, faculty, staff, and public members of the division of recreational sports. The group exercise sessions are designed to focus on fitness/wellness of an apparently healthy population group.
Supervision of group exercise leaders, assistant and program support staff is the major responsibility of this position. This position reports to the program director of Fitness/Wellness. Office location is at the SRSC facility, with sessions scheduled at the SRSC, HPER, and various other satellite locations.

Qualifications: BS in Exercise Science and/or related field; MS preferred. One to two years experience supervising exercise leaders in a college recreational setting preferred. American College of Sports Medicine (ACSM) Health Fitness Instructor certification and American Council on Exercise (ACE) Personal Trainer and/or Exercise Leader certification preferred.

Programming management:

1. Recruit, hire, supervise, and evaluate forty-five group exercise leaders and fitness assistants. Conduct monthly staff meetings and design and implement semester group trainings, new staff training, and individual staff training and development.
2. Maintain records and prepare statistical reports, evaluations, participation reports, and a complete program manual.
3. Assist in determining program fiscal needs and preparing budget recommendations, fee rates, statistical reporting, and documentation; submit bimonthly payroll.
4. Participate in program implementation by leading two to three group exercise sessions per week, working the fitness assessment consultations and meetings with a personal training client.
5. Serve on division, school, or university committees as assigned.
6. Complete monthly report responsibilities and attend weekly Fitness/Wellness and bimonthly division meetings.
7. Assist with staff development, incentive and recognition program.
8. Obtain and maintain appropriate certifications.
9. Perform other duties as assigned by the assistant and associate director or incidental to the work described herein.

Administrative responsibilities:

1. Supervise and evaluate one graduate assistant and one hourly program assistant. Conduct weekly meetings and assign responsibilities.
2. Plan, organize, and schedule 100 group exercise sessions, satellite sessions, and specialty sessions designed to improve the health-related components of fitness.
3. Recommend new programs and make program changes based on current research and industry trends in the fitness industry to assure average contribution of 60 percent to the Fitness/Wellness annual $25,000 targeted income.
4. Conduct quality assurances, equipment inspections, and needs assessments for the group exercise program.
5. Supervise equipment inventory and maintenance for group exercise sessions.
6. Organize, implement, and assure quality of service for satellite group exercise session locations and specialty session offerings (Yoga, Tai Chi, etc.)
7. Develop and oversee programming for two group exercise special events and four wellness education topics per year.
8. Develop and locate appropriate fitness education materials as needed (i.e., educational videos and materials for staff, music library, educational materials for participants, etc.)
9. Assure high quality service by maintaining contact with program participants, responding to their comments and suggestions and acting as a resource to students, staff, and faculty on fitness education topics.
10. Assist program director with publicity and promotion of new and existing services and recruiting new participants.
11. Collaborate with Kinesiology Department in offering high quality instruction through the E119/E102 academic elective programs.
12. Option of teaching P217 Exercise Leadership Methods course with the program director, Fitness/Wellness.

FIGURE 12.1. Sample job description and job specification. Source: Division of Recreational Sports, Indiana University, Bloomington (1999)

organization to increase equal employment opportunities for groups protected by federal equal employment opportunity laws and regulations. This means that it is against the law to discriminate in employment on the basis of race, color, religion, sex, or national origin (Twomey, 1990). Some states, municipalities, and organizations additionally forbid the employment discrimination of gays and lesbians.

To keep within these legal regulations some organizations adopt an affirmative action plan, a written, systematic plan that specifies goals and timetables for hiring, training, promoting, and retaining groups protected by federal equal employment laws. Such plans are required, by federal regulations, in organizations with federal contracts greater than $50,000 and with fifty or more employees. Some states, municipalities, and even individuals have challenged these laws in the courts charging reverse discrimination. Regardless of the status of these laws, it is important that supervisors in a recreation, park, sport, therapeutic, and tourism services organization redress past employment discrimination while balancing efforts to assist women and minorities against the rights of others who may be competing for the same jobs.

Organizing

Assigning jobs to individuals, grouping jobs together to coordinate efforts, assigning work schedules, and assigning authority and responsibility are included in a supervisor's organizational duties. According to Carrell and Kuzmits (1982), organizing involves three broad subcategories of functioning. First, staff jobs must be designed so that the necessary work can be accomplished. Second, individual staff jobs must be grouped into logical and manageable subunits. (This process can result in divisions such as maintenance, crafts center, nature center, and waterfront.) Third, staff persons are assigned responsibilities and delegated authority to perform their jobs and their objectives.

Staffing

Selecting people to fill jobs, placing people on jobs and orienting them, training new staff, and evaluating employee performance are all involved in staffing. Because your staff ultimately determines your success or failure, staffing is a critical element in your supervision functioning.

In some cases the duties involved in staffing will lie within the domain of your organization's personnel department if there is one. Yet in other cases it will be your responsibility. This means that you will recruit, screen, select, employ, and train your staff.

When staffing is your responsibility, your primary pursuit is to obtain a "good fit" between the staff person and the job. A good fit exists when the person has the ability to do the job and likes doing the job. Hiring people who are unable to carry out a job will result in problems. They may require extra training, may become frustrated and quit, may cause frustration among other staff, and may even be required to be dismissed.

Your responsibility in the selection of staff will vary from organization to organization. In smaller organizations you may have almost total responsibility for selecting your staff. Regardless, there are specific steps in the selection process that need to be performed. First, job descriptions and specifications must be approved. Next, a pool of qualified job applicants needs to be attracted. This is labeled **recruitment**. Usually job applicants submit application materials that become a good starting point for determining who is qualified for the job and who is not.

Following the receipt of application materials, interviews, reference checks, and in some cases (e.g., lifeguards) testing procedures are used to lead to the hiring decision. The final step in the selection process is orientation. The new staff person is oriented to the job, coworkers, and the organization.

Selection is an important element in the supervision function of staffing, but it is not the only element. Employees must also be trained and evaluated. Although you may not do all the training, as their supervisor you are ultimately responsible for your staff's performance and must see that they have the necessary job skills. Training implies that you have an understanding of how people learn and that you can teach for learning. (See chapter 11.)

Training of staff may occur away from the job, using such resources as conferences, workshops, and courses. Or training may take place on the job. This is the more common approach for many recreation agencies. In actuality, on-the-job training should be a continuous opportunity for staff throughout their tenure of employment. Such in-service training may be focused specifically on the skills and knowledge needed for the staff position or be of a more general focus enabling the employees to keep up-to-date in their career development.

Performance reviews are also important in the staffing function of supervisors. This involves conferring with your staff on areas of good performance and areas where improved performance is needed. The outcome of these reviews usually affects the employment status of the staff person. More importantly, performance reviews can serve as a way of improving the fit between the employee and the job. This ultimately affects your ability to achieve your recreation service goals. Table 12.1 is a sample form that may aid the supervisor in reviewing employee performance.

Case in Point: How to Conduct an Interview

You have a job vacancy in your unit and need to interview several applicants for the position. What do you do? Here are the steps you should take:

Before the Interview

1. Determine the job requirements. Using the job description and job specification, prepare a list of characteristics that the person will need to possess to perform well in the position.
2. Prepare a written interview guide. You need to plan questions that assess the degree to which the job candidates possess the characteristics needed for the position.
3. Review the candidate's application and/or resume.

During the Interview

4. Establish rapport. Small talk at the beginning of the interview can help put the candidate at ease. For example, select some item on the resume, such as a hobby, that you have in common.
5. Avoid conveying the response you seek. For example, instead of "can you work well with other staff?" say, "we all have some unpleasant experiences with coworkers—tell me about the most difficult time that you have ever had with a coworker."
6. Listen and take notes. The interviewer should talk 20 to 30 percent of the time and allow the interviewee to talk 70 to 80 percent of the time.
7. Ask only job-relevant questions. Especially do not ask discriminating questions, such as asking a female candidate her partner's occupation.

After the Interview

8. Write a short summary immediately after the interview. Score the candidate on the characteristics required for being effective in the job.

(based on Bartol & Martin, 1998, pp. 327–328)

TABLE 12.1. Sample staff performance evaluation form
(Professional Staff Assessment)

Explanation	Below Expectations	Meets Expectations	Exceeds Expectations	Tools/ Resources Used	Comments:
Active Healthy Lifestyles					
Participation levels					
Programming efforts—quality and creativity					
Promotion of the benefits of participation					
Marketing efforts—personal selling/interaction with participants					
Marketing efforts—annual plan and accuracy of information					
Program assessments—process and results					
Staff assessments—process and results					
Assessing outcomes of participation					
Participant recognition					
Program monitoring					
Facility/program scheduling					
Customer satisfaction					
Program diversity					
Outreach to nonusers					
Needs assessment					
Promotion of the division at all events					
Planning					
Enhance a Sense of Community					
Relational service efforts					
Program delivery					
Training					
Education					
Behavior					
Inclusive marketing					

Continued

TABLE 12.1. *Continued*

Explanation	Below Expectations	Meets Expectations	Exceeds Expectations	Tools/ Resources Used	Comments:
Make It Fun!					
Participants					
Staff					
Volunteers					
Risk-Free Environment					
Safe and well-maintained facilities					
Safe and well-maintained equipment					
Properly trained staff					
Monthly in-service safety training					
Documented policies and procedures					
Evacuation process and training					
Safe program offerings					
Routine inspections of facilities and equipment					
Facility security					
Supervision of participants					
Develop Others					
Student staff:					
Quality training					
Recruitment					
Interviewing					
Hiring					
Monitoring					
Scheduling					
Delegation					
Due process					
Diversity					
Educational materials					
Recognition					
Assessment					

Continued

TABLE 12.1. *Continued*

Explanation	Below Expectations	Meets Expectations	Exceeds Expectations	Tools/ Resources Used	Comments:
Mentoring					
Monthly in-service training					
Leadership opportunities					
Participants:					
Educational materials					
Involvement in decision making					
Educational workshops/ seminars for participants					
Participant focused advisory councils					
Volunteers:					
Participant focused advisory councils					
Recruitment					
Selection					
Meeting preparation					
Mentoring					
Monthly meetings					
Leadership opportunities					
Recognition					
Delegation					
Assessments					
Training for volunteers					
Due process					
Full-time staff and graduate assistants:					
Recruitment					
Interviews					
Hiring					
Training					
Due process					
Mentoring					
Delegation					

Continued

TABLE 12.1. *Continued*

Explanation	Below Expectations	Meets Expectations	Exceeds Expectations	Tools/ Resources Used	Comments:
Leadership opportunities					
Project management					
Recognition					
Development workshops and conference attendance					
Professional service					
Stewardship of Resources					
Fiscal:					
Budget preparation					
Budget monitoring					
Income targets					
Expenses					
Fees and charges					
Sponsorships					
Cost/benefit analysis					
Payroll					
Purchasing					
Inventory					
Facilities and equipment:					
Selection of equipment					
Inventory control					
Status of maintenance and repairs					
Cleanliness of facilities and equipment					
Organization of facilities and equipment					
Facility scheduling					
Technology:					
Software use					
Hardware					
Training					
Program development					

Continued

TABLE 12.1. *Continued*

Explanation	Below Expectations	Meets Expectations	Exceeds Expectations	Tools/ Resources Used	Comments:
Balance between technology and personal interaction					
Collaboration and Communication					
Teamwork					
Information sharing					
Honesty					
Personal selling					
Documentation					
Written communication					
Verbal communication					
Attitude					
Use of internal and external resources					

General:

How have you contributed to the vision, mission, and service theme of the division?

How would you like to contribute in the future?

What areas do you consider to be a personal growth opportunity?

How can we assist you in this growth?

Signature of Supervisor ____________________ Date _______

Signature of Staff Member ____________________ Date _______

___ Job Description Updated

___ Certifications Current

Credit: Division of Recreation Sports, Indiana University, Bloomington (1999)

Directing

A supervisor directs by guiding and influencing people to perform well, communicating with them, creating motivation, and handling conflicts and problems. There is little agreement among professionals on the best way to encourage good staff efforts; staff situations vary so widely. Yet several basic techniques are commonly in use in recreation and park organizations today and many of these were discussed in chapters 4–8. These are the important efforts of staff cooperation, communication, innovation, and motivation.

Additionally, staff performance is influenced by two factors. One is ability. Your staff must have the skills and capabilities necessary to do the job they have been assigned. The second factor is motivation. Given two people with the same ability level, the one who is motivated will perform at a higher level. Even capable staff, if they are not motivated to do the job, will do it poorly.

As you know from studying the motivating of participants in chapter 8, motivation is a complex condition. Therefore your supervisory efforts must be grounded in an understanding of the basic motivation process. Beyond this, perhaps the most popular theory of specific work motivation comes from the research of Herzberg (1966). As a result of interviews with a variety of workers in different organizations, Herzberg developed the **two-factor theory of worker motivation.** According to this theory, the absence of certain job factors tends to make workers dissatisfied. These are called maintenance factors. Their presence does not produce motivation, they merely help to avoid dissatisfaction problems. **Maintenance factors** include:

- Fairly administered organizational policies
- Supervisor who knows the work
- Good supervisor-worker relationship
- Good coworkers relationship
- Fair salary
- Job security
- Good working conditions

To build higher levels of work motivation, Herzberg maintains that a different set of factors is additionally necessary. These are called motivator factors. If these factors are absent, motivation on the job will be reduced, but dissatisfaction may not necessarily result. **Motivator factors** include the following:

- Opportunity to accomplish something important
- Recognition for significant accomplishments
- Chance for advancement
- Growth and development on the job
- Opportunity for an increased level of responsibility

Although Herzberg's theory on work motivation has been criticized, it can be useful to your supervisory efforts of directing staff. Perhaps most importantly it emphasizes the difference between staff satisfaction and staff motivation. If you wish to increase a staff person's motivation, build more motivator factors into the job.

Controlling

Controlling involves comparing staff work to organizational standards and taking corrective action where necessary. Control of staff can be considered a three-part process. First is the establishment of standards such as employee goals, performance objectives, or policies. Next the staff person's performance is compared to the standards. Finally, if needed, the supervisor and staff person correct deviations from the standard. What can be done to correct employee performance deviations once they occur?

Suppose, for example, that you are responsible for the shadowboxing program at a membership fitness club. Under your supervision are four part-time instructors. Lately you have noticed that one of your instructors has begun to be late to meet with her early morning class. Let us further assume that you have talked with her, discussed the causes of her lateness, and emphasized the importance of meeting her classes on time. The tardiness, however, continues. What do you do? What are your options for correcting this deviation from the standard?

When someone breaks the rules, many approaches may be used to correct the problem. Most of the techniques supervisors use in dealing with staff discipline situations may be grouped into three categories: preventive discipline, punitive discipline, and positive discipline (Carrell & Kuzmits, 1982).

Perhaps **preventive discipline** is the most desirable. This technique attempts to prevent staff discipline from becoming necessary. To do this the supervisor must create a working climate that is conducive to high levels of job satisfaction and staff productivity. This sort of atmosphere is accomplished by carefully completing the planning, organizing, staffing, and directing functions just presented. The preventive approach depends on well-trained and properly assigned staff who have clear job descriptions and frequent performance feedback. In a sense prevention is not discipline but is effective supervision.

In **punitive discipline,** on the other hand, the supervisor may control staff through fear. This involves threats, harassment, intimidation, and browbeating. In the case of the tardy shadowboxing instructor, the punitive discipline approach would be: "If you're late one more time, you can consider yourself no longer working here!" The problem with this approach is that it usually does not work. Although it may result in some immediate improvements, any change is likely not to last. Although some staff may respond best in certain situations with a "get-tough" supervisor, most staff will not respond positively to this approach.

Positive discipline corrects unsatisfactory staff behavior through supervisory support, respect, and people-oriented leadership. This is not, it must be clear, a soft-pedaling or sidestepping of the problem. This approach assumes that most staff are willing to accept responsibility for their performance problems so long as they have their supervisor's support. Being this kind of supervisor requires that you make clear to the staff person your responsibility for discipline, that you define the staff person's expected behavior, that you make clear the agency's policies and rules, that in a nonthreatening but direct way you communicate the staff person's violation of the rules, and that you assume a team approach with the staff person in developing a correction to the problem.

WORKING WITH VOLUNTEERS

Volunteers are an essential resource to many recreation agencies. Without the efforts of volunteers, recreation leaders would be tremendously disadvantaged in their efforts to offer the quantity and quality of services that are currently available. Using the full potential of a volunteer workforce not only can expand your services by providing special expertise and effort not possible by regular staff persons, but can also bring about closer ties with your community and provide a new enthusiasm to your organization and regular staff (Scott, 1998).

Volunteer staff extend leadership resources. There can be no doubt that some organizations would not be in business without them. This has been an important tradition in our field since the beginning of organized recreation services at the turn of the century. Thousands of people who have special talents and interests have provided millions of hours of leadership without pay.

Volunteers, simply defined, are individuals who perform services without financial remuneration. They may, however, receive payment in other ways. For instance, some give their time to receive public recognition or self-satisfaction. Others volunteer to obtain additional training for a career such as a part of college course work. Many volunteer to support programs that serve other members of their families such as a father volunteering to lead a Girl Scout troop. Thus the motivations for volunteering leadership time and skill in a recreation organization are varied.

Not all volunteers will be effective or happy. The ability to appropriately and productively manage volunteered time and energy is often a required skill of the recreation leader.

Roles of Volunteers

What do volunteers do? The 4-H leader, the condominium residents' advisory council member, the American Red Cross swim instructor, the senior center front desk receptionist, and the musician performing to raise money for the local arts commission are volunteers. What are the typical volunteer roles?

If you have volunteers working in or on behalf of your organization or are contemplating using volunteers, it is most likely that they will be involved in one or more of the following functions:

- Direct service to participants
- Clerical or administrative tasks
- Public relations
- Fund-raising
- Policy making and advising

When volunteers provide **direct services** such as coaching in youth sports, driving participants to a senior center program, and helping hospital patients write letters, they

Case in Point: Volunteers at Kirtland AFB

Kirtland Air Force Base in Albuquerque, New Mexico, is the second largest base in the United States, with 85 square miles and more than 2,000 family housing units with a population of children between the ages of 1 and 13 equal to over 1,800. Over the past few years, a number of initiatives have been underway to enhance the quality of family life on the base. Included, were the installation of two play structures. To make sure the play structures met everyone's needs, a cooperative was formed early in the process. Volunteers were enlisted from various base organizations to help with the choice of play apparatus materials and colors—and construction. Everyone from the base commander to the children was involved. However, by using volunteer construction, the cooperative had to find a vendor who was willing to work with volunteer labor. A local equipment vendor experienced with volunteer-installed play structures was found, and they provided the on-site supervision. The installation of the play structures took only one day each. When it was complete, the volunteers, parents, and children knew they had worked together to make a better community for themselves.

extend an organization's services and the work of the agency's staff. It may mean that the range of services can be extended to new populations or to new service types. For example, with volunteer assistance it may be possible for your organization to establish a home visiting program for older homebound persons, to create a teen theater workshop in the school or community center, or to sponsor a minimarathon running race.

Those volunteers who perform **clerical or administrative tasks** may be engaged in computer operations and filing, serving as receptionists, answering the telephone, mailing out brochures, cataloging, and other similar functions. These volunteers also help to reduce the demand on paid staff time and expand the range of tasks performed.

Those persons who volunteer their time and energy in **public relations** extend the capacities of the organization's management and of planning staff. Public relations efforts may include writing publicity or news releases, editing a newsletter, public speaking, and face-to-face interpretation of the organization's activities or missions. For example, a parent might invite other parents over for coffee to discuss a summer camp.

Fund-raising, to many recreation organizations, is fundamental to survival. Without volunteers to plan and organize fund-raising efforts, an agency might not be able to continue providing its services. The thousands of hours required to mount successful door-to-door, telephone, mail, or special event campaigns would divert the paid staff from the tasks for which they were trained and hired. Paid staff involved in fund-raising could also be viewed as self-serving and might not therefore be truly effective.

Volunteers who are involved in **policy making** and organizational advising are often serving as members of boards, commissions, or advisory councils. Also there are persons such as professors, architects, psychologists, and business people whom the recreation leader may wish to involve in ad hoc structures. In such cases volunteers bring prestige and legitimacy to the agency. Volunteers engaged in policy making and advising can serve in other areas as well. They may act as a buffer between your organization and others in the community. They can also add to the brain power of the staff, contributing new ideas and reflecting the interests of various groups in the community.

Managing Volunteers

Although it is certain that there are invaluable benefits to an organization and to the volunteer, without conscientious and appropriate management there can also be some disadvantages to this resource. Negligence in selecting, supervising, and evaluating volunteers can result in workers who are less responsible, less accountable, more sensitive to criticism, and overall less valuable.

1. **Recruitment and placement.** The best possible volunteers should always be actively recruited for specific needs in your organization. A prerequisite for recruiting volunteers is an identifiable need for them. Any organization that uses volunteers should first define their potential roles and then determine the kinds of individuals needed to carry out these responsibilities. Of foremost importance is the selection and placement of volunteers according to the needs of the volunteers, the service receivers, and the organization. Never should volunteers be recruited as a replacement of paid staff.

   Where do you find people with the needed talents? Recruitment appeal methods are numerous. They are either directed to the public at large or to groups or organizations serving specific populations or functions. Recruitment techniques usually fall under the following categories:

- General publicity addressed to the community at large through such media as television, radio, newspapers, posters, bulletin boards, and other similar methods
- Appeals in the form of letters, invitations or speakers who target specific organizations, service clubs, sports groups, college classes, and professional associations as potential sources of volunteers
- A volunteer recruitment fair
- Indication of the need for volunteers in the bulletins, newsletters, or brochures published by an organization as part of its overall public relations effort
- Development of special cooperative programs with appropriate organizations such as a Boys' Club having a special arrangement with a Kiwanis Club that furnishes volunteers on a regular basis
- Seeking direct volunteer assistance from those who have an important stake in the work of an organization such as a teen drop-in center obtaining parent volunteer help
- Personal contact or appeal by organization staff to specific persons
- Development of internships for students attending nearby colleges or universities
- Affiliation with a central recruitment and referral agency that coordinates the assignment of volunteers to varied social agencies

The important ingredient, no matter what your recruitment recipe, is to make the appeal to that audience that is most likely to be able to respond with the needed talents. For example, when seeking volunteers to conduct travelogues for nursing home patients, a recruitment appeal to the local retired teacher's association would likely be more productive than to a college sorority.

Volunteers should be assigned to those roles that adequately reflect their skills, abilities, and needs and that are nondiscriminatory and nondemeaning. They should be provided tasks that are sufficiently challenging, that give a sense of loyalty and dedication to the organization, and that offer an opportunity for personal growth. Volunteer work assignments should be made with minimal delay after initial contacts. A mutually signed contract—tailored to the needs and abilities of the volunteer—can be useful. In some situations it might also be beneficial to give prospective volunteers the opportunity for a probationary placement before making a long-term commitment.

2. **Orientation and training.** As with paid staff, volunteers should receive an initial, planned orientation and continued training that will prepare them to better perform their responsibilities. A volunteer who knows exactly what the organization expects is a more productive volunteer.

   Volunteer orientations should provide a conceptual overview and an operational description of the organization, its programs, practices, and objectives. Volunteers should also be made aware of volunteer rights, volunteer-staff relationships, and the available avenues of volunteer service advancement. Volunteers should be given adequate background information about the clientele such as their characteristics, abilities, and preferences. Volunteers will function best if they feel they are an integral part of the organization. Therefore they should also have ample opportunity to meet and establish working relationships with other organization staff.

Initial and ongoing training should offer the volunteer an opportunity for growth and challenge. Ongoing training should update knowledge and skills and offer the opportunity for staffwide participation and recognition. It should include acquainting the volunteer to specific procedures and functions of the organization, specific responsibilities, and trends in the field. Volunteers should receive continuing assistance and training opportunities. The goal of initial orientation and continued training is to strengthen volunteer leadership skills and give them a fuller sense of involvement in the organization's work.

3. **Supervision.** Too frequently, volunteers are not given adequate supervision. Contrary to customary practice, volunteers should be conscientiously and regularly observed and assisted by professional staff members. Clearly defined avenues of supervision and lines of support should be communicated so that volunteers will know to whom and for what they are responsible.

   Supervision should be a continuing process, with regular contact between volunteers and their supervisors. Specific ways to facilitate supervision are to provide each volunteer with a written job description and to assign a specific staff person the responsibility for supervising volunteers in fulfilling this job description. Supervisors should discuss with each volunteer his work, focusing on recognition for positive efforts and strengthening areas of weakness.

4. **Evaluation.** An important element in any staffing process is the evaluation of work performance. A strong evaluation component should be built into the organization's volunteer supervision. Volunteer performance should be evaluated on a regular basis to determine the volunteers' potentials, their needs, their satisfaction, and their contribution to the organization. Careful record keeping and personal and public communications will aid in determining the overall value of volunteer activities.

   Also the organization's policies and practices of recruiting, training, and supervising volunteers should be periodically reviewed to determine success in meeting volunteer and constituency needs. When evaluating volunteer workers, feedback should be shared with them on areas of strength and areas requiring correction or redirection.

   Evaluation, like all aspects of staff supervision, should be a continuous process. Praise your volunteers where and when earned. Do not be afraid to correct them when and where needed. They deserve to be evaluated honestly. As with any member of the staff, it is important for them to know if they are or are not performing adequately to have opportunities to make corrections and to grow.

5. **Recognition and retention.** Successful management of volunteers must include formally and informally applied motivation. To reward and retain positive volunteer contributions, systems for their recognition must be developed. The best ways to do this include showing volunteers that their efforts are needed and appreciated; offering guidance to build interest, increase skills, and instill confidence; involving volunteers in the planning and evaluation of programmed recreation activities; and making sure volunteers feel free to communicate with their supervisors as a part of the staff team.

   More extrinsic systems for recognizing the value of your organization's volunteers entail identifying volunteers with badges, pins, mugs, name tags, smocks, or other forms of special recognition; holding award meetings; fostering newsletter or newspaper publicity; awarding certificates or sending letters of appreciation; and sponsoring volunteer parties or picnics.

Recognition of your organization's volunteers must not only be done for adequate rewarding of time and energies freely given but also for continual improvement of the volunteer program and for the retention of an excellent recreation leadership resource.

MAXIMIZING PUBLIC RELATIONS

Leader Profile: The Past
Morris Udall
U.S. Representative. Significant achievements in resource conservation and recreation access—including the eight-year struggle for passage of the Alaska Lands Conservation Act (1980), which set aside more than 100 million acres for national parks and wildlife refuges.

Public relations can serve as a valuable resource for the recreation leader. Every effort that you make and action that you take will be reflected in what others think of you. In turn, the success of your efforts and actions to some degree depends on what others think of you. This is important, but it also goes beyond this individual level. The community's opinions of you, the recreation leader, also have an impact on the image of your organization in the entire leisure services field. Developing favorable opinion is public relations. It should not happen to you; instead you must make it happen.

As a resource for recreation leaders, public relations should be seen as those endeavors that maintain sound, favorable, and productive relations with others. It involves establishing and strengthening goodwill. It is anything we do to yield positive public opinion.

When a participant leaves your facility and is satisfied, that is good public relations. When a parent concludes the phone conversation with one of your staff feeling happy about the way the children's programs are being handled, that is good public relations. When you leave a favorable impression after your report to the board of commissioners, that is good public relations. *Public relations* are those continuous and planned images that cause others to think well of you, your organization, and your profession.

We consider positive public relations to be desirable, but more than this the recreation leader should consider it a vitally needed resource. Why should we nurture public relations as a resource? As in any human endeavor, success depends largely on the light in which these endeavors are viewed by others. Recreation leaders should develop skill in public relations for at least the following reasons (Kraus, Carpenter, & Bates, 1981):

- Creating a more favorable public image for your organization may help to encourage official support such as legislative action.
- Participant attendance at programs or in facilities may be enhanced.
- Volunteers may be easier to recruit.
- Public misunderstandings about your organization and its services may be dispelled.
- Financial donations for facilities, staff, or equipment may be more readily offered.

Who is "The Public"?

For the recreation leader there are many **publics.** Your efforts to promote positive public relations should be focused on those groups of people affected by your decisions and actions. For most leaders these groups may be identified as the participants, colleagues, supervisors, and the general public.

As pointed out by Edginton and Ford (1985), the **participants** or clients you lead have certain expectations of your leadership. They arrive expecting you to be prepared, to be pleasant and clean, to know what you are doing, and to treat them with courtesy and fairness. Beyond this they also have expectations for a satisfying, enjoyable recreation experience under your leadership. Public relations with participants means that you respond to their needs with professional sincerity, are courteous, make a special effort to help each one feel welcome, and have a positive attitude toward them as a person.

Those other professionals who work with you in the same organization require your public relations attention. Your **colleagues** also place expectations on you. Good public relations with them means that they think of you as cooperative, thoughtful, and considerate. They have respect for you. You do not gossip about them or criticize them in an unfair and unproductive way.

Your **supervisors** are another public. Supervisors think highly of staff who are prompt, self-initiated, dependable, honest, cooperative, and thorough. Good public relations requires that you not only be these things but also communicate them through good work.

Finally, all recreation leaders represent both themselves and the organization in the goodwill image to the **general public.** In fulfilling this image the leader should be prepared to answer questions courteously and factually; to assume a professional appearance and demeanor; and to refrain from promoting personal political or religious philosophies.

Participants, colleagues, supervisors, and the general public are the primary objective of recreation leaders' public relations, but in certain situations there are other important publics. These may include other recreation organizations, persons being supervised, advisory and governing boards, legislators, special interest groups, and media representatives.

Regardless of which public, recreation leaders should base their public relations efforts on an excellent performance. Beyond this, honest and continuous communication of this excellence will help establish a good image and public opinion.

The Tools of Public Relations

The ultimate goal of public relations is to favorably influence opinion. In some cases this may require only maintaining an already good relationship with the various publics. In other cases the task may be to change public opinion in order to create a more favorable relationship.

Whatever the recreation leader's specific need might be, the first step is to plan an approach. This not only means that appropriate publics are identified but also useful techniques or tools are selected. There are many tools available for influencing public opinion. They may be combined under the topics of persuasion, publicity, and advertising, yet they are all based on the principles of communication.

1. **Persuasion. Persuasion tools** are used to make a conscious and deliberate effort to manipulate others by appealing to emotions. This persuasive form of communication usually provides only partial information and the attempt is to make only one side of an issue seem logical. In some situations persuasion is a useful public relations tool. Specific ideas include the following:
   - **The band wagon approach:** The band wagon approach is that suggestion that everyone is doing it or believing it. Getting children to be careful with fire in the woods by telling them that "Smokey's friends don't play with matches" is an example.

- **Card stacking:** The technique of telling only half-truths is card stacking. Publishing a colorful brochure about your organization in which you feature only the successful programs is an example.
- **Loaded words:** Loaded words are a persuasion technique used to add a subtle connotation to what is being communicated. Calling someone an official rather than a politician or a visitor rather than a tourist is more flattering and can help to persuade if managed well.
- **The testimonial:** When someone you perceive should know something about skiing (such as a former Olympic champion) recommends a particular ski resort, it is more likely that you will also highly regard that resort. This is the testimonial.
- **Repetition:** Something repeatedly heard or seen makes an impression on the mind. Slogans, billboard posters, and radio announcements done repeatedly can be persuasive.

When poorly managed or used in untimely situations, public relations through persuasive techniques can be unethical. They can also be overused or ineffectively applied. There are circumstances, however, when persuasion is a legitimate and useful tool. Speaker's bureaus and audiovisual presentations are often appropriate opportunities for persuasion.

2. **Publicity.** This technique is a spotlight that focuses a public's attention on an individual, organization, or an object such as a product (Fazio & Gilbert, 1981). Sometimes publicity can occur in an unplanned, coincidental way and potentially create negative public relations. **Planned publicity,** on the other hand, can be highly effective in creating a good spotlight for you and your agency. The methods of accomplishing planned publicity are as limitless as the imagination. Posters, bookmarks, open houses, exhibits, bulletin boards, grand openings, ceremonies, organization tours, and facility dedications are common ways; but above all you need to make news happen. Publicity puts news about you or your organization in the spotlight. For example, give an award and then publicize the occasion through the appropriate media or publicize your organization's sponsorship of a college scholarship.

   Logos and slogans can help publicize the efforts of your organization by serving as a reminder. They usually appear on literature, signs, badges, patches, vehicles, and equipment. When matched with quality services, symbols can remind publics of that quality.

   Usually **public service announcements** are 10- to 60-second radio or television spots or newspaper advertisement placements. The time or space is donated by the medium in which it appears. If yours is a nonprofit organization, public service announcements can be useful tools in publicizing your news. Other ways include public affairs programs, news programs, and instructional programs.
3. **Advertising. Advertising** is paid publicity. To use this public relations tool the recreation leader purchases the use of desired media. Usually the advertising includes space in a newspaper or magazine or air time on radio or television. Advertising has some advantages over publicity: it can reach particular audience targets, and it will appear exactly as submitted without being edited. The greatest disadvantage is cost. As a sample, a small town daily newspaper may cost an advertiser $1,000 or more for a full page with no color. For organizations that can receive dollar returns for advertising investments, this money may be wisely spent. Private, commercial, and tourism agencies are common users of this public relations tool.

Corporate image advertising promotes the image of an organization in the broadest sense. It also has a positive carry-over effect on public perception of the entire profession.

Advertorials are space or time purchased to present some point of view, usually in an attempt to stir action or consciousness related to social or political issues.

SUPPORTING INTERORGANIZATION COORDINATION

Recreation leaders can help each other. The special groups coordinator for a theme amusement park works with the executive director of the Boy Scout council in setting up Cub Scout Day at the park. The recreation supervisor at the youth corrections facility seeks the advice of a high school volleyball coach and a parole officer before starting a volleyball team. The outdoor recreation specialist for an army base coordinates the white-water rafting trip with the nearby college outings club. These and other examples illustrate how cooperative efforts between recreation leaders can enhance the effectiveness of both. When this cooperation occurs between different organizations, it is called **interorganization coordination** and can be an important resource for the recreation leader.

When leaders from two or more organizations work together effectively, the result is better services to participants, clients, or guests. The result from lack of coordination is often expensive inefficiency for the agencies and confusing gaps or overlaps in services for the participants. Specifically the benefits of interorganization coordination are as follows (Rossi, Gilmartin, & Dayton, 1982):

- Improved staff effectiveness: Interorganization coordination can open up a new complement of resources to the innovative leader.
- Greater efficiency: When done well, interorganization coordination can help a leader deliver more services for the same amount of money.
- Improved public image: Improved efficiency and expanded service positively reflect on you and your organization.
- Reduced fragmentation of services: Constituents have multiple needs. With interorganization coordination a constituent can be treated more as a whole person.

Although there are clear advantages to leaders from different organizations working together, in practice interorganization coordination does not happen often because of unnecessary shortsightedness, laziness, and turf protection. There are many ways in which organizations working in related areas can coordinate with one another without extra expense or difficulty.

The first step is learning about other organizations. Do you know what other recreation, tourism, commercial, health, education, and social service agencies exist in your area? How do they operate; who are their clients? It is hard to coordinate with another organization when you know nothing about it. Learning about other organizations can happen in a number of ways. Joint training workshops, regularly scheduled interorganization meetings, and community organization directories can be helpful. The information gained will enable you to determine whether a coordinated effort would be possible and of interest.

Once organizations have come to know and trust each other and have worked out some common objectives, the next level is coordination to better meet common constituency needs. There are many approaches here, including a system of cross-referrals, staff loans, and colocation. **Colocation** involves two or more organizations having staff and facilities at the same location.

Another approach to interorganization coordination is the mutual gathering and use of information. This is a fundamental type of cooperation. Without information exchange, no other kind of interorganization link is possible. Such efforts as a centralized information clearing house, a periodic community needs assessment, and a joint gathering of information about delivery of services can be useful.

As coordination between organizations grows, eventually it reaches the point where not only information is integrated but the joint administration of programs is possible. This may include such elements as joint program design, operation, and evaluation.

Interorganization coordination is a give-and-take relationship in which recreation leaders are able to offer their participants increased opportunities. They do this by sharing information, facilities, equipment, personnel, land, expertise, or administrative support. It can be thought of as a form of barter. By bartering underused, temporarily idle, or common or widespread resources, recreation leaders are able to resolve common and overlapping problems.

USING INFORMATION TECHNOLOGY

In the outdoor sport of rock climbing, battery-powered electric drills have made bolting widespread (Priest & Gass, 1997). Bolting is the practice of drilling holes in the rock face and hammering expansion bolts into the hole to make secure anchor points for rock climbers. The proliferation of bolts is offensive to some climbers and the constant noise of the drills is disturbing to others, not to mention the deteriorating aesthetic values and damage to the rock face. Some mountain park systems have begun to ban bolting. For example, the leaders responsible for the Boulder Mountain Park system have taken the firm and unilateral position that "bolting, all fixed hardware, and the use of rock drills are strictly prohibited in Mountain Parks" (Kennedy, 1990, p. 10).

Is this an extreme stance by these leaders? Does it prohibit the full recreational potential of rock climbing in these parks, rather than enhance it—which is the goal of recreation leadership? Regardless of your position on these questions, the theme behind this, and millions more stories, is that technology impacts our recreation. This example has to do with technology that impacts the nature of recreation. There are many other examples, such as night vision glasses that extend "daytime" activities into darkness, underwater hotels, and Web surfing. There is an entire category of pastimes that is only possible because of the invention of the computer. Within the context of recreation leadership, however, our discussion of technology necessarily focuses on another use. This is information technology.

Exercise: Your Suggestions Are Sought

You have accepted a position as the director of a large fitness center. Your supervisor, the district manager for the organization, likes to involve others in decisions. During your interviews for the job, she mentioned that if you became center director, she would ask for your views on ways to improve the information technology system in the organization. The supervisor said that she, several assistant supervisors, and all six center directors will soon hold a strategic planning meeting at which they will consider possible plans for the technology system. To prepare for the upcoming meeting, outline the suggestions you will offer. What issues should be considered as part of information technology planning?

Information technology (IT) is an umbrella concept that covers a vast array of computer applications that permit organizations to manage their information resources (Bryan & Young, 1999). Today, it is not uncommon for recreation customers and clients to be served by IT rather than by people. In the future, use of this resource will become more widespread (Schneider & Bowen, 1995). For example, within our recreation, park, sport, and tourism organizations we are seeing changes in the types of services and products we provide to our participants, expectations of employee performance by management and participants, and structure of the organizations (Ross & Sharpless, n.d.). In many park and recreation organizations the use of personal computers has become standard for such applications as word processing, electronic spreadsheets, database management, multimedia, desktop publishing, and others. Information technologies such as digital cameras on computers, improved scanners, optical character recognition (OCR), interactive voice response (IVR), information kiosks, World Wide Web, touch screens, digitizing tablets, plotters, electronic pen-based notepads with voice and handwriting recognition and CD-ROMs are becoming commonplace in the delivery of leisure services. With them we are providing sport tournament scheduling, facility reservations, and program registration, along with other applications as diverse as fitness and wellness and nature interpretation.

The Importance of Information Technology

As a resource, IT means a great deal to the recreation leader. But, if we were to summarize its essential importance, we would come to two main points. It helps us solve problems and be productive. Through these two advantages, information technology is a means to make the connection between the recreation organization and the customers it serves, whether those customers and organizations are in a city, state, park, forest, hospital, university, or athletic field. Information technology and its management is the "value-added" to the enterprise of leisure service delivery (Bryan & Young, 1999). Let us consider each of the reasons for the importance of information technology.

First, information technology helps leaders solve problems. Management of organizations requires the detailed measurement of service delivery and the consequential analysis and review of that service. IT will not make you a better leader, but it will increase the availability and analysis of information that will enable you to make better service delivery decisions and solve service delivery problems. Because of this advantage from information technology, teams are increasingly being used to plan an IT approach to solving organization problems. Often these teams include the director of public relations, the financial officer, members of senior management operational areas, field supervisors, and so on (Bryan & Young, 1999).

Second, IT increases the leader's personal productivity. Information technology skills are the language of managing organizations. Just as leaders are responsible for other organizational resources, so are they responsible and accountable for the information resources. In any recreation organization you will be expected to increase your efficiency by progressively developing your information skills. What are some of the ways IT can help you be more efficient and solve problems?

IT as a Leadership Tool

Every recreation, park, sport, tourism, and therapeutic recreation organization should have an information technology system. Some organizations will have a simple system composed of as little as one personal computer, while others will have a sophisticated system of a variety of networked equipment. An appropriate IT system includes at minimum records management and administrative functions, which might include the tools of Internet, Intranet, messaging, and geographic information system (GIS) (Bryan & Young, 1999).

1. Records management: It is necessary that every organization, regardless of size, have a **records management** system. Typically organizations keep records about finances, personnel, properties, legal documents, accident reports, and program services. Technology can be an efficient tool for this purpose. The primary purpose of record keeping is accountability to the leisure services user and the organization. This means that records management through technology is a stewardship process that accounts for the use and status of the organization's resources. IT is an important tool for gathering, storing, and recalling records information.
2. The Internet. The Internet is an electronic version of "commerce" and is used for retrieving and disseminating information (Bryan & Young, 1999). The **Internet** is a global collection of networks that pass information to each other. For example, the Internet can be useful to the leader as a:
   - means to collaborate to solve problems (such as SPRENET—Listserv@listserv.uga.edu)
   - marketing tool for an organization (such as Michigan travel and tourism—http://206.253.228.155/welcome.htm)
   - way to research a topic (such as the Bitterroot Ecosystem Management Research Project—http://www/umt.etu/ccesp/c&i/nrm/bemrp/geninfo.htm)
   - source for government documents and official statistics (Americans with Disabilities Act—http://janweb/icdi.wvu.edu/kinder/)
   - communications link to consumers (such as to make reservations for a campsite at Hardin Ridge National Recreation Area—http://www.fs.fec.us/rq/hoosier/camp-info.htm # Hardin Ridge Recreation Area)
   - contact with professional organizations (such as the National Recreation and Park Association—http://www.nrpa.org)
3. Intranet. An Intranet is a "private Internet." An **Intranet system** for an organization replaces paper memorandums, employee handbooks, calendars of events, internal job postings, intraoffice newsletters, and paper reports. It makes it possible for the organization to run with little to no paper. The information on an Intranet is not for customers and clients to see. Instead, it is comprised of administrative information maintained by each section or department in the organization.
4. Messaging. Thanks to IT, today's recreation leader sends and receives communications via telephone, fax, e-mail, voice mail, and pagers. These are means of **electronic messaging.** The messaging capability has been sufficient justification for organizations to invest in information technology. This is because not all staff for a particular recreation organization work the exact same days, times, or even locations. To get important notices, announcements, and other messages to the staff, electronic mail (e-mail) has been the tool of choice. **E-mail** is the most versatile of the messaging technologies (Bryan & Young, 1999). E-mail can be used to send messages inside and outside the organization, as faxes or to an alpha pager. It can contain attachments of files (such as documents, databases, and graphics), and to multiple people simultaneously. Many times an e-mail conversation is more efficient than talking on the phone.

5. Geographic Information System (GIS). As we've already discussed, one reason to use information technology is its ability to summarize information for decision making. When decisions need to be based on information that is spatially presented, or mapped, the **Geographic Information System (GIS)** is a useful tool. A GIS is a computer-based tool for mapping and analyzing things that exist or happen on the earth. For example, wildfires can be connected to a map and displayed according to color, which tells us quickly the areas of the region that experienced the most (or least) fire trouble last season. While geographic analysis is not new, it was a skill only a few people had. Now it is available to all of us to help with decision making and problem solving.

Summary

The recreation leader is a multiple-skilled professional. One important skill is the effective use of resources. To be useful, resources must be actively identified, recruited, supervised, and evaluated.

One such resource to the recreation leader is other staff. By helping staff work more effectively, you are also able to make the organization more effective. This chapter discussed the staff supervision functions of planning, organizing, staffing, directing, and controlling.

Volunteers are also an essential resource to many recreation leaders. Volunteer staff extend the leadership resource. The ability to appropriately and productively manage volunteered time and energy requires that the leader be concerned about recruiting, selecting, training, supervising, motivating, and evaluating volunteers.

As another resource for recreation leaders, public relations should be seen as those endeavors that maintain sound, favorable, and productive relations with others. It involves establishing and strengthening positive public opinion. Recreation leaders should develop skill in public relations by using the tools of persuasion, publicity, and advertising. Regardless of the eloquence of the technique, positive public relations is always dependent on high-quality performance by you and your organization.

When leader cooperation occurs between different organizations, an additional resource is available. Interorganization coordination enables leaders to work together for the ultimate result of better services to participants. This can be done by learning about other organizations, coordinating the achievements of common participant needs, mutually sharing information, and jointly administering programs.

However, no resource for the recreation leader has been as revolutionary and as fast growing as the computer. With the help of computers, recreation leaders are able to save time and money in a wide assortment of managing resources tasks.

Questions and Activities for Review and Discussion

1. Why would a recreation leader consider other staff persons to be an important resource? Why is their effective management critical to good organization leadership?
2. In what ways can well-written job descriptions make staff supervision more effective? Acquire two or more job descriptions from different organizations and in a group discuss their role in directing the efforts of staff.
3. How do volunteers increase an organization's leadership resources?
4. Interview a leader working in an organization who manages volunteers. Ask about this person's experiences in recruiting, training, supervising, evaluating, and recognizing volunteers.
5. Define public relations. Why is it an important resource for the recreation leader?

6. As a class project, assist an organization's efforts at public relations by setting up an exhibit, display, or bulletin board or by developing an audiovisual program.
7. Why do you suppose interorganization coordination can be so important to a leader? So difficult to establish?
8. Take a tour of a recreation organization that is making extensive use of computers. What functions are the computers performing? Are they saving staff time and organization money? Ask to see some of the computer functions in operation.

References

Bartlett, J. (1953). *The shorter Bartlett's familiar quotations*. New York: Permabooks.

Bartol, K. M., & Martin, D. C. (1998). *Management* (3rd ed.). Boston, MA: McGraw-Hill.

Bryan, V., & Young, L. (1999). Information technology management. In van der Smissen, B. (Ed.), *Recreation Management*. VA: National Recreation and Park Association.

Carrell, M. R., & Kuzmits, F. E. (1982). *Personnel: Management of human resources*. Columbus: Charles E. Merrill Publishing.

Christenson, C., Johnson, T. W., & Stinson, J. E. (1982). *Supervising*. Reading, MA: Addison-Wesley Publishing.

Edginton, C. R., & Ford, P. M. (1985). *Leadership in recreation and leisure service organizations*. New York: John Wiley & Sons.

Fazio, J. R., & Gilbert, D. L. (1981). *Public relations and communications for natural resource managers*. Dubuque, IA: Kendall/Hunt Publishing.

Garcia, S. (1997, December). Volunteer spirit invades Kirtland AFB. *Parks and Recreation*. Ashburn, VA: National Recreation and Park Association.

Herzberg, F. (1966). *Work and the nature of man*. New York: World Publishing.

Kennedy, M. (1990). Trouble in paradise. *Climbing, 118*, 10.

Kraus, R. G., Carpenter, G., and Bates, B. J. (1981). *Recreation leadership and supervision*. Philadelphia: Saunders College Publishing.

Milkovich, G. T., & Boudreau, J. W. (1988). *Personnel/human resource management* (5th ed.). Plano, TX: Business Publications.

Niepoth, E. W. (1983). *Leisure leadership: Working with people in recreation and park settings*. Englewood Cliffs, NJ: Prentice-Hall.

Priest, S., & Gass, M. A. (1997). *Effective leadership in adventure programming*. Champaign, IL: Human Kinetics.

Ross, C. M., & Sharpless, D. R. (n.d.). *Innovative information technology and its impact on recreation and sport programming*. Unpublished manuscript.

Rossi, R. J., Gilmartin, K. J., & Dayton, C. W. (1982). *Agencies working together: A guide to co-ordination and planning*. Beverly Hills, CA: Sage Publications.

Schneider, B., & Bowen, D. E. (1995). *Winning the service game*. Boston, MA: Harvard Business School Press.

Scott, J. (1998). *Fundamentals of leisure business success: A manager's guide to achieving success in the leisure and recreation industry*. New York: The Haworth Press.

Twomey, D. P. (1990). *Equal employment opportunity law*. Cincinnati, OH: South-Western.

Web Resources

Assistive technology in recreation: www.uic.edu/~kdorwick/sports1999/

Chronicle of Philanthropy: www.philantrhopy.com/

Computers in HPER: http://ci.alexandria.va.us/budget/sd-other.html

Council on Foundations: www.cof.org/

Federal grant programs: www.os.dhhs.gov/progorg/grantsnet/

Fund-raiser directory: www.fundraising-ideas.com/

Grants internet links: http://web.fie.com/cws/sra/resource.htm
www.grantscape.com/omaha/grants/top.html

Human resource management resources on the internet:
www.nbs.ntu.ac.uk/staff/lyerj/hrm_link.htm

Interorganization cooperation case study: http://gcrio.ciesin.org/ocp96/p7box/html

Interorganization cooperation case study: www.r6.fws.gov/igbc/igbcdoc1.htm

Philanthropy resources: www.fundsnetservices.com/

Public relations 101: www.tampa.prsa.org/pr101.html

Public relations agencies and resources on the WWW:
www.impulse-research.com/prlist/html

Public relations links: www.jlmc.iastate.edu/facilities/reading/pubrel.html

Public Relations Society of America: www.prsa.org/

Volunteer and staff relations: www.aspca.org/educate/outbuild.htm

Volunteer management: http://energizeinc.com/total/volmm.html

Volunteer services department: www.mgh.org/vol/help.html

Volunteer staff case study: www.bobo.co.gov/cs/cb/jsvindex/htm

Volunteer staff case study: www.gilwellpark.demon.co.uk/team.htm

Web advertising secrets: www.newsletteraccess.com

CHAPTER 13

Managing the Workload

In order that people may be happy in their work these three things are needed: They must be fit for it. They must not do too much of it. And they must have a sense of success in it.
—LéBoeuf, 1979, p. 1.

Learning Objectives

The purpose of this chapter is to suggest additional ways for being successful in recreation leadership. To get the greatest return on your investment of time, energy, and spirit you must:

- get organized
- make every day count
- manage time
- keep learning
- have personal goals and make progress toward them

Key Terms

concentration p. 246
procrastination p. 248
time management p. 250
ABC Priority System p. 250
time wasters p. 252
external time wasters p. 252
internal time wasters p. 252
maintenance learning p. 255
shock learning p. 255
innovative learning p. 255
long-range goals p. 257

Success in managing workload is not simple. Success can be considered as being able to do what you want to do, accomplishing what you want to accomplish, being who you want to be, and attaining any reasonable objective you have in mind. This chapter maintains that beyond success with the various techniques of recreation leadership discussed in the previous chapters of this section, there is the additional ability to successfully manage the tasks of the leadership position.

Failure is possible. Possible reasons are the following:

- Unwillingness to invest effort in the present for reward in the future
- Not knowing or being able to decide what is wanted out of life
- Personal chaos and disorganization
- Energy draining emotions such as weak self-concept, fear of failure, worry, guilt, and jealousy
- Communication breakdowns and interpersonal conflicts
- The inability to manage resources such as time and other people

Other chapters in this book have dealt with many of these reasons. This chapter is focused primarily on ways to manage your everyday resources: your work environment, your time, and your goals.

GETTING ORGANIZED

Getting and staying organized is perhaps the most important ingredient to success in any endeavor. A person with average ability and drive but who is well organized often can run circles around those with more ability and a higher level of drive who are not well organized. Being well organized is not just desirable and enjoyable; it is essential to the success of the recreation leader. You can provide more qualitative services to participants and customers if the details in your workload are ordered and priorities are set.

In getting and staying organized the first necessary realization is that it takes time to be organized. This is a paradox because those with the least amount of available time are the most in need of being organized. This is the point: being organized liberates time, but it takes time to be organized. Not having the time to get organized is a common complaint. But this lack of time is the effect of not being well organized! In other words being too busy is not the problem; it is only a symptom of the problem.

Another important truism about being organized is that there is no such thing as perfection. No one is perfectly organized. It is instead a matter of degree. Good organization of professional and personal lives is a habit. We must constantly practice it, because everyone can improve to some extent.

Steps to Organization

There is some danger in presenting specific steps to getting and staying organized. The danger is that readers will assume that the task is as simple as one, two, three. It is not. The following ideas can be helpful to you in your organizing efforts, but they will not automatically produce personal organization. They must be applied with common sense, they must be practiced, and most of all they must be taken only as rough guideposts. The four steps discussed can be useful, but it takes your wise application to make them work.

Establish Priorities

Being unable to set priorities on the important tasks is a great effectiveness killer. When you are faced with a number of things to do, ask yourself which are the important ones and make them your first priority. Otherwise, if you respond to every task, your personal and professional existence will be one crisis after another. You will be active without accomplishing much. Computer software exists, such as Microsoft Outlook, to help you keep track of the task priorities you have set.

Organize Your Workspace

Consider the environment in which you will be working. The choice of its location, if you have such a choice, can be critical. The location of where you work should be conducive to the tasks you perform. If you need to concentrate, then the workspace should be quiet and private. If you need to interact with many people, then the workspace should be in a well-traveled location.

Have easy access to the tools you use frequently. Refrain from cluttering your workspace with nonessential items. They may occupy valuable space that is required for more immediately needed work tools and resources.

Plan your workspace so that it is comfortable and ergonomically healthy. Discomfort is a distraction that serves only to hinder productivity. A comfortable workspace refers to good seating, ventilation, and lighting.

Many of us frequently perform some of our recreation leadership work at a desk. A desk is also a tool—frequently an abused and misused tool. Assuming that you do need a desk, you may want to organize this tool as well. How? You can increase your desk work effectiveness by reducing the amount of clutter:

- Have only your top priority project on top of your desk.
- Keep items off your desk until you are ready for them.
- Use file cabinets, drawers, or computer files for projects not being worked on at the moment.
- Use in and out baskets to keep the work flowing.
- Do not be afraid to also use the trash can as a work tool.
- Use information technology, if possible, to help you store, retrieve, and easily use information related to your work.

Develop Your Ability to Concentrate

To the degree that we concentrate our efforts we will succeed in getting what we want. **Concentration** is the quality of continuity or holding power—the ability to stay focused (Tulku, 1994). It is the channeling of thought and action toward a purpose. Everyone knows the importance of concentration, and most of us may assume that we do our work with all the concentration we need to succeed. Although we may notice that scattered thoughts, images, or concerns sometimes interrupt our focus, we tend to think this is natural. But imagine how much more we could accomplish if we could focus without interruption.

Concentration is directed by awareness—being aware of when we are focused and when we are not. How might we do this? One strategy for becoming more aware of how well we are concentrating is to think with a pencil in your hand. When you write down your ideas, you automatically focus your attention on them.

Another aid to concentration is to reserve your workplace exclusively for work. This means that when you take a break, move away from where you work. If you develop the habit of choosing a certain spot to work, you will find yourself getting down to business much more rapidly and automatically when it is time to work.

Developing your ability to concentrate can also mean knowing when and how to stop working. Try to end a work period on a positive note so that you will be more eager to return to it. Try to stop at a natural point of completion. This will reduce your start-up time when you return to the task. If you quit at a point where you are stalled, write down the problem first before leaving it.

Exercise: Focusing on Focusing

For the next week, cultivate a light, steady focus on whatever you do. Be conscious of everything, everywhere, and everyone. Be aware of when you are focused and when you lose your focus. Note the times and conditions when your concentration is especially good. At the end of each day, review your notes. Review them again at the end of the week, looking for patterns.

(from Tulku, 1994)

Master the Art of Follow-Through

Somewhere along the line you must tackle the task and follow through to completion. A tidy desk, a computer, or an ordered file drawer will not single-handedly make you successful. You must be good at finishing what you start. Follow-through is much easier if you are interested in your work. A task that is looked forward to is almost automatically completed. This is basic to follow-through.

What else can you do? Try to imagine the satisfaction that will come from seeing the task achieved. Challenge yourself with self-imposed deadlines for completion. Try to shield yourself from interruptions and distractions. Take part in joint projects with others. When you make a commitment to do something with someone else, you are more likely to follow through.

MAKING EVERY DAY COUNT

Success in your work as a recreation leader is also dependent on your attitude. How you spend your time and energy is in large part a matter of how you think and feel. As LeBoeuf (1979, p. 84) claimed: "Tell me what you think and how you feel and I'll tell you who you are." How much you are able to accomplish in leading others in meaningful recreation experiences is also largely governed by your attitude.

How you approach your work, how you approach colleagues, and how you approach participants will reflect how you think and feel about yourself. This means that strengthening your self-image is also a key to increased effectiveness. A strong self-evaluation gives you the "can do" power that enables you to accomplish the following:

- Put the past in the past.
- Build on your strengths.
- Accept yourself unconditionally.
- Do not allow others to define your worth.

Your interest in your work and your effectiveness in your endeavors are only the overflow of your interest in and your effectiveness with yourself. You are in control of your life's successes because of who you are in thought and attitude.

What is stopping you? First, there are certain common emotions that can create barriers to your leadership effectiveness. When we suffer from guilt, worry, and procrastination, our ability to be a success in what we attempt is diminished. Second, pressures and demands on our efforts can be debilitating if we let them. Constructively coping and positively redirecting pressure is a basic ingredient in our survival kits.

Effectiveness Killers

Let us look at those attitudes that get in the way of making every day count. Of all the effectiveness-killing emotions, guilt or the "shouldas" is perhaps the most damaging. By definition, the "shouldas" is feeling bad and becoming immobile by an attitude over what has already occurred. This is a waste of your potential. When applied to your work as a recreation leader, the "shouldas" are recognizable as: "I should have started earlier in hiring the camp staff." "I should have checked with the supervisor before closing enrollment in that swimming class." "I should have taken more time to prepare that special event evaluation." Perhaps most common is the guilt over what does not get done. "I should have done everything on my to do list before going home."

This attitude is a waste because it never brings the past back so that you can make the needed corrections. You can only learn from the past and take steps to behave differently in the present and future. Furthermore, expecting to get everything done is absolutely futile; you could spend your entire life and never get everything done.

Common sense prescribes the following remedies for a guilt attitude:

- Recognize the past for what it is. Are you convinced that pasts can never be changed? Then why bother to try?
- Accept your past mistakes and misfortunes and resolve to learn something from them. Although you have the right to be wrong, you also have the responsibility not to repeat wrongs.
- Pay no attention to the guilt mongers. The world is full of people who will be quick to call your attention to your past errors. Ignore them; your self-worth is not defined by others.

Worry and anxiety are two other attitudes that can kill your effectiveness as a recreation leader. Worry is a mirror reflection of guilt. Instead of feeling guilty about the past, worriers fret over the future. When teamed up, both ways of thinking and feeling ensure that nothing worthwhile will be accomplished in the present.

About worry, Mark Twain once remarked, "I've suffered a great many catastrophes in my life. Most of them never happened" (LaBoeuf, 1979, p. 94). Worrying about whether anyone will show up for the pet show, worrying about whether anyone will drown while you are guarding at the pool this summer, and worrying about whether your supervisor thinks you are doing a good job are merely fantasies. Worrying will not bring people to the pet show or compliments from your supervisor. But it can get in the way of those efforts and abilities that will. Whatever does come to pass will not be prevented or achieved by worrying.

Again, common sense prescribes the following remedies for worry:

- When you are worried about something, confront it head-on. When you do this, you realize that the worst that could happen is not so bad.
- Replace worry with action. If you are so interested in the future, then spend your time and energy in doing something about it. Set useful and realistic goals and then begin now and go after them.

Procrastination is another effectiveness killer. This is perhaps the most common and universal attitude that gets in the way of our accomplishments as recreation leaders. Occasional procrastination is normal and usually harmless. Most of us have a tendency to postpone tasks we do not like such as washing the dishes or scheduling a dental checkup. But, when out of control, procrastination can stop you from achieving your goals.

What is the root of procrastination? Fear—fear of rejection, embarrassment, or failure. People who procrastinate a great deal are usually perfectionists. They often become immobilized by their desire to achieve nothing short of perfection. Tasks that seem overwhelming or distasteful such as preparing a budget or cleaning out the crafts storage cabinet are the easiest to put off. This is because there exists an unconscious desire to avoid risk—the risk of failure.

What is the solution? It relies on placing value on the intermediate steps in a task and not just the finished project. Ways that you may find useful in reducing procrastination are as follows:

- Slice the project into smaller, more manageable subtasks. The key is to make each subtask so simple that you cannot possibly justify not doing it.
- Reward your nonprocrastinating behavior. A tangible, small reward for the accomplishment of a tangible, small task can be motivating. For example, a cup of tea for an hour of studying the new computer tournament scheduling program or a sauna for writing an extensive evaluation report could help give you a sense of worthwhileness and progress.
- Use the buddy system. Turn to others for support. Find a buddy who either shares your task or is willing to help. Report to your buddy each day on what you have accomplished and how you feel about it.
- Practice good time management. Give yourself deadlines, avoid overcommitment, and set realistic time schedules.

Exercise: Stopping Excuses

A. Whenever you give a reason for not doing something at school, work, or home, ask yourself: "Is this an excuse or not?" If you catch yourself making an excuse, try stopping, even if it means breaking off in the middle of a sentence. What are you protecting by making excuses? If you stop making as many excuses, how do those you work and live with react? Be prepared for their possible discomfort.

B. Here is a more radical version of the same exercise. Set aside an entire day for this. For the whole day, whenever somebody asks you to do something, say yes, and do it right away!

(from Tulku, 1994)

Responding to Pressure

We all have pressures in life. If you claim you have no pressures, then you are not a part of your life. Expectations on what we accomplish as recreation leaders can serve as important motivators, but too much pressure or pressure that is not constructively handled can be debilitating.

Did you ever stop to think about how much of the pressure that surrounds you is your creation? People who talk about how they are overworked and under constant and unrelentless pressure are talking about what they have done to themselves. Again, part of responding successfully to the pressures of work and life is found in attitudes.

Approach your work with a relaxed attitude. If you find yourself terribly tense, stop and ask yourself what all that tension is accomplishing. Then slow down; move calmly and deliberately toward your goals. Take relaxation breaks when needed.

Enjoy your work. No matter how successful at what you are doing you say you are, if you do not enjoy it, your real success can be questioned. When you do enjoy your career, you feel a sense of harmony, purpose, and a sense of internal success. This soon translates into success as others see it as well.

It is useful to remember that most things seem more important than they are. The immediacy of the present tends to make us nearsighted. As you encounter pressure-inducing situations in your work, keep your perspective. Is it do or die? Most of the time we find things far less drastic than they seemed. This realization makes it easier to take things in stride.

TIME MANAGEMENT

There are 86,400 seconds in each twenty-four hour day. Each is either used or lost. There can be no storage of time or borrowing from tomorrow. Everybody gets the same amount of time, and everybody gets all there is. It would not make sense if we said, "Sure George can get more cultural art programs successfully going than I can because he has twenty-eight hours every day and I only have twenty-four." Nonetheless most of us would agree that nothing is more scarce than time. Time is a paradox: we never seem to have enough time, yet we have all the time there is.

The solution to the paradox of time, then, is to focus on the most important things first. This is labeled **time management.** Managing time means managing oneself in relation to time; it is how we relate to time. There is time for everything we want to do if we use our time wisely. Time is a resource as plentiful as air but nonrenewable once used.

Exercise: Condensing Time

Imagine that an average human lifespan is only one year. Think about the richness of a whole lifetime—the growth, the accomplishment, the understanding—being condensed into twelve months. Think about how precious this brief life is and how urgent it is to make good use of the time you have left. Now, condense the human lifespan even farther. Imagine that the week to come will be a lifetime. Does thinking about this help you to wake up to the realities of time right now?

(from Tulku, 1994)

Planning Your Time

Leader Profile: The Present
Harriet E. Rice
Public Affairs Officer for the U.S. Army Community and Family Support Center. Harriet's busy international agenda requires her to focus on effective time management skills.

Planning saves time. Often people plan activities but fail to plan time. Planning time means setting a time frame to a planned activity. The process of establishing a plan to your work requires that you identify and set priorities for your tasks. Lakein (1974), a renowned time management consultant, recommended an **ABC Priority System.**

According to this system, you first list all tasks you would like to accomplish in a day or week or month. Complex projects requiring an extended period are broken down into smaller, more specific tasks. Second, you establish priorities by labeling tasks that are of the greatest benefit to your success and effectiveness "A," those tasks of medium benefit "B," and those of low benefit "C." Additional priority may be indicated by numbering the tasks A-1, A-2, B-1, B-2, and so forth. An example of what this might look like for a recreation leader's day is presented in the boxed material on p. 251. This example could be expandable to any period: a week, month, quarter, or year.

This categorized list of tasks, according to Lakein, should then become your guide for performing the work. Since "A" tasks are most important, you should strive to accomplish these first. When "A" tasks are completed, your focus can shift to "B" tasks. Remember, your best use of time is when you complete "A" tasks before "B" tasks and "B" tasks before "C" tasks.

Once the priority of tasks has been determined, it is then important to schedule these projects within available periods. When scheduling high priority "A" tasks, the following is offered as advice:

- *Schedule "A" tasks during prime time*: Prime time is that specific part of the day when you are at your peak. It is when you think your clearest and accomplish the most. Some people prefer early morning hours; others are more productive in late afternoon. Try to schedule your most important tasks when you are most likely to do a good job. Other "B" and "C" tasks such as completing daily routine reports and returning telephone messages should be scheduled when you are not required to be functioning maximally.

- *Schedule whole blocks of time for "A" tasks*: Another way of assuring enough time for high priority work is to set aside one or two hours of uninterrupted time each day for "A" tasks. This may mean that you close your office door, if you have one, and decline phone calls for a while.
- *Leave some unscheduled time in your day*: It can be a frustrating mistake to schedule every minute. Leave some time open to handle unexpected problems, requests, or opportunities. According to Beeler (1984), most people working in supervisory or administrative positions will have between twenty-five percent and fifty percent of controllable time—time in which to accomplish "ABC" priority work. This range of controllable time increases, she has claimed, in lower level positions.

When planning your time for accomplishing your workload, it is a good idea to put your schedule in writing. You cannot remember everything you are planning to do or when you plan to do it in the midst of a hectic day. This written schedule should be on a single sheet, not on numerous little notes. If you use computer software for getting organized, your schedule of when tasks are to be done could be included. Writing things down will help you clarify your thoughts and focus on what you are trying to accomplish with the day.

Another good idea when planning your time is to schedule thinking time every day. More thinking never hurts. You should develop the habit of thinking regularly about what is happening and what you would like to be happening. If you do not build time for thinking and planning into your schedule, you will have difficulty doing an adequate amount of either.

ABC Priority System

Step 1: List all tasks you would like to accomplish

Call police department about ten-kilometer road race.
Order new clay for ceramics classes.
Set up display in community center.
Select new aerobics music.
Write evaluation report on wheelchair sports program.
Return water cooler to Jeff.
Preview new adventure films for teen group meeting.
Draw route map for ten-kilometer race.
Recruit volunteers for new softball league.
Read new issue of *Parks and Recreation* magazine.

Step 2: Categorize tasks according to benefit to your effectiveness

"A" Tasks:
Call police department.
Draw route map.
Order new clay.
Write evaluation report.
Recruit softball volunteers.
"B" Tasks:
Return water cooler.
Set up display.
"C" Tasks:
Select aerobics music.
Read new magazine issue.

Reducing Time Wasters

Successful time management depends on more than a carefully planned schedule. You must also take positive action against those **time wasters** that threaten to destroy your plans. By improving your time planning ability and eliminating many of your time wasters, you have a dual approach to getting on top of your job and using your time effectively. Figure 13.1 illustrates the dual approach. If either part of the formula is neglected, you will not be successful in managing your time productively.

What is a time waster? You waste your time when you spend it on something less important when you could be spending it on something more important. Time wasters can be divided into two groups: external and internal (Douglass & Douglass, 1980). **External time wasters** are generated by someone or something else. Many external time wasters such as traffic jams are beyond your control. **Internal time wasters** come from within. Procrastination, socializing, and the inability to say no are examples of internal time wasters. They are often difficult to identify and conquer.

Leader Profile: The Present
Kathryn Spatz
Director of Chapel Hill Parks and Recreation Department, North Carolina. Recreation leaders at all position levels must learn to reduce time wasters in order to best use their skills and talents.

What are some of the common internal and external time wasters? The following discussion offers suggestions on reducing the time wasted by common interruptive and unproductive situations. The main point of this presentation is that successful recreation leaders are not able to eliminate time wasters, but they are able to hold wasted time to a minimum.

Drop-in Visitors

People interruptions are a part of your job. In addition to a considerable number of interruptions generated by participants, supervisors and subordinates also place constant, usually unplanned, demands on your time. What can you do? First, work on your attitude. Instead of being upset when an interruption occurs, think of it as part of your job. You cannot eliminate all your interruptions. Many are necessary and some are even important.

When planning your day, be sure to allow time for interruptions. Do not schedule activities back to back all day so that one interruption will completely throw you off schedule.

Learn to close your door occasionally for important, high-priority tasks. It will give the potential visitor a brief moment of second thought: "Do I really need to bother this person now?"

Be candid when someone asks, "Have you got a minute?" Learn to say no. Since no is the most time-saving word in your vocabulary, you should strive to use it whenever appropriate.

FIGURE 13.1. Time management formula

Messaging Technology

The ironic truth about the telephone, e-mail, faxes, and voice mail is that they can be your biggest helper and your biggest time waster. They can save a great deal of time if you use them appropriately. For example, you can minimize the troublesome side of telephones by remembering a few important points.

Screen and group your outgoing calls. Set aside a particular time each day to make three to five calls. Ask the people you regularly call for times when they are usually available to receive calls. Record their availability time next to their phone number. Before you make a call, prepare a brief outline of what you want to say. The outline will give your conversation focus and will keep you from forgetting the main reason you called in the first place.

In many recreation settings leaders answer their own phones. In those situations, however, where you have a receptionist, use the expertise of this person to help organize your incoming calls. Remember, though, if others are to answer your telephone, they must be properly trained. You must work with them to develop an appropriate telephone system and protocol.

Paperwork

There are always too many reports to write and too many letters to answer. To get through the volumes of paper requiring your time, consider the following ideas.

In getting efficiently through reports such as evaluation reports, accident reports, or personnel reports, plan what you are going to say before you say it. Taking the time to preplan an outline is always useful. When you write, use short, simple, and clear sentences. Say what needs to be said and no more. Long reports are a double time waster—they take longer to write and to read. Do not make revisions in the name of perfectionism if the added benefit is small. If it must be perfect, take the time; but more likely quick, accurate information is more important than a flawlessly presented report.

In responding to mail and memos develop the in-today, out-tomorrow habit. Try to respond immediately to correspondence to avoid backlog. This will be easier if you handle (touch and look at) each letter or memo only once. Much time is wasted in shuffling and reshuffling paper.

Use electronic mail and the dictaphone more and write less. Sometimes an immediate response by e-mail will enable you to complete a task without all the time spent on writing a letter, waiting for a reply, and reading and answering a second letter. Make handwritten responses in the margins of letters. In some cases an instant reply in the margin is even more useful than a carefully prepared letter.

Use form letters and form paragraphs for routine correspondence. With word processing through a computer, form letters can be more personalized and individualized.

Travel

If you travel as part of your job, you can save time and energy if you consider your trips as exactly that—part of the job. Accept that there will be lines, delays, bad weather, and traffic jams. Many of your most time-consuming tasks can be broken down into smaller steps, and some of these small steps can be reserved for travel time activities.

Listening to tapes is a valuable way to spend your time while traveling. There are tapes available on all subjects of personal and professional concern, and some tape machines are small enough to carry in your pocket. Use travel time for quiet thinking time. No phones will ring, and no one will drop in to visit!

Leader Profile: The Present
Michael A. Kane
Deputy Director of Fairfax County Park Authority, Virginia. Ask any recreation leader about the role of time management in his work and the reply will be unanimous—it is a critically important skill to have.

Meetings

Time wasted in meetings must be approached from two perspectives: those meetings you call and those meetings you do not call but must attend.

When you are responsible for calling a meeting, first be certain that there is something to call the meeting for and that you are prepared. Know what you hope to accomplish at the meeting and try to state your goals in terms of actions to be taken rather than points to be discussed. Be certain that you have all necessary information and papers with you. If you proceed without the forgotten material, you will handle the discussion awkwardly, confuse the group, and waste a great deal of time. Resist any interruptions and aim to stay on course.

Discourage unnecessary meetings. When you must hold a meeting, be certain you have a prepared agenda. Distribute it a few days before the meeting and designate those who will be called on to discuss or present certain points. This will allow you to delegate responsibility for the meeting and give them time to consider the important agenda points ahead of time.

Set a time limit for all meetings. Start and end at the times indicated on your agenda. Do not wait for everyone to show up before starting. If you delay a meeting by waiting for stragglers, you guarantee that people will be late in the future.

As a meeting participant you can also make meetings more useful. Know the purpose of a meeting before you attend and identify your role in it. Come on time to the meeting. Be the kind of participant you would like to see at your own meetings. If you have a grievance about a meeting, tell the meeting chair about it. It is precisely because meeting participants accept ineffective meetings that they continue. It is your valuable time that is being wasted.

Other Time Wasters

There are other time wasters of course. Although meetings, travel, paperwork, telephones, and drop-in visitors are among the main ones, a time waster list could certainly also include topics discussed elsewhere in this book such as ineffective communication, ineffective delegation, poor participant management skills, and an inability to lead groups.

Everyone wastes time. Even the most organized and self-disciplined people have wasted moments. But there is a difference between people who consistently produce good results and people who do not. Those who produce manage to hold their wasted time to a minimum. You cannot control everything. The trick is to accept the uncontrollable and control the controllable.

KEEP LEARNING

One thing is clear about success as a leader. Leaders are made at least as much by their experiences and their understanding and application of experiences as by any skills or knowledge. The experiences I'm talking about are not, however, the rote events of daily life. I mean, instead, paying attention to our daily experiences so that we learn something from them. Some experiences are especially significant for learning. I'm sure that you can easily think of some experiences in your life from which you've learned a great deal. No doubt these include education and travel experiences, for example. While it may seem foolhardy, or at least a waste of time, the point in this section is that successfully managing your workload depends on your continuing to learn and grow.

Types of Learning

In chapter 12, we discussed the strategies and skills you need for teaching so participants learn how to be successful at recreation activities. Here, however, we look at learning differently. Let's talk about your lifelong learning—how learning can and should be experienced after you've finished the formal education requirements of your profession. In the book *On Becoming a Leader*, the author Warren Bennis (1989) reports that in learning there is a "human gap." He defines this as the distance between growing complexity in our work, family, and personal lives and our capacity to cope with it. He calls it a human gap because it is a dichotomy between a growing complexity of our making and a lagging development of our capacities. Accordingly, he describes the two principal modes of conventional learning (Bennis, 1989, p. 75):

- **Maintenance learning:** the acquisition of skills and knowledge for dealing with known situations. It is the type of learning designed to maintain an existing system or established way of doing things. We could view your university training and the continuing education credits offered by professional organizations (such as the continuing education program of the National Recreation and Park Association) as contributing to our maintenance learning.
- **Shock learning:** occurs when experiences or events teach people by overwhelming them. This is learning through the shock of something that has occurred. For example, we learn how much more time and effort college work takes than high school following the shock of our first semester freshman grade report. Or, the playground leader might never forget the importance of keeping accurate accident reports following the lawsuit filed by the parent of an injured child.

You need both types of learning throughout your life. But Bennis maintains that maintenance learning and shock learning are less genuine—that they are a matter of accepting conventional wisdom. While Bennis acknowledges that these types of learning are necessary to remain relevant and useful in a particular profession, he argues that to be ahead of the complexity of today's world (or at minimum keep up), our learning must be more than this.

What he calls for in addition, then, is innovative learning. **Innovative learning** is in essence conscious participation in life. Bennis states the principal components of innovative learning are:

- Anticipating by being active and imaginative rather than passive and habitual
- Learning by listening to others
- Participating in shaping events, rather than being shaped by them

Innovative learning requires that you be self-directed rather than other-directed in your life and your work. Such learning means that we make new connections, generate useful syntheses of experiences, and as a result our understanding increases. Creative problem solving is a form of innovative learning.

How to Be an Innovative Learner

The key to relying on active and conscious learning to help you manage your workload essentially means that you spend your life in pursuit of knowledge, not the gathering of information. How can this be accomplished?

1. *Inquire and dialogue.* Our experiences are filled with things that we do not understand. This is why we need to constantly ask questions and initiate dialogues (Siegel, 1994). We ask questions of friends, colleagues, and experts. We ask questions of books, nature, and spiritual entities. But dialogue is more than asking questions. It also includes listening. Good listening leads to good understanding.
2. *Do and experiment.* Questioning and listening are not enough. To be an innovative learner, you also need to do something (Siegel, 1994). You need to experiment with new ideas and concepts. You need to solve a lot of problems. For example, is it sufficient in learning to ride a bicycle that you ask questions? No. You may learn about the biomechanics of bicycling, but to learn how to ride, you must get onto the bike and try it. You may fall, but you will learn how to ride it. This means that you are developing your knowledge through involvement.
3. *Evaluate and conclude.* No matter the source of your information—from books, research reports, professional journals, or from your own observation, you must evaluate it (Siegel, 1994). To illustrate, trace the studies on coffee: first, coffee is bad for the heart. No, it is not bad at all. Only the caffeine is bad. Not really—decaffeinated is worse than regular coffee. No—only certain types. Now, we're not sure. New information is produced at astonishing rates every day. Should you pay attention to it? Definitely. But evaluate it by asking:
   - Who paid for the study? There may be bias in the results.
   - How was the study performed? Was it rigorous and scientific?
   - Are conclusions warranted logically? Do the conclusions apply in only certain cases?
   - What kind of sample was used? Was the sample relevant to your situation?
   - What type of information was gathered in the study? Is it relevant to you?
4. *Amend and try again.* After you have reached an understanding, you amend your mental framework according to what you have learned (Siegel, 1994). If your understanding is satisfactory and meaningful to you, follow it with action. Now that you have learned something, use it. Nothing is accomplished without action.

SETTING GOALS

Above all else, becoming an effective recreation leader—becoming an effective human being—begins with goal setting. It would not be difficult to insist that goals and the sense of purpose that accompanies them are necessary for your survival. We need personal and professional goals.

Despite this mandate, in reality few of us undertake the task of setting some definite goals for our life. Yet it has been demonstrated over and over that doing this would increase the odds of working less while accomplishing more. Until we decide what we want, it is not likely that we will get it. Goals protect you from aimless effort and point you in a positive direction.

Having personal and professional goals also has great value in time management. Goals are the building blocks of better employment of your time. It is impossible to make good use of your work time without a set of well-clarified goals.

Goals are also an important element in maintaining personal stability. Your life must contain something meaningful to live and work for. Without goals, you lose your purpose and direction. People who say that life is not worth living are saying that they have no worthwhile goals.

Case in Point: The Hectic Life

Louise:
My life is hectic! I'm running all day—meetings, phone calls, paperwork, appointments. I push myself to the limit, fall into bed exhausted, and get up early the next morning to do it again. I'm getting a lot done, but I get this feeling sometimes, "So what? What am I doing that really counts?" I have to admit, I don't know.

There is too little of me to go around. I feel like I am being torn apart. My family is important to me; so is my work. I live with constant conflict, trying to juggle the demands of both. Is it possible to be successful—and happy—at the office and at home? I don't feel in control of my life. I try to figure out what's important and set goals to do it, but other people—my boss, my work colleagues, my partner—continually throw wrenches into the works. What I set out to do is blocked by what other people want me to do for them.

For every one thing I do, I can think of ten things I don't do, and I feel guilty. How can I know what's most important? How can I do it? How can I enjoy it? How can I translate what counts into my daily life?

Questions:
What is wrong for Louise? Besides the issue of setting and achieving goals, what other issues relevant to this chapter is Louise dealing with? How would you advise her to solve these things?

(based on Covey, Merrill, & Merrill, 1995)

The Goals Hierarchy

The goals for your efforts as a recreation leader should relate to one another. Long-range goals are the foundation for more immediate goals. They exist in a hierarchy as illustrated in figure 13.2.

As this figure indicates, the accomplishment of daily tasks should lead ultimately to the accomplishment of bigger, more long-range goals. This means that if daily goals are met, weekly goals can be met. If weekly goals are met, monthly goals can be met. If monthly goals are met, longer range goals can also be met. How far into the future are long-range goals planned? As far into the future as possible. The farther ahead goals are projected, the easier it is to know what to do now.

Where do you start? With long-range goals. To use the goals pyramid you first consider your most important desired achievements. Then you break down these **long-range goals** into yearly goals, which are broken down into monthly goals and so forth. Finally, by the time you have carried on this process to the daily level of the pyramid, you have specific and simple actions that can be handled within a day, which when added together lead to the ultimate accomplishments. See figure 13.3 for an example of the goals pyramid applied to a recreation leader. The main thing is to keep the main thing the main thing!

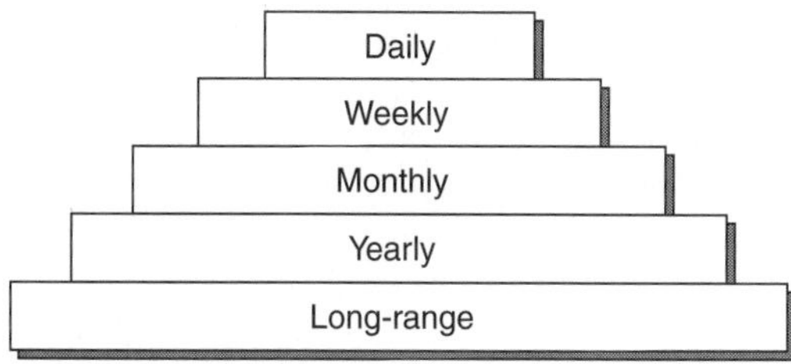

FIGURE 13.2. Goals pyramid

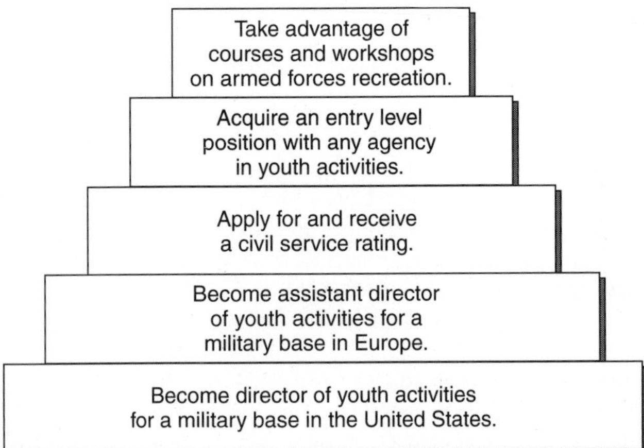

FIGURE 13.3. Example of the goals pyramid for a recreation leader

Setting Your Goals

Developing your goals can be difficult. A useful goal is one that motivates you to action and also provides direction for that action. The secret is to have goals that really work for you. When setting up your goals, several principles need to be adhered to for best results.

Goals Should Be Yours

Set the goals yourself. Take charge of what you want to accomplish according to what is meaningful to you. Do not allow your goals to be set by parents, employers, friends, spouses, children, or society. You should be open to the ideas and suggestions of others, but you should also do your own thinking and deciding. The more the goal is yours, the greater will be your commitment to its achievement.

Goals Should Be Challenging But Attainable

If the goal you set for yourself is unrealistic or unattainable, it is not a goal. This means that setting goals too low or too high can cause you to be unmotivated in achieving them. Goals should make you stretch and grow. But they should also be set at a level

Case in Point: The Gardener

Michael:

Some time ago, a friend of mine—a busy executive for a large company—was moving into his new home. He decided to hire a friend of his to landscape the grounds. She had a doctorate in horticulture and was experienced and knowledgeable. He had a great vision for the grounds around his new home, and because he was busy and traveled a lot, he kept emphasizing to her the need to create his garden in a way that would require of him little or no maintenance. He pointed to the necessity of automatic sprinklers and other labor saving devices, for example. He was constantly looking for ways to cut the amount of time he'd have to spend taking care of the things in his garden. Finally, his friend stopped and said, "Larry, I can see what you're saying. But there is one thing you need to deal with before we go any farther. If there's no gardener, there's no garden!"

(based on Covey, et al., 1995)

at which you are able and willing to work. What is an attainable goal? That is a decision only you can make. If you think you can do it, then you probably can.

Goals Should Be Written Down

Read and reread each goal frequently. The purpose of writing down the things you want to accomplish is to clarify them. Writing goals helps you identify more clearly what you want. Written goals are also less likely to be forgotten or lost in the pressures and shuffle of daily events. Writing down goals also increases your commitment to them, and the degree of commitment to a goal is pivotal in its realization.

Goals Should Be Flexible

As an alive, growing person, your needs and values will be constantly evolving. As a result, you will legitimately have to reevaluate, modify, replace, or even discard some of your goals. This is normal and desirable. If you cannot do this to at least some degree, you are being too rigid in your views of yourself and where you are going.

Goals Should Be Compatible

Goals must not directly conflict with each other. For example, wanting to be outstanding in your profession may conflict with wanting to spend half of each year in adventure traveling. If your goals are not compatible, accomplishing one may prevent you from accomplishing another. This can lead to indecision and frustration, and you will end up accomplishing nothing.

Summary

This chapter's concern is success in managing your workload. Success in being a recreation leader is doing what you want to do, accomplishing what you want to accomplish, being who you want to be, and attaining any reasonable objective you desire.

Several recommendations for how to be successful in this professional pursuit were offered. These suggestions include having goals and meeting them, managing time, getting organized, continuing to learn, and having a positive and productive attitude.

Supporting every effective recreation leader is a thought-out system of goals. Having goals increases the odds that you will work less and accomplish more. Goals protect you from aimless effort and point you in a purposeful direction. Your goals should be partitioned into short-range or immediate aims that ultimately support more long-range aims. Regardless of how thoroughly goals control your personal and professional life, they should be challenging, attainable, flexible, compatible, written down, and all your own.

Time management is also an important skill needed for success and happiness as a recreation leader. You will never have enough. Managing time means managing yourself in relation to time so that there is time for everything you want to do. The foundation of time management is essentially an ability to decide and schedule priorities, while eliminating time spent on less important things.

Productive time management is dependent on another skill—getting and staying organized. Being organized takes time. But this is the point! Being organized liberates time. Lack of time is the result of being unorganized.

We also discussed in this chapter how successfully managing your workload depends on you continuing to learn and grow. Specifically, we compared the two principal modes of conventional learning—maintenance and shock learning—with innovative

Successful Leading Questionnaire

	True	False
1. Most people are overworked because of the nature of their job.	______	______
2. Your job is unique and not subject to repetitive time patterns.	______	______
3. Further delay will probably enable you to improve the quality of your decisions.	______	______
4. Managing time better is essentially a matter of reducing the time spent in various activities.	______	______
5. Your job deals with people, and because all people are important, you cannot establish priorities.	______	______
6. Delegating will probably free a great deal of your time and relieve you of some responsibility.	______	______
7. People who concentrate on working efficiently are the most effective performers.	______	______
8. Most of the ordinary day-to-day activities do not need to be planned, and most people could not plan for them anyway.	______	______
9. It is not always possible to work on the basis of priorities.	______	______
10. The busy and active people who work the hardest are the ones who get the best results.	______	______
11. It is not necessary to write out your goals.	______	______
12. Most of the results you achieve are produced by a few critical activities.	______	______

learning. Innovative learning is conscious participation in life. It means that we approach our personal and professional lives with vigor for: inquiring and dialoguing, doing and experimenting, evaluating and concluding, and amending and trying again.

Finally, how you spend your time and energy is a matter of how you think and feel. This means that how much you are able to accomplish in leading others in meaningful recreation experiences is largely governed by your attitude. How you approach your work, how you deal with colleagues, and how you influence participants will reflect how you think and feel about yourself. Strengthening your self-image is key.

Questions and Activities for Review and Discussion

In the above boxed material is a list of assumptions about success. Read the list and decide which are generally true and which are generally false. Discuss your decisions with classmates and professionals working in the recreation fields. Based on your understanding of this chapter, be able to defend your opinions.

As with many situations, there is no absolute "right" or "wrong" answer to this list of assumptions. However, some answers are generally more true or more false for your effectiveness as a recreation leader even though you can probably find exceptions to each. Check your ideas with the generally considered correct responses: all are false except for statement twelve.

References

Beeler, C. (1984). Time management: mastering the monsters. *Parks and Recreation, 19*(1), 64–65.

Bennis, W. (1989). *On becoming a leader*. Reading, MA: Addison-Wesley.

Covey, S. R., Merrill, A. R., & Merrill, R. R. (1995). *First things first: To live, to love, to learn, to leave a legacy*. New York: Simon & Schuster.

Douglass, M. E., & Douglass, D. N. (1980). *Manage your time, manage your work, manage yourself.* New York: AMACOM.

Lakein, A. (1974). *How to get control of your time and your life*. New York: New American Library.

LeBoeuf, M. (1979). *Working smart: How to accomplish more in half the time*. New York: McGraw-Hill.

Siegel, P. (1994). *Design your future: Live your vision in the ever-changing learning society*. Long Beach, CA: Learning Society Publications.

Tulku, T. (1994). *Skillful means: Wake up*! Oakland, CA: Dharma Publishing.

Web Resources

Day-to-day management: www.lowe.org/

Getting good grades: www.campuslife/utoronto.ca/

Getting organized: www.duncanresource.com/
http://cave3.r5i.com/
www.mindspring.com/
http://techroad.com/
http://organizedhome.com/

Getting organized software: www.hotfiles.com/

Goal setting: www.goalmap.com/
www.psychwww.com/
www.topachievement.com/

Job search goals: www.gov.nf.ca/

Personal success coaching: www.advantagecoaching.com/

Procrastination: www.carleton.ca/
www.angelfire.com/
http://expage.com/
http://wsrv.clas.virginia.edu/

Society for Creative Procrastination: www.dartmouth.edu/

Society for Laziness, Effortlessness, and Procrastination: www.cs.mcgill.ca/

Study skills: http://ads.i33.com/

Time management: www.balancetime.com
www.timedoctor.com/
www.mindtools.com/

Time management books: www.timemanagementbooks.greatbooksplus.com/

Time management internet resources: www.selfgrowth.com/

Time management seminars: www.selfhelp.com/

Time management software: www.journyx.com/
http://business.software-directory.com/

CHAPTER 14

According to Age Groups

We do not cease playing because we are old:
we grow old because we cease playing.
—Joseph Lee in *Butler,* 1965.

LEARNING OBJECTIVES

To highlight the differences and similarities of leading people in different stages of the life cycle, this chapter places recreation leadership techniques and skills into the context of the specific participant groupings of:

- children
- youth
- adults
- older adults

KEY TERMS

human development p. 264
maturation p. 264
motor development p. 265
prosocial development p. 267
moral development p. 267
permissive style p. 268
authoritarian style p. 268
authoritative style p. 268
adolescence p. 270
personal identity p. 272
friendships p. 273
cliques p. 273
crowd p. 273
young-old p. 279
old-old p. 279
primary aging p. 280
secondary aging p. 280

A child is born. Day by day and month by month, from childhood to adolescence to adulthood, the human organism develops and experiences life in a variety of ways. The life cycle is characterized by many changes. Most individuals achieve many developmental milestones such as speaking a first word, learning to read, and riding a bicycle. Many social changes also occur. Making friends, falling in love, being a parent, and retiring from work are life events many individuals experience.

DEVELOPMENT

We tend to look forward to these and other changes in our lives according to a chronological scheme. Figure 14.1 summarizes this chronology. When human development is studied, such an arbitrary, compartmentalized view can also be useful in specifying life's major stages for all people.

Blanketing this notion of developmental stages is the notion of continuity. What happens between birth and death is individual. Each of us has her own unique timetable

Life stage	Approximate period
Prenatal period	Conception to birth
Infancy	Generally up to 2 years of age
Toddlerhood	2–3 years of age
Early childhood	Generally 3 or 4 to about 5 years of age
Middle childhood	Generally 6–12 years of age
Adolescence	13–19 years of age
Young adulthood	20–40 years of age
Middle adulthood	40 to about 60 years of age
Young older adulthood	60–75 years of age
Old older adulthood	76+ years of age

FIGURE 14.1. The chronology of human development

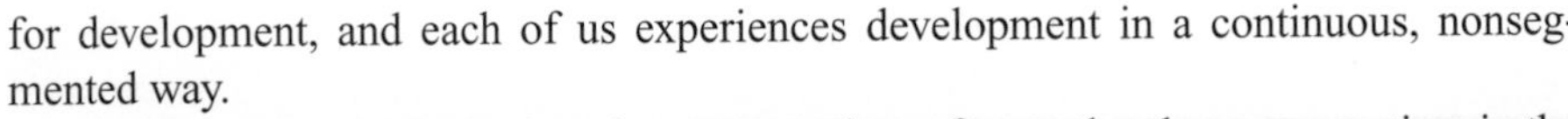

for development, and each of us experiences development in a continuous, nonsegmented way.

Human development, then, is a process that refers to the changes over time in the structure, thought, or behavior of a person. These changes are progressive and cumulative and are considered to be a result of both biological and environmental influences.

Leader Profile: The Past
Ethel Mori, 1959
Former Assistant Director of Recreation, City of Honolulu, Hawaii. With responsibility for recreation programs citywide, Mori was aware of the different needs and interests of varying-aged participants.

Biologically, all living organisms develop according to a genetic plan. In the human the plan is flexible and allows for some physical and much behavioral alteration. When psychologists refer to the process of growing from the genetic plan, they use the term **maturation.** Physical structures and motor capabilities, for example, mature at different rates. Any single structure or capability usually has its point of optimal maturity. Growth refers to the increase in size, function, or complexity to that point of maturity. Aging refers to the kind of biological change that occurs beyond the point of optimal maturity. This does not necessarily imply decline or deterioration. Some qualities, such as judgment and insight, increase as we grow older.

The environment influences us every minute of the day. Environmental influences can stunt an individual's growth or promote it; they can create long-lasting anxieties or help form complex skills. The basic process by which the environment causes lasting changes in behavior is through learning. Learning as a result of experience is the basic developmental ingredient of change in the individual. Learning occurs over an enormous range of activities such as avoiding hot toasters, factoring algebra equations, running interference in football, or losing one's temper. We learn not only skills and knowledge but attitudes, feelings, prejudices, values, and patterns of thought.

IMPORTANCE TO THE RECREATION LEADER

The study of human growth and development has been of interest to psychologists, sociologists, and educators for many years. Recreation leaders work with a variety of people in play settings; therefore a knowledge of the processes of development is also foundational to recreation leadership competency. Whether in the gymnasium, the day-care center, the playing field, the swimming pool, the nature center, or the hospital, leadership must have an understanding of the way participants behave at different stages in life. Without this you can only guess at the workable techniques and procedures for leading people in recreation experiences.

This chapter pays attention to the changes in thought, physical structure, and behavior of people as they travel from the world of a child to the world of the aged. These understandings are then linked to the techniques of recreation leadership so that what we accomplish with participants is more appropriately matched.

LEADING CHILDREN

Those participants who are toddlers or in early and middle childhood are a typical responsibility for many recreation leaders. Historically, children have represented a major participant group, but recreation and park organizations have corrected this by conscientiously expanding services to persons of all ages and abilities. Who is the child? Should children be taught to swim using different teaching strategies than those used with adults? What is unique to recreation leadership with children?

Physical Abilities

A great deal of psychomotor development occurs in infancy; however, because children do not usually become participants in organized recreation until they are at least three to four years of age, the discussion of the development of motor abilities in children will begin at toddlerhood. Knowing what children are physically capable of undertaking and the degree of efficiency that they can exert is important, particularly to leaders who will be structuring children's physical activities.

Let us begin with early childhood. In physical play characterized by such activities as running, tumbling, skipping, rope jumping, tricycle riding, and climbing, the development of motor skills rapidly accelerates. The ability to do these more diversified and strenuous physical activities is primarily a result of rapid muscular growth. Before age four, muscular development is only proportionate to overall body growth; after this, approximately 75 percent of the child's weight gains are a result of muscle development (Helms & Turner, 1981).

Other noteworthy developments evident in early childhood include increases in reaction times, refinements in eye-hand coordination, and improvements in manual dexterity. The number and diversity of new motor skills are significant for young children.

The implications of this **motor development** summary are directly useful to those who lead young children. For successful motor development, movement experiences are important. Recreation leaders who work with this group should place much emphasis on rhythm, body awareness, and unstructured large movement opportunities.

Movement has many important meanings to the young child (Russell, 1996). It means life, because they think things that move are alive. Movement helps the child to discover his body and to form a body image. Controlled movement brings pleasure and the satisfaction of mastery.

Recreation leaders help preschool-age children with motor development by arranging the physical environment so that it encourages running, crawling, jumping, pushing, pulling, and throwing. You can also help them by being supportive and enthusiastic rather than only showing them how to execute a movement. Ask them questions rather than telling them. Set up situations that encourage exploration and practice. Children should be encouraged to discover different ways of throwing, catching, or carrying a ball or different ways of moving around, into, and out of a circle.

Dance movement is an excellent means to motor development. Music and rhythm provide links between movement, emotional expression, creativity, and self-awareness. Despite their limited verbal capacities young children can use music—and the leader's suggestions—to move happily or sadly, to express experiences, and to understand relationships with space.

What about the middle years of childhood? Surely one of the first things that impresses any observer of school-age children is their high activity level. Children's active games and sports provide an opportunity to further develop strength, coordination, agility, and flexibility. Thus in neighborhood playgrounds or in camps children can be seen testing their balance by riding bicycles through homemade obstacle courses. They improve their hand-eye coordination, strength, and speed in games of baseball and basketball. They increase their flexibility and agility by climbing trees or attempting feats of daring. Skateboarding or practicing karate, learning the latest dances, or imitating the exploits of TV heroes helps to improve physical-motor development.

The success that a school-age child experiences in motor skill activities depends on a number of factors, including rates of physical maturity, environmental opportunities to engage in physical activity, and the degree of self-confidence. Recreation leaders must remember that six- to twelve-year-olds are still in the process of refining coordination abilities and mastering grace of movement. Improvement is gradual, and clumsiness and awkwardness can still be expected. It is at this age level that the degree to which a motor skill is mastered can affect the child's sense of achievement and peer acceptance.

Although children learn much through imitation and practice, they also gain from good leadership. This includes teaching for body awareness, for variety and flexibility of movement, and also for skills. For example, a recreation leader can help a child to jump high by asking her to get a ball that is suspended overhead rather than by saying "Jump as high as you can."

During these middle childhood years fitness becomes increasingly more important (Russell, 1996). Fitness includes flexibility, endurance, and strength; it is an indication of the total health of the child. Exercise, especially outdoor exercise, contributes to the development and maintenance of fitness.

The years from six to twelve are also a time of life when children want to be good at what they do. They need to learn to do something they can look back on with the pride of accomplishment (Dennis & Hassol, 1983). In the area of motor skills recreation leaders can help by encouraging, appreciating, teaching, and giving opportunities for learning many skills. If the leader enjoys these activities along with the children, then the children adopt the general attitude that motor skills make a pleasant and important contribution to life. Neither too much nor too little leader intervention should be your watchword.

Sometimes a recreation organization, with good intentions, promotes the development of specialized skills in a few children to the exclusion of all-around motor development in all children. This can happen when the leader's emphasis is on the development of winning teams or "star" athletes. If everyone gets a chance to play and the emphasis is on sportsmanship and fun, then the games are healthful. If the competition is more important and the best athletes are featured, then the majority of children are restricted in movement and diminished in self-concept.

Social and Emotional Abilities

During early childhood youngsters are able to expand their social horizons and develop considerable independence and autonomy. The preschoolers' enlarging social sphere is interrelated with other factors of their development. This socialization process is a gradual one, with some situations causing the child to be aware of new insecurities and unsettling emotions.

Children begin to emerge during early childhood as "individuals," gaining insight into their unique self-concepts and personality traits. Children's developing self-concepts consist in part of their evaluation of how their personal attributes compare with those that the culture conceives of as "good." The valued attributes in our culture include power. The degree to which children feel that they possess this is determined by their social experiences. Power or strength will be evaluated to some extent by a child's ability to defeat a rival in a game, to resist peer pressure, or to dominate others.

Children must also learn to handle a wide range of emotions in these early years. Some are good feelings such as joy, affection, and sensuality. Others such as anger, fear, anxiety, jealousy, frustration, and hurt are not pleasant. The manner in which the child learns to cope with emotions is also a developmental process.

For example, the way in which anger is expressed changes with age. After the age of two, angry outbursts of an undirected physical nature such as kicking and hitting begin to decline. Temper tantrums, which started during toddlerhood, continue to persist into the preschool years. The use of threats and insults tends to increase. Thus, although the amount of anger and aggression appears to remain stable, the child's manner of expressing it changes (Helms & Turner, 1981).

Being sensitive to the needs and feelings of one's peers is also an important facet of social development for young children. Contemporary child psychologists call such sensitivity **prosocial development** (Smart & Smart, 1982). This term encompasses cooperation, altruism, sharing, and helping others. The child's early prosocial behavior appears to be greatly influenced by exposure to an adult role model and certain social situations (Dennis & Hassol, 1983). This means that children who are exposed to altruistic recreation leaders are more likely to imitate such behaviors, especially if the leader is warm and nurturant. Positive reinforcement by leaders can also affect the expression of prosocial behavior in children.

This development of cooperative behavior is accompanied by a parallel growth of the competitive spirit. This naturally occurs as children begin to strive for accomplishment. As children grow older, competitive behavior becomes more apparent. Normal competitiveness can be fostered by careful recreation leadership. For instance, Boy and Girl Scouts are urged to earn merit badges that are awarded when the individual has achieved something. Like cooperative behavior, competition may be increased through a leader's positive reinforcement and modeling behavior. A child who receives praise for winning a contest from a recreation leader will be eager to compete again.

Although the early years are important to social-emotional development, it is during the school years that children experience a critical period of personality and social maturation, especially in developing self-concepts (Craig, 1983). On reaching the middle years of childhood, the energies are turned to a newly expanded world. Reaching the age of school attendance brings freedom and an expansion of the network of social relations.

This expansion of worlds brings with it an increase in the importance of **moral development.** During early childhood a sense of morality is born when youngsters realize that certain behaviors are classified as good whereas other actions are considered bad. As children become older, morality begins to encompass a more complex set of ideas, values, and beliefs about such factors as guilt, shame, lying, and religion (Russell, 1996).

Appropriate adult role modeling from recreation leaders can assist children in their moral development. In addition, Duska and Whelan (1975) suggested the following as specific ways recreation leaders can help children participants develop higher levels of moral judgment:

- Establish the recreation setting (e.g., the camp or the playground) as a place where participants can feel respected.
- Allow participants to help in establishing rules.
- Explain the effect of a child's action on the entire group and choose a punishment that fits the offense.
- Provide chances for group play and help participants consider the feelings of others.
- Make an attempt to role-play or discuss moral dilemma situations that occur so that participants can see the event from a perspective other than their own.

These suggestions indicate that the recreation leader must make a concerted effort to help child participants deal with moral issues.

Another important area of social development in middle childhood is the achievement of a sense of industry, a perception of duty and accomplishment. Approximately at the ages of six to twelve the child learns to take pride in doing tasks well and in finishing them. During the early years the child was good at starting but not at finishing—in exploring but not in following through. Success results in the child's knowing the pleasure and satisfaction of a job well done. Recreation leaders on playgrounds and in camps and in other similar situations have an opportunity to allow children to produce, achieve, and accomplish by themselves. For example, encourage children to complete craft projects in their own way.

Children in recreational situations are usually exposed to different types of leader control, from authoritarian types to more liberal approaches. As a child works to gain a greater sense of accomplishment, what type of leadership control is most appropriate? A study of parental styles by Baumrind (1971) may be instructive in this regard. In this study three styles common to persons working with children were identified. The **permissive style** is one in which control is abdicated. The permissive leader, then, is nonpunitive and gives positive support to a child's behavior but does not offer much guidance or direction. The **authoritarian style,** on the other hand, is where the leader sets up too many regulations, permitting no questioning or deviations. Finally, the **authoritative style** is one where firm but reasonable limits are set. Judicious guidance is combined with warmth and support.

Which style is most useful for promoting a sense of industry in a child? Dennis and Hassol (1983) considered the authoritative style to be best. In contrast to the authoritarian leader's "Do as you are told because I said so," the authoritative leader respects the child's right to autonomy—within limits. Children are given ample opportunity to "try their wings" but with the security of knowing that an adult is willing to provide a "landing net" if needed.

Remember that each child is unique, and thus there is no general prescription for leaders working with them. The exact leadership atmosphere usually depends on the match between the values, temperaments, and the personalities of the leaders and those of the children. The results of your leadership will differ from one group to another. From the experience of a Girl Scout leader for several troops of same-age girls, an example can be cited. Thinking that she consistently brought the same values and leadership behaviors into each troop situation, she found one troop to be highly cooperative with each other and herself, full of creativity and enthusiasm. Another troop was full of interpersonal conflicts and tensions; and a third troop was active and enthusiastic but very uncreative.

Child's Play

Playful behavior comprises a large portion of the life span of human beings. For children play occupies the majority of daily activity. Why do children play? The many theories that have been proposed range from explaining play as a way to use up the surplus of energy that is no longer needed for basic survival to explaining play as the attempt to express an internal locus of control.

Regardless of the accuracy of the numerous theories in understanding children's play, observing children at play makes it clear that to children play is serious business. It is this seriousness of purpose that provides life's meaning for the child. Play is the way in which children explore and experiment with the world around them as they learn to understand that world and themselves. Children at play are learning to cope with the tasks of life, to master new skills, to gain confidence, and to get along with others.

Play provides an avenue through which children learn to share, to have personal worth, and to move their bodies. Early play behavior paves the way for more fully developed physical and social skills. Certain forms of expressive play (such as music and drama) strengthen the child's entire personality, further creativity and the joy of living, and even advance learning and cognitive development (Russell, 1996). Play is unarguably good for children!

When studying the play behavior of children, a predictable sequence of development is apparent. There are characteristic forms of play at different ages. The beginnings of play can be traced to the infant's third or fourth month, when she begins to actively explore. Centered primarily around the child's body, this exploratory play is a source of amusement and the early beginnings of self-concept (Craig, 1983). Later within the first year the child uses play to begin interactions with parents or siblings.

During toddlerhood, because of increased confidence, coordination, and motor skill ability, the child's exploratory behavior becomes more diverse. The play of toddlers is primarily egocentric; it is confined to the child and does not involve much interaction with others.

For children under three or four years of age, play may be characterized primarily as exploratory activity that appeals to their senses and fundamental motor skills. Early group play situations reflect children's social inexperience. In the play of the preschool years, children realize that their behavior must conform to the group situation in which they are placed (Craig, 1983).

A fascinating aspect of play during the preschool period is the development of imaginative abilities. The child's use of imagination has been claimed as a strong indication of originality and inventiveness. By making toys come alive, pretending to be an airplane pilot, and turning a box into a car, the child presumably can also resolve inner conflicts and begin to develop a better understanding of people and events (Craig, 1983).

School-age children enjoy many of the same activities of preschoolers but begin to exhibit increasing ability to play with others in small groups. They are also more interested in active games and table games with rules. Their imagination, however, is often less vivid than preschoolers. Children between the ages of six to twelve also enjoy discovery play and problem solving.

Children will play with or without adult leadership. Cautions have been raised regarding direct intervention in children's play. Within specific circumstances, however, the recreation leader may wish to enhance environmental conditions that maximize the playfulness of a situation. The criteria identified by Newmann (Ellis, 1973) might serve the recreation leader well in this regard.

The leader should ensure that the following conditions are met:

- The focus of control for the play situation remains with the child.
- The behavior of the child is intrinsically motivated; that is, giving rewards or prizes for playing is avoided.
- The child is unrestrained in expressing fantasy or imaginary behavior.

When we attempt to teach children to play, for example, by demonstrating a sports skill, this process is seldom realized as play to the child. Such teaching may, however, lead to play opportunities. This indicates that leaders should allow for free, unintervened play for children of all ages.

LEADING YOUTH

Youth, or adolescents, also represent a participant group that recreation leaders frequently include in their careers. The term **adolescence,** from the Latin word "adolescere," means to grow into maturity (Helms & Turner, 1981). It is the life stage between childhood and adulthood. It is a transitional period marked by numerous and complicated developmental tasks that require an adaptation to physical, social, and emotional changes.

In our society adolescence may be considered to have early, middle, and late stages (Craig, 1983). The period of early adolescence finds most individuals in junior high school. It is a time when youth undergo the bodily changes of puberty and some of the mental changes of cognitive maturity. Middle adolescence is an initial period of seeking new identities and of the beginning of dating; most free time is spent with peers. In the period of late adolescence, decisions are made about careers, further schooling, and the choice of paths toward adult life. The thought processes of those in late adolescence are mature and lack only the experience of adulthood.

Who is the adolescent? What is it about adolescent development and life experience that the recreation leader should understand to help teenagers experience leisure more effectively? What is unique to recreation leadership with youth?

Physical Abilities

Physical ripening gives the adolescent years many of their distinctive characteristics. At the adolescent stage in the life cycle, individuals have accumulated experience, skills, and interests in many motor coordinations. They know how to perform the fundamental physical tasks of running, jumping, balancing, and throwing, although they will continue to improve in these skills throughout adolescence, especially those who train and practice. Youth primarily build on what they have already achieved, according to their interests and to the opportunities offered them.

Physical training and practice, along with the normal growth of this period, make for improvement in the specific motor skills needed in sports, dance, and certain outdoor recreation activities. Youth usually increase in the endurance and strength needed, with boys achieving slightly more in the middle and late stages. Also flexibility, agility, balance, coordination, reaction time, and speed are increased, with girls achieving slightly more in flexibility and balance.

Exercise: Video Games

Eleven-year-old Randy Durham locked his eyes on the target and with arms straight and steady, raised the gun and fired. His victim screamed and staggered to the ground, but he wasn't dead. The bullet had only grazed his arm. As he was trying to crawl to safety, Randy was ruthless. He finished him off with a single bullet to the head. While the victim's body bled and convulsed, Randy had already shifted his attention to a new threat entering through the doorway. Randy has been shooting people for the past two weeks in a video arcade. The game he plays, Mad Dog McCree, is his favorite because it is realistic. Real people replace cartoons. Randy fires electronic bullets at a fifty-inch screen. For $1 per play, he gets to shoot people, making them scream, gasp, and die. (Patterson, 1992; Russell, 1996)

There are arguments on both sides, of course. Are video games destructive or supportive of physical, intellectual, and emotional development in children? Let's hear this debate:

Pros	*Cons*
The games are entertaining. At least they're better than staring at the TV.	A lot of things are more entertaining than TV. Since when is TV a good measure?
They're not passive. They get kids involved.	Between TV, video games, and school, kids are spending most of their time sitting.
They develop good eye/hand coordination. You've got to be fast.	Kids are expert at pushing a button, but that's because they spend so much time at it.
They can play the games solo; the machine becomes the competition.	Machines are a poor substitute for interacting with a human being. Even when they're playing together, kids are playing beside each other, not with each other.
The games help kids develop a greater attention span and train them not to be as easily distracted.	Kids who need flashing lights and beeps to focus on are later going to have a problem with printed pages that just sit there.
The games offer an opportunity to learn problem solving.	The games build a false expectation. Problem solving in life is not as simple as pushing a button.
The games offer a positive release. They are a modern and safe form of fantasy.	The games are aggressive. They focus on violent themes of attack and destroy. Kids are pushed into a prefabricated fantasy rather than creating their own.

Which side of the argument do you think wins the debate? What do your classmates think? Why do you and your classmates support the side you chose?

Do some library research to locate research articles on video and electronic games. What evidence do these studies offer in support of either the pros or cons of the argument?

Take a field trip to your local toy store and/or computer store. As you study the video games available, how would you characterize their play value?

Recreation leaders working with youth in sports can contribute to their motor skill development and to their overall health and fitness by offering wider opportunities for choice and participation. Not only should quality leadership be provided in baseball and basketball but also in tennis, gymnastics, soccer, skating, weights, jogging, volleyball, and golf. Competitive and noncompetitive outlets for physical expression must be in balance in youth programming as well.

More than this, the recreation leader must remember that physical ability affects the adolescent's concept of self. The young person must successfully come to terms with a new body—its boundaries and powers, its beauty or ugliness. In the process of adjusting body image, the young person makes comparisons with peers and ideals. As a result, this process may also involve more interest in dieting, cosmetics, beauty treatments, and clothing. Thus by creating a positive, supportive, and useful social environment for youth, recreation leaders may be aiding the complex transitions of this life period. Research has verified that the social environment can modify the effects of puberty.

Social and Emotional Abilities

Getting it all together is the task of the adolescent. In moving from childhood to adulthood, adolescents often display a curious combination of the mature and the childish (Craig, 1983). This task of developing a sense of identity is not done alone but rather in cooperation and conflict with other people. Social interaction, both real and imagined, is the mode through which youth integrate body, mind, and feelings into a whole person.

Social involvement during the teenage years acquires more meaning and significance than it has had at any previous time. Recreation leaders often observe that for this age group personal relationships become more meaningful, not only because it is important for adolescents to be accepted by their peers but also because of the need to share new feelings and experiences. Peer groups and role models offer support and security to youth as they attempt to make the transition to independence from their families.

In studying the social and emotional abilities of youth, three topics are traditionally of prime concern. The first is the continuing process by which one's sense of personal identity is further established. Another important focus for this life stage is moral development. Peer group interaction and the struggle for group acceptance is the third topic of concern. Recreation leaders who work with youth should possess at least some appreciation for these important adolescent issues.

First, briefly consider the teenager's sense of **personal identity.** This is a central process for the adolescent (Erikson, 1968). It is the procedure of clarifying and becoming aware of one's personal values—of answering the question, "Who am I?" A sense of identity is constructed by the individual by organizing beliefs, values, abilities, thoughts, and history. To achieve a mature identity for adulthood, an "identity crisis" must be experienced.

Frequently, youth create an ideal self, the type of person that they would like to be. Often younger adolescents will select a prestigious or well-known figure in society as an ideal and indulge in hero worship. These heroes help to form the youth's image of the preferred self. Parents, teachers, recreation leaders, and other significant adults do not usually serve as heroes, yet they do serve as important role models.

Also by the time of adolescence the quest for acceptable moral standards of conduct intensifies. Whereas the child's conformity to rules is in an effort to avoid punishment or to obtain reward, the teenager seeks to develop a personally useful set of ethical principles that will govern and direct his behavior. It is at this life stage that youth learn about respecting the rights of others, that they begin to develop a true consciousness, and that they set up an internal system of rules (Kohlberg, 1981).

There are many instances when a teenager's search for useful moral values will occur within recreation settings. This gives the leader a necessary opportunity to help young participants develop and define their values. In some cases the leader may directly program for this through such techniques as leisure counseling, self-contracts, and values clarification exercises (Edginton & Ford, 1985).

More likely, on the other hand, the leader will have a role in youth moral development in a less structured, informal way. This involves providing participants with the environment and support needed to develop values on their own. The way that youthful participants are treated by the leader, for example, can influence their own moral values.

As the adolescent gropes for a sense of personal identity and a set of moral standards, the peer group becomes an indispensable agent of assistance. For most youth, friends of the same age play an even more important part in life than they did during childhood (Craig, 1983). Peers serve as audience, critic, and emotional support for their friend's ideas and behavior.

Different types of peer group relationships exist because the youth subculture is extremely diverse. Representing the smallest type of peer group, **friendships** are best described as the pairing off of two individuals. Girls are usually more attracted to close two-person friendships than boys.

Cliques are similar to friendships in that the individual members share common interests and a strong emotional attachment toward each other. The clique is small in number, is usually composed of like-gender members, and is highly exclusive. Some cliques become formalized into clubs (even fraternities and sororities), but most remain informal and small. Belonging to a clique is more related to status values for girls than it is for boys. High status is relative, therefore excluding others can make the clique members feel even more important. It is important that recreation leaders understand this mechanism without condoning the behavior. Adolescents should be helped to grow beyond the point where they feel the necessity of defending themselves by excluding others. Adult role models need to be strong yet tolerant and judicious.

Similar to the clique but larger in size is the **crowd.** Although the crowd is more impersonal and lacks the strong bonds of attachment that cliques offer, it too maintains rather rigid membership requirements. Being a member of a clique is often a prerequisite for crowd membership. Crowds usually include social interaction; that is the crowd is commonly called on for social events, sitting together at football games, having parties, and for hanging around. There is security and warmth in the company of people who face the same problems, feel the same way, behave the same way, and wear the same symbols of belonging. It feels good to giggle and shout, to be silly, and to be together. Recreation leaders should understand this.

Youth's Play

Late childhood and preadolescence are best characterized as the years of more formalized play. Whether the child pursues recreational interests alone or in the company of others, many of their play activities adhere to some structure or organization. The preadolescent tends to spend more time in organized play groups. For example, involvement in team sports, choirs, and hobby clubs are particularly important.

The popularity and growth of team sports for this age group has been phenomenal. Some estimates put the number of American youth participating in organized sports at 40 million (Ferguson, 1999). But for some, indoctrination into team sports can result in frustration. It becomes the goal of the recreation leader therefore to help foster the proper attitude toward sports. These guidelines may be useful for leaders working in team sports for older children:

- Involvement in team sports should be freely chosen without coercion or external rewards.
- Youth should be encouraged to play for reasons other than winning. Although they should be encouraged to do their best, playing for the fun of the game rather than for victory should be stressed.
- If an adolescent expresses a desire to continue to compete in organized sports, good instruction and practice should be made available.
- Good leadership should stress the value of team play and sportsmanship.

By the time the individual reaches adolescence, recreational interests may change. This may be attributed to a shift in values and a decrease in time available for leisure

Case in Point: Youth Sports

It is not just the number of kids playing an organized sport that's unprecedented. It's the way they're playing it—or to be more exact, the way their parents are arranging for them to play it. Here's an illustration:

Track and Field

What it costs: Equipment = $600 to $1,500 a year
Clubs = $100 first year, $50 thereafter
Travel = $100 to $500 a meet
Clinics = $50 to $100 a day; a three-day stay at hurdle camps is $600
How much time: 2 to 9 hours of practice a day, plus a daylong track meet every Saturday

Soccer

What it costs: Equipment = $85 to $265 for uniforms and cleats
Clubs = $30 to $400 a year
Travel = $50 to $250 for each tournament
Clinics = $400 to $600 for a week at an overnight camp
How much time: 6 to 16 hours a week of practice and games

Basketball

What it costs: Equipment = $200 to $395 for shoes and uniforms
Clubs = $12 to $150 a year
Travel = $60 to $210 a month for a player and parent to attend out-of-town games
Clinics = $100 to $400 a week
How much time: 2 to 6 hours of practice daily, plus games

Baseball

What it costs: Equipment = $150 to $450 for bats, gloves, uniforms, and shoes
Clubs = $25 to $150 a year for league and team fees
Travel = most youth teams play near home, but kids in elite travel squads spend $10 to $100 a week
Clinics = $200 to $600 for intensive summers and spring breaks
How much time: 3 to 12 hours of practice a week, plus 2 to 4 games a week

(Ferguson, 1999, pp. 55–56)

activities. For the most part recreational activities become less strenuous and physical. There is also a marked increase in the amount of social recreation interests.

The recreational interests of the adolescent can be strikingly different from the play behaviors of childhood. The new interests of youth represent increased social maturity; the bicycle of childhood is relinquished for a car, the symbol of adulthood (Godbey, 1981). Activities also become more socially oriented. The interests of the adolescent are more stable, as sampling a wide variety of activities declines. Activities sometimes become introspective, egoistical, and more serious.

During this life stage there is an increase in certain activities that had little significance in childhood. These include dancing, social events, the out-of-doors, music, and reading. The development of lifelong hobbies also begins at about this time. Each of these new interest areas reflects the young person's growing social and intellectual maturity. Recreation leaders can help encourage these altering interests by being flexible and sensitive to changing needs. We must do this while also helping teenagers develop concepts of adequacy, self-respect, and self-confidence. Expressions of new recreational interests should be met with emotional support and facilitation of resources from leaders.

LEADING ADULTS

The period of adulthood may consume as much as 75 percent of your life span, and, adults make up close to 75 percent of the U.S. population. This translates to a sizable client group for recreation leaders. Contrary to historical beliefs, leading adults in recreational experiences requires as much attention to excellence as does leading children and youth. To achieve this an understanding of adult development is necessary.

Adult Life Cycles

Adults, like children and adolescents, have life cycles or developmental stages that can relate to their recreational needs and behaviors. Adult life stages can be times of crisis and disruption, but they can also indicate growth and positive change. The adult years can be the time in which people experience maximal opportunities. Recreation is acknowledged as contributing more and more to these peak years. Understanding and accepting the predictable life events can assist leaders to be more successful in facilitating appropriate and satisfying recreation experiences for adults. The passage from teenager to young adult to middle adult to older adult requires skillful negotiation around biological, emotional, and social milestones.

Late adolescence and early adulthood typically involve leaving the family and finding stability in peers. The main goals of the twenty- to thirty-year-old are searching for a consistent idea of self and personal autonomy. Early adulthood is a time when people begin to remain reasonably stable in personality. As people grow older, their personalities grow and become more complex, but their basic characteristics remain more or less consistent.

Although somewhat immature socially and emotionally, in early adulthood men and women enjoy a peak of vitality, strength, and endurance. Physical strength is at its maximum between ages twenty-five and thirty; after age thirty it declines slowly but significantly (Russell, 1996). Despite signs of aging, most physical skills and capacities remain at a functional level if regularly exercised. Usually, young adults enjoy better health than do children and have not yet begun to experience the health difficulties of middle and older age.

The prime social issues of young adulthood are occupation, intimate sexual interests, and family and friends. Individuals continue to experience new interests, new activities, and new people. A recreation leader would be mistaken to assume that variety in needs and interests is at a minimum for young adults.

The time between the ages of thirty to forty is typically considered to be one of skepticism and self-questioning (Bammel & Burrus-Bammel, 1996). Usually the amount of social life begins to decline as a result of the time and money restrictions of parenting and/or career. At this stage roots are solidly put down, career development becomes a major concern, and for some there begins to be a greater economic capability.

Sheehy (1974) has labeled the years between thirty-five and forty-five as the "deadline decade." For the first time an awareness surfaces that life has a second half. This crossroad brings with it the realization that there is a limited amount of time left in which to find a meaningful existence. Predictably for some at this point in life there results a sense of stagnation, depression, and disequilibrium.

The lack of proper physical conditioning and fitness may intensify this general dissatisfaction. Health problems and a low level of physical fitness will limit the range of possible activities that may be enjoyed. Health will also determine the intensity, frequency, and involvement in recreational experiences.

In addition, other personal and family recreation options are frequently sacrificed as adults in the middle years make vocation advancements. Businesses have acknowledged the importance of recreation in helping employees handle adulthood's developmental issues by more actively guiding them into educational, athletic, and cultural pursuits. A prime role of recreation leadership for persons in middle adulthood is to help them recognize the advantages of hobbies, physical exercise, and recreational experiences of all types for a meaningful and satisfying life.

Equilibrium and a new stability are usually gained somewhere around the ages of forty-five to fifty-five. For many persons a renewal of purpose emerges, and the results can lead to the best years of life. Some persons experience a new warmth and mellowing. People tend to become more aware of the subtleties of their own natures. Married couples begin to rediscover each other as the children leave home; friends have time to establish more constant friendships. People are increasingly interested in joint activities. There is more or less a reestablishment of the role of the peer group in recreational experiences.

Although many important life stages in adulthood are defined by family relationships, particularly in later adulthood shifting family patterns cause many people to rely more on friends than on family. At this period friendships again become a central part of life. Friendship may differ from one life stage to another, but by late middle age it is often a complex, rich, and rewarding part of life.

Fitness continues to be important, as only a minority of people between the ages of forty-five and fifty-five participate in physical activities. Some physical decline or slowing down may likely occur during this period.

Work continues to be a major source of life's meaning and satisfaction for persons in later adulthood stages. By this time an individual's work has in many cases afforded status, companions, financial gain, and structured time use. A major function of recreation leadership with persons in later adulthood lies therefore in retirement counseling.

Through programs on preparation for retirement, leaders have a valuable opportunity for altering attitudes and behaviors concerning the balance between work and leisure. We can have a particular impact in helping people find more meaning and validity in their recreational pursuits. As a part of the recreation leader's overall goal of leisure education discussed in chapter 3, more emphasis should be placed on an even distribution of work and leisure for all participants over the life span.

Adult's Play

Becoming an adult is something that does not happen all at once at a particular age. The same can also be applied to recreation participation; certain options are available at different ages. For example, being able to drive a car for pleasure, enter a nightclub, and buy a television on credit all occur at different ages. Godbey (1981) considered that when teenagers long for adulthood in our society, they are really longing for leisure—the freedom to do what they want when they want.

During the years of young adulthood recreational involvement depends on lifestyle. Going to college, choosing a partner, having children, being unemployed, or other life situations typical of early adulthood have a large impact on recreational pursuits. For example, for adults with children recreation patterns are often disrupted and restricted. Some resent the change from the more adventuresome and carefree lifestyle they enjoyed as college students; others welcome the stable, noncompetitive, and predictable recreation patterns of family life. Introducing young children to various kinds of recreation activities may for some adults be satisfying and challenging.

Recreational involvement during this period usually becomes less spontaneous and more highly regimented and planned. For many parents of preschool children, recreation must be arranged around work and the needs of the young children. Participation in strenuous and high-risk sports gradually decreases because of increased time and responsibility committed to new family activities. On the other hand, skills and knowledge gained during youth can finally serve to make some sports, hobbies, or other recreation abilities even more enjoyable in young adulthood.

However, for some a lack of discretionary income resulting from the expenses of education or the costs of acquiring a house and furnishings may restrict involvement in many types of recreation. Instead young families develop recreation participation patterns that focus on the home. Activities such as television watching, home improvements, reading, playing games, and gardening are common. Trips away from home tend to be restricted to visits with friends and relatives and low-cost commercial facilities such as shopping centers, campgrounds, and parks.

In the middle adulthood period, particularly for those persons with children, recreational involvement may be differently focused from what it was in young adulthood. Recreational interests may include competitive activities and family-centered activities both in and away from the home. For many middle adulthood produces a greater tendency toward consumer recreational behavior. Planned vacations, eating out, and buying a boat or hot air balloon or motor home become major sources of enjoyment for those with the greater discretionary income afforded by expanding careers. The range of recreational activities participated in may also expand because of the increase in free time that is often available as the children start school.

When the children have grown and left home, recreation interests center more on activities that can be done together with partners. Hobbies, traveling, and volunteer activities become more important for some. This postparental stage of life can allow new freedoms that for some adults match greater economic resources. Many will apply these new freedoms and resources to their own enjoyment and satisfaction through recreation.

Case in Point: The Overspent American

The research of economist Juliet Schor (1998) has pointed to the intensification of what she calls "competitive consumption" by American adults. Her point is that by the mid-1990s, the definition of the "good life" and even of "the necessities of life" expanded significantly. For example, in one of her surveys when asked what constitutes the good life, people today focused far more on material goods and luxuries than they did in 1975. Items more likely to be part of the good life now than then include a vacation home, a swimming pool, a color TV, a second color TV, travel abroad, nice clothes, a car, a second car, a home of one's own, a job that pays much more than the average, and a lot of money. Less likely, or no more likely, to yield the good life, according to survey respondents, were a happy marriage, one or more children, an interesting job, and a job that contributes to the welfare of society.

(Schor, 1998, pp. 13–15)

What does all this specifically mean for leadership? Most adults are capable of making their own decisions about their recreational pursuits. In many cases they are interested in self-directed, independent activities, which means that the recreation leader will more often serve as a facilitator or resource provider. Adult participants will commonly be interested in assuming some control over or involvement in the decisions affecting their program services. Leaders working with adults must be attentive to this and respond with an enabling leadership style.

The leader should primarily interact with adult participants in a peer-peer fashion rather than in a superior-subordinate way. Respect for the leader should be based on the leader's knowledge and skills rather than on her position (Edginton & Ford, 1985).

Leader Profile: The Past
Gaylene Carpenter, 1978
Dr. Carpenter focuses her research on adult recreation behavior at the University of Oregon. This photo was taken at the beginning of her career.

LEADING OLDER ADULTS

What is it like to grow old? Many people seem to view old age as a state of only marginal existence. They fear the losses of energy, control, flexibility, sexuality, physical mobility, memory, and even intelligence that they think go hand in hand with aging. Some of the negative connotations of aging are true; the elderly do as a group have a higher poverty rate and a lower education level than the rest of the population. But for the most part failing health and loneliness do not have to be a part of aging any more than acne and social awkwardness have to be a part of adolescence. The population over sixty-five years of age has its marathoners and executives and its hermits and bench sitters.

In the past recreation leaders paid relatively little attention to older adult participants. Traditionally, when our profession did work to bring organized recreation to this participant group, we had a tendency not to take them seriously. We tried to "fill up" the older person's empty time with childish, meaningless diversions. This situation, however, has become historical. Today's leader attempts to facilitate recreation experiences that more accurately match the continued need for enrichment and purpose that older adults have.

This section of the chapter is devoted to correcting many of the negative stereotypes of old age with researched information on the social, physical, and psychological changes of growing old. This information is then relied on to suggest how recreation leaders can better meet the needs of the older adult.

Exercise: Birthday Cards

Do you think there are stereotypes in our society about growing old? Here's one way to check. The next time you are at the mall, stop in the greeting card shop. Go to the birthday card section and spot-read the cards designed for people celebrating their fortieth or more birthdays. Look at at least twenty cards. What is the prevailing message in these cards? Is turning forty, or fifty, or more to be celebrated? Are these cards wishing the birthday person well, or are they poking fun at their age? If there are jokes made in the cards about growing old, what sorts of capability are the targets? Physical decline? Loss of love life? Loss of memory?

Who Is Old?

Old age is a culturally and personally relevant life category. This means that its onset varies according to the life expectancy of the general population, the availability of health care, societal value systems, and individual personality and attitude. As a result of these and other socioeconomic circumstances, developmental psychologists have begun to distinguish different categories of older adults. Neugarten (1976, 1978) laid the groundwork for this with her distinction between the young-old and the old-old. The **young-old** are drawn primarily from ages sixty to midseventies. Their major characteristic is a great deal of free time, because many in this group are retired but healthy, vigorous, and well educated. They are able to use their free time for recreation, self-enhancement, or community activities. The "young-old" enjoy continued and regular athletic activity. They usually require little assistance in making successful adaptations.

The **old-old,** on the other hand, are more likely to have health problems and need assistance. They often live in a more restricted world and suffer from many of the physical and psychological problems typically associated with aging. Persons in their eighties and nineties often require assistance in maintaining social and cultural contacts.

As life expectancy continues to increase, it is possible for old age to be a long, significant, and enjoyable part of life. The aged are not one group but rather a collection of individuals, ranging from the active and happy to the frail and depressed. Like people at other stages of the life cycle, each older adult has unique problems and capabilities that are more associated with who they are as individuals than with their age. Although they do share to some extent the age-related difficulties of reduced income, changing health, and the loss of loved ones, older persons are more individually different than they are the same.

Conditions of Aging

The majority of older persons are reasonably healthy (Russell, 1996). Yet to see oneself growing older can be something of a shock. The skin becomes less elastic, more wrinkled, and thin. Small blood vessels often break producing tiny black-and-blue marks. Age spots may appear, and posture may begin to slump. The cause of these changes is not clear. We know, however, that many individuals can forestall the process of physical aging by regular exercise, improved nutrition, and better ways of dealing with stress. Although some aspects of physical aging are genetically determined (long-lived parents are apt to have long-lived children), it is true that many aspects of physical aging are caused by other factors.

Papalia and Olds (1981) distinguished between primary aging and secondary aging. **Primary aging** results from inborn and inevitable biological changes that are independent of stress or disease. Primary aging does not affect people the same way. **Secondary aging** comes about as a result of accidents and chronic disease. Often what is considered to be a normal part of aging is a characteristic of secondary aging or of disease. Studies (Birren, Woods, & Williams, 1980) have shown that people who remain physically fit and disease free can perform as well as younger people who are not physically fit.

Aging, however, is more than a physiological experience. There are also social and psychological conditions. For example, some contend that of all the events in a person's later years, none in our society has greater impact than retirement.

Retirement is clearly an important passage that requires adjustment to many accompanying changes. Some people eagerly await retirement, whereas others dread it. Whether an individual reacts well or poorly to retirement is the result of many different factors: health, economic status, need for a sense of fulfillment, flexibility, personal history, and the reactions of friends and relatives. On the one hand, we have images of the "golden years" of retirement—travel, recreation, freedom. On the other hand, there are many gloomy portraits of the boredom and meaninglessness encountered by those who retire.

A large body of literature suggests that retirement in this society is an important life phase. Historically, work has been viewed as the central life task, integrating people into the social structure by determining identity, patterns of participation, and lifestyle. Retirement is seen by some as an undermining of social supports and of personal and social identity.

Retirement certainly involves social and psychological trauma for some retirees, but for others retirement is not a problem and in many cases pleasant. Coping styles and patterns of adaptation are well established by this time. Those who have adjusted reasonably well to other significant personal life changes will probably adjust well to this one.

Those people who can anticipate what their lives will be like after they stop working and who actively plan ahead tend to have the richest retired lives. Yet in reality, most people do little definite planning for retirement. Retirement counselors, hired by companies or working independently, are available to work with preretirees to prepare for retirement. Some community agencies also set up formal retirement-planning educational programs.

One important consideration in preparing for retirement is the role of recreation. Learning to live as a retired person is not as simple as it may seem. It involves learning a new role and acting in a new way. No longer will the retiree go to work in the morning and socialize with coworkers; no longer will the retiree have the same function or enjoy the status of work. Rather, the retired person has mostly free time and has to plan how to experience each day. The attitudes that they have about themselves may determine whether they comfortably accept their new role, develop new social acquaintances, and pursue interests and activities.

Older Adult's Play

As retirement provides more free time, people often spend more time in recreation. Such activities as reading, gardening, visiting with friends, clubs, travel, television viewing, swimming, dancing, walking, and hobbies often take on increased meaning. Involvement in recreation can provide older adults with opportunities that can assist the transitions of this life stage.

Many recreation programs provide daily structure by encouraging individuals to become involved on a regular basis and to assume leadership roles. Other recreation activities offer older persons an opportunity for recognition, status, creativity, and a sense of accomplishment and contribution. Also certain recreation experiences can offer older adults opportunities for social interaction and physical and mental fitness. Recreation leaders working with older persons are concerned with enhancing the quality of life. Counteracting physiological changes, retirement adjustment stress, reduced mobility, and loneliness tends to be leadership's major focus.

The recreation leader may work in a variety of settings with older persons. With over 95 percent of those sixty-five years of age and older living in communities (Edginton & Ford, 1985), the most common setting for recreation leaders is with community-based programs such as those offered by public agencies, apartment complexes, voluntary organizations, or adult day health centers. Another setting is the long-term care facility or nursing home, which houses 5 percent of those over sixty-five years of age.

The efforts of the recreation leader should center on two basic areas. First, leaders should work with older persons to help them develop positive attitudes toward themselves and their life experiences. Second, the leader should assist and encourage older persons to become involved in their communities. Here's how your leadership might accomplish these two goals:

- serve as a leisure and social resource
- support the pursuit of former, current, and potential interests
- provide opportunities for physical, intellectual, emotional, and social challenges
- stimulate social interaction
- support creativity and self-expression
- facilitate experiences that enable feelings of self-worth and usefulness
- encourage independence in leisure expression
- provide opportunities for the assumption of leadership roles

Recreation leaders must be particularly alert to meeting the real needs of their older participants—not the stereotypical needs. Stereotypes about older persons often affect the ability of the leader to work with this age group effectively.

Do you automatically plan bingo, card games, and sing alongs? Do you plan activities that are passive and sedentary? Do you find yourself talking down to older participants? Do you approach working with older persons from the perspective of what they cannot do? If so, you may need to examine your attitudes and perceptions. Remember, aging is an individualized life experience. If you do not base your leadership on objective information, you may be inappropriately limiting participant satisfactions.

Summary

The purpose of this chapter is to place recreation leadership techniques and skills into the context of specific participant age groupings to highlight the differences and the similarities of leading people. The umbrella perspective assumed by the chapter is that of life span development. That is, certain stages order the chronology of our lives and these stages can be useful in identifying appropriateness of recreation leadership techniques.

Children are the first participants discussed in the chapter. A major developmental process in childhood that recreation leaders need to be attentive to is physical growth. For most children there occurs a rapid development of motor skills, supported primarily by improvements in eye-hand coordination, reaction time, and manual dexterity. Recreation leaders can facilitate motor skill development in younger children by providing opportunities for rhythmical and unstructured movement and by providing a physical environment that encourages running, jumping, and climbing. For older children motor skill development can be enhanced by opportunities for dance, active games, and sports.

Childhood is also a prime life stage for the development of self-concept, emotional maturity, prosocial behavior, the competitive spirit, morality, and a sense of industry. Recreation leaders can contribute to this development by being a positive role model, by allowing for freedom of self-expression and exploration, by offering appropriate reinforcement, and by remaining sensitive to changing needs.

The play experiences that leaders can present enable the development that is critical to childhood. Children at play are learning to cope with the tasks of life, to master new skills, to gain confidence in themselves, and to get along with others.

Youth, or adolescents, also represent a participant group that recreation leaders frequently include in their careers. In terms of the development of physical abilities, youth primarily build on what they have already achieved according to their interests and to the opportunities offered. Recreation leaders are thus concerned for offering wider options for choice and participation in movement and a balance between competitive and noncompetitive movement expression.

As we may recall, the major socioemotional task of adolescence is the development of a sense of identity. Other important issues at this life stage are moral development and peer group interaction. Recreation leaders can serve as important adult role models to youth. In doing so they must be strong and determined, yet tolerant and judicious.

Within the adolescent context team sports are particularly important. The responsibility of maintaining the helpful role of team sports in adolescent development requires balanced, sensitive, and fun-oriented leadership rather than win-oriented leadership. Additionally, in adolescence there is an increased interest in social recreation. The development of lifelong hobbies such as reading and music also begin at about this time. Each of these new interest areas reflects the young person's growing social, physical, and intellectual maturity. Recreation leaders can help encourage these altering interests by being flexible and by helping to foster concepts of adequacy, self-respect, and self-confidence.

Leading adults in recreational experiences requires as much attention to leadership excellence as does leading children and youth. This is because adults too have life cycles or developmental stages that can affect recreational needs and patterns. Life for persons in young adulthood and middle adulthood can be experienced as times of crisis and growth.

Recreational experiences can affect and be affected by these adult developmental stages. During the years of young adulthood recreational involvement is dependent on lifestyle. For many this means inexpensive, home-centered experiences because of the demands of family and career. Then for some middle adulthood typically produces a greater tendency for consumer recreation experiences away from home. Again, however, this is dictated by the chosen lifestyle.

Finally, like people at other stages of the human life cycle, older adults are individuals with unique experiences and capabilities that are more associated with who they are than with their age. This participant group does share to some extent, however, the age-related difficulties of reduced income, changing health, and the loss of loved ones.

Research and practice have shown that aging is a physiological, sociological, and psychological process. These processes include changes in health and fitness levels, adjustment to retirement, reduced mobility and autonomy, and adjustment to widowhood. These may cause an increased interest in or reliance on recreation. For many older adults recreation is often an important way of maintaining physical and mental capacities. Recreation leaders can play an important role in not only enhancing the quality of retirement life but also in slowing the aging process.

Questions and Activities for Review and Discussion

1. Briefly define the concept of "human development." Why is it important to the recreation leader?
2. Who is the child? What major aspects of child development are important to the success of recreation leadership with children?
3. What three types of peer group relationships exist for adolescents? How might this typology be useful to recreation leaders working with youth?
4. Write a brief autobiography in which you describe the development during adolescence of your own recreational interests and abilities. How did you become exposed to certain recreation pursuits? How did these pursuits change during your teen years? What role did your family and friends have? Which pursuits will you most likely continue through old age?
5. Do adults have developmental stages? Describe adult growth and change.
6. How are the recreational interests and involvements of adults affected by their chosen lifestyle?
7. Suppose you are eighty-nine years of age. Write a brief description of yourself. What are your recreation interests?
8. In the past have recreation leaders been conscientious in serving the recreational needs of older adults? Why or why not?

References

Bammel, G., & Burrus-Bammel, L. L. B. (1996). *Leisure and human behavior* (3rd ed.). Madison, WI: Brown & Benchmark.

Baumrind, D. (1971). Current patterns of parental authority [Mongraph 1]. *Developmental Psychology 4*, 1–103.

Birren, J. E., Woods, A. M., & Williams, M. V. (1980). Behavioral slowing with age: Causes, organization, and consequences. In L. W. Poon (Ed.), *Aging in the 1980s: Psychological issues*. Washington, DC: American Psychological Association.

Butler, G. D. (1965). *Pioneers in public recreation*. Minneapolis: Burgess Publishing.

Craig, G. J. (1983). *Human development*. Englewood Cliffs, NJ: Prentice-Hall.

Dennis, L. B., & Hassol, J. (1983). *Introduction to human development and health issues*. Philadelphia: W.B. Saunders.

Duska, R., & Whelan, M. (1975). *Moral development: A guide to Piaget and Kohlberg*. New York: Paulist Press.

Edginton, C. R., & Ford, P. M. (1985). *Leadership in recreation and leisure service organizations*. New York: John Wiley & Sons.

Ellis, J. J. (1973). *Why people play*. Englewood Cliffs, NJ: Prentice-Hall.

Erikson, E. H. (1968). *Identity: Youth and crisis*. New York: W.W. Norton.

Ferguson, A. (1999, July 12). Inside the crazy culture of kids sports. *Time*, 154(2), 52–60.

Godbey, G. (1981). *Leisure in your life*. Philadelphia: Saunders College Publishing.

Helms, D. B., & Turner, J. S. (1981). *Exploring child behavior*. New York: Holt, Rinehart & Winston.

Kohlberg, L. (1981). *The philosophy of moral development*. New York: Harper & Row.

Neugarten, B. L. (1976). *The psychology of aging: An overview*. Washington, DC: American Psychological Association.

Neugarten, B. L. (1978). The wise of the young-old. In R. Gross, B. Gross, & S. Seidman (Eds.), *The new old: Struggling for decent aging*. Garden City, NY: Anchor Books/Doubleday.

Papalia, D. E., & Olds, S. W. (1981). *Human development*. New York: McGraw-Hill.

Patterson, R. H. (1992, October 20, Lifestyle Section). Interactive video games raise questions. *The Herald-Times*, Bloomington, IN.

Russell, R. V. (1996). *Pastimes: The context of contemporary leisure.* Madison, WI: Brown & Benchmark.

Schor, J. B. (1998). *The overspent American: Why we want what we don't need*. New York: HarperPerennial.

Sheehy, G. (1974). *Passages: Predictable crises of adult life*. New York: E. P. Dutton.

Smart, M. S., & Smart, R. C. (1982). *Children: Development and relationships*. New York: Macmillan Publishing.

Web Resources

ADOL: Adolescence Directory On-line: http://education.indiana.edu/cas/adol/adol.html

American Federation for Aging Research: www.afar.org/

Center for Adolescent Studies: http://education.indiana.edu/cas/cashmpg.html

Center for the Study of Human Development: www.brown.edu/Departments/Human Development Center/

Center on the Economics and Demography of Aging: http://arrow.qal.berkeley.edu/

Directory of agencies and organizations about human development: www.quackwatch.com/04ConsumerEducation/org.html

Early Childhood News: www.earlychildhoodnews.com/

Early Childhood Today online: http://place/scholastic.com/ect/index.html

Earlychildhood.com: www.earlychildhood.com/

Gerontological Society of America: www.geron.org/

Interactive Aging Network: www.ianet.org/

National Association for the Education of Young Children: www.naeyc.org/

National Institute on Aging: www.nih.gov/nia/

Teengay: www.angelfire.com/on/teengay/

The United States Senate, Special Committee on Aging: www.senate.gov/~aging/

CHAPTER 15

According to Special Abilities

To be human is to be handicapped, to be flawed.
—Greenberg, 1981.

Learning Objectives

Becoming a vital recreation leader requires sensitivity to those participants whose life experiences are in some way different. In this chapter participants with

- mental illnesses
- physical disabilities
- mental retardation

are discussed so they may be effectively included in recreation programs and services.

Key Terms

therapeutic recreation p. 286
mental illness p. 287
mental health p. 287
psychoses p. 288
neuroses p. 288
depression p. 288
schizophrenia p. 288
anxiety p. 288
community inclusion p. 289
physical challenges p. 290
arthritis p. 291
cerebral palsy p. 291
multiple sclerosis p. 291
self-concept p. 292
learned helplessness p. 292
self-fulfilling prophecy p. 292
labeling p. 292
mental retardation p. 293
Americans with Disabilities Act (ADA) p. 295

Recreation leaders not only work with persons of all ages but also with persons who have wide-ranging abilities. Children with physical disabilities attend a summer adventure camp sponsored by a university. Elderly residents in a nursing home form their own clown alley. Youth with mental retardation in a state-sponsored special school learn how to play the guitar. In a community-based mental health center, clients are enrolled in wellness classes. Disabled Vietnam war veterans compete in an international wheelchair basketball tournament. High school dropouts spend two weeks wilderness canoeing through a YMCA program. Adults with visual impairments organize themselves into a community improvisational theater group.

From a relatively minor area of concern by recreation and park leaders twenty-five years ago, the enabling of special recreation services to special groups has become a major concern. This is **therapeutic recreation,** a "purposive use of recreation/recreation experiences by qualified professionals to promote independent functioning and to enhance optimal health and well-being of people with illness and/or disabling conditions" (Bullock & Mahon, 1997, p. 136).

Case in Point: Ancient Greece and Rome

The oldest written records of ancient Greece and Rome contain evidence that people with mental illnesses, mental retardation, and physical disabilities existed at that time. From these earliest eras, and even through early parts of the twentieth century, a common belief was that "madness" or "defectiveness" came from demons or evil spirits and was seen as a punishment from an angry God. Thus, Roman law sought to protect the general public from people with mental illnesses and other disabilities, because they were thought to be dangerous (Bullock & Mahon, 1997). This is in direct contrast with today where laws attempt to protect the rights of those with a disability.

Yet similar to today, ancient writings also tell of efforts to use recreation as a curative for persons with disabilities. For example, it is reported that the first Greek physician, Melampus, treated the daughters of Proteus by having them play a game that involved running. This is reported to have cured them of the delusion that they were cows (Avedon, 1974). Also in early Roman and Greek eras, music, drama, reading, and sport were used to ease dysfunction and discomfort of the mind. A number of temples were built as healing centers. One example in ancient Greece is a temple built and continually upgraded through the first century that included a library, a stadium, and a theatre. Sometimes music was played in conjunction with gymnastics and dancing as treatment of mental disorders. In ancient Rome people who were mentally ill were taken from their dark cells; brought into the sunshine; and provided music, games, poetry, and exercise (Avedon).

Exercise: Negative Language

List as many words or phrases that you have heard (or said) that you would consider negative language toward people with disabilities, and indicate what makes them negative.

Negative word/phrase	*Refers to*	*What makes it negative*
1. Cripple	person with physical impairment	based on negative stereotype
2. Mongoloid	person with Down's Syndrome	emphasizes the disability and not the person
3. Deaf and dumb	person who is unable to hear or speak	demeaning
4.		
5.		
6.		
7.		
8.		
9.		
10.		

Some leaders choose therapeutic recreation as their prime career focus and seek specialized training and experience competencies accordingly. These therapeutic recreation specialists use purposeful recreation experiences as an intervention in changing peoples' behavior. A common setting for this specialist is an institution such as a hospital, convalescent center, prison, or school. Yet most individuals with disabilities do not live in institutions. They are in cities, small towns, and rural areas everywhere. They are also appropriate users of community, private, or commercial-sponsored recreation services. Being successful in leading people with disabilities is the responsibility of all recreation and park professionals regardless of organization or setting.

Therefore it is important to your leadership proficiency to be aware of special participants and to be enthusiastic in including them in your service efforts. By doing so you will be able to minimize their "differentness" and offer them equal opportunities for high quality lives. This chapter briefly outlines guidelines for leading these participants.

LEADING PERSONS WITH MENTAL ILLNESSES

Mental illness is a complex form of human disorder that continues to be a major health concern in most societies. It is one of the foremost public health problems in North America (Bullock & Mahon, 1997). For example, it is estimated that some form of mental illness affects approximately 15 percent of Americans. One-fifth of adults have a psychological disorder at any given time, while as many as one-third have had a mental illness at some point in their lives (Kalat, 1990). Psychological disorders affect all ages, social classes, and geographical areas.

Although there has been remarkable progress in the treatment of psychologically impaired persons, the problem of defining mental illness continues to be debated. What is abnormal behavior? Who sets the criteria for what is normal? Where exactly is the line separating mental illness and mental health? If a person leaps up and begins to cheer wildly, do we label this abnormal? In attempting to define psychological impairments, more information about the context or situation and the behavior duration is needed. That is, jumping up and cheering wildly during a goal at a soccer game is often appropriate behavior in our society. Thus mental illness seems to refer to the degrees of inappropriate behavior and also to the duration or persistence of such behavior (Meyer, 1977).

One way to better understand mental illness is to understand **mental health.** Compton (1994, p. 18) suggested that mental health

> . . . is comprised of one's ability to: manage or control daily experience; interact in an acceptable manner with others; exhibit intellectual alertness and reasoning powers; derive a sense of meaning and value from life; achieve a sense of happiness and self-esteem; demonstrate resiliency during and after stressful life events; and develop a sense of maturity in introspective, prospective, and retrospective matters.

People with mental illness are not able to achieve such control of their daily experience. Instead they are presented with significant challenges that do, accordingly, affect their participation in recreation experiences. People with mental illnesses experience some of the most significant barriers to recreation participation and the greatest prejudice from the public and recreation service providers (Bullock & Mahon, 1997).

Therefore, we discuss in this section of the chapter some of the things you will need to know and the implications of these for working with people with mental illnesses.

Types of Mental Illnesses

Although many professionals prefer not to label persons with mental impairments, recreation leaders working with these persons may find the widely used classification system of the *Diagnostic and Statistical Manual of Mental Disorders* (1994), published by the American Psychiatric Association, helpful in increasing their understanding.

The two main categories of mental illness are psychosis and neurosis. **Psychoses** are disturbances in the thinking process that seriously limit judgment and insight and the ability to objectively evaluate reality (Bullock & Mahon, 1997). Some examples of psychoses include Alzheimer's disease, manic-depressive disorder, and schizophrenia. **Neuroses** are more common and less severe than psychoses. It can be difficult to determine whether a mental disturbance is due to a neurosis or just the problems of coping with everyday life. For example, neurosis includes depression, feelings of anxiety, phobias, and obsessive behavior (Nevid, Spencer, & Green, 1994). Let's look at a few of these disorders more carefully.

Depression is a mental illness that can affect people of all ages and seriously disrupt an individual's life for a long time. Depressive disorders are usually viewed as a continuum determined by the frequency, duration, and severity of the symptoms. Some of the symptoms include: depressed mood, significantly diminished interest in the pleasure of most activities, major weight loss when not dieting, insomnia, fatigue, excessive guilt or feelings of worthlessness, inability to make decisions, and recurrent thoughts of death or committing suicide (American Psychiatric Association, 1994, p. 327). Most treatment of depression combines drug intervention along with psychotherapy.

Schizophrenia is a mental illness in which people experience hallucinations, impaired thinking, exaggerated emotions (both positive and negative), and behavioral changes. Affecting about one person in a hundred, the age of onset for schizophrenia is before adolescence and after age forty-five. There are subtypes of schizophrenia: catatonic—disturbances in movement; paranoid—delusions or auditory hallucinations; disorganized—loose and disorganized verbal patterns; undifferentiated—characteristics that do not fit any of the other subtypes; and residual—a person who has one or more episodes of schizophrenia, but who no longer displays any psychotic features. Schizophrenia is typically controlled through a combination of medication and social-psychological treatments (Bullock & Mahon, 1997).

Anxiety disorders include phobias, panic disorders, and obsessive-compulsive disorders. For example, people with phobias exhibit extreme terror when confronted with a specific situation or object and make adjustments in daily activities to avoid these situations and objects. Panic disorders are characterized by sudden, intense feelings of dread for no apparent reason, and people who suffer from obsessive-compulsive disorders will attempt to cope with anxiety by associating it with repeated, unwanted thoughts or ritualistic behaviors (Bullock & Mahon, 1997).

Leadership Guidelines

There can be a tendency to guide people with mental illnesses to take up simple, unskilled recreation activities in segregated settings (Bullock & Mahon, 1997). To the contrary,

I advise community inclusion. **Community inclusion** is probably best accomplished by encouraging participation in a wide range of recreation activities that the client chooses. Leisure education has also been identified as a useful approach to meeting the recreation needs of people with mental illnesses, as has leisure counseling. Exercise programs, too, have been shown to be productive in facilitating wellness and independence. Some of the more general skills recreation leaders should consider when working with persons with mental illness include the following (Carter, Van Andel, & Robb, 1985; Bullock & Mahon, 1997):

- *Be yourself*: At times it is tempting to play a role or fake an attitude. This may stem from our own insecurities and attempts to be in control. Be real; be yourself.
- *Be professional*: Maintain integrity. Do not share confidential information with family or friends outside of your work. Overinvolvement with clients also jeopardizes your ability to be objective and effective.
- *Focus on the individual*: Learn about the person and deal with her on the basis of your knowledge. For people with mental illnesses, there is a mistaken tendency to assume they are not capable of expressing their own opinions.
- *Guard the dignity of the participant*: Help preserve the autonomy and individuality of the client. Although a person appears to be out of touch with reality, there is never an appropriate time to ridicule or downgrade him.
- *Provide only as much structure as is needed to promote a safe environment*: Your leadership should help to stimulate growth toward independence and personal fulfillment. More structure is necessary for the more disturbed clients.
- *Use sequential activity experiences to build toward more socialized levels of group play*: It may be necessary to begin participation on a one-to-one, or parallel interaction, level and then move into small group or larger group activities.
- *Facilitate reintegration*: Do what you can to help individuals with mental illness reenter society. Often it is difficult for them to reintegrate into their own home communities—your practical assistance may be the most important aspect of your leadership.
- *Use physical touch with discretion*: As in any leadership situation, physical touch may be offensive or frightening. Although touch is extremely useful in enhancing communication, it should be used with appropriateness and caution when working with participants with mental illness.
- *Plan a wide variety of activities*: Be well prepared to offer new opportunities for recreation even for those with seemingly limited interests.
- *Encourage participants to be actively involved rather than mere observers*: As much as possible, try to include all participants in some way in the group's recreation activities. This may mean keeping score or serving as a judge.
- *Advocate*: Challenge the inappropriate use of words such as crazy, maniac, and schizo. Tell others what you have learned and insist that people with mental illnesses be treated with dignity and fairness.
- *Motivate through example*: Firm, consistent persistence performed with enthusiasm must match your sincere interest in the participant's well-being.
- *Activities that provide immediate gratification will usually be most effective*: Shorter attention spans, decreased energy levels, and often limited motivation for recreation participation suggest the need to avoid complex, intense activities.

LEADING PERSONS WITH PHYSICAL DISABILITIES

Fred is a 43-year-old quadriplegic diagnosed with multiple sclerosis at the age of thirty-five. Although unable to walk, he is able to move about independently with the use of a battery-powered wheelchair. He requires help when rising from bed and retiring at night. He also needs some assistance in attending to his toilet needs.

One year Fred was given the opportunity to attend a two-week residential camp for adults with physical disabilities. He arrived at camp on a Sunday afternoon and, following the regular check-in procedure, was assigned to a counselor and immediately "wheeled" to his living quarters.

During the first few days of the camp session it was observed that Fred did not participate in any of the planned recreation activities although encouraged to do so by the staff. He was usually seen sitting just outside his living quarters or on the sun deck of another camp building watching other campers swimming or playing table games. After three days of this nonparticipation, he was asked to discuss his experiences to date and how he felt about camp.

He pointed out that when he first arrived, his first inclination was to "turn tail and run." With over one hundred other campers present having all types of disabilities, his previous self-image was apparently shattered. He indicated that at that moment he had said to himself, "My God—am I like these other people?" (adapted from Stein & Sessoms, 1977).

As a member of this camp staff, what would you do now?

Physical Challenges

People experience many forms and degrees of physical limitations. Such physical challenges include cerebral palsy, muscular dystrophy, spinal cord injuries, amputations, arthritis, epilepsy, and multiple sclerosis. A physical disability is any condition that has the potential to physically limit major life activities—including recreation activities. Millions of people in the United States and Canada have some degree of physical disability. They affect a person's coordination, mobility, balance, agility, strength, endurance, and often a combination of these capabilities.

The labeling or "grouping" that exists in our society is clearly evident in the way we deal with individuals having **physical challenges.** They "wear" their disability for all to see. Recognition of individuals with disabilities as whole persons is long overdue. They should never be considered as a homogeneous group because of a disability. Your recreation leadership should be grounded in this philosophical commitment.

For example, leaders should assume that someone with unintelligible speech understands on a higher level than her communication suggests—that a physical disability does not necessarily impede cognitive function. There is a wide range of causes, definitions, and severity of physical disabilities. Such terms as paraplegia are often used but not always helpful to the recreation leader, because individuals with the same condition differ greatly in their level of ability (Bullock & Mahon, 1997). Nonetheless, we should review information on the most prevalent types of physical disabilities.

The *Handbook of Severe Disability* by Stolov and Clowers (1981) identified six significant body systems as nervous system, musculoskeletal system, cardiovascular system, pulmonary system, visual system, and auditory system. When any of these systems alone or in combination with any other system ceases to function at the necessary level, a physical disability is the result. Major disorders of the neuromuscular systems would include, for example, spinal injuries, spina bifida, cerebrovascular diseases, cerebral palsy, lower motor neuron diseases, diseases of muscle, minimal brain dysfunction, and language disorders. Disabilities of the musculoskeletal system include orthopedic syndromes, limb deficiencies, and scoliosis.

Let's discuss several of these a bit more.

The term *arthritis* includes more than one hundred different diseases that cause inflammation of the joints, frequently resulting in pain, swelling, and in more serious cases, loss of mobility and bone damage. Arthritis limits daily activities for nearly 37 million Americans (Bullock & Mahon, 1997).

Arthritis is frequently an invisible disease, and this invisibility sometimes contributes to adverse social and psychological impacts. For example, those with arthritis in the legs will find it difficult to walk any distance. Some, particularly those with arthritis in the hips, cannot climb a bus step or a flight of stairs. Many will find an activity involving prolonged standing difficult. When the wrists and fingers are painful and swollen, they will experience difficulty in gripping small items, grasping articles, or picking up objects (National Institute on Disability and Rehabilitation Research, 1993). We cannot see this pain, and it is easy for friends and coworkers to assume the individual is faking the severity of the symptoms, thinking he wants attention or lacks initiative.

Cerebral palsy is the commonly used term for a category of conditions where there is an inability to fully control motor function. The disability may involve one or more limbs—or any part of the body, including the face and tongue—in a jerky and involuntary motion. It is the result of nonprogressive brain damage at either the prenatal stage or from shortly after birth. With about seven out of one hundred births resulting in cerebral palsy, the condition takes many forms and no two people with it are precisely alike. Some are mildly affected with no obvious disability; others who are more seriously affected may have difficulty walking, with manual manipulation, or with speech. Some also have perceptual difficulties.

Multiple sclerosis (MS) is a chronic, and sometimes progressive, disease of the central nervous system. It most often affects young adults, up to about age forty, with women affected twice as often as men. Symptoms may vary from a mild alteration of sensation to paralysis of limbs, an interference with speech, walking, and other basic functions. MS is variable and not severely disabling for the majority of people who have it.

Such labels and descriptions as these do not give a fully accurate picture of disability and its effects; both the degree of physical disability and the extent to which it has proven to be a major limitation to the individual's life vary widely within each disorder and within each individual. Yet, the great majority of physically disabled persons live in the community, either with their families or independently. Many of them, even those with extremely serious physical impairments, are able to engage in a wide range of recreational interests. Recreation leaders working in a community, a state park, a resort, a hospital, and almost about anywhere are committed to their responsibility for providing services for all persons—including those with disabilities.

Guidelines for Recreation Leaders

Whether the setting is the community or an institution such as a hospital, leaders working with children and adults with physical disabilities must understand the unique situations that can arise between themselves and participants. Important topics of concern include self-concept, learned helplessness, the self-fulfilling prophecy, and labeling.

Your concept of yourself is an important determinant of your behavior. Your **self-concept** affects whether a particular situation is viewed as routine, challenging, or threatening. For example, if we perceive ourselves to be highly competent, we are more likely to be eager for new experiences. If, however, we perceive ourselves as inadequate, new experiences can be threatening and debilitating (Iso-Ahola, 1980).

Leader Profile: The Present
Jamie Messier
Fairlawn Rehabilitation Hospital in Worcester, Massachusetts. Shown here assisting a client in using an adaptive fishing-rod holder to cast the line. Messier is using the activity to help the client succeed in an accepting and safe environment.

Persons with physical disabilities can have strong feelings of inadequacy and lack of control. This will affect the way in which new recreation experiences are approached. Recreation leaders must therefore keep in mind that they can have a great impact on participant's self-concept by enabling more successful recreation experiences and by providing positive yet realistic recreation performance evaluations.

Repeated failure in an activity can produce feelings of worthlessness. This can lead an individual to conclude that no matter how energetic the effort, it is futile. The result is a feeling of helplessness to alter things. **Learned helplessness** refers to inappropriate participant dependency on the leader. A participant who is overly dependent on the leader is not able to reach his potential in the recreation experience.

Thus leaders need to use activities and interactions to provide opportunities for participants to try, succeed, and fail in an accepting and safe environment (Austin, 1991). Here are some ways to do this:

- give participants opportunities to master challenges and learn to cope with frustrations
- be aware of participant demands linked to their lack of confidence to do the task
- while showing acceptance of participant needs, do not give in to their demands if they are excessive or irrational
- help participants see their helpless attitudes

The **self-fulfilling prophecy** is also an issue for recreation leaders working with those with disabilities. It is based on the idea that people will exhibit the behavior others expect of them. Thus, if leaders have an inaccurate assessment about the participants, this may bring about behavior conforming to that falsehood. People learn to see themselves and behave as others treat them and expect them to behave.

If leaders hold negative preconceptions about their participant's abilities, lowered expectations and decreased demands can result, thus resulting in poorer performances and responses. The recreation leader must be aware of his expectations for participants and must be flexible so that expectations can be changed as new information is gained.

Finally, how a recreation leader interacts with a participant with a physical disability can be affected by **labeling.** It is a common practice in our society to assign a categorical term (often negative) to an individual. This can cause stigmatization and does not usually take into account the individual's uniqueness. Labeling can put the focus on categorical differences instead of on the person.

The recreation leader must therefore rely on participant disability labels with caution and openness. Each participant should be treated as an individual with unique abilities. Although labeling can assist recreation and park organizations in organizing services, factual information on the participant's ability instead of a general categorization should form the basis of leadership efforts.

There are perhaps some special qualities that leaders working with people who have physical impairments need to possess. A few examples follow:

- Accept the person first as an individual who has the same basic needs, desires, and problems as other people.
- Maintain an understanding of each person's disability without indulging in pity.
- Demonstrate a capacity for patience. Be patient without being overprotective. A person may not move quickly but may want to complete a project or activity independently.
- Help the participants to help themselves. If you think a person may need help, offer assistance and then wait for a reply. If assistance is needed, the person can tell you what method of help is best.
- Recognize that initial feelings of discomfort when first interacting with persons with disabilities will usually evaporate quickly.
- Avoid the tendency to spread a disability to the total person, thus viewing the person as completely unable.
- Resist being a spectator but instead become actively involved in the recreation experience with the participant.
- Choose activity areas that allow all people to participate and succeed.
- Be yourself—be comfortable—have fun.

In light of this advice consider the case about Fred introduced at the beginning of this section of the chapter. From the issues discussed, what is the case study an illustration of? As a member of this camp staff, what would you do?

LEADING PERSONS WITH MENTAL RETARDATION

Mental retardation is a complex medical, social, personal, and economic problem. The condition, which affects about 3 percent of the population, was for a long time considered an incurable disability that resulted in little potential for development. It is no longer viewed this way. Thanks to research and innovative programs we know that mental retardation is not an absolute trait but can be improved with the right supports (Bullock & Mahon, 1997).

Information About Mental Retardation

Mental retardation is considered to be limitations in cognitive, functional, and social abilities. It results in adaptation difficulties in communication, self-care, home living, community use, self-direction, health and safety, functional academics, work, and recreation (Auxter, Pyfer, & Huettig, 1993). For example, people with mental retardation may have problems in learning, for instance they may learn at a slower rate. Some exhibit socially inappropriate behavior when interacting with other people, while some may have a limited vocabulary. However, these limitations may be due to limited opportunities to learn such skills and restricted experiences in using them.

Adaptation difficulties are usually not measured directly, but instead the observations of parents, teachers, and others who are significant to the person are relied on to determine the severity. There are two levels of mental retardation based on the adaptive skills of individuals. These are mild and severe.

Even more useful, however, are the levels of functioning designations. These are expressed in terms of the levels of support required (Bullock & Mahon, 1997):

1. *No support.* Either self-sufficient or can get needed support on her own.
2. *Minimal support.* Needs intermittent help in particular areas of adaptive skill, such as transportation and employment.
3. *Substantial support.* Needs regular ongoing support that includes instruction, assistance, and supervision within particular areas of adaptive skill.
4. *Consistent support.* Needs constant pervasive care on a twenty-four-hour basis, which may include the maintenance of life-support functions.

Previously the levels of mental retardation were based on intellectual functioning, or the IQ of the individual (mild, moderate, severe, and profound). Now, intelligence test scores are only one part of the assessment process. They may give a general idea about the intellectual level of a person, but they do not indicate that all people with the same score share specific characteristics or even abilities (Bullock & Mahon, 1997). As well the daily functioning of the individual within the environment is also considered. Mental retardation is defined as the interaction between the individual and his environment. Thus supports provided to an individual can improve how she functions (and even change the diagnosis of mental retardation) and can come from either the environment, the individual, or both.

For example, to change the environment, mechanical devices for personal care assistance can improve an individual's function. A change in the educational situation can improve function, or the individual can change—such as learning new coping skills, which can improve the level of functioning.

Purpose of Recreation

Involvement in organized recreation programs enables an opportunity for controlled social interactions and relationships. As a result, interpersonal skills may be acquired. Recreation activities also become the medium through which feelings are identified and expressed. A positive self-concept is developed. Recreation leaders should therefore encourage activities that have alternative means to achieve success and recognition. Opportunities should be given for decision making and independent functioning as a way to the formation of unique selves.

Recreation also provides an opportunity for increasing perceptual-motor skills, rhythm, eye-hand coordination, gross and fine motor control, endurance, and strength. Organized recreation experiences can likewise help in the development of academic skills and the ability to learn.

Activities through which some of these goals may be realized include dramatics, music, dance, singing, team sports, arts and crafts, clubs, parties, outings, and service projects. Social skills may be further enhanced by attending movies, participating in contests, playing board games, camping, and adventure-challenge activities.

Leadership Interaction

The functioning level of the participant determines the leader's responsibility and actions. Those leaders involved with lower functioning clients living in long-term care centers will exhibit some leadership styles that differ from those leaders working with higher functioning persons (Carter, Van Andel, & Robb 1985; Bullock & Mahon, 1997).

Here are some general leadership guidelines applicable to a variety of settings (Bullock & Mahon):

- If you make activity modifications, keep the original reason for doing the activity in mind.
- Use physical guidance, verbal directions, visual cues, and demonstration consistently during leadership. Yet do not use more guidance than necessary; the goal is to have the participant assume as much responsibility as possible.
- Consistency in voice tone, quality, and communication pattern is advised. Participants with mental retardation often take cues from how something sounds rather than from what is said.
- Help your participants distinguish how well a recreation skill is performed from how "good" or "bad" they are as persons.
- Break down complicated, multiple-stepped instructions into one or two steps at a time.
- Say the participant's name before giving them key directions.
- Always state health and safety rules before starting each recreation activity and remind participants of these rules during the activity if necessary.
- Be concise in your word choice. "Over there" is too general. "Stand on the orange line" is more concise.
- Use repetition as a method of teaching participants new skills; they will learn best by doing.
- Help control high and low energy levels by structuring the pace and tempo of the recreation activities.
- Call attention to individual improvements in a recreation skill rather than asking them to compete against each other.
- In activities that require equipment begin with large, stationary objects and then advance to smaller, movable objects.
- The circle is a useful participant formation. It enables you to use modeling, imitation, demonstration, and peer interactions.
- Allow each individual a choice of activities in which she wishes to participate or wishes to learn. Decision making can occur on different levels for people with mental retardation.
- Recognize that some people with mental retardation have limitations. Do not lose your composure or patience if they are not able to comprehend or perform what you want.
- Discuss the type of conduct expected and accepted for the situation or activity. Be consistent and firm when discipline is required.

Leader Profile: The Present
Charlsena Stone
Lecturer of therapeutic recreation in the Department of Leisure Studies at the University of North Carolina—Greensboro. Stone is also completing her Ph.D. in special education. Therefore, her classes for future recreation leaders include instruction about the Americans with Disabilities Act.

THE AMERICANS WITH DISABILITIES ACT (ADA)

The **Americans with Disabilities Act (ADA)** of 1990 makes it illegal to discriminate against a person on the basis of a disability. It has been referred to as the twentieth century Emancipation Proclamation for individuals with disabilities (Bullock & Mahon, 1997). The purpose of this act is to extend civil rights similar to those provided by other laws on the basis of race, gender, national origin, and religion. The ADA guarantees equal opportunity for individuals with disabilities in the areas of employment, public accommodation, transportation, state and local government services, and telecommunications.

You should be well informed about the ADA to be in compliance with the law because you will be responsible for a wide diversity of people as a recreation leader. This law states that you shall not:

- deny a qualified person with a disability the opportunity to participate or benefit from services available to people without disabilities
- offer recreation opportunities of less quality or magnitude for those with disabilities
- provide separate aids, benefits, or services for people with disabilities unless those aids are necessary to make the services available
- aid or perpetuate discrimination in any form
- use facilities or sites that result in the exclusion of people with disabilities (Eichstaedt & Kalakian, 1993)

Essentially, the ADA states that as a recreation services provider you must make reasonable accommodations for people with disabilities to enable full enjoyment and the most interaction possible.

Exercise: ADA Checklist

People with disabilities should be able to arrive on the site, approach the building, and enter the building as freely as everyone else. Try this checklist for the entrance of a recreation services building with which you are familiar, such as a fitness center or community center. For each question where the response is no, think of some possible solutions. You will need a tape measure for this activity.

Building entrance
(ADA Accessibility Guidelines 4.13, 4.14)

1. If there are stairs at the main entrance, is there also a ramp or lift, or is there an alternative accessible entrance? (Do not use a service entrance as the accessible entrance unless there is no other option.)
   ( ) yes ( ) no
   Solution:
2. Do all inaccessible entrances have signs indicating the location of the nearest accessible entrance?
   ( ) yes ( ) no
   Solution:
3. Can the alternate accessible entrance be used independently?
   ( ) yes ( ) no
   Solution:
4. Does the entrance door have at least thirty-two inches clear opening (for a double door, at least one thirty-two-inch leaf)?
   ( ) yes ( ) no
   Solution:
5. Is there at least eighteen inches of clear wall space on the pull side of the door, next to the handle? (A person using a wheelchair needs this space to get close enough to open the door.)
   ( ) yes ( ) no
   Solution:
6. Is the threshold level (less than one-fourth inch) or beveled, up to one-half inch high?
   ( ) yes ( ) no
   Solution:
7. Are doormats one-half inch high or less and secured to the floor at all edges?
   ( ) yes ( ) no
   Solution:
8. Is the door handle no higher than forty-eight inches and operable with a closed fist? (The "closed fist" tests for handles and controls: try opening the door or operating the control using only one hand, held in a fist. If you can do it, so can a person who has limited use of his hands.)
   ( ) yes ( ) no
   Solution:
9. Can doors be opened without too much force?
   ( ) yes ( ) no
   Solution:
10. If the door has a closer, does it take at least three seconds to close?
    ( ) yes ( ) no
    Solution:

Summary

Becoming a vital recreation and park leader requires sensitivity and competency with persons who have wide-ranging abilities. This chapter considers the importance of including special participant groups in your service efforts regardless of the organization setting.

Persons with mental illness, physical disabilities, or mental retardation have an equal right to meaningful and life-enriching recreation experiences. For some, recreation is additionally considered to have a positive treatment or rehabilitative impact. Specific leadership guidelines for accomplishing these goals were outlined in this chapter according to a basic appreciation of persons with these disabilities as individuals.

Questions and Activities for Review and Discussion

1. What is mental illness? As a professional in the field, what should be your attitude about the role of recreation in serving persons with mental retardation?
2. Visit a community mental health center in your area and interview a member of the staff. Discuss the role of recreation in the treatment of persons with mental illness.
3. Discuss specific ways in which recreation leaders can assist persons with physical disabilities in counteracting learned helplessness.
4. The case about Fred is an illustration of what issues pertinent to leaders working with persons with physical disabilities? As a member of the camp staff, what would you do? Form small discussion groups and compare the leader's alternatives.
5. Discuss with classmates any contacts you have had with people with mental retardation. What were the circumstances? How did you react? What were other people's reactions?
6. What is the purpose of recreation for participants with mental retardation?
7. Discuss some of the challenges you might face in trying to integrate a child with mental retardation into a Little League program. How would you go about overcoming these challenges?

References

American Psychiatric Association (1994). *Diagnostic and statistical manual of mental disorders: DSM-IV* (4th ed.). Washington, DC: Author.

Austin, D. (1991). *Therapeutic recreation: Processes and techniques* (2nd ed.). Champaign, IL: Sagamore Publishing.

Auxter, D., Pyfer, J., & Huettig, C. (1993). *Adapted physical education and recreation.* St. Louis, MO: Mosby-Year Book, Inc.

Avedon, F. M. (1974). *Therapeutic recreation service: An applied behavioral science approach.* Englewood Cliffs, NJ: Prentice-Hall.

Bullock, C., & Mahon, M. J. (1997). *Introduction to recreation services for people with disabilities: A person-centered approach.* Champaign, IL: Sagamore Publishing.

Carter, M. J., Van Andel, G. E., & Robb, G. M. (1985). *Therapeutic recreation: A practical approach.* St. Louis: Times Mirror/Mosby College Publishing.

Compton, D. (1994). Leisure and mental health: Context and issues. In D. M. Compton & S. E. Iso-Ahola (Eds.), *Leisure and mental health: Volume I.* Park City, UT: Family Resources Inc.

Eichstaedt, C., & Kalakian, L. (1993). *Developmental/adapted physical education* (3rd ed.). New York: Macmillan.

Greenberg, Rabbi S. (1981, July 25). We are each of us a flawed creation. *The Philadelphia Inquirer*, p. 7-A.

Iso-Ahola, S. (1980). *The social psychology of leisure and recreation*. Dubuque, IA: Wm. C. Brown.

Kalat, J. (1990). *Introduction to psychology*. CA: Wadsworth.

Meyer, L. (1977). A view of therapeutic recreation: its foundations, objectives and challenges. In G. C. Zaso (Ed.), *Therapeutic recreation dialogues in development: Concepts and action*. Durham: University of New Hampshire School of Health Studies, Recreation and Parks Program.

National Institute on Disability and Rehabilitation Research (1993). *Arthritis: An overview of research findings*. Washington, DC: Author, Department of Education.

Nevid, J. S., Spencer, A. R., & Green, B. (1994). *Abnormal psychology in a changing world*. Englewood Cliffs: Prentice Hall.

Stein, T. A., & Sessoms, H. D. (1977). *Recreation and Special Populations*. Boston: Holbrook Press.

Stolov, W. C., & Clowers, M. A. (Eds.). (1981). *Handbook of severe disability*. Seattle: University of Washington.

Web Resources

Adapted recreation & sporting equipment for people with disabilities and the aged: www.users.bigpond.com/achievable concepts/

American Psychiatric Association: www.psych.org/main.html

American Therapeutic Recreation Association: www.atra-tr.org/

Americans with Disabilities Act (document center): http://janweb.icdi.wvu.edu/kinder/

Arthritis (table of contents): www.duq.edu/PT/RA/TableOfContents.html

CARF...The Rehabilitation Accreditation Commission: www.carf.org/

Cerebral palsy links: www.hsl.mcmaster.ca/tomflem/cp.html

Childlife & TR Coalition: www.recreationtherapy.com/childlife/

National Institute of Mental Health: www.nimh.nih.gov/publicat/index.cfm

National Therapeutic Recreation Society: www.nrpa.org/branches/ntrs.htm

Special Olympics: www.specialolympics.org/

Therapeutic recreation association directory: www.recreationtherapy.com/trorg/html

Therapeutic Recreation Directory: www.recreationtherapy.com/

TRAIN (Therapeutic Recreation Access to the Internet): http://perth.uwlax.edu/hper/rmtr/TRAIN.html

Appendixes: Leadership Methods and Resources for Recreation Activities

Contained in this final section of the book are step-by-step procedures for leading particular recreation activity experiences. Depending on the activity, suggestions such as how to organize the event, prepare the group, plan for safety, teach a skill, and promote participation are presented. Also included for each activity are organizational and literature resources for further preparation on these leading skills. The format is a checklist or "recipe." This makes the appendixes useful as a comprehensive yet quick reference on specific how-to procedures.

Appendixes A through E provide a guide to leading the basic recreation activities. This includes leading game, song, dramatic, craft, and dance experiences. Appendixes F through I feature the important procedures in sports leading. This includes tournament conducting, coaching, and leading fitness and aquatic programs. Appendixes J and K concern outdoor activity leading as applied to nature experiences and high-risk adventure experiences. Appendix L focuses on trip leading, and appendix M contains the steps in special event planning and leading. Appendix N features party leadership, and appendix O concludes the section with useful suggestions for enhancing free play opportunities for children.

Appendix A: Game Leading

Duck, Duck, Goose! Red Rover! Lap Sit! Crows and Cranes! Taffy Pull! Pin the Tail on the Donkey! Musical Chairs! Electric Fence! Monolopy!

Games are an essential part of the recreation services for many organizations. They are a part of recreation programs for all ages and ability levels and may include physical, mental, dramatic, musical, literary, dance, or sport activities. Games involve participants in strategy, choice, and interference to compete against or cooperate with other participants, objects, or even themselves.

When participants play *closed games,* the situation is predictable or predetermined such as tossing bean bags into the mouth of a wooden clown face. When participants play *open games*, the situation is unpredictable or not predetermined such as dividing up into teams and stumping each other in charades. Game formats can also differ. Whereas a *conventional game format* specifies the rules as predetermined, an *original game format* encourages the participants to invent or modify the rules before or during the play.

TYPES

NOTE: Specific games may overlap categories.

- Low-organized games: few rules, simple skills required, minimal amount of leader control needed, spontaneously initiated
- Self-test games: competitive games where the opponent is yourself
- Lead-up games: emphasis on practice of one or more skills needed for a more complicated game
- Team games: participants subdivided into groups that cooperate together to achieve the game goal before the other groups
- Table games: equipment that can be set on a small flat surface
- Mental games: competitive focus on mental abilities such as problem solving and puzzle solving
- Wide games: a series of games for a large group of people, in a large physical space, over an extended period, usually according to a theme
- Simulation games: role playing situations simulating real life
- Cooperative games: physical or social, group, cooperative competition with an emphasis on group fun rather than winning
- Group initiative games: initiative taking and decision making involved, certain tasks requiring the joint effort of all group members

- Ropes course activities: individual initiative games applied to a configuration of ropes in the outdoors
- Groups course initiatives: group initiative games applied to high perceived risk experiences

TYPES OF GAME LEADERS

There are three ways to lead a games session:

- The official: The official type of leader walks onto the center of a playing area and announces, "All right, we're going to play Catch the Dragon's Tail. Everyone form lines of eight players and each player lock arms around the person in front." The official's job is to make sure that all the players follow the instructions.
- The coach: The coach type of leader takes eight players in hand and says, "Here, you put your arms around this person; you get behind her, like this; and you stand at the end of the line, like this." The coach helps the players play the game.
- The player: The third way to lead games is to put your arms around someone's waist, look over your shoulder, and say, "Come over here and put your arms around my waist." The player is a part of the game.

All three types of leaders are appropriate in game leading, but it works best when each player is a leader—when everyone assumes responsibility for the game and for the other players.

SUGGESTIONS FOR LEADING

- Select games appropriate to the abilities and interests of each participant group. All games are not successful with all groups.
- Feel free to modify game rules or formats to more effectively achieve the recreation experience goals.
- When safety is not hindered, encourage participants to modify game rules or formats if doing so will enhance the recreational experience.
- Select games designed to eliminate one player at a time with caution.
- Avoid games that cause embarrassment.
- Avoid games that introduce health problems.
- Be sensitive to how participants might react and select games with care.
- In a multiple game session offer both new and familiar games.
- Depending on the game, feel free to assume player roles when appropriate.
- Be enthusiastic; enjoy the game playing yourself.

PRIOR PREPARATION

- Have equipment needed for games ready, at hand, operational, and clean. Have extra equipment in case of breakage.
- Rehearse with yourself and other leaders the game rules and procedures.
- Inspect the physical area where games will be played for such concerns as size, adequacy, and safety hazards before games are selected.
- Alert participants to clothing and footwear needed if the games require this consideration.

- Know something about the participants in terms of ages, ability levels, and interests.
- Develop a time frame to know how many games to prepare.
- Secure leader, referee, or other supervisory assistance if needed.

CREATING AND KEEPING THE PLAY ENERGY

- In starting the play energy do not jump right into the most active games; use instead a moderately physical game before going all out in an active game.
- Do not play too many active games in succession; the built-up energy will fatigue and be dissipated.
- Vary the activity level of the games to keep everyone fresh and energetic.
- In building group energy use games that emphasize group awareness and cooperation.
- The individually expressive games build energy, but the group awareness games help preserve it; therefore intersperse the games that offer individual and group play.
- Maintain the group's play energy by keeping everyone involved in the game.
- Let each game run its natural course, but change to a new one before the players lose their enthusiasm for it.

SAFETY CONSIDERATIONS

- Participants should wear athletic shoes for active indoor and outdoor games.
- Leaders and referees should be well trained and competent.
- Remove potential hazards from the game playing area, or if this is not possible, modify the game.
- Ask every player to be their own referee with regard to safety.
- In games that require players to have their eyes shut be sure that there are enough leaders who remain out of the game as players to watch for hazards.
- Never force participants to play.
- Stop games that get out of hand or become dangerous.
- For active games encourage participants to remove jewelry or sharp clothing objects.
- In games requiring active physical contact between players, match according to similar size and weight.

FORMING AND MANAGING TEAMS

- Create teams only as a momentary way of enjoying the game; do not emphasize team winners or losers.
- Make sure that there are different teams for each game.
- Choose teams at random and not based on skill level.
- Make joining into teams a game. Many games can be used as methods for forming teams. Be creative.
- If you are going to play with a large group of people with multiple leaders, organize the leaders into teams. Have one leader in each team function as the official, setting up and explaining the game, while other leaders help as coaches and players. Make sure that you share the roles.
- Emphasize to the players that there is only one team. Everyone is playing on the same side.

STEPS IN TEACHING

1. Get participants' attention.
2. Arouse interest in the game by explaining the game's background or other interesting features.
3. Organize participants into the formation required of the game such as form relay lines or get in a circle.
4. Tell the object or goal of the game.
5. Explain how the goal is achieved.
6. Demonstrate (or have selected participants demonstrate) any game procedures or skills the players are unclear about.
7. Practice with participants the skill or procedure of the game (first without equipment if complex).
8. Review the game rules.
9. Start play.
10. Add rules, strategies, or changes as the game is played.
11. Stop the game before participant interest begins to diminish.

PRACTICE EXPERIENCES

- Visit a recreation organization in your community and observe the staff leading games. After the session, discuss with the leaders their techniques for leading the games.
- Lead games from as many game types as possible with both small and large groups of classmates. Critique each other.
- Volunteer to lead games with participants from community recreation groups, campers, and playground attendees and ask them for their help in improving your leading ability.
- Organize and conduct a games leading workshop for recreation majors from your college or recreation professionals from your community.
- Visit a recreation agency that sponsors ropes course or groups course initiative activities. Observe the use of these activity areas and discuss with staff the leadership competencies for conducting these games.
- Invite school children to your class and lead them in group initiative games. Discuss the benefits of this type of game with the children's teacher.
- Videotape yourself leading a group in a game. When viewing the film later, identify strengths and improvement areas for your games leading.

RESOURCES

Clements, R. L. (Ed.). (1995). *Games and great ideas: A guide for elementary school physical educators and classroom teachers*. Westport, CT: Greenwood Press.

Fluegelman, A. (1981). *The more New Games book*. Garden City, NY: Doubleday.

Kasser, S. L. (1995). *Inclusive games*. Champaign, IL: Human Kinetics.

Lichtman, B. (1999). *More innovative games*. Champaign, IL: Human Kinetics.

Moore, A. C. (1992). *The game finder: A leader's guide to great activities*. State College, PA: Venture Publishing.

Morris, G. S. D., & Stiehl, J. (1999). *Changing kids' games*. Champaign, IL: Human Kinetics.

Rohnke, K. (1977). *Cowstails and cobras*. Hamilton, MA: Project Adventure.

Sher, B. (1995). *Popular games for positive play: Activities for self-awareness*. Tuscon, AZ: Therapy Skill Builders.

Appendix B: Song Leading

Opportunities for leading in singing are diverse. Singing can occur in settings that are formal or informal, indoors or outdoors, and as a component of other programs or as its own program. Singing activities can occur on a log behind the dining hall or in an auditorium. Ethnic song fests, children's celebrations, songs to travel by bus with, and caroling at holidays are samples. Group singing is an excellent way to set a mood, create group unity, and soothe attitudes. It requires no special equipment or space. It does require leadership.

SONG LEADING PREPARATIONS

- Assume an attitude of enthusiasm and belief in the values of singing.
- Have an ability to create a sense of fun and enjoyment.
- Select a song agenda that includes both songs that are familiar to the participants and songs that are new to participants.
- Select a variety of songs that match the interests of the group and the appropriateness of the occasion.
- Practice the songs ahead of time and be thoroughly familiar with them.
- Determine the value of using accompaniment as a singing support and include it in the singing session if appropriate.

TYPES OF SONG LEADING

There are three ways to lead a song using your hands.

- Beat leading: The leader uses her hands to beat the cadence of the song. This may be done from side to side or up and down. Visually keeping time to the beat of the song is important.
- Action leading: The leader uses the gestures that are a part of the song as a method of leading. Action songs are those in which the singers do something with their hands (or bodies) to act out the words of the song. For the beginning song leader the dramatic appeal of action songs can aid in overcoming self-consciousness.
- Pitch leading: The leader uses the position of his hand to indicate whether the note is high or low. This is done by changing the level of the hand in the direction of the pitch of the song. As the pitch goes up, so does the hand. Pitch leading is not appropriate for leading rounds or harmony singing.

STEPS IN LEADING A SONG

There is no standard way for presenting and conducting song sessions. However, the following sequence can be useful.

1. Get the group's attention.
2. Announce each song's title clearly.
3. Start with a song the group knows and likes to sing.
4. Sing the song or first verse of the song through to give the participants a sense of how the song sounds.
5. Pitch the tune clearly in a distinct, steady tone.
6. Sing the entire song together with the group.
7. If the participants are doing it correctly and enjoy it, continue it until the end. If not, stop them and correct the singing.
8. Praise the participants for singing well.
9. Sing another familiar song.
10. Introduce new songs gradually.
11. End the singing session with a group's familiar and favorite song.

TEACHING NEW SONGS

- Clearly give the title of the new song.
- Give interesting facts or stories about the song to arouse interest.
- Sing the entire song for the group.
- Sing each phrase at a time and have the group sing the phrase after you.
- If the song has complex or difficult words, speak each phrase at a time and have the group speak after you; then add the tune by singing each phrase for the group to repeat.
- For songs with several verses and a chorus, it is best to teach the chorus first.
- In teaching rounds have the group sing the entire song through in unison two or three times, then divide into the number of groups needed to sing in a round.
- Use of song sheets should be limited.
- Stop singing the new song while the interest is still high and go on to a familiar song.

GUIDELINES FOR SUCCESS

- Be careful to pitch the song correctly.
- If the group is singing well, encourage harmony and changes in volume or tempo.
- Encourage all to take part, but do not force anyone.
- Sing along with the group, but do not dominate them, particularly if you have a strong voice or are using a microphone.
- If you correct the group's singing, do it pleasantly and constructively.
- Let your personality shine through in your unique leading technique.

RESOURCES

Allen, J. L. (1994). *Jeffrey Allen's secrets of singing*. Miami, FL: CPP/Belwin.

Bennett, P. D. (1997). *SongWorks*. Belmont, CA: Wadsworth.

Brown, O. (1996). *Discover your voice: How to develop healthy voice habits*. San Diego: Singular Publishing Group.

Frisell, A. (1996). *A singer's notebook: A self-help singing technique manual*. New York: Anthony Frisell.

Mitchell, L. (1991). *One, two, three—echo me!: Ready-to-use songs, games and activities to help children sing in tune*. West Nyack, NY: Parker Publishing.

Page, N. (1995). *Sing and shine on!: The teacher's guide to multicultural song leading*. Portsmouth, NH: Heinemann.

Phillips, K. H. (1992). *Teaching kids to sing*. New York: Maxwell Macmillan International.

Tobbitt, J. (1971). *Counselor's guide to camp singing*. Martinsville, IN: American Camping Association.

Ware, C. (1998). *Basics of vocal pedagogy: The foundations and process of singing*. Boston: McGraw-Hill.

Appendix C: Leading Dramatic Experiences

The leader involved in dramatic activities may sometimes assume a teaching role, act as a facilitator, or may even command the center of the dramatic attention as in storytelling. The leader of recreational dramatic experiences must not only have expertise in the methods of drama but also must be able to bring out the creative talents of participants. Opportunities to lead formal play productions before large audiences are not numerous. Recreation leaders are more often involved in informal, creative dramatic activities with groups of participants where an audience does not exist or at least is minimal.

TYPES OF DRAMATICS

Dramatic experiences are led differently according to the level of structure established by the leader. *Informal dramatics* are more casually experienced with little prior structure or rules established by the leader. A leader in this case is concerned with suggesting themes, providing props and a space, facilitating creative expression by the participants, and being supportive and encouraging. In informal dramatics emphasis is on the satisfaction of the participants directly involved in the drama.

Formal dramatics, on the other hand, obey more standards of performance and require a great deal of structure establishment and autocratic direction from the leader. A leader in this situation is concerned with selecting a script, assigning character roles to performers, establishing sets and costumes, and directing rehearsals. In formal dramatics emphasis is on the satisfaction of the audience.

The following list of types of dramatic activities may be led at either formal or informal levels depending on how much structure and control the leader maintains over the actors:

- Pantomime: Using only facial and body action to tell a story. Suggested activities include a cowboy roping steers, going grocery shopping, a visit to the amusement park, animal imitations, your first date, taking your dog to a first visit to the vet, your first job interview, imitating Santa Claus at a department store, getting in and out of a box, flying a kite, picking up shells from the beach, imitating a machine, watching a tennis match, stifling a sneeze, an ice cream cone on a hot day, and eating grapes full of seeds.
- Puppetry: Using objects as characters and adding the participant's voice. In some puppet play the participant is not even seen by the audience. Puppet dramatics may be done either with a script or improvisationally. Suggested activities include finger puppets, shadow plays, sock puppets, paper bag puppets, papier-mâché puppets, vegetable puppets, spoon puppets, flannel board cutouts, marionettes, and stick puppets.

- Skits: Short plays requiring only simple or improvised props and costumes. They usually have a humorous or suprise ending. Suggested activities include paper bag dramatics, one-line completions, impromptu skits around themes, story enacting, and memorized skits from drama books.
- Storytelling: Orally delivering the contents of a story or book. This may be done from memory or read from books. It may be done with the leader as storyteller or by a group of participants. Suggested activities include going around a group and adding to a story, dramatic readings, telling audience participation stories, fairy or folk tales, nursery rhymes, mystery stories, and ghost stories around the campfire.
- Dramatic games: Group games that use dramatic expression. Suggested activities include charades, guess the animal, guessing gifts, and machines.
- Play production: Rehearsed performances before an audience. Suggested activities include one-act plays, musicals, operas, multiple-act plays, play competitions, children's theater, choral speech, community theater, monologue, pageants, and symphonic drama.

LEADERSHIP GUIDELINES

1. Pantomime
   a. Use to introduce children to characterization.
   b. Use to bring out self-conscious or shy participants.
   c. Only suggest the themes or situations; do not instruct in how to interpret these into a pantomime.
   d. Enable participants to stretch and limber up their bodies before beginning a pantomime session.
   e. Lead participants up to pantomime with exercises that encourage nonverbal communication.
2. Puppetry
   a. Include the making of puppets in the dramatic activity.
   b. For beginning puppeting groups allow participants to develop their theme and characters.
   c. Encourage participants to speak loudly and clearly.
   d. Encourage participants to make large, dramatic movements with their puppets.
3. Skits
   a. Have on hand a repertoire of skit ideas that can be used in impromptu circumstances.
   b. Do not hesitate to change or adapt the skit to match the situation.
   c. Encourage participants to change parts as much as they want.
   d. Stress the participant's expression of the role she is assuming.
   e. Remember that skits are not polished performances; encourage the fun of spontaneity and creativity.
   f. Do not suggest skits that embarrass or ridicule.
4. Storytelling
   a. Get the listener's attention with your first sentence.
   b. Believe in the story yourself and identify with the characters.
   c. Talk on the experience level of the group.
   d. Use silence and pauses for dramatic effect.
   e. Sit where everyone can see and hear you.
   f. Know your story well.
   g. Be aware of the attention span and interest level of your listeners.
   h. Maintain eye contact with the listeners.
   i. Use facial expressions and physical gestures.
   j. Vary the volume of your voice to emphasize the action.

5. Dramatic games
   a. Employ the suggestions for leading games from appendix A.
   b. Emphasize within group cooperation and between group competition.
   c. Focus the participants on the fun and creative aspects rather than the performance aspects of the game.
6. Play production
   a. Encourage all actors to learn their parts quickly.
   b. Provide the needed props and costumes as soon as possible to train the actors in their use.
   c. Hold a full dress rehearsal before the production.
   d. Fully use nonacting participants in important support projects such as staging, publicity, ticket sales, and costumes.
   e. Have simple rules, but enforce them (e.g., no visitors behind stage, gum chewing, or curtain peeking).
   f. Use simple plays or familiar stories for young children.

RESOURCES

Barchers, S. T. (1993). *Readers theatre for beginning readers*. Englewood, CO: Teacher Ideas Press.
Bush, M. (1995). *Plays for young audiences: Feature The Emerald Circle and other plays*. Colorado Springs: Meriwether Publishing.
Cattanach, A. (1992). *Drama for people with special needs*. New York: Drama Book Publishers.
Champlin, C. (1980). *Puppetry and creative dramatics in storytelling*. Austin, TX: Renfro Studios.
Gray, P. G. (1974). *Creative dramatics for the elderly: A guide for residential care settings and senior centers*. New York: Teachers College, Columbia University.
MacDonald, M. R. (1990). *The skit book: 101 skits from kids*. Hamden, CT: Linnet Books.
Reynolds, J. L. (1980). *Skits for seniors only*. Woodbury, CT: Solar Studio.
Shepard, A. (1993). *Stories on stage: Scripts for reader's theater*. Bronx, NY: H.W. Wilson.
Sturkie, J., & Cassady, M. (1992). *Acting it out junior*. San Jose, CA: Resource Publications.
Zeder, S. (1990). *Wish in one hand, spit in the other: A collection of plays*. New Orleans, LA: Anchorage Press.

Appendix D: Art and Craft Managing

Art and craft experiences make up one of our richest and most satisfying recreational areas. As a way of communicating, arts and crafts provide a vehicle for creative expression of our ideas, values, feelings, interests, emotions, and fantasies. They appeal to all ages and to a wide range of cultural interests. Recreation leaders must be alert to the possibilities for including varied forms of arts and crafts into their programs, both as independent forms of activity and in cooperation with other program areas. Leading these activities requires some basic techniques but not always artistic talent.

CATEGORIES OF ACTIVITIES

The distinction between arts and crafts is often arbitrary. One differentiation that may be useful for the leader is that crafts produce a useful form or product, whereas visual art is strictly for appreciation and beauty. Examples follow:

Crafts	*Arts*
Automotive crafts	Batik
Basketry	Etching
Candle making	Finger painting
Ceramics	Painting
Jewelry making	Paper folding
Leather work	Pen-and-ink drawing
Metalcraft	Photography
Needlecraft	Printmaking
Pottery	Sculpturing
Tie dying	Silk screening
Weaving	Sketching
Woodworking	Tapestries

CRAFTS INSTRUCTION

- Have finished objects ready for viewing as samples.
- Break the craft activity down into simple, progressive steps in which the participant is able to enjoy some degree of immediate success.

- Give an initial instruction in the craft project including techniques, preparations, tools, safety, and materials.
- If the craft is complex or difficult, a demonstration by the leader may be helpful to participant learning.
- Help participants get under way on their own projects as soon as possible; do not become so detailed with your instruction that participants become anxious and lose interest.
- Help participants develop their critical judgment and standards for creativity and quality.

MANAGING AN ART AND CRAFT PROGRAM

- Children should at least receive minimal exposure to a variety of art and craft experiences, whether or not they have a special interest.
- Art and craft programs are highly adaptable for those with physical, emotional, and mental disabilities.
- For a well-rounded arts and crafts program stress both variety and depth, which means going beyond the beginning instructional level.
- Project fun into the program while at the same time gradually raising quality standards.
- Develop both individual and group projects within the program.
- Focus the program around each person's development of skill and appreciation rather than on yourself as a skilled craftsperson.
- Divide into groups according to interest and skill rather than by age.
- Have a display or show of all products made by the group; obtain newspaper publicity.

RESOURCES

Better Homes and Gardens. (1993). *Wood weekend toy projects you can make*. Des Moines, IA: Meredith.

Churchill, E. R. (1992). *Holiday paper projects*. New York: Sterling.

Coney, N. (1997). *The complete candle maker*. Asheville, NC: Lark.

Constable, D. (1997). *Beginner's guide to candlemaking*. Tunbridge Wells, Kent: Search Press.

Cusick, D. (1994). *Nature crafts with a microwave*. New York: Sterling.

Dean, A. E. (1998). *Natural creativity: Exploring and using nature's raw materials to craft simple, functional, and attractive objects*. New York: M. Evans.

DeCosse, C. (1992). *More creative sewing ideas*. Chicago: Contemporary.

Medearis, A. S. (1997). *Ideas for entertaining from the African-American kitchen*. New York: Dutton.

Munson, R. S. (1994). *Favorite hobbies and pastimes: A sourcebook of leisure pursuits*. Chicago: American Library Association.

Nelson, J. A. (1989). *Country classics: Authentic projects you can build in one weekend*. Harrisburg, PA: Stackpole.

Wankelman, W. F. (1993). *A handbook of arts and crafts* (8th ed.). Dubuque, IA: W. C. Brown.

Wigg, P. R., Hasselschwert, J., & Wankelman, W. F. (1997). *A handbook of arts and crafts*. Madison, WI: Brown & Benchmark.

Wormleighton, A. (1995). *Pigs, piglets, and porkers: 30 projects to quilt, stitch, embroider, and appliqué*. Radnor, PA: Chilton.

Appendix E: Guiding the Dance Experience

Recreational dance experiences do not require a highly skilled dancer or dance instructor as leader. With only a small amount of training and study you are able to lead dance activities for children in recreational settings and conduct simple folk and square dance activities for youth and adults. However, for more advanced or established dance groups, specially trained leadership is necessary.

Recreational dance experiences are an integral part of any comprehensive recreation program. They may be organized as instructional classes, demonstrations, social recreation gatherings, performances, clubs, festivals, clinics, and workshops. In numerous ways varied forms of dance offer important physical, social, emotional, and intellectual opportunities for participants.

TYPES OF RECREATIONAL DANCE EXPRESSIONS

There are many ways to categorize dance experiences in recreational settings. One is to consider those dances primarily enjoyed as a skill to perform for viewing by others and the other is those dances primarily engaged in as socializing experiences:

Peformance dance	Social dance
Ballet	Round
Jazz	Square
Ethnic	Folk
Modern	Rock
Interpretive	Ballroom
Belly	Clog
Tap	Disco
Ballroom	Line

TEACHING A NEW FOLK DANCE

- Have participants get in the appropriate formation for the dance.
- Stand where everyone can see you; that is, stand as part of the circle rather than in the center of the circle.
- Be in close proximity to your accompanist or recorded music.
- Give the name of the dance, its nationality, and a brief story or history.

- Play a portion of the music and ask participants to listen to the beat and theme.
- Demonstrate the entire dance to its music.
- Teach the whole dance if the steps and sequences are simple.
- Teach parts of the dance one at a time if the steps and sequences are complex or difficult.
- Teach the steps and movements with the music unless practice without it will enhance learning.
- Have the group walk through the dance pattern, giving them verbal cues that keep time to the music's rhythm.
- Play the introduction to the music and indicate where the dance begins.
- If the dance has more than one pattern, dance each pattern separately before proceeding to a next pattern. Each time begin the dance from the beginning.
- Offer special instruction or demonstration for those having trouble.
- Reteach parts of the pattern that may be causing difficulty.
- Have the participants change partners frequently.
- In a folk dance session offer a review of familiar dances and opportunities for learning new ones.
- Teach a variety of folk dances that are appropriate to the ability level of the participants.
- Encourage everyone to take part, but do not insist.
- Teach simple dances in the beginning, with gradual advancement to more complicated dances.
- If the program is a party or social gathering, teach dances that require little instruction and practice and maximize the mixing of participants.

FACILITATING SOCIAL DANCING

- Plan with the group what forms of social dancing they are interested in.
- Offer instruction in social dance forms if appropriate.
- See that the sound system for the music is in good working order and a high quality of sound is available.
- Use dance mixers frequently to provide opportunity for each person to dance with many partners.
- Set the mood for social dancing by using lighting, decorations, and other appropriate atmospheres.
- If a disc jockey is to be used, employ only those with this specific type of talent and thoroughly familiarize them ahead of time about the participants.
- Become involved in the dancing along with participants, instead of standing with arms folded along the side of the dance area.

LEADING SQUARE DANCES

- For beginning groups, offer a brief description of the square dance calls and their formations.
- Demonstrate the smooth, shuffling step done in square dancing and have participants practice it without partners to a selection of square dance music.
- Have the square dance music organized in the order you wish to present the dances.
- Begin with the Grand March as a method for forming the dance squares. (Line the gents and ladies up separately facing one end of the dance area. When the music begins, the first dancer in each line comes to the center of the room, meets his or her partner there with an elbow swing, and moves down the center of the room. Others in the lines follow. At the opposite end of the dance floor the first couple turns right, the second left, and so on to return to the other

end of the floor. The couples next come down in groups of four, then in groups of eight. As soon as the last group of eight participants is complete, stop the music.)

- Explain the positions in the set and how to square the sets.
- Walk through the pattern of the first dance.
- Dance the pattern to the music.
- If you are calling the square dancing yourself, use patter-style music rather than singing-style music.
- Review and begin again from the beginning if the dancers become confused.
- Begin with simpler square dance patterns (such as swing, circle left, and do-si-do), then proceed to more complicated patterns (such as allemande left and grand right and left).
- For the caller, learn the dance first and then memorize the call before presenting it to a group.
- Give the dancers adequate time to dance the pattern, but remember that the call precedes the beginning of the pattern.
- When one set is slightly behind the others, give them time to catch up before calling the next pattern.
- When the group of dancers is large, stand on a platform and use a microphone.
- Add your personality to the calling, making it lively and enthusiastic.

TEACHING CREATIVE DANCE

Unlike the rote learning of specific dance techniques required of participants in square and folk dancing, creative dance encourages the individual exploration of movement.

- Use a variety of approaches to stimulate movement exploration.
- Use suggestions of movement sequences or combinations of actions to assist participants in interpreting individually.
- Suggest images or objects as basis for movement such as moving like animals, machines, characters, or emotions.
- Use a variety of musical or percussive accompaniment to stimulate movement.
- Encourage the movement possibilities of all body parts.
- Use pictures, stories, or poems to suggest movement themes.
- Gradually, specific movement skills may be introduced in which participants deliberately work on such abilities as flexibility, coordination, strength, and balance.
- Encourage different levels of movement, different rhythms, and different directions.
- From exploring movement individually, enable participants to advance to working in pairs or small groups.

RESOURCES

Bannerman, G., & Pugsley, M. N. (1999). *Recreation with dance, movement, and music.* Louisville, KY: Bridge Resources.

Bennett, J. P., & Riemer, P. C. (1995). *Rhythmic activities and dance*. Champaign, IL: Human Kinetics.

Gilbert, D. (1994). *International folk dances at a glance*. Minneapolis, MN: Burgess Publishing.

Lane, C. (1995). *Christy Lane's complete book of line dancing*. Champaign, IL: Human Kinetics.

Levete, G. (1993). *No handicap to dance: Creative improvisation for people with and without disabilities*. London: Souvenir Press.

Lloyd, M. L. (1990). *Adventures in creative movement activities: A guide for teaching*. Petaling Jaya, Malaysia: Federal Publications.

Purcell, T. M. (1994). *Teaching children dance: Becoming a master teacher*. Champaign, IL: Human Kinetics.

Schlaich, J., & Dupont, B. (1993). *The art of teaching dance technique*. Reston, VA: National Dance Association.

Sherbon, E. (1990). *On the count of one: The art, craft, and science of teaching modern dance*. Pennington, NJ: A Cappella Books.

Appendix F: Tournament Conducting

Tournaments are merely methods of organizing competitive recreation activities. There are many types of tournaments because there are many reasons for competition, many types of competitive activities, and many types of competitors. Not everyone desires to participate in organized competition or in organized competition that culminates in the designation of a winner. For those who do, the leader must be prepared to select the most desirable means of organizing it.

Tournaments can be used for most competitive activities for which several teams or participants wish to determine a champion. Some activities, however, such as Four Square and Croquet must have the rules changed for tournament use. Other than modifications such as this required for certain activities, any recreation activity can be formatted by the leader into a tournament. A Euchre tournament anyone?

CATEGORIES OF TOURNAMENTS

- Round Robin tournament
- Elimination tournaments
  - Single elimination
  - Double elimination
  - Consolation
  - Bagnall-Wild elimination
  - Mueller-Anderson playback
- Challenge tournaments
  - Ladder
  - Pyramid
  - King or Crown
  - Funnel
  - Spider Web
  - Round-the-Clock
  - Bump Board
  - Progressive Bridge
  - Tombstone

FACTORS TO CONSIDER WHEN SELECTING AND DESIGNING A TOURNAMENT*

1. Objectives of the tournament (one or more of the following)
   a. Determine a winner quickly
   b. Provide for maximal participation
   c. Encourage social interaction
   d. Determine a true champion
   e. Motivate participants for a long period
   f. Provide for equal number of matches per entry
   g. Increase skills in a sport
2. Characteristics of the participants
   a. Age level
   b. Gender mixes
   c. Playing ability
   d. Interest or desire
   e. Attention span
3. Facility, equipment, and staff requirements
   a. Availability of fields or courts
   b. Condition of fields or courts
   c. Accessibility to locker rooms
   d. Provisions for equipment rental or checkout
   e. Adequate number and competency of officials
   f. Funding
4. Time
   a. Length of time to run the tournament
   b. Available dates and hours
   c. Provisions for rescheduling as a result of weather
5. Others
   a. Medical supervision
   b. Publicity and promotion
   c. Governance procedures
   d. Spectator control

ROUND ROBIN TOURNAMENT

The Round Robin tournament provides for maximal participation, because each entry plays against each other entry an equal number of times. The winner is that participant or team with the highest percentages of wins. It is best used when time and facility space are ample and when there are a small number of participants or teams. If there are more than eight entries, select another tournament format.

1. Formulas (N = Total number of entries)
   a. Number of games per league: $\frac{N(N-1)}{2}$

* Adapted from Bayless, K. G., Mull, R. F., & Ross, C. M. (1983). *Recreational sports programming*. North Palm Beach, FL: The Athletic Institute.

b. Number of games per entry: N − 1
c. Number of rounds
   (1) Even number of entries: N − 1
   (2) Odd number of entries: N
d. Number of games per round
   (1) Even number of entries: $\frac{N}{2}$
   (2) Odd number of entries: $\frac{N - 1}{2}$

2. Obtaining pairings
   a. Arrange all entries, either by name or assigned number, into two vertical columns.
   b. List consecutively down the first column and continue up the second.
   c. When an odd number of entries are scheduled, a "bye" should be placed in the fixed upper-left position.
   d. For subsequent rounds, rotate the names or numbers counterclockwise around the participant located in the upper-left position of the column.

Round 1	*Round 2*	*Round 3*	
Bye-7	Bye-6	Bye-5	
1–6	7–5	6–4	
2–5	1–4	7–3	
3–4	2–3	1–2	and so forth

3. Reasons to select Round Robin tournaments
   a. Tournaments are easily organized and administered.
   b. They allow for complete prescheduling of entries.
   c. Participants can be informed in advance of opponents and game times.
   d. Emphasis is on maximal participation for an extended period.
   e. Tournaments produce a true champion.
   f. They are effective for outdoor sports, because postponed games may be replayed at a convenient time later in the tournament.
   g. The schedule is easily understood by participants.
   h. Participants are able to become better acquainted because of the extended play.
4. Reasons not to select Round Robin tournaments
   a. They are time consuming.
   b. Tournaments require large amount of facility space.
   c. A significant number of forfeits may occur toward last rounds when an entry realizes there is no chance of winning.
   d. Tournaments are not useful with a large number of entries.
5. Leading tips
   a. Try to schedule each entry to play at least once a week.
   b. Designate open dates for rescheduling purposes.
   c. If several entries have similar playing time conflicts, group these entries together for easier scheduling.

SINGLE ELIMINATION

Elimination tournaments are, as the name suggests, designed to eliminate players or teams who have lost games until there is only one player or team remaining. It is useful when players or teams are fairly skilled, there is not much time, and there is a large number of entries. In a single elimination tournament all entries compete in the first round, but only the winners of each round compete in the subsequent rounds until an ultimate winner is determined.

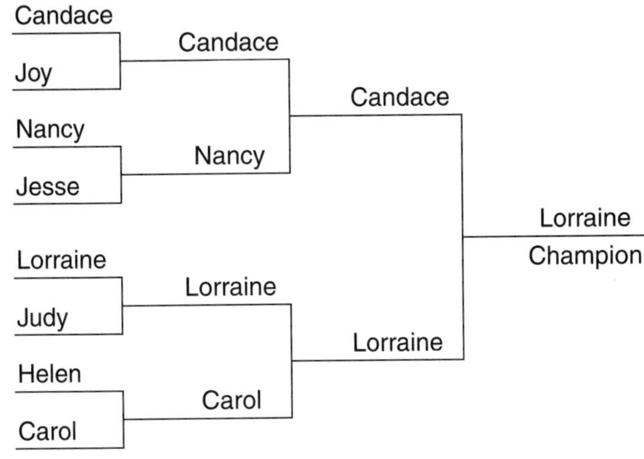

1. Formulas (N = Total number of entries)
   a. Number of tournament games: N − 1
   b. Power of two: Number of times 2 has to be multiplied to equal or exceed the number of entries (e.g., if there were eight entries, $2 \times 2 \times 2 = 8$ or the power of two is 3 for eight entries).
   c. Number of byes: (Power of two) − N
   d. Number of first round games: $\dfrac{\text{N} - \text{No of byes}}{2}$
2. Setting up
   a. Complete the determination of the entries.
   b. Double-check to make sure all entries are accounted for.
   c. Determine the "seeds" or better players so that they may be placed initially in the tournament so as not to play each other.
   d. Determine the number of byes.
   e. Place all byes in the first round so that they are distributed as evenly as possible between the upper and lower brackets.
   f. Number the games; all games in the first round should be numbered first before proceeding to the second round.
   g. List the date, time, and location of each game on the bracket sheet.
3. Reasons to select single elimination tournaments
   a. Easily understood by the participants.
   b. Simple to conduct.
   c. Recognize excellent playing ability.
   d. Take a short amount of time.
   e. Can accommodate a large number of entries.
   f. Interesting for spectators.
   g. Appropriate for a one-day event.
4. Reasons not to select single elimination tournaments
   a. Minimize participation.
   b. Place emphasis on winning.
   c. Not conducive for outdoor sports because of scheduling difficulties caused by weather-related postponements.
   d. Possibility of good players being eliminated early.

5. Leading tips
   a. Remember, round one must be completed before progressing to game round two.
   b. Assignment of positions on round one of the bracket sheet may be determined at random, on the basis of known ability (seeding), or in the order the entries were received.
   c. The date, time, and place of all games on the schedule should be incorporated in the original bracket chart.

LADDER TOURNAMENT

Challenge tournaments are ongoing tournaments that place emphasis on participation rather than on winning. Players issue and accept challenge matches from each other with the ultimate goal of winning all challenges and advancing to the top of the tournament structure. All entrants continue to play regardless of the outcome of the challenge. It is used primarily with individual and dual activities. The most popular challenge tournament is probably the ladder.

Al
John
Peter
Michael
Hal
Ted
Dick

1. Setting up
   a. The entries' names are listed on a horizontal rung and placed in a vertical column, usually with the best player at the bottom.
   b. Similar to climbing a ladder, the rungs are used to advance players from one position to another in accordance to challenge procedures.
   c. The winner of the tournament is that individual at the top rung of the ladder when play is stopped.
2. Challenge rules: Movement to the top of the ladder is gained by a player issuing a challenge to an individual on a higher level, defeating that individual, and changing positions.
   a. Participants initiate their own challenges.
   b. All challenges must be accepted and played within or by an agreed time.
   c. A participant may challenge only those one level above.
   d. If the challenger wins, the individuals exchange positions on the ladder.
   e. If the challenger is defeated, both individuals remain in their original position.
   f. It is the winner's responsibility to update the ladder tournament board.
   g. Challenges may not be refused.
   h. Challenges should be met in the order that they were issued.
   i. If a challenge has been accepted and one of the contestants fails to appear, declare a forfeit and exchange positions.
3. Reasons to select ladder tournaments
   a. Easily organized and led.
   b. Require a minimal amount of supervision.
   c. Emphasize maximal participation.
   d. Does not eliminate any participant.
   e. Yield opportunities for social interaction.

   f. Convenient for participants.
   g. No formal scheduling required.
4. Reasons not to select ladder tournaments
   a. Communication between participants to set up play dates and times can be a problem.
   b. Tournaments are suited best for small number of entries.
   c. The procedure can be confusing to participants.
   d. Security of the challenge board may be a problem.
   e. Poorer players who remain constantly at the bottom are singled out and may be discouraged.
5. Leading tips
   a. Establish a minimal and maximal number of contests that may be played during the tournament period.
   b. Announce a definite date for completing the tournament before the start of play.
   c. Add late entries to the lowest rung.

RESOURCES

Bailey, D. C., Greaves, E. C., Holsberry, W. M., & Reznik, J. W. (1985). *Management of recreational sports*. Corvallis, OR: The National Intramural-Recreational Sports Association.

Horine, L. (1999). *Administration of physical education and sport programs* (4th ed.). Boston: McGraw-Hill.

Leith, L. M. (1990). *Coaches guide to sport administration*. Champaign, IL: Leisure Press.

Martens, R. (1995). *NRPA special edition of youth sport director guide*. Champaign, IL: Human Kinetics.

Paciovek, M. J., & Jones, J. A. (1994). *Sports and recreation for the disabled* (2nd ed.). Carmel, IN: Cooper Publishing Group.

Parks, J. B., Zanger, B. R. K., & Quarterman, J. (Eds.). (1998). *Contemporary sport management*. Champaign, IL: Human Kinetics.

Appendix G: Coaching Sports

In considering the types of recreational activities that leaders are responsible for conducting in organized programs, it is evident that the most popular and widely found activities involve sports. Critically important to the success of any sports program are the coaches who assume the responsibility for the teams. Coaches should be able to instruct participants in the sport, demonstrating techniques and teaching the rules of the sport so that all participants can realize success. The coach should also be able to motivate each team member to perform to her highest capabilities.

GENERAL COACHING PRINCIPLES

- Respect the individuality of each participant.
- Maintain discipline without being dictatorial.
- Be fair and lead rather than drive.
- Be more concerned with finding the right way than your own way.
- Develop a sense of mutual responsibility in all team members.
- Have one team, not regulars and substitutes.
- Make all criticism constructive and avoid sarcasm.
- Never sacrifice a player to make an example.
- Be quick to praise and slow to blame.
- Seek to develop the skill of all participants.
- Make arrangements so that all participants can play and compete at their appropriate ability level.

TEACHING GAME RULES

- All players must know and understand that game rules are necessary for safe play.
- Demonstrations showing how rules are broken and what happens when they are afford splendid ways to help players learn rules.
- The coach should help the group know each rule, why it is a rule, and the penalty for breaking it.
- All practice and competitive games should be played according to the rules.
- The game should be stopped during practice periods at teachable moments when rule infractions occur.
- The use of clinics and workshops is often a successful way to teach rules to large groups.
- The best way to teach game rules is in relation to skills to be mastered.

TEACHING SPORT SKILLS

- When possible, group participants according to skill and ability levels for teaching sport skills.
- Emphasis is on learning the correct way to perform each skill, but the leader should be able to accept individual styles or unique movements.
- When demonstrating or explaining, be sure to have the complete attention of participants.
- When demonstrating or explaining, locate participants in a single line so that all may see and hear.
- Briefly explain what you are doing and how to do it, then encourage participants to copy you as you continue to slowly perform the skill.
- Give individual assistance to all who are having difficulty copying the movements.
- Help each individual evaluate his progress.
- It is important to demonstrate skills correctly so that participants do not copy an incorrect movement pattern.
- Break skills down into their component parts and teach each part first before combining them into the whole skill.
- The priority for teaching is the concept that movement accuracy should precede the development of agility, speed, timing, and body flexibility.
- Drills, relays, and novelty games are useful for skill practicing; make sure the emphasis is on the mastery of the needed skills.
- Periods of demonstration and practice should be followed as quickly as possible with periods of play to keep participants motivated.
- Do not hesitate to interrupt practice play sessions to make improvements or take advantage of teachable moments.
- As the basic skills are learned, the leader can move participants on to such more advanced skills as scoring and game strategy.
- Use positive reinforcement rather than negative criticism to urge participants to higher skill competency.

TEACHING GAME STRATEGY

- The techniques of offensive and defensive play may be taught by first helping participants discover the object of the game and how points are made.
- Chalk talks, movies, filmstrips, and magnetic boards may be useful teaching aids in showing possible plays in a game situation.
- Drills of set plays and variations to use when the first-learned combinations fail are helpful methods for teaching game tactics.
- Help participants to develop healthy and constructive attitudes toward competition and good sportsmanship. They should be taught how to accept the rules of the game and how to win and lose with grace and good humor.
- Teach the proper use of equipment, the role of officials, and game winning strategies.

CONDUCTING PRACTICE SESSIONS

- Start and finish the sessions on time.
- Establish a plan for each practice session.
- Each session should include warm-up, review, introduction of new skills, practicing fundamentals, active play, skill drills, theory work, and physical conditioning.

- When making use of parental help in the practice session, ensure that parents are aware of what is expected of the session and how they can best enhance this.
- End each practice with a brief summary of the session and a word of encouragement to the participants.
- Make practices fun. Be creative in developing practice techniques.

OFFICIATING

Although the recreation leader is not usually expected to serve as an official, she may have to do so on occasion or may have to supervise officials. When this occurs, you must remember that there is far more to good officiating than a mere knowledge of the rules.

- Be alert at all times; follow every play closely.
- Be ready. Decisions must be made in a split second. Keep your mind on the game.
- Make your call in a decisive way that leaves no doubt as to the correctness of your judgment.
- Do not socialize with participants during the game.
- Do not hold valuables for participants.
- Control your own temper. Be patient and cool no matter how angry those around you may be.
- Do not behave in a sarcastic or antagonistic way toward participants, coaches, or spectators.
- Do not point your finger, charge after, or yell at participants.
- Control the game.
- Assume a teamwork attitude with other officials. Help each other.

ACTIVITY MODIFICATION FOR THOSE WITH DISABILITIES

- Walking or wheeling may be substituted for running.
- A bounced throw or underhand toss may be used instead of a regular throw.
- Positions such as sitting, kneeling, or lying down may be substituted for standing.
- The dimensions of playing areas may be reduced.
- Participants may be restricted to an assigned position on the playing field.
- Runners may be used for the participant with a disability.
- Rules can be modified such as the number of hits allowed in volleyball.

RESOURCES

Hacker, P., Malmberg, E., & Nance, J. (1996). *Gymnastics fun and games*. Champaign, IL: Human Kinetics.

Jones, B. J. (1981). *Guide to effective coaching: Principles and practices*. Newton, MA: Allyn & Bacon.

Lee, M. (Ed.). (1993). *Coaching children in sport: Principles and practice*. New York: E & FN SPON.

Martens, R. (1997). *Successful coaching* (2nd ed.). Champaign, IL: Human Kinetics.

Zulewski, R. (1994). *The parent's guide to coaching physically challenged children*. Cincinnati, OH: Better Way Books.

Appendix H: Leading Aquatic Programs

Using water for play is one of the most popular sources of recreation. Aquatic activities can occur in swimming pools, on lakes, at ocean beaches, and on rivers and can include swimming, boating, water skiing, water ballet, water games, and sailing. To be a leader of aquatic activities requires a great deal of responsibility for the safety of participants. This means that the goal of the aquatics leader is to provide participants with enough knowledge, attitudes, and skills to enable them to participate in water activities safely.

CERTIFICATION AND TRAINING PROGRAMS FOR AQUATIC WORKERS

Swimming: Universities, American National Red Cross, YMCA, Boy Scouts, Canadian Red Cross Society

Swimming for preschoolers: YMCA

Lifeguarding: Universities, United States Lifesaving Association, YMCA, American National Red Cross, Royal Lifesaving Society (Canada)

Competitive swimming: Universities, YMCA, U.S. Masters, United States Swimming, American Sport Education Program

Springboard diving: Universities, YMCA, United States Professional Diving Coaches

Swimming for persons with disabilities: American National Red Cross, YMCA

Scuba: Universities, YMCA, National Association of Underwater Instructors, commercial dive shops

Small craft: Universities, American National Red Cross, YMCA, U.S. Coast Guard Office of Boating Safety, Canadian Yachting Association, U.S. Sailing Association, American Canoe Association, National Outdoor Leadership School

Surfing and windsurfing: YMCA, United States Windsurfing Association, Association of Surfing Professionals, United States Surfing Federation

Synchronized swimming: Universities, YMCA

Water polo: Universities, YMCA

Water skiing: American Water Ski Association

Aquatic fitness: Aquatic Exercise Association, Maternity Fitness, Inc., WW Enterprises of Wisconsin

Aquatic facilities management: Universities, YMCA, Aquatic Certification and Training Association, National Spa and Pool Institute, National Recreation and Park Association

GENERAL LEADERSHIP GUIDELINES

- Attempt to gain as complete an understanding as possible of the capabilities and limitations of each participant.
- Position yourself so that all participants can see you without having to look into the glare of the sun.
- Many aquatic activities are best taught with the leader in the water.
- Although fun and informality are a part of waterfront experiences, rules are more important and must always be enforced.
- Select and use appropriate water safety methods such as the buddy system, the check board system, colored caps, and whistle signal systems.

EFFECTIVE GUARDING

- Report, ready for your guarding shift, at least ten minutes early.
- Know the rules and serve as a role model in following them.
- Enforce all rules promptly and consistently—making requests of swimmers in a courteous yet serious manner.
- Be well groomed and dressed in a neat bathing suit.
- Watch your assigned waterfront area carefully. Do not engage in any other activity (such as smoking or talking) except watching your assigned area.
- Always have a whistle and wear appropriate lifeguard identification.
- Do not teach swimming or diving while responsible for guarding a specific waterfront area.
- Do not leave your guarding position except in cases of emergency or when properly relieved.
- Make sure that the waterfront area is neat and clean and that all equipment is in good repair.
- Instruct all swimmers to leave the water area in the event of an electrical storm.
- Know the emergency procedures for the waterfront area and follow them exactly.
- If possible make sure that the entrances to the waterfront area are closed during non-swimming hours.

TEACHING SWIMMING

- The temperature of the water should be comfortable.
- Never hurry progress or show impatience.
- Keep the lessons short; gauging the exact time to coincide with the interest and age level of the students.
- The use of any support aids should be restricted to periods of instruction and supervised practices.
- Keep the instruction fun by using games and stunts to aid in skill learning.
- Use terminology that is familiar to the age or experience of the students so that they may form more accurate visual images of what you are asking them to do.
- Be ready to change to a new activity or to practice another skill when the students become distracted, restless, or bored.
- Do not ridicule or threaten the student.
- Demonstrate skills yourself slowly and correctly.

- Keep a constant eye out for the safety of all participants in the instructional session even while working with only a few.

GENERAL SAFETY RULES

- All aquatic leaders must be properly certified in the specific aquatic skill and in first aid.
- Keep basic rescue and lifesaving equipment available and repaired at all times.
- Post emergency instructions and telephone numbers conspicuously.
- Always have a first aid kit available.
- Clearly mark deep and shallow sections and hazards.
- Be on the lookout for dangerous or inappropriate activities and stop them immediately.

EMERGENCY ACTION STEPS

1. Accident or emergency occurs.
2. Staff person (lifeguard) recognizes the situation as a potential or actual emergency, quickly determines the initial action to be taken, and then alerts other staff persons.
3. One staff person leaves his post and reaches the victim as quickly as possible, while other persons assume their assigned emergency duties.
4. The remaining persons assist the primary respondent, either by participating actively in the rescue, by readying necessary equipment, by beginning an alternate plan of action, or by remaining at their assigned duties.
5. Summon medical aid and supervise bathers.
6. Complete the accident report, including statements from witnesses.
7. Notify appropriate persons in the organization.
8. Study the incident and make necessary modifications for the handling of future situations.

RESOURCES

American Red Cross. (1996). *Swimming & diving*. St. Louis: Mosby.

Clayton, R. D., & Thomas, D. G. (1989). *Professional aquatic management* (2nd ed.). Champaign, IL: Human Kinetics.

Guzman, R. J. (1998). *Swimming drills for every stroke*. Champaign, IL: Human Kinetics.

Katz, J. (1992). *Swimming for total fitness*. New York: Doubleday.

Kochen, C. L., & McCabe, J. (1986). *The baby swim book*. Champaign, IL: Human Kinetics.

Langendorfer, S. J., & Bruya, L. D. (1995). *Aquatic readiness: Developing water competence in young children*. Champaign, IL: Human Kinetics.

Sova, R. (1992). *Aquatics: The complete reference guide for aquatic fitness professionals*. Boston: Jones and Bartlett.

Thomas, D. G. (1989). *Teaching swimming: Steps to success*. Champaign, IL: Human Kinetics.

Whitten, P. (1994). *The complete book of swimming*. New York: Random House.

YMCA of the USA. (1997). *On the guard II: The YMCA lifeguard manual*. Champaign, IL: Human Kinetics.

Appendix I: Leading Group Fitness Sessions

Today, persons of all ages, body types, and recreational preferences are demonstrating interest in the elements of an active, healthy lifestyle. More and more people are turning to recreation organizations for opportunities to participate in organized fitness programs. These programs are leader directed, with structured activities and events to motivate and satisfy participant interests. Some of the most popular activities include aerobic dancing, step aerobics, aquarobics, shadow boxing, and cycle fit. These activities are scheduled to occur several times a week. Fitness program leaders must have the training necessary to conduct the activity properly.

BENEFITS OF FITNESS

Cardiovascular
- More blood cells produced
- Expansion of blood vessels
- Stronger heart muscle
- Lower heart rate
- Reduction in blood pressure
- Improved coronary circulation
- Less chance of heart attack

Body fat
- Greater lean body mass
- Less body fat
- Greater work efficiency
- Improved appearance

Strength
- Greater muscular endurance
- Greater work efficiency
- Reduced chance of muscle injury
- Less chance of low back problems
- Improved ability to meet emergencies
- Decreased muscle tension
- Resistance to fatigue

Flexibility
- Less chance of joint injury
- Less chance of muscle injury
- Greater flexibility in everyday activities

Respiratory
- Increased ability to use oxygen
- Quicker recovery after hard work
- Greater respiratory efficiency
- Increased lung capacity
- Stronger respiratory muscles

Other physiological
- Regulation of release of adrenalin
- More regular elimination of solid wastes

Mental
- Relief of depression
- Fewer stress symptoms
- Ability to enjoy leisure activities
- Possible work improvement
- Improved sense of well-being
- Improved self-concept
- Opportunity to recognize and accept personal limitations

Social
- Opportunity for social interactions
- Ability to enjoy leisure activities
- Healthier society

EXAMPLES OF ORGANIZED FITNESS PROGRAMS

Marathon races
Jogging clubs
Massage clinics
Hiking programs
T'ai Chi Ch'uan classes
Lunchtime demonstrations
Injury prevention clinics
Circuit training sessions
Fitness planning centers
Stop smoking support groups
Aerobic fitness sessions
Deep water exercise classes
Weight training consulting
Street aerobics
Yoga classes
Nutrition seminars
Acupuncture seminars
Shi-Atsu classes
Fitness testing
Stress management workshops
Weight control groups
Fitness during pregnancy classes
Self-directed fitness programs
Stretch and Fit programs
Presport conditioning workshops

COMPONENTS OF A FITNESS PROGRAM

A well-rounded weekly fitness program should consist of regular participation in all three of the following components:

- Cardiovascular and respiratory fitness: The goal is to increase the oxygen supply to all body parts, including the heart and lungs, through continuous movement of large muscles. This type of movement conditions the body's oxygen transport system (the heart, lungs, blood, and blood vessels) to process the use of oxygen more efficiently.
- Flexibility: The ability of the body to bend and stretch is the result of a fitness program that includes activities of flexibility. Flexibility is the range of motion of a certain joint and its corresponding muscle groups. The greater the range of movement, the more the muscles,

tendons, and ligaments can flex or bend. Flexibility is maintained or increased by movement patterns that slowly and progressively stretch the muscle beyond its relaxed length.

- Muscular strength and endurance: This involves activities that thicken the muscle fiber mass to enable individuals to endure a heavier workload. Muscular strength is the ability of a muscle to exert a force against a resistance. Activities such as weight training can develop strong muscles. On the other hand, muscular endurance is the ability of muscle to work strenuously for progressively longer periods without fatigue.

Other components of a fitness program include:

- Balance: The ability to maintain body position while standing and while moving
- Agility: The ability to change the direction of the body or body parts rapidly
- Power: The ability to transfer energy into a fast rate
- Coordination: The harmonious integration of muscular movements necessary to execute a task smoothly
- Speed: The rate at which a person moves her body or body parts from one point to another
- Reaction time: The amount of time required to initiate a response to a particular stimulus

ROLE OF THE FITNESS LEADER

- Directs the exercise program
- Trains and supervises support staff
- Markets the exercise program
- Develops individual exercise prescriptions for participants
- Develops strategies for keeping participant motivation high

LEADERSHIP GUIDELINES

- Have adequate medical information available to properly assess participant health status before and during the program.
- Know physical fitness and exercise principles.
- Set realistic short-term and long-term goals for the participants.
- Give advice to participants on proper attire and equipment.
- Be careful to watch for and intervene on participant overexertion.
- Help participants monitor their fitness progress.
- Educate the participants in the principles of exercise.
- Develop strategies to help participants remain motivated for regular exercise

SEQUENCING THE FITNESS SESSION

There are four essential aspects of a well-sequenced fitness session:

1. Warm-up: Execute warm-up and stretching exercises for at least five to ten minutes. This is important to help assure a safe and comfortable session. Its function is to help the muscles prepare for the stresses of vigorous activity by increasing the blood flow to muscles and connective tissues. All parts of the body need to be warmed up. Without a warm-up period the risk of tearing or pulling a muscle is increased. The warm-up sequence of exercises needs to be designed with the following phases:
   a. A gradual increase in intensity of exercise as the warm-up progresses

b. Exercises that stretch the muscles and put joints through a whole range of motion but do not strain them against resistance
c. Exercises that are rhythmic with a natural flow from one to the next
d. A variety of exercises to make the warm-up enjoyable
e. A combination of muscle stretching with increased activity of the cardiovascular system
f. All body segments and natural motions included

2. Main exercise workout: The major segment of the session is the active movement of the body. Moving continuously in three-minute intervals, with heart rate monitoring in between, will allow the new unconditioned participant a safe way to begin exercising. After sufficient conditioning is achieved, participants can exercise on a continual high-intensity basis. As participants make progress in increasing their fitness levels, continue to increase the duration, frequency, and intensity of the active portion of the session. The three principles for increasing fitness levels are as follows:
   a. Fitness target zone: Identify a range of participation from the minimal amount necessary to bring about improvement in fitness to a maximal amount, beyond which activity may be counterproductive. This continuum constitutes the fitness target zone.
   b. Overload principle: To improve an aspect of fitness, engage in more than normal participation.
   c. Threshold of training: Identify the minimal amount of participation that will produce improvements in each component of total fitness.
3. Cool down: Following the main exercise workout is an important cool-down period. Its purpose is to help prevent muscle stiffness and to give the body the opportunity to readjust to the resting state. Abrupt stopping of the main exercise workout may cause stress to the body. Include in the cool down the following:
   a. Slow down large muscle activity with an appropriate activity or stretching exercise
   b. Begin by walking for a minute or two
   c. Follow with sitting and then lying down while performing stretching exercises
   d. Gradually diminish the intensity level
   e. Cool down for a minimum of five minutes
4. Relaxation: Conclude with a few quiet, meditative moments with the body completely at rest. Incorporate three to ten minutes of relaxation into the ending of the fitness program. During this time, the tension previously held in all muscle groups is eliminated as much as possible.

SIGNS OF OVEREXERTION

- Severe breathlessness
- Poor heart rate response (such as too high during exercise or too slow a recovery rate)
- Undue fatigue during exercise
- Inability to recover from a workout later in the day
- Inability to sleep at night
- Persistent severe muscle soreness
- Nausea, feeling faint, dizziness
- Tightness or pains in the chest

AGENCIES FOR ASSISTANCE

Aerobics & Fitness Association of America
15250 Ventura Boulevard, Suite 310
Sherman Oaks, CA 91403
(818) 905-0040
(818) 990-5468 (FAX)

Amateur Athletic Union (AAU)
Physical Fitness Program
Poplars Bldg.
Bloomington, IN 47405
(800) 258-5497

American Council on Exercise
5820 Oberlin Drive, #102
San Diego, CA 92121
(619) 535-8227
(619) 535-1778 (FAX)

American Running and Fitness Association
4405 East-West Highway, Suite 405
Bethesda, MD 20814
(301) 897-0197

IDEA, The International Association of Fitness Professionals
6190 Cornerstone Court East, Suite 204
San Diego, CA 92121-3773
(619) 535-9879
(619) 535-8234 (FAX)

National Strength and Conditioning Association (NSCA)
P.O. Box 81410
Lincoln, NE 68501
(402) 472-3000

President's Council on Physical Fitness and Sports
701 Pennsylvania Avenue, NW, Suite 250
Washington, DC 20004
(202) 272-3421
(202) 504-2064 (FAX)

RESOURCES

American Alliance for Health, Physical Education, Recreation and Dance. (1995). *Physical best activity guide: Elementary level*. Champaign, IL: Human Kinetics.

American Alliance for Health, Physical Education, Recreation and Dance. (1999). *Physical best activity guide: Secondary level*. Champaign, IL: Human Kinetics.

Collingwood, T. R. (1997). *Helping at-risk youth through physical fitness programming*. Champaign, IL: Human Kinetics.

Franks, B. D., & Howley, E. T. (1998). *Fitness leader's handbook* (2nd ed.). Champaign, IL: Human Kinetics.

Hinson, C. (1995). *Fitness for children*. Champaign, IL: Human Kinetics.

Howley, E. T., & Franks, B. D. (1997). *Health fitness instructor's handbook*. Champaign, IL: Human Kinetics.

Miller, P. D. (Ed.). (1995). *Fitness programming and physical disability*. Champaign, IL: Human Kinetics.

Thompson, M. K. (1993). *Jump for joy: Over 375 creative movement activities for young children*. West Nyack, NY: Parker.

Appendix J: Leading Through Nature

A recreation program area requiring leadership that has expanded dramatically is outdoor activities. Outdoor recreation includes those experiences that offer a meaningful relationship between the participant and the out-of-doors. It includes going to camp, climbing a tree, taking a canoe trip, identifying a wild flower, and fishing. The variety of outdoor recreation activities is limitless, and new forms are becoming popular at a rapid rate.

As with the other recreation program areas, there are no specific rules for success in the leadership of outdoor activities. However, there are some general guidelines. Perhaps foremost is that the leader must have expertise in nature. It is not possible to facilitate meaningful experiences for others in the out-of-doors without a solid background of knowledge on the natural environment. Improvement of this competency can be accomplished by course work in the natural sciences, attendance at workshops, independent reading, and studying under a naturalist.

TYPES OF OUTDOOR LEADERS

Two types of leadership are of importance to the success of outdoor-oriented programs:

- Organizing leader: The leader possesses a genuine enthusiasm for the outdoors and general knowledge about outdoor recreation activities and skills. Responsibility is in organizing and implementing outdoor programs that meet the needs of the participants and the goals of the agency.
- Knowledge leader: The leader possesses an expertise in a specific aspect of outdoor life or activities. She often serves as a resource person to a program, skill instructor, or staff trainer. Responsibility is to support the organizing leader's overall programming efforts by offering specialized knowledge and ability in the natural sciences or in an outdoor sport or skill.

PRINCIPLES OF OUTDOOR LEADING

- Outdoor leaders should portray a liking for the natural world and an exuberance for outdoor experiences.
- Outdoor experiences are at their best when there are no more than ten participants per leader.
- Leaders should know how to caution the overly bold and encourage the overly timid.
- Leaders should encourage participants to relate to the out-of-doors through primarily first-hand experiences.

- Outdoor leaders seek to build activities around local materials and the common, everyday, unseen miracles of nature.
- Outdoor experiences are best when they are based on seasonal opportunities.
- Helping the participant know what is ecologically happening in the out-of-doors is more important than helping them know the names of the plants and animals.
- Much learning in the out-of-doors comes from discovery and use of "teachable moments" when the unexpected occurs.

TECHNIQUES FOR LEADING NATURE PROGRAMS

- When on the trail, one leader should be at the beginning of the group and place another leader at the end to ensure that no one gets behind and becomes lost.
- When explaining something to the group, position yourself in the middle so that equal attention can be given to all participants.
- The human voice does not carry over the noise of a waterfall, the surf, a rapidly flowing river, or strong wind; therefore move the group to a more sheltered area to explain and discuss.
- In discussing an event or object of nature, encourage participants to relate with all their senses.
- Seek a balance between giving information and encouraging participant questions.
- Be aware of participants' feelings and comfort when guiding a nature walk; they may experience fatigue or discomfort before you do.
- Do not be afraid to admit you do not know; but also show an interest in learning or finding out.
- Give participants plenty of time to explore on their own and to appreciate nature on their terms.
- Demonstrate appropriate respect for nature by not tearing branches, picking specimens, or disturbing animals in behalf of your presentation or display.

ROLES OF CAMP COUNSELORS

The chief functions of a camp counselor are to serve as teacher, arbitrator, and friend to participants in an organized day or resident camp program. Specifically, the responsibilities of this type of leader include the following:

- Promote the healthy development of the group.
- Lead outdoor program activities.
- Work with those campers who develop problems.
- Maintain an appropriate level of constructive behavior and discipline.
- Oversee the health and safety of the campers.
- Facilitate the physical and mental growth of the campers.

*RANKED LEADER COMPETENCIES: OUTDOOR SKILLS**

1. First aid and safety
2. Physical fitness
3. Personal and group equipment

*From Buell, L. (1983). *Outdoor leadership competency: A manual for self-assessment and staff evaluation.* Greenfield, MA: Environmental Awareness Publications.

4. Water safety procedures
5. Hiking and trail techniques
6. Campcraft
7. Expedition behavior
8. Food preparation
9. Navigation and route planning
10. On-the-trail activities
11. Search and rescue
12. Environmental awareness
13. Survival
14. Ropecraft
15. Weather
16. Automobile and van use
17. Physiology and nutrition
18. Special modes of travel
19. Toolcraft

*RANKED LEADER COMPETENCIES: OUTDOOR SPORTS**

1. Backpacking
2. Hiking and walking
3. Orienteering
4. Survival
5. Rock climbing
6. Flat-water canoeing
7. Mountaineering
8. Cross-country skiing
9. Bouldering
10. White-water canoeing

RESOURCES

Dougherty, N. J., IV. (1998). *Outdoor recreation safety*. Champaign, IL: Human Kinetics.

Logue, V. (1995). *Camping in the '90s: Tips, techniques, and secrets*. Birmingham, AL: Menasha Ridge Press.

Lotter, D. (1993). *Earthscore: A personal environmental audit & guide*. Lafayette, CA: Morning Sun Press.

Meier, J. F., & Mitchell, A. V. (1993). *Camp counseling: Leadership and programming for the organized camp* (7th ed.). Madison, WI: Brown & Benchmark.

Woodson, R., & Woodson, K. (1995). *The parents' guide to camping with children*. Cincinnati, OH: Betterway Books.

*From Buell, L. (1983). *Outdoor leadership competency: A manual for self-assessment and staff evaluation*. Greenfield, MA: Environmental Awareness Publications.

Appendix K: Leading Outdoor Adventure Activities

Outdoor adventure activities include pursuits that relate directly to a particular outdoor environment and that require a certain amount of risk. Rock climbing, scuba diving, hang gliding, kayaking, and other high-challenge outdoor activities demand a special kind of knowledge, strength, endurance, and flexibility of both participants and leaders. Successful outdoor adventure experiences, however, require that the magnitude of the challenge be proportional to the skill of individual participants. In these experiences competition between individuals and groups is minimal, whereas competition between people and their environment is the major focus.

TYPES OF OUTDOOR ADVENTURE ACTIVITIES

Adventure running
Backpacking
Board sailing
Bushflying
Cross-country skiing
Hang gliding
Horseback riding
Ice climbing
Jumaring
Kayaking
Mountain biking
Mountaineering
Off-road vehicles
Parachuting
Parasailing
Rock climbing
Scuba diving
Skydiving
Snowshoeing
Spelunking
Surfing
Ultralight flying
White-water canoeing
White-water rafting
Wilderness solos
Winter camping

DEGREES OF RISK IN OUTDOOR ADVENTURE ACTIVITIES

- Low risk: The low-risk level of outdoor adventure activities provides minimal danger to the individual's life. People interested in these activities have minimal fear of the immediate possibility of physical danger. Hazards from these activities arise primarily from unusual accidents. Activities in this category include horseback riding and backpacking.
- Medium risk: The medium-risk level of outdoor adventure activities provides a moderate amount of danger to the individual's life. There is a certain degree of risk inherent in such

activities as snowshoeing and wilderness solos. It is important for participants of medium-risk outdoor activities to be aware of the potential dangers. They should be able to react positively to increasing degrees of physical danger.

- High risk: The high-risk level of outdoor adventure activities involves a high degree of danger and poses a constant threat to the participant's safety and well-being. Not only leaders but also participants should be well trained. They must possess the appropriate physical skills, and they must be ready to react quickly and positively to high degrees of life-threatening dangers. Activities such as hang gliding, rock climbing, spelunking, white-water rafting, and scuba diving are included in this category.

BENEFITS: WHY IT'S WORTH THE RISK

Personal

New experience
Personal growth
Escape
Improved self-image
Personal success
Physical fitness
Self-confidence
Emotional stability

Social

Socializing
Sense of unity with others
Cooperation
Trust
Closer to nature

LEADER'S ROLE

- Guarantee that the danger involved is minimized
- Keep the excitement level high
- Accurately assess participants' suitability for the activity
- See that only those participants who are prepared take part in the activity
- Moderate the level of control, diversity of situations, and the variety of resources
- Provide the proper activity sequencing
- See that the experiences are not psychologically harmful

LEADERSHIP COMPETENCIES

Expert knowledge of the activity content
Interpersonal relations skills
Behavioral management abilities
Ability to teach
Ability to remain calm in stressful situations
Outdoor survival skills competency
Decision-making skills
Ability to communicate with all types of people
At least twenty-one years of age
Expedition experience for extended periods
Broad life experiences such as travel or unique jobs
Strong commitment to the values of the activity
Emotional stability
Problem-solving skills

GUIDELINES FOR LEADING OUTDOOR ADVENTURE ACTIVITIES

- Provide for all the basic needs of life (food, shelter, warmth, and group acceptance) before anything else.
- Show confidence and respect, not dictatorial control, when handling situations.
- Be fair and consistent in handling participants and situations.
- Do not become too close to any one group or individual, or other participants will be alienated and communication will break down.
- An ideal leader-participant ratio is approximately one to six; it is better to work with smaller groups than larger ones.
- Check all cuts, bruises, and other complaints related to health no matter how seemingly small or insignificant.
- Be sure that participants are thoroughly aware of the risk before beginning the activity. In this way participants assume responsibility for the risk once they are in complete understanding of it.
- Know and like the activity you are leading.
- Move slowly and conscientiously when teaching a new skill; do not rush participants into new activities.
- Choose activities suitable for the participants according to their age, physical ability, size, fatigue level, emotional stability, and environmental conditions.
- Vary the program and be prepared to change it at a moment's notice.
- Practice conservation; do not collect samples or souvenirs.
- Plan for sufficient rest and refreshment breaks.
- Avoid technical nomenclature when working with beginning participants.

REDUCING ACCIDENTS*

1. Nature of activity
   a. Have a clear understanding of the potential danger of the activity.
   b. Be able to predict dangerous situations before participants become involved.
2. Leadership
   a. Be alert to the needs of the participants.
   b. Maintain a one-to-six leader-participant ratio.
   c. Never leave the group unsupervised.
   d. Never allow untrained participants to participate in spotting or belaying duties.
   e. Become familiar with students' abilities in relation to skill development and physical limitations.
   f. In those activities that require it, be sure that participants wear certified headgear.
3. The environment
   a. Never allow participants to proceed into an area without prior knowledge of that area.
   b. Know the rules and regulations of the area you are using.
   c. Be familiar with weather conditions, river currents, avalanche dangers, falling rock, and other hazards.
   d. Never overestimate a participant's ability with respect to distances of hikes, classification of rock faces, and classification of white water routes.

*Modified from Darst, P. W., & Armstrong, G. P. (1980). *Outdoor adventure activities for school and recreation programs*. Minneapolis, MN: Burgess Publishing.

4. Health
   a. Participants in high-risk level activities should have medical examinations immediately before the experience.
   b. Maintain sound hygienic practices.
5. Transportation
   a. Provide transportation to and from the area for participants rather than allowing them to drive their cars.
   b. Leaders should ride with participants while en route to and from the area.
6. Equipment
   a. Never make substitutions for specialized activity and safety equipment.
   b. Always check ropes, climbing hardware, life jackets, and so on, before they are used.
   c. Never allow participants to handle dangerous equipment without expert supervision.
   d. Check participants before the experience to ensure that adequate personal equipment is ready.
7. First aid
   a. Leaders should be chosen who have certification in first aid, CPR, water safety, and other life-saving competencies.
   b. Give only immediate and temporary care in treating injuries and seek professional medical assistance as soon as possible.
   c. Take a good first aid kit on all outings.
   d. Indicate where you are going and your time table to local safety officials before departing.
   e. File thorough and accurate accident reports with your agency as soon as possible.
   f. A list of contact persons for each participant should be maintained.

LEADERSHIP TRAINING PROGRAMS

American Camping Association
Bradford Woods, 5000 State Road 67 North
Martinsville, IN 46151-7902

Association of Experiential Education
CU-Box 249
Boulder, CO 80309

Boy Scouts of America
1325 Walnut Hill Lane
Irving, TX 75062-12906

Girl Scouts of the USA
830 Third Avenue
New York, NY 10022

National Outdoor Leadership School
Box AA
Lander, WY 82520

Outward Bound, Inc.
384 Field Point Road
Greenwich, CT 06830

Project Adventure
P.O. Box 157
Hamilton, MA 01936

Wilderness Education Association
Box 89
Winona Avenue
Saranac Lake, NY 12983

YMCA
101 North Wacker Drive
Chicago, IL 60606

RESOURCES

Bennett, J. (1996). *The complete whitewater rafter*. Camden, ME: Ragged Mountain.

Burns, B., & Burns, M. (1999). *Wilderness navigation: Finding your way using map, compass, altimeter, and GPS*. Seattle, WA: The Mountaineers.

Ewert, A. W. (1989). *Outdoor adventure pursuits: Foundations, models, and theories*. Columbus, OH: Publishing Horizons.

Ford, K. (1995). *Whitewater and sea kayaking*. Champaign, IL: Human Kinetics.

Goodman, D., & Brodie, I. (1994). *Learning to sail*. Camden, ME: International Marine.

Kuhne, C. (1995). *Whitewater rafting: An introductory guide*. New York: Lyons & Burford.

Leubben, C. (1999). *How to ice climb*. Helena, MT: Falcon.

Logue, V. (1995). *Backpacking in the '90s: Tips, techniques, and secrets*. Birmingham, AL: Menasha Ridge Press.

Meier, J., Morash, T. W., & Welton, G. E. (1980). *High adventure outdoor pursuits: Organization and leadership*. Salt Lake City, UT: Brighton Publishers.

Oakley, B. (1994). *Windsurfing: The skills of the game*. Wiltshire, UK: The Crowood Press.

Olsen, L. D. (1998). *Outdoor survival skills*. Chicago: Chicago Review Press.

Ray, S. (1992). *The canoe handbook: Techniques for mastering the sport of canoeing*. Harrisburg, PA: Stackpole.

Rea, G. T. (1992). *Caving basics: A comprehensive guide for beginning cavers*. Huntsville, AL: National Speleological Society.

Renfrew, T. (1997). *Orienteering*. Champaign, IL: Human Kinetics.

Watts, P. (1996). *Rock climbing*. Champaign, IL: Human Kinetics.

Appendix L: Leading Trips

Whether it is a picnic to a nearby woods or a trip to Kathmandu, travel is a favorite pastime. Today many recreation organizations are providing trips for participants. These trips can be elaborate and expensive, involving a great deal of preplanning on the part of the leader, or they can be brief and simple. The degree of effort required of the leader will depend on the destination and the number of participants. Leading a small tour group to a local area will not require complicated arrangements; however, leading a large group to a distant destination will require more complex efforts by the leader.

GENERAL LEADERSHIP GUIDELINES

- Trips should not be extemporaneous; they should be carefully planned.
- Make sure participants are well oriented to the trip's purpose and logistics before departure.
- While on the trip group leaders should be easily identified.
- Do not attempt to include too much activity within one trip.
- The leader should remain pleasant regardless of any problems that arise when leading tour groups; problems must be handled firmly and cheerfully.
- The tour leader must exhibit integrity by following the rules of the destination being toured.
- Contingency arrangements should be established in case of problems with arrangements.
- A useful leader-participant ratio for touring with children is one-to-eight.

TRIP TO DO LIST

Before the trip

- Let the group be involved in making the plans as much as possible.
- Select a destination, date, and time.
- Decide on a departure meeting place.
- Contact the destination to make reservations if necessary.
- Secure transportation.
- Make arrangements for collecting participant fees.
- Pay reservation deposits if needed.
- Publicize the trip.
- Establish a system for receiving participant reservations and begin registrations.

- Secure parent permission if necessary.
- Arrange for an adequate number of assistant trip leaders according to the number of participants.
- Hold a pretrip orientation meeting with participants to discuss clothing, luggage, spending money needs, and trip manners.
- Prepare a risk management plan for dealing with emergencies while on the trip.

During the trip

- Know the whereabouts of all trip participants at all times.
- Be alert to safety hazards.
- Introduce the participants to the hosts at the trip destination and make any last minute arrangements.
- If giving information to the participants about the destination, do so with knowledge and enthusiasm.
- Give each participant in the tour group equal attention.
- Insist that tour participants behave in a mannerly and appreciative way.

After the trip

- Send thank you letters to the sponsors of the destinations visited.
- Thank and/or pay assistant trip leaders.
- Reinforce the recollective value of the trip with group discussions, parties, slide shows, and scrapbook making.
- See that all equipment is cleaned and stored properly.
- Complete accident reports if necessary.
- Evaluate the trip and begin planning another trip if interest warrants.

IDEAS FOR LOCAL TRIPS

Airport
Amusement park
Antiques auction
Aquarium
Arboretum
Art museum or gallery
Bakery
Bank
Beach
Canning or bottling company
Christmas tree farm
City hall
College or university
County courthouse
Driver's education school
Farm auction
Farm or dairy
Festival or fair
Fire station
Fish hatchery
Florist
Forest
Garden
Greenhouse
Historical home
Historical site
Hospital
Ice creamery
Lake
Library
Lumber mill
Marina
Museum
Nursery
Observatory
Outdoor education center
Parade
Park
Pet store
Police station
Post office
Radio or TV station

Shopping mall
Sporting event
Theater
Train station
Veterinary hospital
Water park
Zoo

IDEAS FOR ADVENTURE TRAVEL

By land
- Backpacking
- Bicycle touring
- Covered wagons
- Dog packing
- Horse packing
- Llama packing
- Mule packing
- Off road touring

By water
- Boat charters
- Jet boating
- Offshore sailing
- River touring
- Windjammers

In the winter
- Dog sledding
- Ski touring
- Snowmobiling
- Snowshoeing
- Winter backpacking

By air
- Ballooning
- Hang gliding
- Parachuting
- Soaring

RESOURCES

Browkaw, M., & Gilbar, A. (1995). *The Penny Whistle traveling with kids book: Whether by boat, train, car, or plane—how to take the best trip ever with kids of all ages.* New York: Simon & Schuster.

Burns, D. (1997). *Tips for the savvy traveler*. Pownal, VT: Storey Communications.

Colwell, S. D., & Shulman, A. R. (1996). *Trouble-free travel: And what to do when things go wrong*. Berkeley, CA: Nolo.

Davidson, N. N. (1999). *Travel with others: Without wishing they'd stayed home*. Los Angeles, CA: Prince.

Portnoy, S., & Portnoy, J. (1995). *How to take great trips with your kids*. Boston: Harvard Common.

Smith, D. L., & Kniskern, N. V. (1997). *The traveler's sourcebook: A practical guide to information on recreational and business travel in the United States*. Detroit, MI: Omnigraphics.

Wade, B. (1994). *The New York Times practical traveler handbook: An A-Z guide to getting there and back.* New York: Times Books.

Appendix M: Special Event Leading

Another important function of recreation activity leadership is the ability to organize and lead special events. As recreation professionals have often claimed, special events are those occasions that give "spice" to the regular program. They are those moments when talents are honored, seasons are celebrated, new participants are intrigued, ideas are exchanged, friendships are begun, and endings are noted. The variety of types and themes for special events are limitless—bounded only by the creativity of those in charge.

TYPES OF SPECIAL EVENTS

Campfires
Carnivals
Ceremonies
Conferences
Contests
Dedications
Demonstrations
Exhibits
Fairs
Festivals
Fests
Field days
Fiestas
Hunts
Jamborees
Openings
Pageants
Parades
Performances
Races
Rallies
Retreats
Round-ups
Sales
Seminars
Shows
Workshops

SPECIAL EVENT THEMES

Themes for special events are usually dependent on local traditions, customs, folklore, and interests. There are unlimited possibilities. As a starter, the following offers a categorization of theme subjects:

- Holidays: A celebration of a day or a time—Holidays may include a religious, local, regional, national, or international focus. For example, a Fourth of July parade or a Christmas pageant.

- History: A celebration of an historical event or an historical individual—Historical events are based on political themes of local or national significance. For example, a Martin Luther King Rally, Daniel Boone Days, or a Pioneer Crafts Demonstration.
- Cultural arts: A celebration of the visual or performing arts—Cultural arts special events focus on such expressions as painting, sculpture, computer arts, dance, music, literature, and drama—For example, Lunch with the Arts, Dancing Under the Stars, an Arts and Crafts Fair, Mystery Writer's Workshop, and Quilting Demonstration.
- Ethnic: A celebration of a particular ethnic group—For example, an Alpenfest, Swiss Winter Festival, Prospectors Jamboree, and Mexican Fiesta.
- Geographical: A celebration highlighting an interesting feature of the local area—Special events that focus on a river; a mountain; or other natural feature offer numerous opportunities for themes for example, the South River Raft Race, a Rhododendron Festival, and a Gold Beach Summer Carnival.
- Food: A celebration featuring a food item of local significance—Special events that celebrate harvests or foods particularly important to the area offer good ideas for themes for example, the Oliver Winery Festival, a Buckwheat Cakes Feast, a Cherry Festival, a Chili Cook-off, and a Crawfish Hunt and Eating Day.
- Sports: A celebration that culminates a sporting program—The Olympic Games, the Super Bowl, and Wimbledon Tennis Tournament are well-known examples. Sporting special events can offer an opportunity to recruit participants to regular programs and offer a finale to the season. At the local level, such events as a Minimarathon, Fishing Rodeo, Spirit of Sport All-nighter, and Wheelchair Tennis Tournament provide uplifting variety to the agency's sports program.
- Novelty: A celebration of anything—Novelty special events are based on unique ideas that are primarily for the purpose of celebrating fun. Such ideas as an Ugly Dog Contest, a White Elephant Auction, and a Rummage Superbowl often attract great interest because of their novel qualities and opportunities for unusual fun.

STEPS IN PLANNING

The planning and conducting of special events can be complex depending on the size and scope of the event. Planning usually begins months in advance and usually involves committees.

1. Decide the main purpose of the event. This includes the theme and what the event is to accomplish.
2. Decide the type of event that is most likely to portray the purpose.
3. Identify members of a planning committee and invite their participation.
4. With the planning committee, decide the time of year in which the event should take place.
5. Compare this date selection with other community special event dates to ensure that they do not conflict.
6. Determine the length of the event: several hours, one day, several days?
7. Determine an alternative rain date or an alternative rain location.
8. As the planning committee takes shape, various subcommittees for organizing purposes may be identified. These subcommittees could include responsibility for the areas of program, facilities, safety, publicity, concessions, and funding.
9. The program subcommittee should be responsible for accomplishing the following:
   a. Locate entertainment, exhibitors, and speakers.
   b. Formulate the program structure and format.
   c. Develop the program schedule.
   d. Reconfirm with entertainment, exhibitors, and speakers.
   e. Oversee the program during the event.

10. The facilities subcommittee has responsibility for the following:
    a. Secure the facility.
    b. Secure props and equipment needed.
    c. See that reservation deposits are made if needed.
    d. Handle necessary permits.
    e. Ensure that the facility is accessible by all participants.
    f. Prepare facility before the event.
    g. Develop plans for transportation and parking.
    h. Prepare plans for cleanup and teardown.
11. The safety and security subcommittee should be responsible for accomplishing the following:
    a. Coordinate safety and crowd control procedures with local police and fire officials.
    b. Secure necessary licenses and permits.
    c. Provide rest areas away from the main area of the event—including restrooms.
    d. Develop a plan and assistance for traffic control.
12. The publicity subcommittee is important to the ultimate success of any special event. This committee's duties include:
    a. Identify the target audience.
    b. Develop methods for promoting the event.
    c. Coordinate these plans with local mass media such as newspapers, radio stations, TV stations, outdoor advertising firms.
13. The funding subcommittee has duties that include the following:
    a. Prepare the budget for the entire event.
    b. Coordinate the financial needs of the other subcommittees.
    c. Determine ticket pricing.
    d. Sell advance tickets if desired.
    e. Handle the bookkeeping of receipts and bills.
    f. Handle the banking arrangements.
    g. Coordinate fund-raising if necessary.
14. The concessions or food operations subcommittee has the following responsibilities:
    a. Plan the food to be theme related.
    b. Handle food purchasing, preparation, sales, and cleanup, or handle the contracting of a concession food vendor.
    c. Make sure that food service and preparation areas are clean and accessible.
    d. Check local health regulations and make sure they are obeyed.

IDEAS FOR PROMOTING SPECIAL EVENTS

Before the event

News releases
Posters and signs
Flyers
Bumper stickers and buttons
Logos on novelty items
Radio talk shows
Invitations
Newspaper supplements
Endorsement by important persons
Ticket drawings
Sandwich boards
Table tents
Mass media advertising
Billboards
Selling talks to local groups
Fund-raising drives
Airplane banners
Contests
Street banners
Sponsorship by local firms
Discount tickets
Searchlights
Cartop announcements

After the event
- News releases
- Postevent reunions
- Thank you letters
- Volunteer recognitions
- Favorable letters to the editor
- Newspaper picture stories
- Postevent programs
- Video tape or slide shows
- Contest winner announcements
- T-shirts with logo to attendees

RESOURCES

American Sport Education Program. (1996). *Event management for sport directors*. Champaign, IL: Human Kinetics.

Goldblatt, J. J. (1997). *Special events: Best practices in modern event management*. New York: Van Nostrand Reinhold.

Heath, A. (1995). *Windows on the world: Multicultural festivals for schools and libraries*. Metuchen, NJ: Scarecrow Press.

Heath, A. (1996). *Common threads: Festivals of folklore and literature for schools and libraries*. Lanham, MD: Scarecrow Press.

National Intramural-Recreational Sports Association. (1992). *Special events*. Corvallis, OR: Author.

Surbeck, L. (1991). *Creating special events*. Louisville, KY: Master.

Wiersma, E. A. (1995). *Creative event development: A guide to strategic success in the world of special events*. Indianapolis, IN: Elizabeth A. Wiersma.

Appendix N: Planning and Conducting Parties

Although most recreation is social in value, directed social recreation experiences provide increased opportunities for people to share good fun and fellowship. Every age level enjoys parties—either to celebrate holidays, birthdays, and special themes or to have fun in an informal way. Successful party leadership depends on careful preparations, wisely selected activities, an appropriately motivating atmosphere, and delicious refreshments. There are many reasons to give a party, but the leader's prime focus needs to remain on the sociability of the participants.

GENERAL PARTY LEADERSHIP PRINCIPLES

- Remember the size of the group, their age, and the nature of the facility when planning parties.
- Always center a party around a theme.
- Balance the party agenda so that all participants feel comfortable in enjoying the activities.
- Balance the party leadership so that no one person is too obvious.
- Strive to have smooth transitions from one party activity to the next.
- Structure parties to allow for simple activities in the beginning, more complex activities in the middle, and a tapering off of activities in the end.
- Keep refreshments simple but make sure they fit into the party theme.
- Set the party atmosphere to match the party theme.
- Build up anticipation and interest about the coming party through word of mouth, impromptu skits, posters, invitations, bulletins, and other forms of publicity.

THEME IDEAS

Holiday themes

Abraham Lincoln's Birthday
April Fool
Arbor Day
Bastille Day
Birthday of Johann Sebastian Bach
Birthday of Paul Cezanne
Christmas
Cinco de Mayo
Columbus Day
Easter
Father's Day
George Washington's Birthday
Groundhog Day
Halloween

Independence Day
June Brides
Kamehameha Day
Kentucky Derby
Labor Day
May Day
Memorial Day
Mother's Day
New Year's Eve
Orville Wright's Birthday
Passover
St. Patrick's Day
Super Bowl
Thanksgiving
Valentine's Day
William Shakespeare's Birthday
Yom Kippur

Topical themes

Anniversary
Backward
Bar Mitzvah/Bas Mitzvah
Barnyard
Birthdays
Bon Voyage
California Gold Rush
Card party
Circus
Clam bake
Country faire
Crazy hat
Garden party
Gay Nineties
Gypsy
Hard times
Hawaiian
High tea
Hobo
Homecoming
House warming
Indoor beach
International
Johnny Appleseed
Mother Goose
Nautical
Olympics
Pioneer
Pirate
Pizza
Progressive Dinner
Resort Weepers Party for Stay at Homes
Sand castle
Scavenger hunt
Shipwreck
Space
Spring
Starving artists
Take a cruise
Treasure hunts
Weddings
Wine tastings
Winter Wonderland

PLANNING STEPS

The process of planning any social event includes the following tasks:

1. Determine the purpose of the party.
2. Define the participants and their needs.
3. Determine the date and the times of the event.
4. Select an appropriate theme and use it as the focus for the remainder of the planning.
5. Select the program agenda.
6. Make arrangements for the facility.
7. Select and produce publicity and invitations.
8. Choose and prepare decorations.
9. Determine and make arrangements for refreshments.
10. Make financial plans for paying for the event.
11. For large events, prepare for safety and crowd control.
12. Plan for afterevent cleanup.
13. Make arrangements for evaluating the event.

PLANNING DETAILS

Facilities
- Number of rooms
- Size of rooms
- Utilities and equipment (such as tables, chairs, electrical outlets)
- Proximity of rest rooms
- Availability of drinking fountains
- If outdoors, suitability of site
- Parking spaces
- Availability of transportation to and from the area
- Safety and police support

Publicity
- Degree of publicity (such as simple invitation or an elaborate series of fliers)
- Form of invitation (such as telephone calls or formal engraved notices)
- Timing of publicity releases
- R.S.V. P. procedure

Decorations
- Selected according to theme
- Degree of complexity (simple or elaborate)
- Purchasing and gathering supplies
- Timing of putting up
- Arrangements for taking down

Refreshments
- Selected according to theme
- Degree of complexity (simple or elaborate)
- Purchasing ingredients
- Preparing recipes
- Serving equipment
- Storing and reheating
- Timing of serving
- Cleanup and dish washing
- Handling of leftovers
- Arrangements with caterer, servers, and cleanup staff

PROGRAM AGENDA

- Firstcomers: For those persons who arrive before everyone has assembled, an activity is usually available. Firstcomer activities can be entered into at anytime by one or more persons, and they last until the last person arrives and takes part. An example of a firstcomer activity for a children's birthday party might be the involvement of guests, as they arrive, in the creation of a scrapbook for the birthday guest.
- Icebreakers: An icebreaker activity is designed to break down initial social shyness and insecurities through a social activity that causes mutual amusement and fun. Games and other activities that help people feel at home and a part of the group are useful icebreakers.
- Mixers: A social mixer is designed to encourage participants to move among each other and to socialize. Often games that help people to get acquainted informally are useful mixers.
- Main activity: Near the middle of the party the main reason for the party is celebrated. Perhaps this is dancing, game playing, group singing, viewing a film, playing a sport, tasting wines, or contests.

- Refreshments: After the main activity, slow the pace of the action without diminishing the sociability of the gathering by serving refreshments.
- Quiet activity: To slow the pace even farther and begin to prepare guests for the end of the party, have ready quiet activities such as mental games, small group conversations, quiet singing, or quiet music.
- Ending: For some parties it is appropriate to have a definite party closing activity such as the singing of a special song, a formal toast to the guest of honor, a concluding game, or formal expressions of thanks.

DECORATING IDEAS

Balloons
Bunting
Candles
Comic book pages
Crepe paper
Doilies
Dry ice in buckets
Fishnet
Flags
Fresh flowers
Fresh fruit in baskets
Fresh greenery
Garlands
Gauze
Grape garlands
Hawaiian flower lei
Hay bales
Japanese lanterns
Kerosene lamps
Mexican pottery
Oriental rugs
Paper bag lanterns
Paper chains
Papier mâché
Parachutes
Parasols
Pennants
Pompons
Sawdust on the floor
Sea shells
Sparklers
Table centerpieces
Theatrical masks
Tie-dyed table cloths
Travel posters
Tree lights

RESOURCES

Amos, J. S. (1992). *Entertaining children: Theme parties, activities, games, and fun ideas for groups*. Jefferson, NC: McFarland & Co.

Boteler, A. M. (1986). *The children's party handbook: Fantasy, food, and fun*. Woodbury, NY: Barron's.

Campbell, A. (1992). *Great games for great parties: How to throw a perfect party*. New York: Sterling.

Harbin, E. O. (1986). *The new fun encyclopedia (Volume 2—Parties and banquets)*. Nashville, TN: Abingdon Press.

Litherland, J. (1990). *Absolutely unforgettable parties: Great ideas for party people*. Colorado Springs, CO: Meriwether.

Reynolds, R. (1992). *The art of the party: Design ideas for successful entertaining*. New York: Viking Studio Books.

Sachs, P. (1993). *52 totally unique theme parties*. Minneapolis, MN: Celebration Creations.

Warner, P. (1992). *The best party book: 1001 creative ideas for fun parties*. Deephaven, MN: Meadowbrook Press.

Wills, M. (1988). *Fun games for great parties*. Los Angeles, CA: Price Stern Sloan.

Appendix O: Leading Children's Free Play Experiences

For recreation leaders working with young children, there are opportunities to manage free play sessions. Prime among the regular and necessary experiences of the child are those various activities referred to as free play. A well-run program of free play arouses the child's curiosity and learning and stimulates her creativity. It helps the child grow intellectually, emotionally, and socially. Successful free play sessions come about only by careful planning and management by the leaders. As distinguished from other forms of organized recreation for children, free play is managed by the leader but not directly led by the leader. The leader's role is primarily in setting up a conducive environment for meaningful play and then remaining to supervise for safety.

FRAMEWORK FOR FREE PLAY SESSIONS

The free play period in children's recreational programming should offer a variety of activities to accommodate the stages of developmental play. These include the following:

- Solitary play: The child plays alone.
- Parallel play: The child plays alongside another child and usually enjoys being with him but is primarily interested in her own activity.
- Cooperative play: The child is interested in other children as integral parts of the play experience.

LEADERSHIP GUIDELINES

- Move about the free play area giving encouragement, support, and guidance to the children as needed.
- Constantly analyze and evaluate activities and the use of equipment and space to offer the best possible learning environment for these particular children.
- In the beginning of a free play program the session should be short, perhaps twenty minutes.
- The length of the free play session can be increased as the program progresses and the children become able to participate in more complex activities.
- When children begin to give such signals as loss of interest, leaving the activity, high and loud voices, and general pandemonium, it is time to end the free play session and go on to organized, leader-directed play activities.

- At the end of a free play session the children should be given an opportunity to report and to talk about the activities they have been involved in. Devote only a few minutes to reporting time.
- Develop a way of getting the children's attention when needed. Such methods as a chord on the piano, a series of tones on the xylophone, a raised hand, or the first few lines from a song are useful.
- Show genuine interest in each child and in his endeavors.
- When opportunities arise, ask questions and encourage the children to ask questions of each other, thus generating thinking and encouraging intellectual development.

CRITERIA FOR SELECTION OF PLAY MATERIALS

- Be sure that the toys serve a purpose and are not just decorative.
- If sharing is an important experience for these children, do not have one of everything for every child. This ratio depends on the age of the child. For younger children, have a higher ratio of play materials per child.
- Select play materials that reflect the interests and abilities of each particular group of children. For example, the number of pieces in a puzzle would depend on the ability of the children.
- Select play materials that have good durability. For example, hardwood play materials are preferred to fragile plastic toys.
- Include some play materials that do not look exactly like a specific object, but are an undefined form. For example, the wood is carved to suggest a vehicle, but it could be a car, a truck, or even a train if the child wants it to be.
- Toys as safe as possible are the best. Watch for roughness in material, for sharp edges, for detachable parts, and for toxic paint.

IDEAS FOR PLAY MATERIALS

Table Activities

Alphabet games
Beads
Blocks
Counting frames
Dollhouse
Greeting cards
Lotto games
Modeling clay
Nests of boxes
Nests of rings
Pegs and pegboards
Picture dominoes
Picture postcards
Puzzles
Sewing box
Spelling blocks
Story boards
Table games
Touching box
Variety of puppets

Housekeeping

Cereal boxes
Doll equipment
Dolls
Empty food cans
Full-length mirror
Old adult clothes
Plastic dishes
Plastic soap bottles
Small cupboards
Small grocery cart
Small rocking chair
Small stove, sink, refrigerator
Small table and chairs
Telephone

Library

Book lists
Bookcase
Books
Bulletin board about books
Dioramas
Flannel board
Floor pillows
Magnetic board
Stories on tape
Stories on video
Story board
Tape recorders

Art

Blunt scissors
Chalk
Clay
Clothes bar for hanging pictures
Construction and poster paper
Crayons
Easels
Felt tip markers
Large brushes
Manila paper
Newsprint
Paint containers
Paste
Pencils
Poster paints
Ribbons
Shelf paper
Smocks
String
Tape
Tempera paints
Tissue paper

Music

Cassette tapes and players
CDs and Players
Drum
Rhythm band instruments
Sand blocks
Shaker
Tambourine
Tone blocks
Triangle
Xylophone

Water Play

Egg beaters
Galvanized or plastic tub
Ladles
Measuring cups
Plastic aprons
Plastic boats
Plastic bottles
Plastic containers
Sieves
Sink
Soapsuds
Sponges
Squirt plastic bottles
Various lengths of hose

Sand Play

Balance scales
Bulldozers
Dump trucks
Funnels
Measuring cups
Paper bags
Plastic containers
Sand table or sand box
Sieves
Sifters

Science

Ant farm
Barometer
Bulletin board displays
Cocoon holder
Container for small insects
"Do you know?" table
Gardening bench
Leaves
Magnets
Plants
Prism
Pulley
Rabbit hutch
Rulers
Science pictures
Terrarium
Thermometer

RESOURCES

Cowe, E. G. (1982). *Free play: Organization and management in the pre-school and kindergarten*. Springfield, IL: Charles C. Thomas.

Hart, C. H. (1993). *Children on playgrounds: Research perspectives and applications*. Albany, NY: State University of New York Press.

Lear, R. (1996). *Play helps: Toys and activities for children with special needs*. Boston: Butterworth Heinemann.

Sher, B. (1992). *Extraordinary play with ordinary things: Recycling everyday materials to build motor skills*. Tuscon, AZ: Therapy Skill Builders.

Stumbo, N. J. (1992). *Leisure education II: More activities and resources*. State College, PA: Venture.

Thompson, D., & Bowers, L. (Eds.). (1989). *Where our children play: Community park playground equipment*. Reston, VA: AAHPERD.

Wortham, S. C., & Frost, J. L. (1990). *Playgrounds for young children: National survey and perspectives*. Reston, VA: AAHPERD.

Credits

Chapter 1
TA 1.1, TA 1.2, Joseph Lee Memorial Library and Archives. National Recreation and Park Association. Ashburn, Virginia.
Figure 1.3 Robert A. Blake and Jane S. Monton. The Managerial Grid®, Houston, Gulf Publishing, 1985, p. 12.
TA 1.3 Indiana University Photographic Services, Christopher Lake.

Chapter 2
TA 2.2 Joseph Lee Memorial Library and Archives. National Recreation and Park Association. Ashburn, Virginia.
TA 2.1 *Parks and Recreation*, November 1998, page 12.

Chapter 3
TA 3.1 Joseph Lee Memorial Library and Archives. National Recreation and Park Association. Ashburn, Virginia.

Chapter 4
TA 4.1 *Parks and Recreation*, July 1998, page 8.
TA 4.2 *Parks and Recreation*, March 1999, page 20.

Chapter 5
TA 5.1 *Parks and Recreation*, November 1998, page 8.
TA 5.2 Joseph Lee Memorial Library and Archives. National Recreation and Park Association. Ashburn, Virginia.

Chapter 6
TA 6.1 *Parks and Recreation*, April 1999, page 31.
TA 6.3 *Parks and Recreation*, January 1999, page 8.

Chapter 7
TA 7.1 Joseph Lee Memorial Library and Archives. National Recreation and Park Association. Ashburn, Virginia. Florida State News Bureau.
TA 7.2 Joseph Lee Memorial Library and Archives. National Recreation and Park Association. Ashburn, Virginia. Courtesy of *Recreation.*
TA 7.3 *Parks and Recreation*, December 1998, page 80.

Chapter 8
TA 8.1 *Parks and Recreation*, August 1998, page 63.
TA 8.2 Joseph Lee Memorial Library and Archives. National Recreation and Park Association. Ashburn, Virginia.

Chapter 9
TA 9.1 Joseph Lee Memorial Library and Archives. National Recreation and Park Association. Ashburn, Virginia.
Figure 9.1 Division of Recreational Sports, Indiana University—Bloomington (1999).
TA 9.2 *Parks and Recreation*, February 1999, page 49.

Chapter 10
TA 10.1 *Parks and Recreation*, December 1998, page 8.
TA 10.2 *Parks and Recreation*, August 1998, page 14.
TA 10.3 *Parks and Recreation*, December 1998, page 18.

Chapter 11
TA 11.1 Joseph Lee Memorial Library and Archives. National Recreation and Park Association. Ashburn, Virginia.
TA 11.2 *Parks and Recreation*, February 1999, page 20.
TA 11.3 *Parks and Recreation*, June 1998, page 14.

Chapter 12
TA 12.1 *Parks and Recreation*, September 1998, page 72.
TA 12.2 Joseph Lee Memorial Library and Archives. National Recreation and Park Association. Ashburn, Virginia.

Chapter 13
TA 13.4 *Parks and Recreation*, July 1998, page 60.
TA 13.5 Joseph Lee Memorial Library and Archives. National Recreation and Park Association. Ashburn, Virginia.

Chapter 14
TA 14.1 Joseph Lee Memorial Library and Archives. National Recreation and Park Association. Ashburn, Virginia.
TA 14.2 Joseph Lee Memorial Library and Archives. National Recreation and Park Association. Ashburn, Virginia.

Chapter 15
TA 15.1 *Parks and Recreation*, July 1998, page 33.
TA 15.2 *Parks and Recreation*, July 1998, page 14.

Index

Note: Page numbers in *italics* indicate illustrations; those followed by t indicate tables; and those followed by b indicate boxed materials.